RESEARCH METHODS IN
EDUCATIONAL
LEADERSHIP &
MANAGEMENT

Education at SAGE

SAGE is a leading international publisher of journals, books, and electronic media for academic, educational, and professional markets.

Our education publishing includes:

- accessible and comprehensive texts for aspiring education professionals and practitioners looking to further their careers through continuing professional development

- inspirational advice and guidance for the classroom

- authoritative state of the art reference from the leading authors in the field

Find out more at: **www.sagepub.co.uk/education**

3RD EDITION

RESEARCH METHODS IN EDUCATIONAL LEADERSHIP & MANAGEMENT

Edited by
ANN R. J. BRIGGS, MARIANNE COLEMAN
& MARLENE MORRISON

Los Angeles | London | New Delhi
Singapore | Washington DC

SAGE Publications Ltd
1 Oliver's Yard
55 City Road
London EC1Y 1SP

SAGE Publications Inc.
2455 Teller Road
Thousand Oaks, California 91320

SAGE Publications India Pvt Ltd
B 1/I 1 Mohan Cooperative Industrial Area
Mathura Road
New Delhi 110 044

SAGE Publications Asia-Pacific Pte Ltd
3 Church Street
#10-04 Samsung Hub
Singapore 049483

Library of Congress Control Number: 2011938814

British Library Cataloguing in Publication data

A catalogue record for this book is available from the British Library

ISBN 978-1-4462-0043-8
ISBN 978-1-4462-0044-5 (pbk)

Typeset by C&M Digitals (P) Ltd, Chennai, India
Printed and bound by CPI Group (UK) Ltd, Croydon, CR0 4YY
Printed on paper from sustainable resources

Contents

Notes on Contributors

Professor Michael Bassey is now retired, but still active. His formal academic career ended as Professor of Education at Nottingham Trent University. Elected Academician of the Academy of Social Sciences in 2001, he has published extensively in the fields of education, research, environment and sustainability. He lives in Nottinghamshire.

Dr Judith Bell is now retired but has worked as a college lecturer, head of department and vice-principal, as a lecturer in several universities, as a course team writer in the Open University and as one of Her Majesty's Inspectors specialising in further and higher education.

Dr Ann R.J. Briggs is Emeritus Professor of Educational Leadership at Newcastle University, UK. She has published on research methods, middle leadership, 14–19 education and management structures in post-compulsory institutions. Ann is a past Chair of British Educational Leadership, Management and Administration Society (BELMAS) and is currently National Secretary of New Zealand Educational Administration and Leadership Society (NZEALS), having retired to New Zealand in 2009.

Professor Sir Robert Burgess is Vice-Chancellor of the University of Leicester. He has engaged in a wide range of research, writing and teaching on research methods in the Social Sciences. He was Director of the Centre for Educational Development, Appraisal and Research (CEDAR) at the University of Warwick from 1987 to 1999.

Professor Tony Bush is Chair of Educational Leadership at the University of Warwick, UK, and Visiting Professor of Education at the University of the Witwatersrand, Johannesburg, South Africa. He has published more than 30 books and 70 articles in refereed journals. He is the editor of the leading international journal, *Educational Management, Administration and Leadership*.

Dr Hugh Busher is a Senior Lecturer in the School of Education, University of Leicester, with extensive experience of teaching and examining at Masters and Doctoral level. He is currently researching students' and teachers' perspectives on education, and teaches courses on research methods and on leadership, inclusive schooling and learning communities.

Dr Marianne Coleman is an Emeritus Reader in Educational Leadership and Management at the Institute of Education, University of London. She has taught extensively at Master's and doctoral level and is now retired, but maintains her research interest in how gender and other aspects of diversity relate to leadership. Her latest book is *Women at the Top: Challenges, Choices and Change* (Palgrave Macmillan, 2011).

Professor Shirley Dex is Emeritus Professor of Longitudinal Social Research in Education, University of London. She previously held posts at the Universities of Cambridge, Essex and Keele. Much of her research has involved the secondary analysis of large-scale longitudinal data on topics such as life course trajectories, family policy and cross-national research and she has taught courses in quantitative methods in social science.

Professor Clive Dimmock is Visiting Professor at the National Institute of Education, Nanyang Technological University, Singapore, where he is leading a major research project on leadership across the Singapore school system. He is also Emeritus Professor and former Director of the Centre for Educational Leadership and Management, at the University of Leicester.

Dr Pauline Dixon is a senior lecturer in International Development and Education at Newcastle University. Her research in developing countries investigates education for the poorest living in slums. She presents worldwide and has more than 30 publications in academic journals including *School Effectiveness and School Improvement*, and *Educational Management, Administration and Leadership*.

Professor Tanya Fitzgerald is currently Professor of Educational Leadership, Management and History at La Trobe University, Melbourne. She has researched widely in the area of the history of women's higher education, gender and leadership, and teachers' work and lives. Tanya is editor of *History of Education Review* and co-editor of the *Journal of Educational Administration & History*.

Dr Alan Floyd is Senior Lecturer in Educational Leadership and Management at the University of Reading. His research interests include the role of the academic HoD, how people perceive and experience being in a leadership role, and professional identity formation and change throughout the life course.

Professor Margaret Grogan is currently Professor of Educational Leadership and Policy, and Dean of the School of Educational Studies at Claremont Graduate University, California. She has published many articles and chapters on educational leadership and has authored, co-authored or edited five books. Her latest one, co-authored with Charol Shakeshaft, is entitled *Women in Educational Leadership* (Jossey-Bass, 2011).

Dr Elaine Hall is a Senior Research Associate in the Centre for Learning and Teaching at Newcastle University. Elaine's major research interests are the development of teachers' enquiry skills; the impact that an enquiry has on pedagogy and learners' experience and the role of the university in supporting a process of enquiry in schools, colleges and universities.

Mary F. Hibberts is a PhD student in Instructional Design and Development at the University of South Alabama. She works in the Center for Evaluation, Measurement and Statistics and assists in quantitative methods courses in the college of education. She plans on becoming a professor in Instructional Design with an emphasis on research, statistics and program evaluation.

Dr Nalita James is lecturer in Employment Studies at the Centre for Labour Market Studies, University of Leicester. Her substantive research interests lie in the broad field of young adults' and teachers' work, identity and learning in informal and formal educational settings, as well as the methodological capacities of the Internet.

Professor Veronica James is a medical sociologist with a particular interest in qualitative research and the study of emotional labour. She is currently Executive Dean and Pro Vice Chancellor at the School of Health and Life Sciences, Glasgow Caledonian University.

Professor R. Burke Johnson, a research methodologist, has co-authored three books on methodology: *Educational Research: Quantitative, Qualitative, and Mixed Approaches* (Sage, 2007); *Research Methods, Design, and Analysis* (Pearson, 2010); and *Dictionary of Statistics and Methodology* (Sage, 2011). He was an editor of *The Sage Glossary of the Social and Behavioral Sciences* (2009), and guest-edited two special journal issues on mixed methods research (for *Research in the Schools,* and *American Behavioral Scientist*).

Dr Martha Lam is Associate Director of the Language Centre at the Hong Kong University of Science and Technology. She is the recipient of the 2008 Ray Bolam Doctoral Thesis Award from BELMAS for her thesis, *Senior Women Academics in Hong Kong: A Life History Approach*.

Rachel Lofthouse is Head of Teacher Learning and Development in the School of Education, Communication and Language Sciences, and Partnership Development Director for the Centre for Learning and Teaching at Newcastle University. Her research has centred on the development of reflective practice for teachers both in training and in their ongoing professional lives. She has written most recently on the role of coaching practice to support professional learning.

Professor Jacky Lumby is Professor of Education at Southampton Education School, University of Southampton. She has taught in a range of educational settings, including secondary schools, community and further education. She has researched in the UK, South Africa, China and Hong Kong and published extensively on leadership.

Professor Marlene Morrison is Emeritus Professor of Education at Oxford Brookes University. A sociologist of education, her interests are in critical interpretations of education leadership and management, policy and practice, for diversity, social justice and inclusion. She has conducted funded research in all sectors of education, including adult and postgraduate education, and at the 14–19 interface. Her publications reflect her substantive and methodological interests. Recent works include *Leadership and Learning: Matters of Social Justice* (IA Publishing, 2009) and with David Scott, *Key Ideas in Educational Research* (Continuum, 2006).

Professor Daniel Muijs holds the Chair of Education at the University of Southampton. He is an acknowledged expert in the field of Educational Effectiveness and School Leadership and is co-editor of the journal *School Effectiveness and School Improvement*. He has published widely in the areas of educational effectiveness, leadership and research methods.

Dr Jane Perryman is currently the course leader for the PGCE Social Science at the Institute of Education, University of London. She also contributes to the EdD and the MA in School Effectiveness. Her research interests are accountability and performativity in secondary education, school leadership and management, and how schools respond to policy.

Professor David Scott is Professor of Curriculum, Pedagogy and Assessment at the Institute of Education, University of London. His most recent books are *Education, Epistemology and Critical Realism* (Routledge, 2010) and *Critical Essays on Major Curriculum Theorists* (Routledge, 2008).

Dr Juanita M. Cleaver Simmons is an associate professor at the University of Missouri-Columbia. She works with the leadership development and preparation of Pre-Kindergarten to 12th grade educators.

Professor David Stephens is currently Professor of International Education at the University of Brighton. For the past 40 years, he has worked in universities in the UK, Norway, East and West Africa. He is particularly interested in the role of culture in the research process and is currently writing a book on narrative in the research process.

Professor Anna Vignoles is a Professor in the Economics of Education at the Institute of Education, University of London. Her research interests include quantitative methods, equity in education, school choice, school efficiency and finance and the economic value of schooling. Anna has advised numerous government departments and is the economist member of the NHS Pay Review Body.

Dr Kate Wall is Senior Lecturer in Education at Durham University. She is committed to research partnerships between teaching and research communities to generate better understandings of 'what works'. She has written extensively around the process of collaborative research, focusing on how visual methods can support effective learning conversations between researchers, teachers and students.

Dr Rob Watling has worked at the Universities of Nottingham, Nottingham Trent and Leicester where he conducted qualitative research for a wide range of government departments, NGOs, Local Authorities and Trades Unions. He now runs Momentum Associates, providing executive coaching, organisational consultancy and project evaluations across the public sector.

Jacqui Weetman DaCosta has worked in academic libraries in the UK and USA for over 25 years, where she has taught hundreds of students the skills associated with literature searching. She holds an MBA in Educational Management (with distinction) from the University of Leicester.

Dr Pam Woolner is a Lecturer in Education in the Research Centre for Learning and Teaching at Newcastle University. Formerly a secondary school mathematics teacher, she now teaches research methods and supervises postgraduate students. Her research interests centre on investigations of the learning environment and have included evaluations of learning innovations.

FOREWORD

The previous editions of *Research Methods in Educational Leadership and Management* have proved to be a worldwide success. The book addresses the specific needs of researchers in educational leadership and management, particularly of new researchers, and has been adopted as a core text in many UK universities as well as in Canada, Australia and Hong Kong. One strength of the book is that it identifies a specialist niche in the field of research methods, namely a book that is required by researchers – including practitioner researchers – who are working in the field of educational leadership and management throughout the world. A second strength is that it contains specially commissioned pieces that are appropriate for the field of educational leadership and management, and addresses issues of concern to the experienced researcher, the new researcher and those engaged in practitioner research.

The third edition draws on the strengths of the previous volumes. Responding to reader evaluations, Ann Briggs, Marianne Coleman and Marlene Morrison have sought updated chapters from many of their authors, and new chapters from others, in response to the needs of the field. New chapters introduced in the third edition include: research design, grounded research, ethnography and mixed methods as well as other major topics in chapters that have been updated. The contributions provided by various authors demonstrate a rich range of methodologies that social scientists use when studying educational settings. As with any volume on research methodology, the authors indicate the 'different voices' in which research methodology can be discussed.

The range of chapters provided within this third edition is indeed impressive. The philosophical issues that underpin our rationale for conducting research, and our approaches to it, are addressed; there are technical appraisals of validity, reliability and triangulation as well as discussions of a wide range of research approaches, such as case studies and practitioner research, as well as thought-provoking chapters about research tools and research ethics. A particular feature of this book is the way in which it focuses on data analysis, writing and dissemination as well as some of the standard topics associated with research techniques and data collection.

This volume, like its predecessors, is an important contribution to the literature, which enables students to engage with the wide range of issues which affect and underpin their research, before consulting specialist texts on particular aspects of research methods. It is this facility that this collection provides. Overall, it is a volume that will be of great value to those engaged in teaching and learning about the research process and research methods. I am sure that the third edition of this collection will become essential reading for students engaged in the study of educational leadership and management.

Professor Sir Robert Burgess
Vice-Chancellor
University of Leicester
July 2011

CHAPTER 1

Introduction

*Ann R.J. Briggs, Marianne Coleman and
Marlene Morrison*

Chapter objectives

This third edition of *Research Methods in Educational Leadership and Management* has been written specifically for researchers in the area. Many will be Masters and Doctoral students in educational leadership, and others will include the increasing range of practitioner-researchers in education throughout the world. In this introductory chapter, we have the following aims:

- To consider the nature of educational leadership and management research.
- To introduce the book as a whole.
- To give an overview of the process of designing and undertaking research in this field.

We welcome a new editor to the team – Professor Marlene Morrison – and many new authors, who have substantially added to the range of perspectives and subject matter presented in the chapters.

We have introduced in this third edition website materials, where you can find additional material for five of the chapters. The website is at: http://www.sagepub.co.uk/briggs

Introduction

This book offers insight and guidance concerning research paradigms, research methodology and research practice which are relevant to any social science researcher. However, our primary focus is on the field of educational leadership and management, and the book draws extensively upon research in this field. In this third edition, we have further strengthened the international focus of the book, and drawn in new international writers. With the increasing use of international comparators for school achievement, and the interplay of policy and practice between countries across the world, there is a worldwide consideration of what constitutes effective leadership and management of educational institutions. Although specific local contexts differ greatly between countries, there are shared concerns about how to lead effectively for the best possible levels of student achievement.

In many countries, there is currently a strong focus upon school and college improvement being addressed through small-scale empirical research, potentially providing a direct link between research and practice. This book has therefore been designed for readers with a range of research experience and levels of theoretical and practical knowledge, and we hope that the various sections and chapters provide a stimulus for thought and action across this spectrum of experience. All of our authors have their own insights and areas of research expertise, and one of the strengths of this and earlier editions of this text has been the range of author voices presented. We hope that the spectrum of approaches, writing styles and individual voices which you will find in this edition enable you to consider your research from a wide variety of perspectives. In addition, this edition has a companion website, where you will find supplementary data and worked examples to support individual chapters.

What is educational leadership research?

Educational leadership research may be seen as twin-focused. It is a systematic enquiry that is both a distinctive way of thinking about educational phenomena, that is, an *attitude*, and a way of investigating those phenomena, that is, an *action* or *activity*. The published outcomes of educational leadership research form the bedrock from which most postgraduate researchers start their own research journeys. Tendencies towards academic elitism, the inaccessibility of research outcomes and the perceived irrelevance of educational research may have left some education leaders, managers and teachers in 'a vacuum, with the so what? or what next? factors failing to be addressed' (Clipson-Boyles, 2000: 2–3). The growth of professional doctorates and research-focused postgraduate degrees is seen as a counterpoint to such tendencies. Educational leaders might now feel that they have an ownership of research knowledge and practice. Yet, becoming researchers rather than research recipients brings other challenges.

One potential stumbling block is training in educational research that is almost totally associated with the narrow acquisition of research skills that enable individual small-scale researchers to collect, process and analyse research data. If educational leadership research *is* both an attitude and an activity, then the task of this book is to invite readers to consider and re-consider educational research not just as a 'rule-driven' means of 'finding out' what educators did not know before, but as an approach to skilful and intellectual enquiry that is rooted in and shaped by a number of research traditions, and by multiple ways of viewing the educational worlds we inhabit.

Why undertake research into educational leadership and management?

Educational leadership and management as a research field is relatively new, having been developed over the past 40 years (Bush, 1999). It draws upon theory and practice from the management field and from the social sciences. The fields of leadership and of management overlap to some extent, but educational management research may be taken to be a study of the organisational structures of educational institutions, and the roles and responsibilities of staff in organising and directing the work of the institution, including 'work activities, decision making, problem solving, resource allocation' (Heck and Hallinger, 2005: 230). Educational leadership research involves analysing the concept of leadership itself, the types and styles of leadership and their relevance to educational settings. Ribbins and Gunter (2002) claim that two important areas of leadership research are under-represented: first, studies of *leading:* 'what individual leaders do and why they do it in a variety of specific circumstances, how and why others respond as they do, and with what outcomes' (Ribbins and Gunter, 2002: 362). Secondly, Ribbins and Gunter call for more studies of *leaders*: 'what leaders are, why and by whom they are shaped into what they are, and how they become leaders' (Ribbins and Gunter, 2002: 362). Thirdly, we might also call for more studies of leadership and management as perceived by those who are most affected by their decisions and actions, for example, learners, an issue pursued by Jacky Lumby in Chapter 16. Finally, we need to move beyond what leaders and others *say* they think and do, towards more ethnographically centred observations of leadership practices, within and beyond institutional locales.

Research activity seeks to extend our knowledge, and a typology for educational leadership research offered by Gunter (2005: 166) enables us to distinguish between different approaches to knowledge. She offers five such approaches:

- technical – field members log the actualities of practice
- illuminative – field members interpret the meaning of practice
- critical – field members ask questions about power relations within and external to activity and actions
- practical – field members devise strategies to secure improvements
- positional – field members align their research with particular knowledge claims.

The type of knowledge sought links closely with the purpose of the research. For example, a technical study could be undertaken with the purpose of producing a rich description of leadership or management practice, an illuminative study would seek to interpret meanings from the data collected, whilst the purpose of a practical study would be to use the knowledge gained in order to achieve organisational improvement. A critical approach would examine the power relations within the leadership or management activity, for example taking diversity into account, and a positional approach would assess practice against a particular theoretical framework. These different approaches to knowledge affect the type of data collected and the analysis to which the data are subjected.

Research in educational management and leadership is often focused upon potential improvements in leadership activity which could impact positively upon learner achievement. At the very least, undertaking research contributes to the professional development of the individual, but it may also encourage small changes in practice, such as the development of a policy; it may even underpin a major change in the ethos that affects the whole institution, particularly where multiple research projects are involved (Middlewood et al., 1999).

Challenges in researching educational leadership and management

Research in this field presents challenges, and this short section introduces some of them. The educational research field has been criticised for its lack of relevance to the work of educational organisations (see Gorard, 2005: 155 for a summary of these criticisms). In addition, leaders and leadership relationships are difficult to define, and causal factors associated with leadership and management practice are complex, presenting problems for the small-scale researcher, and the range of different types of research undertaken can make it difficult to draw upon previous findings. An insider researcher may have difficulty in accessing the views of more senior staff, particularly in high power distance cultures (Hofstede, 1991).

The educational leadership researcher encounters difficulty in defining who are leaders, who are 'followers,' and what their relationship is. Is leadership a construct of the leader (or leaders), created by those whom they lead? And how do we take account of the intricacies of leadership and management of schools, colleges and universities, where an individual may be a leader in one context and a 'follower' or team member in another? It is important to acknowledge these complexities, and not to adopt simplistic definitions of leadership too readily.

A further problem met by researchers in the educational leadership and management field is the difficulty (especially for the small-scale researcher) of linking causal factors: for example, linking leadership or management activities to improvement in student learning. The meta analyses undertaken by Hallinger and Heck (1998) and Witziers et al. (2004), which reviewed 40 and 37 research studies respectively, found only weak or indirect effects of leadership on student attainment in the studies reviewed.

However, the literature offers researchers some indication of likely areas for investigation, and two examples are offered here. Firstly, Robinson and her colleagues (2009), in their *Best Evidence Synthesis* (BES) of literature on the relationship between school leadership practice and student outcomes, identify five leadership dimensions which are perceived to have a direct impact upon student outcomes. They are listed here in order of magnitude of their perceived impact, with the greatest at the top:

1   Promoting and participating in teacher learning and development
2 = Establishing goals and expectations
2 = Planning, coordinating and evaluating teaching and the curriculum
4   Resourcing strategically
5   Ensuring an orderly and supportive environment

It is of particular interest in the context of this book that teacher learning and development – which includes the activity of practitioner research – is seen as having a strong impact upon student outcomes. The BES document offers substantial guidance to educational leaders for acting on these findings, and the five dimensions quoted above indicate areas of leadership activity which could usefully form the focus of institutional improvement research.

A much broader conceptual framework is offered by Leithwood et al. (2010: 14–26), who propose four paths of leadership influence on student learning:

The *rational path*, where variables are rooted in the knowledge and skills of staff about curriculum, teaching and learning.

The *emotional path*, which encompasses factors affecting the emotions and morale of staff, and thereby their efficacy as teachers.

The *organisational path*, where variables include the organisational structure, culture, policies and standard operational procedures.

The *family path*, where influences such as home environment and parental involvement in school are located.

Leithwood et al. discuss the need for leaders to be aware of their potential to influence variables positively across all four of these paths. Educational leadership researchers could usefully examine variables from one or more of the paths to understand better their effect on learner achievement.

Finally, as this book exemplifies, research in the educational leadership and management field encompasses a wide range of possible purposes and approaches. Heck and Hallinger (2005: 232) warn that:

Researchers employing different conceptual and methodological approaches often seem to pass each other blindly in the night. They ask different questions and base their enquiry on widely differing epistemological assumptions. For the field as a whole, greater diversity has not added up to greater accumulation of knowledge.

In considering your own research design, therefore, do not limit your reading and thinking to researchers who 'think like you'. Through reading papers by investigators who have adopted a particular stance towards their research, or have collected and analysed data sets unlike your own, you will broaden your insight into your own investigation, its conceptual basis, purpose and methodology.

Designing your research: focus and purpose

Gunter (2005: 168) suggests the following interests which educational leadership and management researchers might have:

> *Learners*: who are they, how do they experience learning, how do they progress, and why?
>
> *Staff*: who are they, how do they experience their work, how are they developed, and why?
>
> *Organisation*: what formal structures are there in the division of labour, how do they function, and why?
>
> *Culture*: what informal structures are there, how do they function, and why?
>
> *Communities*: what direct (parents, governors) and indirect (businesses, charities) participation is there by local people, how do they participate, and why?
>
> *State*: what are the purposes of schools and schooling, and how is the school as a public institution interconnected with citizenship and democratic development?
>
> *Connections*: how are local, regional, national and international communities interconnected, what impact does this have on learners and staff, and why?

This list provides a useful starting point in developing a research focus. A research focus could combine some of the interests outlined above, for example: how do staff create and experience culture? An interest in 'State' could investigate the impact of an educational policy on an institution, in relation to the needs of the local community. When combined with Gunter's list (2005: 266), cited earlier, of approaches to knowledge – technical, illuminative, critical, practical, positional – both the focus and the purpose of the research can be located. You do not have to use Gunter's terminology or classification, but you can use it to establish what you wish to investigate and why. If you wish to investigate how staff experience their work, do you wish your research outcomes to be a detailed description of staff roles and activities? Do you wish staff to evaluate their motivation to work, or their satisfaction with their working environment? Do you think that some staff (women or those from minority ethnic groups perhaps) may experience their work differently from others? Do you need to find out how staff could be better led, or how they could improve their own management of learning? Does your research purpose include the analysis of student perceptions of the staff who teach them? These various suggestions for research focus and purpose demand different research approaches and different data.

Exploring the concept of research

The thinking above leads us to an important question: what is the focus for my research? It is important to define as carefully as possible the issue or research problem that is to be investigated, and the context within which it is set. The way that you frame the problem will both influence, and be influenced by, the research paradigm within which you work. Part A of this book, *The Concept of Research,* challenges you to consider not only the research problem which you are about to investigate, but how to think about it: how to understand it as research before making choices concerning research approaches and tools.

Part A therefore considers the wider questions related to research which underpin any choice of research approach and research tool. In Chapter 2, Marlene Morrison introduces us to research paradigms, challenging us to think about the nature of knowledge and being, and how this relates to the methodological issues that will occupy your mind as a researcher. The themes of this chapter are replayed throughout the book, as they underpin the many choices we make as researchers. Chapter 3 adds another layer to this process of reflexivity in asking whether we are to adopt a particular stance towards our research, and towards the area of our investigation. You may see research as being a neutral, objective activity; however, Margaret Grogan and Juanita Cleaver Simmons open our minds to critical stances adopted by social science researchers who are likely to operate at the subjective, interpretivist end of the research paradigm spectrum. It is important also to consider the context of our research. Our thinking about research is strongly influenced by the prevailing culture of the society we live in, and our understanding of research objectives and practice may largely be based upon Western concepts of social structure and ethical purpose. In Chapter 4, David Stephens shows not only that research is seen differently in different cultures, but that the focus of any research can only be fully understood within its cultural context. Reflection upon these three chapters will lead you to consider deeply the nature and purpose of research, and the importance of its cultural context.

In order to understand your research problem more fully, you will need to review the existing research-based knowledge and the theoretical and conceptual areas that relate to your chosen area. In Chapter 5, Jacqui Weetman DaCosta guides you through the process of systematically reviewing educational literature, making use of all available sources to provide a secure foundation for your work. As your research focus becomes clear, and you frame your research questions, two important issues need to be addressed: how can I ensure that this investigation is reliable and valid, and what are the ethical issues presented by this research? In Chapter 6, Tony Bush discusses reliability, validity and triangulation – what he calls the 'authenticity' of research – and in Chapter 7, Hugh Busher and Nalita James consider the ethics of research in education. These chapters deal with two of the book's most consistent themes. Virtually every chapter invites you to consider some aspect of validity, very often incorporating Michael Bassey's notion of the 'trustworthiness' of the data. Similarly, the desire to ensure that research is carried out with due regard to ethics, and that no one is damaged by your research, is a theme that is consistent throughout the book.

It is useful at this point to consider the recommendations of the US National Research Council (Shavelson et al., 2003, cited by Gorard, 2005: 160), which state that good research would:

- pose important questions that it was possible to answer
- relate research to available theory and seek to test that theory
- use methods allowing direct investigation of the questions
- create a coherent, explicit chain of reasoning leading from the findings to the conclusion
- be replicable and fit easily into syntheses
- be disclosed to critique, rather than playing to a gallery of existing converts.

Approaches to research

The advice offered above exhorts us to use research methods that allow direct investigation of the research questions: methods which are appropriate to purpose. This leads us to consider the overall concept of research design and the methodological approaches available to researchers in educational leadership and management. Having used the first part of this book to consider the type of research you are to undertake – what its philosophical, ethical and conceptual basis is – Part B, Approaches to Research, enables you to link those understandings to appropriate research design and choice of methodological approach. We have substantially expanded this section of the book in the third edition, to bring new authors into a wider discussion of a range of research approaches.

First, in Chapter 8, David Scott establishes the links between the philosophical basis of research – its ontology and epistemology – and the choices involved in research design. The chapters which follow discuss a broad range of approaches to research which are not mutually exclusive: for example, practitioner research might be conducted through a mixed method approach and grounded research undertaken through life history. These chapters discuss the fundamental choices to be made about your research, and the need to consider your own values and understanding in making those choices.

Mary Hibbert and R. Burke Johnson explore the challenge of mixed method research (Chapter 9), where seemingly conflicting research ontologies and epistemologies may be combined within a single study. In Chapter 10, Daniel Muijs takes us through the issues involved in conducting surveys, and ways of achieving reliability and generalisability through appropriate sampling strategies. Michael Bassey presents an authoritative account of an approach that will be taken by many insider researchers, that of the case study (Chapter 11), and shows ways of achieving trustworthiness through the design and operation of the study. Rachel Lofthouse and her colleagues draw upon their experience of stimulating and supporting practitioner research (Chapter 12) to demonstrate ways in which such research can be an integral part of organisational improvement.

Postgraduate researchers often seek a grounded approach to their research, drawing theory out of the data presented: in Chapter 13, Clive Dimmock and Martha Lam set out the theory behind grounded theory research, and demonstrate the rigour of its practice. The worked example of Chapter 13 is of the life histories of educational leaders, and this theme is echoed in the next two chapters. In Chapter 14, Marlene Morrison considers the deep, critical insights which an ethnographic approach can provide into organisational life and leadership. She summarises key methods, notably participant observation, and provides examples, including recent developments in virtual ethnography. Narrative and life history approaches are the specific focus of Chapter 15, where Alan Floyd demonstrates how both approaches can offer a personal perspective on leadership practice and enable the researcher to understand the inner experience of individuals. Finally in this section, Jacky Lumby challenges us to consider the views of those who are the intended beneficiaries of education: the learners. In her chapter on learner voice (Chapter 16), she questions the view that learners can contribute little to educational leadership research and considers ways in which barriers to learner involvement might be addressed.

Choosing your research tools

The train of thought which started with research paradigms – the philosophical underpinnings of the process of research – through to considering research purpose, research design and methodological approach, leads us through to the practical choice of the research tools themselves. Part C of this book is therefore concerned with the *research tools* that may be used within any of the wider approaches discussed above. Researchers into educational leadership and management are often seeking opinions, perceptions and evidence of day-to-day practice from active participants in the field, and Chapters 17 and 18 provide clear practical guides to using two of the most commonly used types of research tools: interviews and questionnaires. Chapter 17 by Marianne Coleman provides valuable practical advice on the practice of interviewing, drawing on her considerable experience of interviewing in the field of leadership. In Chapter 18, Judith Bell and Pam Woolner offer guidance for the process of designing questionnaires, including online surveys, and indicate how questionnaire design links back to the research questions and forward to data analysis. Both chapters relate to the survey method, particularly to the issues of sampling discussed in Chapter 10, and also refer to validity and reliability and the ethics of research.

The final four chapters in Part C are concerned largely with text and with existing data sets. In the excitement of collecting 'fresh' data to explore a research theme, existing data may sometimes be overlooked. In the field of education, there is a rich seam of such data, both in the form of statistics and text documents. Whether they form the whole basis of the research, or are used to establish contextual factors for an investigation, these data should not be overlooked. In Chapter 19, Anna Vignoles and Shirley Dex discuss ways of making use of existing data which may be of particular interest to those who lead educational institutions, and to those who wish to conduct unobtrusive research. In Chapter 20, Tanya Fitzgerald invites us as educational leaders and practitioners to consider making use of documents and documentary analysis, again particularly when unobtrusive research is advisable. Similarly, Jane Perryman in Chapter 21 invites us to consider how discourse analysis can be used to uncover the socially constructed context in which words are spoken and written, enabling us to understand the real dynamics of leadership structures. In Chapter 22, the final chapter in this section, Marlene Morrison draws on her extensive experience with the use of diaries as research instruments. She demonstrates how diaries and blogs, as an increasingly interactive and experimental genre, have a growing potential to illuminate a range of leadership issues.

Whichever research tools you use, it is important to consider their fitness for purpose, and your own expertise in using them and analysing the ensuing data. It is very important that the tools you use properly address the research purpose and the research questions. Consider your research questions carefully: what kind – and what range – of data do you need to elicit in order to pursue this enquiry? And how are you going to analyse your data? Although the part of this book which considers data analysis is placed last, its consideration should take place early in the research design process. The choice and design of your research tools are inextricably linked to the ways in which the data are to be analysed.

Making sense of your research

The final section of the book, Part D, Analysing and Presenting Data, considers the analysis of your data and the presentation and dissemination of your research. Although research is carried out sequentially, it is vital that you consider at the outset how your work is to be analysed and in particular whether you have the resources to undertake the sort of analysis that your data sets will require. Transcribing even one interview is a painstaking process and the extraction of themes from a number of transcriptions should develop as the work progresses rather than being left to the end. Similarly, inputting and analysing a large amount of quantitative data requires skills that may have to be learnt and practised. Two new chapters in this volume, Chapters 23 and 24, take us through the processes of analysing quantitative data. In Chapter 23, Pauline Dixon and Pam Woolner offer practical advice – with worked examples – on undertaking quantitative data analysis using SPSS, while Daniel Muijs introduces and works through the more advanced quantitative data analysis methods in Chapter 24. Similarly, in Chapter 25, Rob Watling and Veronica James show the steps that can be followed in the analysis of qualitative data, including the use of data analysis software, while reinforcing the point that analysis is not necessarily something that you only consider towards the end of a research project.

While research is seemingly a linear process, from considering the research problem and purpose, to considering research approaches and design, through to the collection and analysis of data, in practice these thought processes, choices and actions are all inter-dependent, and the researcher may move back and forth, considering analysis alongside research design, and ethical issues together with research outcomes. Moreover, although the research questions may have set out what the researcher wished to discover, the most important findings may have been unsought and unexpected. Research is, after all, an exploratory process: if the outcome could be predicted, there would be little point in undertaking the research.

Chapter 26, on academic writing, has been written by Ann Briggs with you, the practitioner and student researcher, very much in mind. She encourages you to consider both the nature of academic writing and the writing process itself: the ways in which text is created from a range of working documents to present an appropriate flow of argument. She demonstrates how the process of writing is inextricably linked with the process of analysis, and offers examples of conceptual modelling to illustrate this point.

The book as a whole has been written mainly for Masters and Doctoral students and for practitioner researchers of educational management and leadership. We hope that your research will lead to the achievement of your desired qualification, and offer insights into leadership which result in improvements for learners. Publication of your research will also enable the dissemination of your findings, adding to the wider understanding and improvement of educational processes and their leadership and management. In this Introduction, we have taken you through the stages in thinking which underpin your research, and indicated some of the choices and understandings that are needed. We trust that you will read and re-read the various chapters as you progress in your research, and move on to consult the many associated texts recommended by the chapter authors. Above all, we hope that you enjoy your research, and that from it you will gain both practical insight and personal growth.

Reminder

The website materials for this book can be found at http://www.sagepub.co.uk/briggs

Here you will find additional materials for Chapter 13, 19, 23, 24 and 26. We hope that you find it useful.

References

Bush, T. (1999) Introduction: setting the scene, in Bush, T., Bell, L., Bolam, R., Glatter, R. and Ribbins, P. (eds) *Educational Management: Redefining Theory, Policy and Practice*. London: Paul Chapman.

Clipson-Boyles, S. (2000) Introduction in Clipson-Boyles, S. (ed.) *Putting Research into Practice in Primary Teaching and Learning*. London: David Fulton.

Gorard, S. (2005) Current contexts for research in educational leadership and management. *Educational Management, Administration and Leadership* 33(2): 155–64.

Gunter, H.M. (2005) Conceptualising research in educational leadership. *Educational Management Administration and Leadership* 33(2): 165–80.

Hallinger, P. and Heck, R.H. (1998) Exploring the Principal's contribution to school effectiveness: 1980–1995. *School Effectiveness and School Improvement* 9(2): 157–91.

Heck, R.H. and Hallinger, P. (2005) The study of educational leadership and management: where does the field stand today? *Educational Management, Administration and Leadership* 33(2): 229–44.

Hofstede, G.H. (1991) *Cultures and Organizations: Software of the Mind*. London: McGraw-Hill.

Leithwood, K., Anderson, S.E., Mascall, B. and Strauss, T. (2010) School leaders' influences on student learning: the four paths, in Bush, T., Bell, L. and Middlewood, D. (eds) *The Principles of Educational Leadership and Management* (2nd edn). London: Sage.

Middlewood, D., Coleman, M. and Lumby, J. (1999) *Practitioner Research in Education: Making a Difference*. London: Paul Chapman.

Ribbins, P.M. and Gunter, H.M. (2002) Mapping leadership studies in education: towards a typology of knowledge domains. *Educational Management and Administration* 30(4): 359–86.

Robinson, V., Hohepa, M. and Lloyd, C. (2009) *School Leadership and Student Outcomes: Identifying What Works and Why. Best Evidence Synthesis Iteration*. Wellington, New Zealand: Ministry of Education.

Shavelson, R., Phillips, D., Towne, L. and Feuer, M. (2003) On the science of education design studies. *Educational Researcher* 32(1): 25–8.

Witziers, B., Bosker, R. and Kruger, M. (2004) Educational leadership and student achievement: the elusive search for an association. *Educational Administration Quarterly* 39(3): 398–425.

Part A

The Concept of Research

CHAPTER 2

Understanding Methodology

Marlene Morrison

Chapter objectives

- This chapter seeks to enable researchers to consider the rationale which forms the philosophical basis for their research.
- It introduces key concepts which are fundamental to research activity: epistemology, ontology and methodology.
- The concept of paradigms is presented, together with a consideration of positivist and interpretivist paradigms.
- The relationship between these two paradigms and quantitative and qualitative research is explored.
- A main aim of the chapter is to enable researchers to knowingly choose the methodological approach which best fits their research study.

Epistemology, ontology and methodology

Research enquiry is full of challenges and uncertainties. As researchers, we want to know if the conclusions we reach are the 'right' ones; at the same time, our literature searches and reviews tell us that the history of published research into education leadership and management, as for other educational areas, is one in which a range of published authors appear to reach different as well as similar conclusions about the same or very similar phenomena. As McKenzie (1997: 9) points out, 'research is embedded in a churning vortex of constructive and destructive tensions in which old educational "certainties" are replaced by new "certainties"'. That tension is historical. For researchers, two questions are key:

What is the relation between what we see and understand [our claims to 'know' and our theories of knowledge or *epistemology*] and that which is reality [our sense of being or *ontology*]?

In other words, how do we go about creating knowledge about the world in which we live? (McKenzie, 1997: 9)

Epistemology, then, is central to research endeavour. All researchers ask questions about knowledge – how we find it, how we recognise it when we find it, how we use it and how it distinguishes truth from falsehood. In other words, researchers seek to 'know' the 'reality' they are describing. Educational researchers bring a wide range of theoretical perspectives to their work. Perhaps the widest of these is *ontology*. This consists of a range of perceptions about the nature of reality and is important because it affects the way in which researchers *can* 'know'. Together, ontology and epistemology affect the methodologies that underpin researchers' work: *methodology* is based upon critical thinking about the nature of reality and how we can understand it. As Scott and Morrison (2006: 153) explain:

> Methodology is the theory (or set of ideas about the relationship between phenomena) of how researchers gain knowledge in research contexts and why. The 'why' question is critical since it is through methodological understanding that researchers and readers of research are provided with a rationale to explain the reasons for using specific strategies and methods in order to construct, collect, and develop particular kinds of knowledge about educational phenomena.

Crucially, then, methodology provides a rationale for the ways in which researchers conduct research activities.

From this perspective, methodology is much more than *methods* or *techniques* or *tools* for research, like 'conducting an interview' or 'keeping a research diary'. The methodological rationale provides researchers with underlying reasons for 'conducting an interview'; as importantly, in choosing to conduct serial life-history interviews with a secondary school head of science, for example, rather than a questionnaire survey with a number of heads of science, the researcher is arguing that interviews provide a 'more informed' way of claiming knowledge than a questionnaire could provide in order to address one or more of his/her specific research questions.

Epistemological and methodological concerns are implicated at every stage of the research process. There might be a tendency to think that the information collected by researchers is transformed into 'data' and then into 'knowledge' as if this were both automatic and linear. Not so. Information is transformed into data by the process of analysis; information is collected in a range of forms, as qualitative or quantitative information, or as combinations of both.

Paradigms

In making sense of research information and transforming it into data, researchers draw implicitly or explicitly upon a set of beliefs or epistemological assumptions called *paradigms*. In educational research, these are sometimes called epistemes (following Foucault, 1972) or traditions (following MacIntyre, 1988) about how research evidence might be understood, patterned, reasoned and compiled. Researchers who adhere to a specific paradigm hold a kind of consensus about what does or should count as 'normal' research.

Somekh and Lewin (2005: 347) describe a paradigm as:

> An approach to research which provides a unifying framework of understandings of knowledge, truth, values and the nature of being.

In the field of educational research, a range of paradigms has been developed. Scott and Morrison (2006: 170) point to four of these:

- *Positivism/empiricism*, where it is accepted that facts can be collected about the world; language allows us to represent those facts unproblematically; and it is possible to develop correct methods for understanding educational processes, relations and institutions.
- *Phenomenology* as a form of interpretivism, where the emphasis is placed on the way human beings give meaning to their lives; reasons are accepted as legitimate causes of human behaviour; and agential perspectives are prioritised.
- *Critical theory*, where it is accepted that values are central to all research activities; describing and changing the world are elided; and the researcher does not adopt a neutral stance in relation to the world.
- *Postmodernism*, which rejects universalising modes of thought and global narratives; understands knowledge as localised; and seeks above all else to undermine the universal legitimacy of notions such as truth.

The ways of thinking which underpin such beliefs are often referred to in terms of philosophical positions. This means that all discussions about the methodology of educational research require researchers to familiarise themselves with philosophical debates about the nature of educational enquiry, and whether that enquiry will be influenced by individual ontologies. In the following sections, discussion turns to the respective influences of positivism and interpretivism upon educational research activities and environments. The core aim here is to introduce readers to epistemological and methodological issues that are frequently reduced to matters of 'quantity' and 'quality'.

Introducing positivism

Positivism is a social theory. Its basic tenet is to view the natural science as *the* paradigm for educational enquiry. Four issues confront readers who wish to explore the term *positivism* for the first time:

1 As Bryman (2004) articulates, there is a range of definitions attributed to positivism.

2 The term is not always recognised by educational researchers, who may work implicitly within the paradigm. Especially with regard to first-time researchers, it is not always easy to discern whether the approach being used is seen 'simply' as the most appropriate or 'scientific' way of conducting research, and/or whether this reflects a cultural preference for one paradigm or methodology over another.

3 The term is sometimes used pejoratively, particularly by those who would reject this paradigm in favour of (an) alternative(s).

4 The educational community includes researchers who, for reasons that might be ideological, technical or pragmatic, engage in 'mix-and-match' approaches to research methodology and method. They may not perceive, or indeed value, the need for a specific distinctiveness in paradigmatic approaches to research activities.

Readers will be invited to consider 'combination' frameworks in Chapter 9, which discusses mixed methods. Meanwhile, 'mix-and-match' approaches may also be viewed as a research response to criticisms from research sponsors who berate the boldness or 'exaggeration' of research claims emanating from one paradigm, frequently but not always interpretive.

The key point about positivist approaches to educational research is their adherence to the scientific method. The positivist tradition has a number of key features:

- People – pupils, students, heads of departments, principals and parents – are the *objects* of educational research, notwithstanding their uniqueness as one from another and from the other objects of the natural world.

- Only educational phenomena that are amenable to the researcher's senses, in other words, that are *observable* through experience, can validly be considered as knowledge. 'Feelings' as the objects of educational research activity, therefore, need to be ruled out, unless they can be rendered observable and measurable.

- Scientific knowledge is obtained through the collection of verified 'facts'. Such facts can be observed 'out there' in an educational world that is distinct from the observer. These facts feed into theories about educational leadership and management, for example; theories, in turn, represent the accumulated findings of educational research. Theories are likely to have law-like characteristics because they are based upon empirically established *regularities*. The notion that a theory of educational management ... or learning ... or leadership can be built upon an edifice of empirically established facts is called *inductivism*.

- Theories also provide a backdrop to empirical research because *hypotheses* can be generated from them, usually in the form of postulated *causal connections*. This implies that educational research is also *deductive*.

- Positivists take a particular stance with regard to values. As Bryman (1988: 15) articulates, they do so in two senses. The first involves the need for educational researchers to 'purge' themselves of values that may impair their objectivity and undermine the validity of the research. The second is to draw a distinction between scientific statements and normative ones. Thus 'whilst positivists recognise that they can investigate the implications of a particular normative position, they cannot verify or falsify the position itself' (1988: 15). In such ways, factual statements can be separated from value statements, so that:

  > Secure knowledge of the world can be obtained free from any type of values. Observations can be theory-free, and thus it is possible to construct a science of education, which consists of enduring law-like statements. (Scott and Morrison, 2006: 174)

- Human characteristics and attributes can be considered as *variables*. When combined, they can capture the essence of either human beings or the educational activities in which they are engaged. Discoveries about the relationship between variables should enable positivists to explain the world they have uncovered. Again, Scott and Morrison (2006) describe this in terms of 'atomism': 'generalizations refer to the constant conjunction of atomistic events ... these generalizations refer not to causal relations but to empirical regularities' (Scott and Morrison, 2006: 174). Because positivists do not consider themselves as 'inside' the research milieux they investigate, then it should not matter who does the research, provided that others are as 'expert' as they are in applying the scientific method. One would expect that other researchers handling similar data would come to similar conclusions.

- Positivists may predict, in the sense that observations in the past may enable them to predict what will happen in the future, given similar circumstances and significant associations between variables.

What is the relation between positivism and quantitative research?

Quantitative research as a rational, linear process has been heavily influenced by the application of the scientific method which has, in turn, been seen mainly in positivist terms. Bryman (2004: 63) provides an 'idealised' model of this process in which he reminds us that actuality may vary from the ideal, with theory playing a smaller role in quantitative research than is frequently assumed. Quantitative research has a number of core features:

1 The relation between *concept formation*, observation and *measurement* is central. How we objectify, observe and measure 'leadership styles', 'intelligence', 'educational attainment', 'reading ages' and 'home–school partnerships', for example, are key concerns; with this comes the important notion of 'breaking down' the research problem into manageable 'bits'

that can be observed and measured. The use of structured observation and questionnaires is common in educational research for measurement purposes (see Chapters 14 and 18 respectively).

2   Quantitative research is also interested in *causality*. So, quantitative researchers make frequent use of independent and dependent variables, frequently associated with experimental and cross-sectional survey design, and more recently, mathematical modelling. What makes a school 'effective'? How can we tell a 'good school' from a 'bad school'? How do we know that a school has 'improved'? By 'how much' and 'why'?

3   Three conditions have to be met in order to establish causal relations. First, researchers need statistical techniques to show that there is a relationship between variables; second, they need to show that the relationship is non-spurious; third, the analyst needs to show that there is a temporal order to the data being studied.

4   Following the model of the natural sciences, quantitative researchers have a central interest in showing that their findings can be *generalised* beyond the location of their project. Hence the concern among such researchers about the representativeness of survey samples, or the extent to which the results of experiments can be generalised beyond the circumstances of the original experiment.

5   Few educational researchers, whether disposed towards qualitative or quantitative research, subscribe to the view that research can be *entirely* value-free. Therefore, the interest of the quantitative researcher turns more generally on whether the research can be (rather than is) replicated.

6   In quantitative research, the emphasis is very much upon the individual as the object of research; the aggregation of individualised data provides overall measures. Thus in a survey sample of 300 women managers and 300 male managers designed to ascertain a 'measure' of gendered leadership styles, individual responses may be aggregated in order to give a summative measurement. Following Bryman (1988), there may be a kind of perversity in reifying aggregated data on 'gendered management styles' on the one hand, and placing an emphasis upon individual, unconnected and discrete responses on the other.

Introducing interpretivism

Interpretivism has made an important impact upon education research. It is most strongly signalled in an approach to research that is called symbolic interactionism (see also below). The basis of the approach is expressed succinctly by Scott and Morrison (2006: 130) as one in which:

Social actors negotiate meanings about their activity in the world. Social reality therefore consists of their attempts to interpret the world, and many other such attempts by those still living and those long since dead.

These are real and constitute the world as it is. Thus interpretivists subscribe to a realist ontology. Educational researchers insert themselves into this continual process of meaning construction in order to understand it.

As with positivism, a range of issues confronts readers who may be exploring the term 'interpretivism' for the first time:

1. The term 'interpretivism' encompasses a number of philosophical traditions. The substitute term *anti-positivism* sets interpretivism in binary opposition to positivism. In the following section, the terms 'phenomenology', 'ethnomethodology', 'symbolic interactionism', 'naturalism' and 'ethogenics' are introduced; boundaries overlap and some traditions are excluded (see Silverman, 2001: 38–40 for additional terms and approaches, for example). For some, ethnography is also a branch of this paradigm, although it is not always clear that there is agreement about whether ethnography is a philosophy or a method (Pole and Morrison, 2003). For further discussion of ethnography, see Chapter 14 of this volume.

2. The term is not always recognised by educational researchers who work within the paradigm. Recognising the inter-subjectivity of educational research may be viewed as 'obviously' the most appropriate way of conducting research on, with or for human beings.

3. As noted in the discussion of positivism above, the educational community includes researchers who, for reasons that might be ideological, technical or pragmatic, engage in 'mix-and-match' approaches to research methodology and method. Some researchers may not perceive, or indeed value, a specific distinctiveness in paradigmatic approaches to research activities.

The starting point for interpretive researchers is to operate within a set of distinctive principles regarding what it means to conduct educational research *with* people. Thus, the world of the educational researcher is different from the world of the natural science researcher – all educational research needs to be grounded in people's experience. For interpretivists, reality is not 'out there' as an amalgam of external phenomena waiting to be uncovered as 'facts', but a construct in which people understand reality in different ways. (It may be that some human groups perceive reality similarly, but this does not diminish the potential for reality to be construed differently.)

There are a number of implications that flow from this, not least of which are the ways in which education researchers 'work' with and on their data. First, interpretive researchers recognise that they are part of, rather than separate from, the research topics they investigate. Not only does their work impact upon research participants but participants impact upon researchers. Second, for interpretivists, the core task is to view research participants as research subjects and to explore the 'meanings' of events and phenomena from the subjects' perspectives. Third, a related issue for educational researchers is the extent to which it is possible to present the accounts that research participants give in a different language, namely those accounts contained in research reports and theses in education leadership and management as being accounts by them, and whether or not researchers' accounts represent or distort what research participants have said or written.

How these issues are tackled shows some variation; in part these relate to the use of data as advocated by early proponents, such as the following:

- *Phenomenologists.* From the writings of the 'father' of *phenomenology*, Albert Schutz (1967), and from recent proponents, comes the view that 'the phenomenologist attempts to see things from the person's point of view' (Bogdan and Taylor, 1975: 14). The emphasis is upon how people in educational settings build understandings of their world by continually trying to interpret sense data. Reality is viewed as a social construction. In recent years, it is a research position inhabited most closely by those who follow critical and postmodernist schools of thought.

- *Ethnomethodologists* have also been influenced by the work of Schutz; early work drew largely upon participant observation, unstructured interviews and ethnographic studies in specific settings (see, for example, Schutz, 1967). More recently, emphases have been upon conversation analyses and breaching experiments. In the former, recordings of conversations with subjects are presented in as unadulterated a form as possible, with an emphasis upon how taken-for-granted conversations might be understood. In the latter, proponents such as Garfinkel (1988), with some notoriety, encouraged researchers to act in ways which violated everyday constructions of reality in order to shed light on how that reality was constructed.

- *Symbolic interactionists* view life as an unfolding process in which individuals interpret their environment and act upon it on the basis of that interpretation. Best-known proponents of this approach are G.H. Mead (1934) and Herbert Blumer (1969). Blumer (1969: 2) argued that symbolic interactionism rests upon three premises:

> The first premise is that human beings act towards things on the basis of the meanings that the things have for them ...

> The second is that the meaning of such things is derived from, or arises out of, the social interaction one has with one's fellows [*sic*] ...

> The third premise is that these meanings are handled in, and modified through an interpretative process used by the person in dealing with the things he [*sic*] encounters.

A key implication of this approach has been an emphasis upon participant observation, a common feature of school ethnographies of the 1980s (Ball, 1981; Burgess, 1983) in which the researcher becomes a participant in the activity he or she is observing.

- *Naturalism* implies reluctance among researchers to interfere 'artificially' in the world around them and in particular emphasises the need to record the educational world in a way that would be consistent with the images of the world that participants carry with them.

- A key aspect of *ethogenics* is the understanding of 'episodes' in social life. An early study by Marsh, Rosser and Harre (1978) of disorder in classrooms, and on football terraces, is cited by Bryman (1988: 61) as an example of the ways in which ethogenics provides a framework for the analysis of social action:

  > The material collected on schools and football terraces reveals that the apparently disordered events that often occur in these milieux can be seen as 'conforming to a very distinct and orderly system of roles, rules, and meanings' (1978: 97); in other words, people's accounts of particular episodes and the observation of their acts ... reveal a structure in the midst of apparent disorder.

Interpretivism and interpretation

As with positivism, interpretivism is subject to a number of criticisms, some of which reveal problems with the approach, especially in its purest form. The first issue is whether 'lay' accounts can ever be represented as 'reality'. In part, this is because reality is multi-perspectival and also because the way that humans create meanings is by offering accounts of what they do, and this is, in turn, affected by context. To give an example, the way a school headteacher describes his relationship with his senior management team might be described by him differently to members of that team, to an Ofsted inspector, to a researcher or to a family member at home.

Second, it is still relatively unusual for humans to reflect in a structured manner upon their behaviour. Most often, behaviour is routinised. It is only when, for example, the researcher asks for reflection on an event or situation that it happens. So, descriptions of reality that are untainted by the process of the researcher asking are not possible – the best one can hope for is a re-description or a re-evaluation.

Third, it has been argued that people's accounts of themselves, of others, and of events, are incomplete in the sense that research participants may be unaware of the broader structures that govern the interpretations they give or of the conditions that underpin their actions. An illustrative example might be a mixed gender focus group of young people invited to respond to a researcher's question about how their behaviour is controlled in class. They note that, in the school attended by them, male and female teachers treat them differently in relation to discipline and tolerance of different kinds of behaviour. Much more difficult to unpack, because they are assumed, are the broader stereotypical assumptions that such young men and young women might have about what should or does constitute 'a male teacher' or 'a female teacher' and/or assumed distinctive characteristics of their behaviour. Such stereotypifications extend far beyond the confines of school to include socialisation that derives from broader familial, employment, economic and political structures.

Notwithstanding such problems, it is probably fair to point out that many educational researchers 'use interpretation as distinct from the interpretive paradigm' (Scott and Morrison, 2006: 132) in its purest form. This is especially common in qualitative forms of interviews, for example, when interviewees are asked to explain what they think about activities and actions: as, for example, in sequenced questions to a senior staff member in a school who has previously described collegiality as an aspect of how the school operates. Questions to follow might be: Why do you think that practices among staff in this school are based on collegial relations between them? Would you provide an example to illustrate practice that, in your view, derives from collegial relations? It is also a feature of biographical/autobiographical perspectives that might, for example, focus upon the career trajectory of a headteacher. Interpretive approaches are also used as part of first-phase exploratory studies in order to understand educational processes and procedures; for example, how and why some students, rather than others, are formally excluded from school.

What is the relation between interpretivism and qualitative research?

What is apparent from the previous section is that there is an over-arching view that all human life is experienced and constructed from a subjective perspective. For an interpretivist, there cannot be an objective reality which exists irrespective of the meanings human beings bring to it (though they may disagree about the extent to which reality is re-constructed by researchers). Therefore, the data collected and analysed have qualitative rather than quantitative significance.

Qualitative research has a number of key features:

1 Strategies that take the subject's perspective are central and draw heavily from the philosophical traditions introduced above. Understanding those perspectives is critical, regardless of whether the subjects are children or adults. Recent research, which emphasises the importance of children's perspectives, as research 'with' and 'for' rather than 'on' children (for example, Mayall, 2000, and Chapter 16 of this volume), reflects the need both to empathise with research subjects and to penetrate the meaning frames in which they operate. Researchers observing, for example, school management meetings are obliged therefore to acquire and understand a specialised language. The need to penetrate the subject's world suggests the need for lengthy immersion 'in the field'. The approach is replete with challenges, not least of which may be seeing 'through *whose* eyes' and the pressure to produce research outcomes over reduced time spans. Nonetheless, the aim is to investigate 'from the inside' through a process of *verstehen* or empathetic understanding.

2 Qualitative researchers pay much attention to detailed observation. Indeed, the essence of their work is 'rich' and 'deep' description. This provides contexts for description and interpretation when researchers ask, 'What is going on here?' Few details are excluded. Thus, the layout of the chairs and tables in a principal's office in preparation for a senior management meeting, for example, can offer important descriptive insights about the ways in which a principal might construe the purposes and operation of such a meeting.

3 In qualitative research, detailed consideration is given to the holistic picture in which the research topic is embedded. This is more than attention to setting; the approach taken is that researchers can *only* make sense of the data collected if they are able to understand the data in a broader educational, social and historic context. For example, school improvement studies look at individual institutions 'as a whole' in order to understand the processes of change that have led to improvement in that school, but not necessarily in other schools.

4 Because qualitative research is frequently concerned with process(es) – of learning, adaptation, innovation, change, professional development, etc. – there is often a longitudinal element to the research, and no shrinking from the commonplace, or what Miles and Huberman (1994: 6) describe as the 'banal':

> Qualitative research is conducted through an intense and/or prolonged contact with a 'field' or life situation. These situations are typical 'banal' or normal ones, reflective of the everyday life of individuals, groups, societies, and organizations.

5 There may be a reluctance on the part of qualitative researchers to impose prior structures on their investigation so as not to foreclose issues which may be invisible at the start of the research. Moreover, 'the researcher is the main "measurement device" of the study' (Miles and Huberman, 1994: 7). An absence of foreclosure should not be misconstrued as a reluctance to be systematic, and a case can be made for 'tight prestructured qualitative designs' (especially for those new to qualitative studies) as well as for 'loose, emergent ones' (1994: 17).

6 Linked to the previous point, there may be a reluctance to impose prior theoretical frameworks. Instead, notable writers in the field discuss the importance of 'sensitising concepts' (Blumer, 1954) and 'conceptual frameworks' (Miles and Huberman, 1994). 'Frameworks can be rudimentary or elaborate, theory-driven or commonsensical, descriptive or causal' (Miles and Huberman, 1994: 18).

7 In contrast to quantitative research, the emphasis in interpretivism is upon words rather than numbers. This should not, of course, be exaggerated from either perspective, but the key issue for qualitative researchers is that textual analysis predominates: 'Words can be broken into semiotic segments. They can be organised to permit the researcher to contrast,

compare, analyse and bestow patterns upon them' (Miles and Huberman, 1994: 7). More recently, photographs and video images have complemented rather than replaced words (for example, Harrison, 1996).

What this chapter has sought to do is to encourage readers to think about the variety of ways in which researchers can investigate the educational world. In important respects, 'qualitative' and 'quantitative' have been seen not only as different ways of researching education but also as if in competition with one another, or as 'largely uncontaminated "bundles" of epistemological assumptions, sufficiently divergent to constitute different ways of knowing and finding out about the social world' (Scott and Morrison, 2006: 155). More recently, arguments in support of combining approaches have been advocated, and draw on arguments that are both technical and epistemological. 'Combining approaches' has been likened to 'a third methodological movement' (Gorard with Taylor, 2004: Ch. 1).

The position is best described in terms of four main points:

- Qualitative or quantitative represents only one way of classifying methods.
- Choice of method is determined by the needs of the investigation and not the personal preferences or fears of the investigator.
- All researchers need to be able to use a range of methods.
- Completely different methods can have the same research aim. (Adapted from Gorard with Taylor, 2004: 3)

In the field of education leadership and management, there have been calls for change that include the incorporation of research perspectives from more disciplines and 'a wider range of methodologies, within qualitative and quantitative domains, and also ... mixed methodologies where appropriate' (Foskett et al., 2005: 251). Chapter 9 in this volume therefore continues this discussion in its consideration of mixed methods.

Key points

In presenting the philosophical traditions that underpin *positivism* and *quantity*, *interpretivism* and *quality* in educational research, a tendency to under-estimate the degree of overlap, and indeed, similarity between them has been noted. In part, this is a consequence of establishing, for analytical purposes, a distinction between 'qualitative' and 'quantitative'; hopefully, evaluative distinctions between 'good' and 'bad' have been avoided.

Perhaps the key issue for all educational researchers is to engage with research approaches knowingly and self-consciously as a counterpoint to naivety. According to Brown and Dowling (1998: 83):

The naive use of quantitative methods imagines that statistical techniques themselves will guarantee the quality of the work. Correspondingly, naive qualitative research tends to substitute narrative for analysis. On the other hand, the adoption of a dual approach involving both qualitative and quantitative techniques can help in overcoming such tendencies to what we might refer to as naive empiricism. The qualitative imagination will tend to demand that quantitative analysis explains itself in terms of non-statistical concepts that it is claiming to measure. The quantitative imagination will demand a degree of precision in definition that qualitative work may want to slide away from.

Again, caution needs to be exercised in relation to the view that using a combined approach to educational research *necessarily* provides a balance between the shortcomings of one approach and the strengths of another. The critical issue for researchers is to choose the approach that best addresses the questions asked; and, as importantly, that researchers are aware of the implications of choosing one approach over another (or combining them), and its impact upon the things that researchers will find. Hammersley (1992: 172) evokes the image of the research journey:

> What is involved here is not a cross-roads where we go left or right. A better analogy is a complex maze where we are repeatedly faced with decisions, and where paths wind back on one another.

Such methodological awareness, I would argue, has seldom been more necessary. Researchers need to be very clear not only about *how* they are doing research about educational leadership and management but also '*why* this approach rather than another?' Such confidence and clarity about the robustness of our studies will relate to all approaches.

Questions and reflections

1 What features would characterise educational leadership research for which a positivist stance was appropriate?
2 What features would characterise educational leadership research for which an interpretivist stance was appropriate?
3 How can we best justify a chosen stance, and its ensuing methodology, to ourselves and to others?

Recommended further reading

Punch, K.F. (2009) *Introduction to Research Methods in Education*. London: Sage.

A comprehensive text which links research theory and method in an accessible way. Of particular interest is the chapter focusing on research questions.

Scott, D. and Morrison, M. (2006) *Key Ideas in Educational Research.* London: Continuum.

This ingeniously organised book gives insightful definitions and discussions of research concepts and terminology.

Thomas, G. (2009) *How to do Your Research Project.* London: Sage.

A practical guide which enables you to think your way through your research project, addressing the 'Why?' questions as well as 'What?'

References

Ball, S.J. (1981) *Beachside Comprehensive: A Case Study of Secondary Schooling.* Cambridge: Cambridge University Press.

Blumer, H. (1954) What is wrong with social theory? *American Sociological Review* 19 (1): 3–10.

Blumer, H. (1969) *Symbolic Interactionism.* Englewood Cliffs, NJ: Prentice–Hall.

Bogdan, R. and Taylor, S.J. (1975) *Qualitative Research for Education: An Introduction to Theory and Methods.* Boston, MA: Allyn and Bacon.

Brown, A. and Dowling, P. (1998) *Doing Research: Reading Research – A Mode of Interrogation for Education.* London: Falmer Press.

Bryman, A. (1988) *Quantity and Quality in Social Research.* London: Routledge.

Bryman, A. (2004) *Social Research Methods.* Oxford: Oxford University Press.

Burgess, R.G. (1983) *Experiencing Comprehensive Education: A Study of Bishop McGregor School.* London: Methuen.

Foskett, N., Lumby, J. and Fidler, B. (2005) Evolution or extinction? Reflections on the future in educational leadership and management. *Education Management Administration and Leadership*, 33(2): 245–53.

Foucault, M. (1972) *The Archaeology of Knowledge.* London: Routledge.

Garfinkel, H. (1988) Evidence for locally produced, naturally accountable phenomena of order, logic, reason, method, etc. in and as of the essential quiddity of immortal ordinary society (I of IV): an announcement of studies. *Sociological Theory*, 6: 103–9.

Gorard, S. with Taylor, C. (2004) *Combining Methods in Educational and Social Research.* Maidenhead: Open University Press.

Hammersley, M. (1992) *Deconstructing the Qualitative Divide: What's Wrong with Ethnography?* London: Routledge.

Harrison, B. (1996) Every picture 'tells a story': uses of the visual in sociological research', in Lyons, E.S. and Busfield, J. (eds) *Methodological Imaginations.* London: Macmillan Press for the British Sociological Association. pp. 75–94.

MacIntyre, D. (1988) *Whose Justice? Whose Rationality?* London: Duckworth.

McKenzie, G. (1997) The age of reason or the age of innocence?, in McKenzie, G., Powell, J. and Usher, R. (eds) *Understanding Social Research: Methodology and Practice.* London: Falmer Press.

Marsh, P., Rosser, E. and Harre, R. (1978) *The Rules of Disorder.* London: Routledge and Kegan Paul.

Mayall, B. (2000) Conversations with children: working with generational issues, in Christensen, P. and James, A. (eds) *Research with Children: Perspectives and Practices.* London: Falmer Press.

Mead, G.H. (1934) *Mind, Self and Society*. Chicago, IL: University of Chicago Press.

Miles, M.B. and Huberman, A.M. (1994) *Qualitative Data Analysis* (2nd edn). London: Sage.

Pole, C. and Morrison, M. (2003) *Ethnography for Education*. Buckingham: Open University Press.

Schutz, A. (1967) *The Phenomenology of the Social World*. Evanston, IL: Northwestern University.

Scott, D. and Morrison, M. (2006) *Key Ideas in Educational Research*. London: Continuum.

Silverman, D. (2001) *Interpreting Qualitative Data*: *Methods for Analysing Talk, Text, and Interaction* (2nd edn). London: Sage.

Somekh, B. and Lewin, C. (2005) *Research Methods in the Social Sciences*. London: Sage.

CHAPTER 3

Taking a Critical Stance in Research

Margaret Grogan and Juanita M. Cleaver Simmons

Chapter objectives

- To situate the critical stance as applied to research within the context of traditional research paradigms to explain the ontological and epistemological foundations of such research.
- To briefly outline the main concepts and tenets that have been used to characterise the most common critical stances today that are or can be employed in educational leadership/management studies, including postmodernist, critical race-related, feminist, queer and postcolonial.
- To introduce some examples of studies already conducted and/or ideas for studies that could be undertaken.
- To include helpful references for further reading.
- Our overall aim is to place critical research firmly within the traditions of the academy and to encourage research on educational leadership that has the potential of creating meaningful change for participants and their constituencies.

Introduction

As Marlene Morrison has made clear in Chapter 2, researchers carry certain philosophical assumptions about the world into their research even if such assumptions are not acknowledged or made explicit. Most scholars describe these ways of thinking as paradigms. Research paradigms in the human and social sciences range along a continuum from positivist to critical realist to interpretivist to postmodern to pragmatic, including action or applied research (see Grix, 2004; Heppner and Heppner, 2004; Mertens, 2005, among many others). Not everyone agrees on the terms for each paradigm or on the discrete nature of each. However, most would agree that taking a critical stance in research is embedded in paradigms at the opposite end of the continuum from the positivist paradigm. Within these paradigms, researchers define the nature of the world subjectively and use methodologies that define knowledge from a subjectivist point of view. Researchers who take a stance in research are conscious of the relationship between the researcher and the object of the research. There is an acknowledgement of the researcher's belief systems and of the impact a researcher can have on the object of the research. Most important to all these critical stances in research is the desire to transform existing forms of social organisation. The purpose of research conducted within the critical paradigms is not just to describe or understand social phenomena but also to change them. This is in contrast to the purposes of traditional research which are most often to explain or understand the social world.

Foundations of research

It is generally acknowledged that a research paradigm includes three dimensions: an ontological perspective, an epistemological perspective and methodological approaches that are most often associated with the paradigm. The paradigms that are grounded in the critical perspectives or theories above are most often labelled transformative, postmodern, emancipatory or simply critical theorist (all hereafter referred to as transformative). Research continua that include action research often identify another paradigm labelled participatory or pragmatic that also includes transformative perspectives along with traditional perspectives. The ontological underpinnings of such paradigms address the question of what the nature of reality is. The epistemological foundation addresses the nature of knowledge and the relationship between the knower and what is to be known. Appropriate methodologies follow from the notion of how the knower can best learn the desired knowledge or understandings (Mertens, 2005).

Ontological foundations range from the belief that there is a reality out there that can be apprehended objectively to the belief that all realities are constructed by the perceiver. A critical stance embraces the latter. A critical perspective also takes the epistemological position that there is no knowledge that is value neutral in contrast to the belief that there is an objective truth. Thus, researchers operating under transformative paradigms accept that reality is shaped by conditions – historical, social, political, cultural, religious, economic, race- and/or gender-related, determined by sexual orientation, and ability-related. And unlike researchers who adopt a post-positivist or constructivist or interpretivist stance, transformative researchers create knowledge 'with' instead of 'for' powerless populations such as students, teachers, parents, custodial or secretarial staff. In particular, they investigate issues of marginalisation that are related to gender, race, poverty, disability, sexual orientation, religious difference and/or other marginalising structures. Often of interest are the intersectionalities between and among such structures.

As will become clear, there is no one philosophy or theory that characterises transformative research paradigms. Theories labelled poststructuralist and, later, postmodernist emerged in the late 1960s, the 1970s and 1980s to challenge modernist notions of certainty and truth. Other critical theories that derived from the feminist movement at about the same time introduced another set of constructs that questioned patriarchy and its many outcomes, though not all feminist theories take a critical stance. More recently, individuals whose ethnicities separate them from the dominant white populations around the world have developed and tested critical race theories and postcolonial theories. In addition, there is a growing research tradition using queer theories to help challenge the heteronormative view of the world that has dominated modernity.

This is not an exhaustive list of critical stances. However, these stances can and do provide us with many useful insights into the practices and policies surrounding educational leadership. To date there are more examples available in English of research informed by feminist, postmodern, feminist postmodern/poststructural and critical race theories in educational leadership than of research using postcolonial or queer theories. We offer some examples.

Postmodernist/poststructuralist stances

French writers such as Michel Foucault, Louis Althusser, Jacques Derrida and Jean-François Lyotard, among others, introduced a critique of modernism that has gained considerable popularity in the latter part of the twentieth century and on into the twenty-first century. Although the meaning of the terms is contested and the way each writer conceptualised his ideas differs, postmodern and poststructural labels have been applied to their ideas (see English, 2004; Turner, 1990). For the most part, postmodern and poststructural are used interchangeably in this chapter though the theories and constructs that characterise them are not entirely synonymous. An exception is the reference to feminist poststructualism (Weedon, 1997).

Central to most postmodern theories is an interest in language, subjectivity and meaning. They also share a suspicion of the 'grand narratives' or theories that are claimed as having universal application – such as functionalism, liberalism, Marxism, scientific theories, Western philosophy, and so on. Therefore, researchers taking a postmodern stance would shy away from utilising grand or formal theories in their work.

Postmodernism abandons the modernist tradition of seeking truth and objectivity in research. It also denies the idea of 'progress' that is accompanied by the steady 'enlightening' and 'civilising' of human beings across the globe. '[P]ostmodernism has been distinguished by its distrust and rejection of such totalizing discourses of modernism in favour of limitless diversity and difference' (King, 1999: 475).

A postmodern stance on educational leadership questions the very notion of foundational knowledge of administration and management of schools. 'Indeed, such theories in management science represent attempts to solidify the power base of those presenting them' (Littrell and Foster, 1995: 36). Using the postmodern critique of who is best served by the way things are, it becomes clear that educational administration is dominated by the white, male, middle-class scholars who are in the business of defining knowledge in the field.

A knowledge base is unnecessary since postmodernism asserts that meanings of social phenomena are continually shifting and being re-assessed. This critique rejects the modernist approaches to organisational analysis that are based on positivist studies of management processes. Capper (1995) argues that from a poststructuralist perspective, the very definition of leader would be contested since it has emerged from a rationalist, narrowly construed idea of top-down decision making. Also suspect is the totalising and de-personalising experience of working and learning in organisations as modernist theories describe them. In the traditional scientific discourse of administration and management, 'social institutions come to control through language the very people who compose them' (Maxcy, 1994: 12).

Drawing on Foucault's (1977) concept of the Panopticon, researchers of educational leadership begin to understand in more complex terms the relations of power and discipline as they are played out in schools (McKinney and Garrison, 1994; see also Chapter 21 in this book). These ideas provide some of the earliest critiques in the late 1980s of the narrow focus of accountability and the damage of high-stakes testing in the USA. The concept of technocratic education and its attendant instrumentality emerged (Foster, 1986).

Many of these themes are taken up and further complexified by the intersections of postmodern thought with the critical stances that follow. Further examples of postmodernist approaches to studies in educational leadership include English (2004) and Sugrue and Furlong (2002).

Critical feminist stances

Feminist theories have a common focus on gender inequities and women's rights. Two specific feminist theoretical approaches can be included in transformative paradigms as they have been defined here: feminist standpoint theories and feminist postmodern theories.

Standpoint

The basis of feminist standpoint theory is that all knowledge is dependent on the social and historical context of the individual knower. In other words, an individual's standpoint influences her knowledge of the world and her standpoint is shaped by the economic and political situation in which she is situated. As with most critical feminist theories, attention is paid to the question of power at the intersections of gender with race, class and sexuality. Nancy

Hartsock (1983) and Sandra Harding (1991, 2004) are probably the best-known proponents of feminist standpoint theory. Harding (1993) states: 'Standpoint epistemology sets the relationship between knowledge and politics at the center of its account ...' (cited in Mertens, 2005: 21). Patricia Hill Collins (2000) problematises the social and economic location of black women through standpoint theory, arguing that they are better situated not only to understand their own lived experiences, but are also able to shed light on privileged others' views of the world. Consequently, standpoint theory provides an opportunity for black women to define themselves in a framework that includes their personal and cultural beliefs while suggesting transformative actions that might acknowledge and/or remediate the oppression. It provides 'conceptual and representational tools that explicate deep meanings of the very bases of educational research and leadership, its ontologies, epistemologies, pedagogies, and its ethical concerns' (Dillard, 2003: 131).

Feminist standpoint theorists encourage researchers to generate research questions that arise from the lives and experiences of marginalised people. The purpose of such research would be to help generate power for those without it (Mertens, 2005). Women's experiences, knowledge and subjectivities (their standpoints) ground their research (Hammers and Brown, 2004).

Postmodern

Many feminist researchers have found inspiration in postmodern ideas. One of the best-known examples is Chris Weedon (1997), who combined poststructuralist theories with feminism. Originally published in 1987, her book *Feminist Practice and Poststructuralist Theory* paved the way for researchers in many of the social sciences to use the critical tools of language, discourse, subjectivity and common sense (commonly held beliefs used to maintain the status quo) introduced by poststructuralism to studies of gender power relations. She posed an agenda for feminist poststructuralism which centred on an investigation into why women tolerated 'social relations which subordinate their interests to those of men, and mechanisms whereby women and men adopt particular discursive positions as representative of their interests' (Weedon, 1997: 12).

Postmodern feminist researchers are often interested in 'textual analysis and the role of the text in sustaining the integration of power and oppression' (Mertens, 2005: 22). There is an emphasis on deconstructing binary categories such as leader/follower, light/dark, order/chaos, man/woman, etc. The notion is that instead of seeing the world dichotomously, a more fluid blurring of distinctions is productive. Postmodernism also questions the implied privileging of the first of these binary oppositions. Moving out from the text, some researchers investigate the various institutional discourses within which women and other marginalised individuals are situated (see Davies, 1994; Grogan, 1996). The purpose of a focus on discourse is to discover how the discourse shapes participants' subject position. We are all situated in different discourses, but particularly for women and individuals of colour, the discourses often conflict with each other. As Davies (1994: 26) explains:

My intention in elaborating feminist poststructuralist theory in relation to education … is to enable the participants to have a different way of seeing that does not necessarily replace other ways of seeing, but enables the student and the teacher to *position themselves differently* in relation to existing discourses. (Emphasis in the original)

Importance is placed on the understanding that the product of any research is a construction of reality, not a representation of it. An effective tool that allows critical feminist researchers to attend to this point is reflexivity. A reflexive approach is one where the researcher critically reflects on her academic, race, class or other privileges, and on her methodologies, to be sure that she is not creating knowledge from her own life (mind).

As with all critical stances, both quantitative and qualitative methods are used in feminist research. Those who employ quantitative tools have been careful to use critical perspectives in framing questions and/or in understanding data. Feminist researchers using quantitative methods have also departed from the positivist tradition by examining the impact on their research of their own values and social class or otherwise privileged positions. Fonow and Cook (2005) make the point that feminist researchers have sought to bridge the gap between quantitative and qualitative methods by doing collaborative research and by searching for more nuanced and sophisticated ways to measure complex issues. Qualitative tools allow the feminist researcher to probe social phenomena in depth and to hear participants' own accounts of their lived experiences. Good use has been made of mixed methods where a large enough sample has been surveyed to permit generalisation, and in-depth interviews or observations have followed particular quantitative findings in order to enrich understanding. Ethnography has often been chosen by those wishing to study marginalised populations over time. In addition, participatory action research offers excellent opportunities for collaborative research with participants (see Lather and Smithies, 1997). (See also Chapter 14 for further discussion of ethnography.)

Examples of feminist standpoint or postmodern studies pertaining to educational leadership include: Ah-Nee-Benham (2003); Blackmore (1999); Brunner (2002); Coleman (2002, 2011); Dillard (2006); Gardiner et al., (2000); Grogan (1996, 2000); Hall (1996, 1997); Mendez-Morse (2003); Scott (2003); Sherman (2010); Simmons and Johnson (2008) and Skrla (2003).

Critical race theory

Studies highlighting issues of race and racism in education that are informed by critical race theory (CRT) have been prominent in North America for the past decade or more and are now appearing in the UK. Many more scholars have employed this approach to research on education and educational leadership in the USA than have used the other critical stances discussed here. Therefore, we go into more depth on CRT and its offshoot LatCrit (Iglesias, 1999) to do justice to this growing body of research.

Gloria Ladson-Billings and William Tate (1995) published an article that first brought attention to the need for race-related critical analyses in education. CRT has its roots in critical legal studies in the USA, which critiqued American jurisprudence from a Marxist/postmodern perspective. But it did not go far enough. A growing number of scholars of colour realised the necessity of foregrounding and centring race. For instance, as Ladson-Billings and Tate (1995) and in the UK Gillborn (2005) argue, even though class and gender and their intersections with race are important categories contributing to our understanding of many school achievement issues, they still do not account for all inequalities between whites and students of colour. Many researchers of colour and others have begun to investigate educational issues through a CRT framework so as to question the dominant white causal conceptions and theories. Parker and Lynn (2002: 10) define three main goals for CRT:

(a) to present storytelling and narratives as valid approaches through which to examine race and racism in the law and society

(b) to argue for the eradication of racial subjugation while simultaneously recognising that race is a social construct

(c) to draw important relationships between race and other axes of domination.

The notion of institutionalised racism is a very important understanding brought to the fore by CRT. Scholars using the theory have argued that race is a permanent force in the USA, and that racism is not limited to individually perpetrated acts of discrimination, exclusion and/or violence. Influenced by postmodern critiques of societal structures, race and racism are seen as permeating laws and everyday policy and practice (see Young and Laible, 2000). Lopez (2003) argues that allowing racism to be defined as hateful acts or disparaging language encourages the idea that a decrease in those acts means a decrease in racism. This is essentially naïve because societal racism is far deeper and more systemic. Institutional racism is best understood when race is placed at the centre of research.

Another tenet of CRT is interest convergence, which emerges out of a Marxist view that the proletariat will only benefit from legal advances if the bourgeoisie stand to gain more power and privilege. Interest convergence is the understanding that changes in the law and in policies and practices that help to improve the social, economic or political situation of racial minorities only occur when such changes are also in the interests of the white, middle-class society (Kohn, 1998). For instance, during the Second World War, when it was in the interests of the country to mobilise as many troops as possible to fight foreign enemies, African-American men were readily accepted into the US military, and given some status even though segregation was alive and well in the South. Another example includes the landmark US Supreme Court decision *Brown* v. *The Board of Education* (1954; this was the US Supreme Court case that ended the legal separation of black students from white students in the US public schools). Using the framework of CRT, it becomes clear that it was politically important for the United States to be seen abroad as sensitive to the segregated conditions of schooling for African-Americans. The United States needed Third World allies in their Cold War struggle and they wanted to improve their racist image abroad (Bell, 1995; Lopez, 2003; Taylor, 2006).

The value of narratives and counter-stories is another key feature of CRT. Taylor (2006) argues that it is important to hear about experience of school from non-white students, teachers, administrators and parents. For instance, the practices of ability grouping and tracking in schools coincide with the racial identities of students – few African-American and Latino students are in US college preparatory classes. What happens when minority students read little about themselves that is positive in their texts? Pernicious stereotyping of children of colour (with the exception of some Asian-American groups) as less academically capable and uninterested in school affects teachers' expectations in the classroom. CRT urges researchers to provide students' stories that illustrate their experiences. A powerful example is DeCuir and Dixon's (2004) study of African-American high school students struggling in an elite private preparatory school.

Another critical stance taken by researchers who centre race is critical spiritualist (see Dantley, 2005; Dillard, 2006). Dantley argues that this approach is most important for African-American educational leaders in urban settings where the majority of students are students of colour. '[T]heir work is not only intellectual but can also be political and grounded in spirituality ... a spirituality that promotes dealing with pressing social issues through a mind-set that creates ways for leaders and the rest of the learning community to unravel and overcome obstacles they may face' (p. 662). He urges the inclusion of the idea of critical spiritualism in leadership preparation programmes.

Additional examples of CRT/LatCrit-informed research pertaining to educational leadership include: Cooper (2009); Fernandez (2002); Gillborn (2005); Lewis (2001); Rodriguez and Alanis, (2011); Solorzano and Delgado Bernal (2001); Solorzano and Yosso (2002) and Theoharis (2007).

Queer theory

Queer theory is a fairly recent addition to the critical stances that have informed research and data analysis. Derived from a postmodernist deconstruction of the stable identity, queer theory calls into question and problematises such binary constructions as straight/gay and male/female. That sexuality is naturally, as opposed to socially, produced is also critiqued. Just as feminist poststructuralists do, queer theorists abandon the notion of a fixed identity. Instead they use the idea of unstable and multiple subjectivities: 'Queer theory has established sexual identity as a central axis of contemporary critical discourse about personhood and agency' (Hostetler and Herdt, 1998: 250).

The origins of queer theory are thought to be in the gay and lesbian studies of the late 1980s and 1990s as gay and AIDs activists sought appropriate theoretical perspectives to counter the discrimination and violence associated with homosexuality and the disease (Hostetler and Herdt, 1998). Informed by poststructuralist and feminist theories, queer theory centres on the notion of sexuality to challenge the restrictive and damaging heteronormative and homophobic social order. Hammers and Brown (2004) offer the insight that a feminist queer alliance can provide a very productive approach to research that aims to transform social constructions. They emphasise that such research should employ 'a reflexive and critical stance, praxis, and the use of participatory methods' (p. 100). By adopting sexuality as an analytic category, queer theory opens up a space for interrogating commonly held assumptions of sex, sexuality, pleasure, desire and how each of these intersects (Sumara and Davis, 1999). One key purpose in using queer theory in education is to provide an opportunity for resistance to the strongly heteronormative cultures of schools.

From a management perspective, Lugg (2003) observes that public school districts in the USA not only fail to address queer and gender issues, but they also make a conscious effort not to employ queer people. She uses queer legal theory to show how, historically, public schools have been particularly homophobic. This intersection between queer theory and critical legal studies, like the intersection that created CRT, provides an effective theoretical lens through which to understand discrimination and the abrogation of human rights in educational settings.

Critiquing pedagogy and curriculum through the lens of queer theory offers an opportunity to broaden the notions of what counts as knowledge. Sumara and Davis (1999) explain that in examining the forms of curriculum, researchers can identify what counts as difference or *other* within the prescribed texts, materials and teaching/administrative practices. And:

> Rather than defining queer identities in strict reference to particular bodily acts and aberrant or quirky lifestyles, queer theory asks that the continued construction of narratives supporting that unruly category 'heterosexual' be constantly interrupted and renarrated. (p. 192)

Qualitative methodologies have been most often used in studies informed by queer theory. Critical ethnography offers important transformative dimensions to such research. However, this is not in the traditional sense. Both queer theory and postmodern theory insist on researcher accountability and sensitivity to the representation of participants. King (1999) insists that it is the duty of the ethnographer to shy away from deciding what and how change should occur. Instead, in the ethnographic account, the key is the opportunity for participant self-examination that may or may not be transformative.

Studies from a critical queer perspective have investigated different aspects of education. King (1998) studied male elementary school teachers to understand the gender and sexual identity issues that surrounded males teaching in an overwhelmingly female environment. With a group of self-identified gay, lesbian and transgendered teachers, Sumara (1996) conducted a study of literary texts written by and about authors who identified as queer. The purpose of the study was to learn from the group's identifications to, and interpretations of, the texts. And Koschoreck (2003) studied gay principals in American public schools.

To further understand how queer theory is used to illuminate issues in educational administration, see Capper (1998), Lugg (2003) and Lugg and Tooms (2010).

Postcolonial theory

There is not much evidence of the use of postcolonial theory in the USA to inform studies of educational leadership yet. However, the theory offers interesting and important insights into the epistemological foundations of education, which have implications for educational leadership around the globe. Since the study of leadership and management in business and education has been and continues to be informed largely by Western concepts and ideas, it is appropriate to introduce a critical perspective that challenges the dominance of Western practice and policy (cf. the critique offered to Western concepts in Chapter 4 of this book).

As the name suggests, postcolonial theory emerged from a critique of the way Eurocentric colonial practices and policies shaped colonised societies. The theory has a historical dimension, referring to the Western colonialism that spread across the world in the wake of the Industrial Revolution. This modern Western colonialism (distinguishing it from the continuous conquest and colonisation of earlier empires such as the Byzantine, Inca, Mongol, Roman, etc.) is particularly powerful because: '[it] represents a unique constellation of complex and interrelated practices that sought to establish Western hegemony not only politically, militarily, and economically, but also culturally and ideologically' (Prasad, 2003: 5). As a critical stance, postcolonialism questions and explores the multiple and layered experiences of colonisation and people's resistance to it both in the (former) colonies and in the West.

But the theory is not limited to a narrow interpretation of colonisation. It includes the notions of neo-colonialism, which pertain to the continued economic dependence of independent nations on their former European power, and the newer forms of imperialism such as those associated with US economic, political and cultural global dominance. In addition, it provides a powerful lens to study immigrant experiences in the West (Nguyen, 2006). The theory offers researchers opportunities to understand more fully how Western culture, knowledge and epistemology profoundly affect non-Western societies, and how the complex dynamics of Western hegemony contribute to the continued international regime of exploitation and deprivation (Prasad and Prasad, 2003).

Postcolonial theory has had a significant impact on studies of literature in English. New understandings have emerged about language as English (capitalised to denote the language of the coloniser) becomes replaced and intertwined with english (small 'e' to denote the language enriched by local languages and usages). Important insights include: the expanded, contested, yet fluid sense of identity and thought english contributes, and the multi-layered concepts of place and displacement experienced by both colonisers and the colonised (Ashcroft et al., 2002). Nguyen (2006) expands the lens of colonisation in her interrogation of this same notion of place and displacement with the children of Vietnamese immigrants in a US school.

Like the other critical stances identified in this chapter, postcolonial theory offers epistemological and methodological approaches that question and challenge the traditional. Research that employs postcolonial theory often uses qualitative tools and designs. Postcolonialism exposes even more blatantly the challenge of representation with which critical feminism and queer theory are also concerned. When the researcher is an outsider or even an outsider 'within' a community, especially one bringing Western knowledge and practice, it becomes extremely important (a) that the researcher does not exploit the participants for her own academic purposes, and (b) that the researcher reflexively interrogates whose knowledge is being produced by the study. Echoing the cautions found in queer theory, postcolonial theory cautions that change must be owned by and be in the interests of the participants. Nagar (2003) explores these tensions as she writes about two studies in which she has been involved in North India. For instance, she makes the point that the women she has been studying must be trained as community researchers so that they can continue the research to solve their own problems without relying on outside experts.

Some examples of cross-cultural educational research that is informed by postcolonial theory are: Abu-Rabia Quader and Oplatka (2008); Blackmore (2010); Fitzgerald (2003); Johnson (2005); London (2004); and Tikly (1999).

Conclusion

The degree to which these varied stances in critical theory have contributed to educational leadership research is difficult to measure. Although some researchers have been cited in this chapter as examples of positive knowledge production from their critical stance research (see, for example, Blackmore, 1999; Collins, 2000; Johnson, 2005; Ladson-Billings 1999), acceptance of their work by the educational research community continues to be challenged by those who adhere to traditional educational research theory. It is also suspected that the works of several other critical stance researchers have been silenced from the outset. One may never realise the numerous contributions that might have added value to the educational leadership preparation discourse, but were rejected, instead, by the establishment, by those who did not value research diversity. It is hoped, nonetheless, that a new dynamic of possibilities in educational leadership may be allowed that includes reconsiderations, questions and debates about what is 'empirically legitimised'. These discussions must also include in-depth analyses of world views that disparage anything that is contextually/socially constructed; or non-universal/specific to certain lived experiences that may be emotional, literary or intensely personal. This would end colonised restrictions that have been used for too long as extreme common devices not just by which subject positioning is obscured, but by which agency and responsibility are befuddled, and would replace such with democratic freedoms that might contribute to a new way of preparing for true educational leadership.

Key points

- To take a critical stance in research is to critique the status quo.
- Most critiques offer possibilities for change or transformation so that those who have been marginalised and disenfranchised by current practices and policies will be better served.
- Critical stances include, but are not limited to, postmodernist, critical race-related, feminist, queer and postcolonial.
- A critical stance accepts that realities are constructed by the perceiver and that there is no knowledge that is value neutral.
- Postmodernist/poststructuralist theories use constructs such as power, subjectivity and language to question anything considered universal.
- Critical feminist theories embrace reflexivity to understand women's lived experiences, in all diverse forms, as other than and often subordinate to men's lived experiences.
- Critical race theory, including LatCrit, grounded in critical legal theories and discourse, foregrounds race and exposes the inequalities and inequities associated with institutional racism.
- Queer theory problematizes such binary constructions as straight/gay and male/female and allows insights into the negative effects of homophobic stereotyping.
- Postcolonial theory critiques Eurocentric colonial practices and their legacies to better understand postcolonial societies.
- Not enough leadership research in education has been conducted using any or all of these critical stances.
- When more leadership research in education is informed by these and other critical stances, and when such research is truly valued, the preparation of leaders will be greatly enhanced.

Questions and reflections

1 To what extent do those that provide your leadership programmes adopt a critical stance and/or provide materials for you to read that are based on any of the critical theories mentioned in this chapter?
2 As we move further into the 21st century, what other marginalising conditions, not mentioned in this chapter, do we need to become more aware of?

Recommended further reading

For recommended reading on critical feminist stances, critical race theory, queer theory and postcolonial theory, see the end of each section in this chapter. For further reading, see below.

English, F.W. (ed.) (2011) *Sage Handbook of Educational Leadership*. Thousand Oaks, CA: Sage.

This new text provides several chapters grounded in critical theories.

Grogan, M. and Shakeshaft, C. (2011) *Women and Educational Leadership*. San Francisco CA: Jossey-Bass.

Women leaders bring diverse lived experiences to the exercise of leadership. Researchers and practitioners will find good examples of ways to harness this diversity to address the needs of marginalised people in this book.

Marshall, C. and Oliva, M. (2005) *Leadership for Social Justice*. Boston, MA: Allyn and Bacon.

This is a textbook that provides good examples of how leadership can address issues that affect various marginalised populations in the USA, offering researchers an excellent starting point for further research to benefit those who have not been well served by current educational systems.

Ngunjiri, F.W. (2010) *Women's Spirtual Leadership in Africa*. Albany, NY: SUNY Press.

This is another thought-provoking book drawing on women's leadership. It uses black feminist standpoint theories and intersectionality to understand women's leadership under postcolonial conditions in Africa.

References

Abu-Rabia Quader, S. and Oplatka, I. (2008) The power of femininity: exploring the gender and ethnic experiences of Muslim women in a Bedouin society. *Journal of Educational Administration* 46(3): 396–415.

Ah-Nee-Benham, M. (2003) In our mother's voice: a native woman's knowing of leadership, in Young, M. and Skrla, L. (eds) *Reconsidering Feminist Research in Educational Leadership*. Albany, NY: State University of New York Press. pp. 223–46.

Ashcroft, B., Griffiths, G. and Tiffin, H. (2002) *The Empire Writes Back: Theory and Practice in Post-colonial Literatures* (2nd edn). New York: Routledge.

Bell, D.A. (1995) *Brown v. Board of Education* and the interest convergence dilemma, in Crenshaw, K., Gotanda, N., Peller, G. and Thomas, K. (eds) *Critical Race Theory: The Key Writings that Formed the Movement*. New York: The New Press. pp. 20–9.

Blackmore, J. (1999) *Troubling Women: Feminism, Leadership and Educational Change*. Buckingham: Open University Press.

Blackmore, J. (2010) Disrupting notions of leadership from feminist, post-colonial positions. *International Journal of Leadership in Education: Theory and Practice* 13(1): 1–6.

Brunner, C.C. (2002) A proposition for the reconception of the superintendency: reconsidering traditional and nontraditional discourses. *Educational Administration Quarterly* 38(3): 402–31.

Capper, C.A. (1995) An otherist poststructural perspective of the knowledge base in educational administration, in Donmoyer, R., Imber, M. and Scheurich, J.J. (eds) *The Knowledge Base in Educational Administration: Multiple Perspectives*. Albany, NY: State University of New York Press. pp. 285–99.

Capper, C.A. (1998) Critically oriented and postmodern perspectives: sorting out the differences and applications for practice. *Educational Administration Quarterly* 34(3): 354–79.

Coleman, M. (2002) *Women as Headteachers: Striking the Balance*. Stoke on Trent: Trentham Books.

Coleman, M. (2011) *Women at the Top: Challenges, Choices and Change*. Basingstoke, Palgrave Macmillan.

Collins, P. Hill (2000) *Black Feminist Thought: Knowledge, Consciousness and the Politics of Empowerment* (2nd edn). New York: Routledge.

Cooper, C.W. (2009) Performing cultural work in demographically changing schools: implications for expanding transformative leadership frameworks. *Educational Administration Quarterly* 45(5): 694–724.

Dantley, M.E. (2005) African American spirituality and Cornel West's notions of prophetic pragmatism: restructuring educational leadership in American Urban Schools. *Educational Administration Quarterly* 41(4): 651–74.

Davies, B. (1994) *Poststructuralist Theory and Classroom Practice*. Geelong: Deakin University.

DeCuir, J.T. and Dixon, A. (2004) 'So when it comes out, they aren't that surprised that it is there': using critical race theory as a tool of analysis of race and racism in education. *Education Researcher* 33(5): 26–31.

Dillard, C.B. (2003) The substance of things hoped for, the evidence of things not seen: examining an endarkened feminist epistemology in educational research and leadership, in Young, M.D. and Skrla, L. (eds) *Reconsidering Feminist Research in Educational Leadership*. Albany, NY: State University of New York Press. pp. 131–59.

Dillard, C.B. (2006) *On Spiritual Strivings: Transforming an African-American Woman's Academic Life*. Albany, NY: State University of New York Press.

English, F.W. (2004) *Theory in Educational Administration*. New York: HarperCollins.

English, F.W. (ed.) (2011) *Sage Handbook of Educational Leadership*. Thousand Oaks, CA: Sage.

Fernandez, L. (2002) Telling stories about school: using critical race and Latino critical theories to document Latina/Latino education and resistance. *Qualitative Inquiry* 8(1): 45–65.

Fitzgerald, T. (2003) Changing the deafening silence of indigenous women's voices in educational leadership. *Journal of Educational Administration* 41(1): 9–23.

Fonow, M.M. and Cook, J.A. (2005) Feminist methodology: new applications in the academy and public policy. *Signs: Journal of Women in Culture and Society* 30(4): 2211–36.

Foster, W. (1986) *Paradigms and Promises: New Approaches to Educational Administration*. Buffalo, NY: Prometheus Books.

Foucault, M. (1977) *Discipline and Punish: The Birth of the Prison*. New York: Pantheon.

Gardiner, M., Enomoto, E. and Grogan, M. (2000) *Coloring Outside the Lines: Mentoring Women into Educational Leadership*. Albany, NY: SUNY Press.

Gillborn, D. (2005) Education policy as an act of white supremacy: whiteness, critical race theory and education reform. *Journal of Education Policy* 20(4): 485–505.

Grix, J. (2004) *The Foundations of Research*. New York: Palgrave Macmillan.

Grogan, M. (1996) *Voices of Women in the Superintendency*. Albany, NY: State University of New York Press.

Grogan, M. (2000) The short tenure of a woman superintendent: a clash of gender and politics. *Journal of School Leadership* 10(2): 104–30.

Hall, V. (1996) *Dancing on the Ceiling: A Study of Women Managers in Education*. London: Paul Chapman.

Hall, V. (1997) Dusting off the phoenix: gender and educational management revisited. *Educational Management and Administration* 25(3): 309–24.

Hammers, C. and Brown, A.D. III (2004) Towards a feminist–queer alliance: a paradigmatic shift in the research process. *Social Epistemology* 18(1): 85–101.

Harding, S.G. (1991) *Whose Science? Whose Knowledge? Thinking from Women's Lives*. Ithaca, NY: Cornell University Press.

Harding, S.G. (ed.) (2004) *The Feminist Standpoint Theory Reader: Intellectual and Political Controversies*. New York: Routledge.

Hartsock, N.C.M. (1983) The feminist standpoint: developing the ground for a specifically feminist historical materialism, in Harding, S. and Hintikka, M. (eds) *Discovering Reality: Feminist Perspectives on Epistemology, Metaphysics, Methodology, and Philosophy of Science*. Boston, MA: D. Reidel Publishing. pp. 283–310.

Heppner, P.P. and Heppner, M.J. (2004) *Writing and Publishing Your Thesis, Dissertation and Research*. Belmont, CA: Brooks/Cole–Thompson Learning.

Hostetler, A.J. and Herdt, G.H. (1998) Culture, sexual lifeways, and developmental subjectivities: rethinking sexual taxonomies. *Social Research* 65(2): 249–90.

Iglesias, E.M. (1999) LatCrit theory: some preliminary notes towards a transatlantic dialogue. Available at: http://personal.law.miami.edu/~iglesias/transatlantic.htm (accessed 30 May 2011).

Johnson, G.G. (2005) Resilience, a story: a postcolonial position from which to [re] view Indian education framed in 'at-risk' ideology. *Education Studies* 34(2): 182–97.

King, J.R. (1998) *Uncommon Caring: Learning from Men who Teach Young Children*. New York: Teachers College Press.

King, J.R. (1999) Am not! Are too! Using queer standpoint in postmodern critical ethnography. *International Journal of Qualitative Studies in Education* 12(5): 473–90.

Kohn, A. (1998) Only for my kid: how privileged parents undermine school reform. *Phi Delta Kappan* 79: 568–77.

Koschoreck, J.W. (2003) Easing the violence: transgressing heteronormativity in educational administration. *Journal of School Leadership* 13(1): 27–50.

Ladson-Billings, G. (1999) Just what is critical race theory, and what's it doing in a 'nice' field like education? In Parker, L., Deyhle, D. and Villenas, S. (eds) *Race Is… Race Isn't: Critical Race Theory and Qualitative Studies in Education*. Boulder, CO: Westview. pp. 7–30.

Ladson-Billings, G. and Tate, W.F. IV (1995) Towards a critical race theory of education. *Teachers College Record*, 97.

Lather, P. and Smithies, C. (1997) *Troubling the Angels: Women Living with HIV/AIDS*. Boulder, CO: Westview.

Lewis, A.E. (2001) There is no 'race' in the schoolyard: color-blind ideology in an (almost) all-white school. *American Educational Research Journal* 38(4): 781–811.

Littrell, J. and Foster, W. (1995) The myth of a knowledge base in educational administration, in Donmoyer, R., Imber, M. and Scheurich, J.J. (eds) *The Knowledge Base in Educational Administration: Multiple Perspectives*. Albany, NY: State University of New York Press. pp. 32–46.

London, N. (2004) School inspection, the inspectorate and educational practice in Trinidad and Tobago. *Journal of Educational Administration* 42(4): 479–501.

Lopez, G.R. (2003) The (racially neutral) politics of education: a critical race theory perspective. *Educational Administration Quarterly* 39(1): 68–94.

Lugg, C.A. (2003) Sissies, faggots, lezzies, and dykes: gender, sexual orientation, and a new politics of education. *Educational Administration Quarterly* 39(1): 95–134.

Lugg, C.A. and Tooms, A. (2010) A shadow of ourselves: identity erasure and the politics of queer leadership. *School Leadership and Management* 30(1): 77–91.

Maxcy, S.J. (1994) Introduction, in Maxcy, S.J. (ed.) *Postmodern School Leadership: Meeting the Crisis in Educational Administration*. Westport, CT: Praeger. pp. 1–16.

Mendez-Morse, S. (2003) Chicana feminism and educational leadership, in Young, M. and Skrla, L. (eds) *Reconsidering Feminist Research in Educational Leadership*. Albany, NY: State University of New York Press. pp. 161–78.

Mertens, D.M. (2005) *Research and Evaluation in Education and Psychology: Interpreting Diversity with Quantitative, Qualitative, and Mixed Methods*. Thousand Oaks, CA: Sage.

Nagar, R. (2003) Collaboration across borders: moving beyond positionality. *Singapore Journal of Tropical Geography* 24(3): 356–72.

Nguyen, T.S.T. (2006) 'They don't even know what Vietnam is!': The production of space through hybrid place-making and performativity in an urban public elementary school. Unpublished doctoral dissertation, University of Texas at Austin.

Parker, L. and Lynn, M. (2002) What's race got to do with it? Critical Race Theory's conflicts with and connections to qualitative research methodology and epistemology. *Qualitative Inquiry* 8(1): 7–22.

Prasad, A. (2003) The gaze of the other: postcolonial theory and organizational analysis, in Prasad, A. (ed.) *Postcolonial Theory and Organizational Analysis: A Critical Engagement*. New York: Palgrave Macmillan. pp. 3–46.

Prasad, A. and Prasad, P. (2003) The postcolonial imagination, in Prasad, A. (ed.) *Postcolonial Theory and Organizational Analysis: A Critical Engagement*. New York: Palgrave Macmillan. pp. 283–95.

Rodriguez, M. and Alanis, I. (2011) Negotiating linguistic and cultural identity: one borderlander's initiative. *International Journal of Leadership in Education: Theory and Practice* 14(1): 103–17.

Scott, J. (2003) The linguistic production of genderlessness in the superintendency, in Young, M. and Skrla, L. (eds) *Reconsidering Feminist Research in Educational Leadership*. Albany, NY: State University of New York Press. pp. 81–102.

Sherman, W. (2010) Special issue: Globalization expanding horizons in women's leadership. *Journal of Educational Administration* 48(6).

Simmons, J.M. and Johnson, W.Y. (2008) African-American female superintendents speaking the language of hope: reconstructing the multi-dimension of passions, in Hoy, W. and DiPaola, M. (eds) *Improving Schools: Studies in Leadership and Culture*. Charlotte, NC: Information Age. pp. 223–49.

Skrla, L. (2003) Mourning silence: women superintendents (and a researcher) rethink speaking up and speaking out, in Young, M. and Skrla, L. (eds) *Reconsidering Feminist Research in Educational Leadership*. Albany, NY: State University of New York Press. pp. 103–28.

Solorzano, D.G. and Delgado Bernal, D. (2001) Examining transformational resistance through a critical race and LatCrit theory framework: Chicana and Chicano students in an urban context. *Urban Education* 36(3): 308–42.

Solorzano, D.G. and Yosso, T.J. (2002) Critical race methodology: counter-storytelling as an analytic framework for educational research. *Qualitative Inquiry* 8(1): 23–44.

Sugrue, C. and Furlong, C. (2002) The cosmology of Irish primary principals' identities: between the modern and the postmodern. *International Journal of Leadership in Education* 5(3): 189–210.

Sumara, D.J. (1996) *Private Readings in Public: Schooling the Literary Imagination*. New York: Peter Lang.

Sumara, D. and Davis, B. (1999) Interrupting heteronormativity: toward a queer curriculum theory. *Curriculum Inquiry* 29(2): 191–208.

Taylor, E. (2006) A critical race analysis of the achievement gap in the United States: politics, reality and hope. *Leadership and Policy in Schools* 5: 71–87.

Theoharis, G. (2007) Social justice educational leaders and resistance: towards a theory of social justice leadership. *Educational Administration Quarterly* 43(2): 221–58.

Tikly, L. (1999) Postcolonialism and comparative education. *International Review of Education* 45(5/6): 603–21.

Turner, B.S. (ed.) (1990) *Theories of Modernity and Postmodernity*. Newbury Park, CA: Sage.

Weedon, C. (1997) *Feminist Practice and Poststructuralist Theory* (2nd edn). Cambridge, MA: Blackwell.

Young, M.D. and Laible, J. (2000) White racism, anti-racism, and school leader preparation. *Journal of School Leadership* 10(5): 371–415.

CHAPTER 4

The Role of Culture in Interpreting and Conducting Research

David Stephens

Chapter objectives

The chapter is divided into two parts. The first, which is more theoretical, is guided by three questions:

- What is culture?
- To what extent is educational research a Western activity?
- What is the role of culture in the research process?

The second part focuses further upon the question of how such research might be carried out, making use of a recent example of a completed cross-cultural research project to identify some of the issues involved in conducting cross-cultural research.

Introduction

The purpose of this chapter is to examine the nature of cross-cultural educational research and to argue that at the heart of such research is the concept of culture. As researchers, it is important, wherever we carry out our research, to be aware of the cultural factors that shape our endeavour, whether these are epistemological, such as the type of knowledge we are seeking to discover, or linguistic, such as the language we are using to describe and discuss our findings. This is never more so than when a researcher from a Western cultural background carries out research in a non-Western context or vice versa.

Part 1: The importance of culture in research

Before we look in some detail at the notion of culture, let me present a brief overview of how I understand and interpret cross-cultural educational research.

At the heart of my meaning is a paradox, namely the desire to be sensitive to a particular research context, epitomised by Clifford Geertz's (2000) valuing of 'local knowledge', whilst at the same time using an analytical framework that is comparative, useful and reflexive.

An example may help here. In the late 1990s, a colleague and I set out to research issues of the quality of education in five very different cultural settings, which nonetheless included some similar features (Nepal, Lesotho, Kenya, Malaysia and Indonesia). Following Geertz, we valued local or 'micro level' knowledge and set out to generate as much evidence as we could 'on the ground'. But we did so by developing a 'macro level' comparative model which, at the time, we argued would: 'reflect the complexity of the elements which determine quality and qualitative improvement and indicate their inter-relation and inter-dependence' (Hawes and Stephens, 1990: 43).

These elements included:

- the goals and principles of practice, such as social and economic needs
- the conditions necessary for successful implementation, such as realism
- the agents of implementation, such as the community and its leaders.

Crucial to the interplay between the micro and macro levels is reflexivity; to be context-sensitive at the lower level, but equally reflexive at the macro-conceptual level. This is particularly the case when applying what are largely Western concepts and models of research to a non-Western context. Western here refers to Europe and North America and other Anglophone nations such as Australia and New Zealand. An alternative grouping is to refer to the Northern and Southern hemispheres: a useful differentiation as the Northern hemisphere countries are largely better off than the Southern. It should also be remembered that cultural contexts are not necessarily synonymous with national boundaries, reflecting instead, perhaps, urban–rural or formal–non-formal cultural divisions.

Let us begin with an exploration of the central concept that underpins cross-cultural research, namely culture.

The concept of culture

In 1969, as a sixth-form student, I remember one rainy afternoon our young history teacher giving each of us a blank sheet of paper and asking us to 'define culture'.

I am comforted to learn that others, more renowned than I, have also found the task problematic. Raymond Williams informs us that 'culture is one of the two or three most complicated words in the English language' (Williams, 1976: 77). This view is echoed in Eagleton's provocative study on *The Idea of*

Culture (2000). Culture, though, does seem to have something to do with *meaning*. In his examination of the methodology of cultural studies, Pertti Alasuutari (1995) expresses the view that 'qualitative analysis always deals with the concept of culture and explaining meaningful action' (1995: 2).

Others have focused upon the avoidance or sidelining of culture in contemporary study, it being referred to as 'the forgotten dimension' (Verhelst, 1987) and the 'neglected concept' (Smith and Bond, 1993; Thomas, 1994). Culture is often perceived as an overly complex concept that is not particularly usable or useful, and is the prerogative of the anthropologist and ethnographer rather than the researcher working, for example, in educational leadership and management.

But if we seriously want to carry out educational research – particularly of a qualitative kind – then, I would argue, the concept of culture must be foregrounded in both *what* we study and also in the *way* we design, execute, write up and disseminate our results. The whole nature of our research I suggest *is* cultural. This is particularly so when researching issues in educational leadership and management in that these fields are essentially concerned with how individuals change and grow in a particular learning environment, and how such individuals are managed and led.

Much of what has been written about the term *culture* indicates that there are different dimensions to the concept. First, culture exists on both an individual and social level, being concerned with what particular individuals think, learn and do and, second, it is about what a society considers important or meaningful. Third, culture as a concept has come to relate to both the desirable – for example, ideas of *kultur* and 'civilisation' in the eighteenth and nineteenth centuries – and the descriptive, current use of the term by sociologists and anthropologists when identifying specific cultures and sub-cultures.

In 1990, the Dutch Centre for the Study of Education in Developing Countries (CESO) produced a position paper on Education, Culture and Productive Life in Developing Countries, in which they argued that the concept of culture is more than Ralph Linton's 1964 'configuration of learned behaviour', arguing that it is fundamentally *ideational*, culture not being behaviour and customs, but the ideas which are used to shape behaviour and customs (CESO, 1990). I would argue that we can apply such ideas to the research endeavour. Culture, then, is a system of shared ideas, concepts, rules and meaning that underlie and are expressed in the ways that people live (Keesing, 1981).

Thierry Verhelst (1987) writing from a grassroots non-government organisation (NGO) development perspective extends this *ideational* view by suggesting that culture as a concept must not only be descriptive but useful, a concept embodying change, empowerment and the process of decision making. I would argue that some types of cross-cultural research (see the example of NGO-funded research later in this chapter) mirror such concerns, particularly in their desire to be useful and in their attention to problem solving.

Culture then impacts upon the interpreting and conducting of research in the following ways:

- It is central in the generation of 'important or meaningful' concepts we choose to research, for example, patterns of leadership.
- It gives meaning to the purposes and ideals that underpin research.
- It recognises the importance of context and local knowledge in the generation of both research questions and research responses.
- It relates to epistemological and linguistic aspects that shape the research enquiry, for example, how terms like 'management', 'observation' and 'consent' are understood in different socio-cultural settings.
- It encompasses issues of power and ideology within the research process from design to publication and dissemination, for example, who is setting the research agenda? Whose career will benefit from this research?

So bearing all this in mind, in hindsight, how might I now define culture as I was asked back in 1969? I would first draw upon Brian Bullivant's (1981) brave attempt to present a comprehensive definition of culture embracing all the aspects discussed so far:

> Culture is a patterned system of knowledge and conception embodied in symbolic and non-symbolic communication modes which a society has evolved from the past, and progressively augments to give meaning to and cope with the present and anticipated future problems of its existence. (Bullivant, 1981: 3)

And then add my own summary (Stephens, 2007) which suggests that culture is also concerned with two things, namely the: knowledge and ideas that give meaning to the beliefs and actions of individuals and societies; and its use as an ideational tool which can be used to describe and evaluate those beliefs and actions.

Culture, then, is both about what people think and do and conditions how we describe and evaluate those beliefs and actions.

Having focused on the concept of culture and its relevance to research, I now turn to consider the extent to which Western cultural values tend to dominate educational research.

To what extent is educational research a Western activity?

The theory and practice of educational research is generally rooted in Western culture. Linda Tuhiwai Smith (1999: 44) puts it bluntly:

> to a large extent theories about research are underpinned by a cultural system of classification and systems of representation, by views about human nature, human morality and virtue, by conceptions of space and time, by conceptions of gender and race. Ideas about these things help determine what counts as real.

The Western cultural system rests, to a large extent, upon technological–scientific forms and ideas shaped, since the Reformation, by the transformative forces of scientific rationalism and industrialisation (Odora Hoppers, 2002). Perhaps it is not only an epistemological question but an ideological and political one involving questions of ownership and the purpose of research. For Tuhiwai Smith (1999: 216): 'the term research is inextricably linked with European colonialism: the way in which scientific research has been implicated in the worst excesses of imperialism.'

It is important to recognise that Western researchers learn from questioning their own standpoint and being open to the viewpoints of non-Western cultures. It is also worth reminding ourselves of the cultural difficulties in using basically Western approaches in non-Western cultures and also in the increasingly multi-cultural contexts of Western societies. A number of these challenges relate to the status, gender, perceived wealth and education of the researcher. Another way of looking at this is to consider reasons why an interview carried out in an authoritarian context might be perceived as an interrogation. Or why an out-of-school girl in a male-dominated society might only be prepared to respond to questions from an older male interviewer, or why an economically poor rural teacher might legitimately enquire about his financial reward for completing a questionnaire.

Perhaps it is possible to steer a course that is both critical of Western epistemological stances and practical, in that it is appropriate to the specific culture. Odora Hoppers (2002) suggests that the way to the future is towards political and epistemological co-determination and *rapprochement*, an integrative coming together of world views that is not just pluralistic tolerance but affects the emergence of a new synthesis for acknowledging and incorporating cultural diversity.

On a more practical level: the development of a strong sense of researcher reflexivity; a fore-fronting of the purposes of the research; and a recognition of the importance of context and culture in the framing and carrying out of the research – from initial idea through to publication – would at least go some way to ensuring that research has cultural integrity.

It is worth noting here that particular research paradigms, quantitative or qualitative, for example, have more cultural 'weight' in different cultural settings (Denzin et al., 2006: 770). It is clear that in certain countries of the world, more and less credibility, kudos and status are given to scholars working from predominantly quantitative or qualitative approaches. However, this is not a simple divide between Western and non-Western research. The USA, for example, currently funds positivist, statistically heavy research in the field of educational leadership and management to a far greater extent than it does ethnographically inclined research. Denzin et al. (2006: 770) remind us of the relatively inimical attitude to qualitative research in current climates:

> Qualitative research exists at a time of global uncertainty. Around the globe governments are attempting to regulate the scientific inquiry by defining what good science is. Conservative regimes are enforcing evidence, or scientifically-based biomedical models of research. These regulatory activities raise fundamental philosophical issues for scholarship and freedom of speech in the academy. These threats constitute a challenge to qualitative inquiry.

However, all research and not just qualitative research needs to be understood within its political and ideological contexts.

What role does culture play in the research process?

Reviewing the literature – and there is a growing body of material coming out of UNESCO's activities worldwide as well as some interesting work in multi-cultural education and culturally conscious research in the USA, UK and elsewhere (see, for example, Dimmock and Walker, 2005; Ladson-Billings and Gillborn, 2004) – it is possible to gain a picture of what high quality, culturally appropriate research might look like. There are five key questions to be addressed:

- *What* in terms of cultural factors need to be identified in the content and methodology of research?
- *Where* will the research and publication be carried out?
- *Why* is the research being done?
- *Who* in terms of personnel will be involved in the research, and to what extent will research be both empowering and reflexive for researcher and researched?
- *How* might such research be achieved?

What in terms of cultural factors need to be identified in the content and methodology of research?

A way of addressing the 'what' question is to pose a number of reflexive questions during the initial brainstorming about the proposed focus of the research.

A few years ago, a colleague and I undertook an externally funded research project in South Africa. The project's aims were to investigate the relationship between schooling and cultural values in black, and what were termed in South Africa, coloured, urban and rural areas in the Western and Eastern Cape. We took a general cultural view of what we intended to research. Here are some of the questions we posed to ourselves and our local research partners in the field:

Q: *What can theories about culture tell us that is useful in framing the research problem? Are such theories predominantly Western? Will they 'fit' the cultural context in which we will be working?*

Q: *Which research traditions will we draw upon at the design and question framing stage?* (Interestingly, my colleague, a scholar of African literature, immediately started to draw inspiration from novels written about the places we would work, whereas I, as an historian, found myself wondering about the chronology of events that had influenced the communities and townships chosen for the research.)

Q: *To what extent will language and discourse shape and determine the focus and its interpretation?* (It was clear to us from the beginning that even a term as relatively well known as 'schooling' had very different connotations in different contexts. For example in Langa, a black township of Cape Town, the term was associated with ideas of social mobility, Christianity and the 'white' values of an aspiring middle class.)

It is the adopting of a cultural approach to the design of a research project that is significant. In posing the question, for example, 'How can we improve teacher education?', a cultural orientation to this question demands that we also first make a number of pre-requisite enquiries, such as how do research informants of a particular culture understand what it means to 'teach' or be trained?

Where will the research and publication be carried out?

In terms of *where* research is best carried out, it is worth remembering that 'all cultural data ... must be considered as belonging to somebody' (Rose, 1990). A proper use of context needs to be all-pervasive, to allow cultural factors to give meaning to the research environment.

In the early 2000s, I carried out several research and evaluation studies in two very different cultural contexts: Afghanistan (during and after the fall of the Taliban) and the People's Democratic Republic of Laos. A particular focus of the work involved evaluating the quality of educational leadership and management in the two national contexts. With colleagues from both countries, we identified cultural and contextual factors that we deemed important in shaping the design of the study. In Figure 4.1, I present a summary of some of the factors we decided to 'foreground':

Afghanistan 2002 and 2007

- High context culture (a society with close connections; Hall, 1976): meanings of events, phenomena and behaviour interpreted in terms of contexts in which they occur
- Collectivist rather than individualist culture (Hofstede, 2001)
- Importance of historical events, for example, Russian invasion, role of war lords
- Cultural issues surrounding security and post-Taliban nation-building
- Significance of religion (Islam) in values, attitudes towards knowledge, curriculum etc.
- Importance of external/globalising agents shaping educational policy, for example, USAID.

Laos 2000 and 2007

- High context, collectivist culture with strongly defined gender roles within education
- Importance of religion (Buddhist) and political culture (Communist) in shaping leadership/ management cultures in education
- Historical factors, for example, Vietnam War
- High levels of poverty, particularly in rural areas
- Research culture and epistemologies shaped by use of indigenous language/English.

Figure 4.1   Contextual factors foregrounded in the design of two research projects

Why is the research being done?

Why research is being done is a question that, curiously, is not always asked, perhaps because the answer is obvious, such as to acquire a PhD, or perhaps because the answer takes us into the realm of ethics, accountability and power. One view, taken by George (1984) for example, is that even posing the question has to be considered ideologically and in relation to the research approach being taken. Researchers and research informants need to relate to one another in ways which are, as far as is possible to ascertain, actionable and underpinned by informed consent and mutual respect. Researchers will be changed by the results of their research and also change the contexts they study, not least by their presence and the questions they ask. They must be accountable to the people who form the subjects of their work; and must be prepared to see the worth of that work evaluated according to the relevance it has to the lives of the community in question. Assessments of worth may vary considerably according to interpretations of the research outcomes by the various parties involved. Such interpretations are not necessarily understood in similar ways.

Who in terms of personnel will be involved in the research, and to what extent will research be both empowering and reflexive for researcher and researched?

There are a number of hurdles in terms of the personnel involved in cross-cultural research.

First, there is the philosophical problem of cultural objectification and relativism (Van Nieuwenhuijze, 1987). Faced with a different culture, researchers may easily fall prey to the tendency to objectify the new, perceiving the confronted culture from 'some mental distance' (Van Nieuwenhuijze, 1987: 4) and in so doing create a situation where 'two cultures in encounter, both operating as frames of reference in their own right, inevitably vie for pre-dominance as the provider of the criteria for the validity of the imponderables involved in their interaction' (Van Nieuwenhuijze, 1987: 14).

Second, there is the problem of Westernised notions of 'high' and 'low' culture and a possible association of Western researchers with reaction and colonialism. Associated with this is a third problem of the possible misuses of culture in the research process. Cross-cultural data can often feed stereotypes, can endorse a static and uniform view of 'culture' and could even promote segregation (Klitgaard, 1994). For example, in South Africa in the 1950s, many (white) South African researchers argued forcefully for education to be tailored to local cultures. This, they claimed, meant taking seriously language differences, levels of ability and cultural traits. The resulting Bantu Education Act fortified apartheid and instead of tailoring education to student needs, it tried to tailor children to a racist society's needs. The normative dimension of cultural analysis is, therefore, both valuable and worrying when applied to sensitive educational issues.

It has been suggested (Klitgaard, 1994; Verhelst, 1987) that reflexivity on the part of researchers is highly significant in allowing researchers to counteract the tendencies described above, and requires researchers to consider fully their own values, preferences and assumptions. At best, this will enable researchers to act as cultural conduits; 'coming from one culture but trained to penetrate another, they can serve as interlocutors – telling them, telling us, what each other really care about, is good at, can contribute' (Klitgaard, 1994: 18).

This people-centred view of development with its research corollary in giving voice to those so often marginalised, particularly in larger development projects, has implications for research methods and the need for pre-requisite training for all concerned that is necessary for any research to be culturally sensitive and participatory. Perhaps a start is to do what Klitgaard suggests and begin any research enquiry by critiquing our own values, preferences and assumptions, something that is easier said than done.

How might such research be achieved?
In order to address this question, I draw, in Part 2, upon an illustrative case study example of cross-cultural research, sponsored by a large international development agency, Save the Children, Norway (SCN).

Part 2: The Quality Education Project (QEP)[1]: a case study example

A particular focus of the project was its action orientation, specifically its emphasis upon building education leadership and management capacity at district and school level.

Background to the research project

In the 1980s and 1990s, much of the concern for national governments and development agencies, such as Save the Children, was to ensure that all children had access to schooling, particularly in the first cycle. This led to a rapid expansion in initiatives to generate school building and teacher training, and increased efforts to bring education to the poor and minority groups, particularly girls and young women. As expansion continued, concerns shifted to quality, particularly in sub-Saharan Africa (Hawes and Stephens, 1989).

Echoing calls for action at the Dakar Education for All conference (2000), SCN instigated a large multi-country, cross-cultural project aimed specifically at raising the quality of teaching and learning in selected primary school classrooms in four of sub-Saharan Africa's poorest countries: Ethiopia, Mozambique, Zambia and Zimbabwe. The project was called the Quality Education Project (QEP).

Quality in the QEP was defined not as a set of inputs to the education system (because SCN realised in the early 2000s that quality had to be more than new buildings and resources) or as a focus upon identified learning outcomes but rather concerned the interaction between teacher, student and the curriculum. The project was large and complex.

Project aims and objectives

The project aimed to transform the way adults teach and children learn in some of the most challenging environments in sub-Saharan Africa. The ideas involved teachers relying less on solutions from external consultants and more on participants investigating their own problems through participatory action research, observing each other teach and then devising, implementing and monitoring the effectiveness of their solutions. Teachers were encouraged to be more reflective of their professional practice, and work together with support from a range of stakeholders from the school inspectorate, local teachers' colleges, and Save the Children national offices in each of the four countries to acquire expertise and confidence. The participating teachers gradually acquired the expertise and confidence to improve the quality of teaching and learning in the classroom.

If we consider this from a *cultural* perspective, we can see that much of what QEP set out to do was – and is – fundamentally concerned with values, priorities and policy options available to educational leaders and managers at different levels of the respective educational hierarchies.

In 2009, Clive Harber and I were funded to evaluate the impact of the project by means of a participatory research exercise involving four 10-day field visits to the four countries to collect evidence supported by the International Resource Group (IRG) who had supported the original project. Data were collected from the partners involved in the QEP project, i.e. schools, Teacher Training Colleges, National and District Ministries of Education, parents and pupils, and SCN field staff (see Figure 4.2).

Generally, the results of the evaluation were positive. We concluded that action research had significantly changed the ways many teachers approach educational change. Many respondents reported that they now realise that with effective training and support, for example from the district inspectors

---

Ethiopia – Interviews: 13 teacher educators (individually and focus groups – all QEP); 49 teachers (41QEP – 8 non-QEP); 6 children (a focus group); 7 Ministry of Education officials at regional and district levels; 14 parents (focus groups); 11 observations (6 QEP, 5 non-QEP)

Mozambique – Interviews: 84 teachers (individually, in small and large groups); 9 teacher educators; 14 Ministry of Education officials; 8 parents; 2 observations

Zambia – Interviews: 15 teacher educators (all QEP); 69 teachers (individually and in focus groups – 52 QEP and 17 non-QEP); 138 children; 14 education standards officers and other education officials; 2 parents; 21 observations (11 QEP, 10 non-QEP)

Zimbabwe – Interviews: 45 teacher educators (individually and focus groups – all QEP); 68 teachers (individually and in focus groups – 55 QEP and 13 non-QEP); 9 Ministry officials; 20 children (in focus groups); 7 observations (all QEP)

Figure 4.2   The size and nature of the evaluation samples in each country

in Zambia, they can take the initiative about teaching and learning in the classroom rather than wait for someone else to do so. Some imaginative and inspiring change was recorded by teachers and children working in some daunting circumstances. On a cautionary note, the research also found that a clear distinction needs to be made between areas a teacher can improve, such as improved teaching methods, more relevant content of lessons; and what remains the responsibility of others, such as improved teacher salaries and enhanced political stability.

Research methodology: questions of how?

The plan for the evaluation research was based around three principles: that the research would be *participatory* (involving teams from each of the national contexts who would be involved in evaluating all the sites), *comparable*, and largely *qualitative* to reflect the cultural and contextual realities, although examination and classroom test data were collected to provide some indication of relative success over the years QEP ran in each country and to present some limited comparisons between countries.

It is important to note that for this study, setting or context was not something to be pushed to the background but was treated as integral to the holistic character of qualitative research. With that in mind, a decision was taken to ground the evaluation of QEP, as far as practically possible, in the realities as faced by teachers and children 'on the ground'. The qualitative methods included not only individual and focus group interviews (see Figure 4.2 above) but also observation and child-sensitive research methods, for example encouraging pupils to draw their impressions of their schools to establish if they perceived any differences as a result of the QEP project.

Lessons for cross-cultural research drawn from the evaluation

There are three clusters of methodological issues I will focus upon:

- The use and interpretation of ideas and concepts such as 'leadership' and 'management' in different cultural contexts.
- Language and discourse: the role of English in the research process, the use of academic discourse, etc.
- Fieldwork including: management of field relations, culturally sensitive research methods, the role of insiders and outsiders, the sequencing of the data collection, and ethical concerns (Stephens, 2009).

Ideas and concepts
The evaluation of QEP indicated how understanding of terms such as leadership, quality or effective pedagogy may be contested. Amongst those participating in the QEP project, the concept of *leadership*, for example, tended to be viewed in communal rather than individual terms, a leader

being somebody with social responsibilities and possessing cultural attributes associated with age, gender and political affiliation. It was clear also that understanding of what was meant by *quality* teaching and learning involved a huge shift for many teachers from a chalk and talk transmission model, in some cases underpinned by an acceptance of physical punishment as a predominant means of control, to one more recognisable in a child-centred primary school.

Language and discourse issues

Research, particularly that involving leadership from outside the research field, involves issues of language and power. Earlier we mentioned the importance of *voice* and *ownership*. In the QEP evaluation, care was taken in establishing and maintaining a balance between building the capacity of the research team and producing a set of robust findings as set out in the terms of reference of the project.

There were two specific language issues, the first concerning the relationship of indigenous languages to the widely spoken second language, English (with the exception of Mozambique where English is a third language to the second, Portuguese), and second the relationship between the research discourse or register and what might be called the day-to-day language used, for example, by parents, children and teachers. (See also Chapter 21 for further discussion of discourse analysis.) Where necessary, interpreters were used, and with the children a raft of non-verbal data collection methods, including drawing, were used. The draft and final reports were presented in English, which raises further issues of power and status of the findings produced.

Fieldwork issues

There are a number of fieldwork issues common to all researchers conducting research, not least of the qualitative kind. Arguably, these are magnified in cross-cultural settings.

There are particular sensitivities about the role of evaluator in some contexts. For example in Zimbabwe the tense political climate meant that great sensitivity and diplomacy were required when discussing education with those in official positions. The role of the International Resource Group (IRG) was valuable here: insiders easing the way for the 'outsider' lead researchers. However, there was an implicit challenge in involving the IRG in the evaluation of a development project where they had a vested interest. The fact that the final evaluation was both critical and fair says a great deal about the IRG who acted throughout in a professional and supportive manner.

Another important field issue concerned the sequencing of the data collection. It was decided that the best strategy was to evaluate country by country in the order in which the countries had embraced QEP. As the evaluation progressed, it became clear that changes and fine tuning would be required and lessons carried from country to country. The challenge here was to maintain a core set of research questions and approaches for the purposes of a valid comparison yet at the same time to allow for variations to 'fit' the particular circumstances at local level.

Finally, there were a number of ethical challenges involved in the fieldwork, particularly with regard to interviews with children. Save the Children have carried out pioneering work in the development of child-friendly research methods, several of which were used in the field.

Lessons drawn from this evaluation specifically refer to a large-scale cross-national and cross-cultural exercise, but they have relevance for all researchers including single individuals engaged in a small-scale individual project.

Conclusion

Where there are cross-cultural elements involved in research, it is possible to identify three core dimensions: first, the *content* of the research which will involve a variety of different ways in which the issues and concepts, for example, leadership, are understood from context to context; second, the *process* by which the research is carried out, for example the employment of particular research methods and the language in which the data is collected and analysed; and third, the knowledge and interpretations brought to the research by the *researcher*, for example the discipline background of the researcher, the previous experience the researcher has of the contexts involved, and the level of reflexivity attained.

Key points

- Culture plays a central role in both the content and methodology of all educational research, but particularly cross-cultural research.
- Theories and practice of research in educational leadership are largely grounded in Western ideas that may carry a cultural heritage of imperialism.
- Cross-cultural research is growing in importance as there is greater movement and exchange of individuals and ideas across national boundaries.
- Context matters in cross-cultural research – it is important to identify background factors and make use of cross-cultural theories. These factors and theories may well relate to institutional values, policy priorities and interpretations of individuals, particularly leaders, of the decision-making processes and agendas.
- Researcher reflexivity is vital in successful cross-cultural research.
- Preferences for quantitative and qualitative research differ across cultures.
- There are a number of challenges involved in carrying out cross-cultural research, for example objectification, a narrow focus upon those affected by decision making (rather than those setting the agenda), and stereotyping.

Questions and reflections

1 Reflect upon the cultural variables and value choices that shape the field in which you are working.

2 If your research is cross-cultural, what are the background factors that should be foregrounded in your research? Reflect upon the historical, ideological and institutional contexts and the relative importance each may have in shaping your research.

3 What are the likely fieldwork issues and challenges you are going to face? Reflect upon the experiences and skills you are bringing to the research. If you are working as part of a team, do you have a good balance of competencies?

Recommended further reading

Dimmock, C. and Walker, A. (2005) *Educational Leadership: Culture and Diversity*. London: Sage.

This text provides a good overview of the issues.

Somekh, B. and Lewin, C. (2005) *Research Methods in the Social Sciences*. London: Sage.

This is an excellent introduction to a range of methods available. Unlike many method books, it is not overly prescriptive, instead offering chapters on appropriate approaches and tools with an eye for culture and context.

Stephens, D. (2007) *Culture in Education and Development: Principles, Practice and Policy*. Oxford: Symposium.

This book, by the author of this chapter, sets out the role of culture in the development of education (Ch. 1) and in Chapter 2 focuses upon the methodologies and methods to be used in the framing and conducting of cross-cultural research in education.

Stephens, D. (2009) *Qualitative Research in International Settings: A Practical Guide*. London: Routledge.

In this second book, I emphasise the importance of context or setting as foreground rather than background, arguing that context matters whether at a micro or macro level.

Tuhiwai Smith, L. (1999) *Decolonizing Methodologies: Research and Indigenous Peoples*. London: Zed Books.

This book is worth reading for its questioning of some of the fundamental assumptions that underpin the dominance of Western models of research.

Note

1 Full details of the research evaluation can be found in Harber and Stephens (2010). Acknowledgement also to Tove Nagel of Save the Children, Norway, who with Harber and Stephens led the original research from which the evaluation is drawn.

References

Alasuutari, P. (1995) *Researching Culture: Qualitative Method and Cultural Studies.* London: Sage.

Bullivant, B.M. (1981) *The Pluralist Dilemma in Education.* London: Allen & Unwin.

Centre for the Study of Education in Developing Countries (CESO) (1990) *Education, Culture and Productive Life* (eds A. Boeren and K. Epskamp). The Hague: CESO.

Denzin, N.K., Lincoln, Y.S. and Giardina, M.S. (2006) Disciplining qualitative research. *International Journal of Qualitative Studies* 19(6): 769–82.

Dimmock, C. and Walker, A. (2005) *Educational Leadership: Culture and Diversity,* London: Sage.

Eagleton, T. (2000) *The Idea of Culture.* Oxford: Blackwell.

Geertz, C. (2000) *The Interpretation of Cultures.* New York: Basic Books Classics.

George, S. (1984) *Ill Fares the Land: Essays on Food, Hunger and Power.* London: Writers and Readers.

Hall, E.T. (1976) *Beyond Culture.* New York: Anchor Books.

Harber, C.M. and Stephens, D.G. (2010) *From Shouters to Supporters.* Oslo: Save the Children, Norway.

Hawes, H. and Stephens, D. (1990) *Questions of Quality: Primary Education and Development.* Harlow: Longman.

Hofstede, G.H. (2001) *Culture's Consequences.* Thousand Oaks, CA: Sage.

Keesing, R. (1981) *Cultural Anthropology: A Contemporary Perspective.* New York: Holt, Rinehart and Winston.

Klitgaard, R. (1994) Taking culture into account from 'Let's' to 'How', in Serageldin, I. and Tabaroff, J. (eds) *Culture and Development in Africa.* Washington: World Bank.

Ladson-Billings, G. and Gillborn, D. (2004) *The RoutledgeFalmer Reader in Multicultural Education.* London: RoutledgeFalmer.

Odora Hoppers, C.A. (ed.) (2002). *Indigenous Knowledge and the Integration of Knowledge Systems: Towards a Philosophy of Articulation.* Claremont: New Africa Books.

Rose, D. (1990) *Living the Ethnographic Life.* Thousand Oaks, CA: Sage.

Smith, P. and Bond, M. (1993) *Social Psychology Across Cultures: Analysis and Perspectives.* Hemel Hempstead: Harvester Wheatsheaf.

Stephens, D. (2007) *Culture in Education and Development: Principles, Practice and Policy.* Oxford: Symposium.

Stephens, D. (2009) *Qualitative Research in International Settings: A Practical Guide.* London: Routledge.

Thomas, E. (1994) *International Perspectives on Culture and Schooling: A Symposium Proceedings.* London: Department for International and Comparative Education, University of London Institute of Education.

Tuhiwai Smith, L. (1999) *Decolonizing Methodologies: Research and Indigenous Peoples.* London: Zed Books.

Van Nieuwenhuijze, C. (1987) The cultural perspective: icing on the cake or Pandora's Box? *Development* 1: 13–17.

Verhelst, T. (1987) *No Life without Roots: Culture and Development.* London: Zed Books.

Williams, R. (1976) *Keywords: A Vocabulary of Culture and Society.* London: Fontana.

CHAPTER 5

Reviewing Educational Literature

Jacqui Weetman DaCosta

Chapter objectives

- To outline the need to review the literature in the disciplines.
- To recommend systematic review processes when searching for relevant literature.
- To provide an overview of a variety of valuable resources in print and electronic formats.
- To encourage sensible management and ethical use of information.

Introduction

Reviewing the literature relating to educational leadership and management has become more challenging over the years as a substantial body of international publications in an ever-growing range of formats has become available. However, by following a systematic approach, a search can be conducted both efficiently and effectively yielding a treasure trove of information.

This chapter will outline the literature searching process providing the tools to source, manage and critically evaluate available material. This practice enables researchers to justify their work and set it within the context of other studies and, ideally, advance the body of knowledge on a particular subject. The digital age has brought vast changes to the way in which we conduct research and to the availability of resources. The emergence of digital publications and the 'blogosphere' means that research products are being shared with the public more quickly and widely than ever.

Research is an iterative process and sufficient time needs to be allowed to review the results and, if necessary, modify the search strategy to improve its effectiveness. It is never too soon to begin the literature search for a dissertation or other major piece of research. 'The key to finding and using information successfully for research is good planning, organisation and knowing where to go for help' (Keeble and Kirk, 2007: 70). This chapter is designed to guide you through a systematic process to help save time and produce better results.

Why undertake a literature search?

A literature search is a systematic gathering of information relating to a particular topic. The process is similar for most subjects but the type of information and format may change depending on the topic. Working systematically helps you retrieve a wide range of resources within date parameters that are appropriate to your topic. It also gives you a logical sequence to follow as you progress from one research source to another.

There are many reasons why people conduct literature searches:

1　They can help you to become familiar with a subject about which you know nothing, or very little; to help you understand it better or to determine whether it is a subject on which you want to conduct further investigation.

2　A short and simple literature search may be conducted to answer a particular question when you have to validate your answer with reputable sources.

3　Researchers are required to keep up-to-date in their subject areas and need to run searches regularly to check for recent additions to the literature.

4　Maintaining a level of current awareness in a field can help a seasoned researcher to be stimulated by fresh ideas.

5　At the doctoral level, a researcher needs to scour the literature to ensure that they are producing original research and to determine where it fits within what is already known.

Your supervisor may say that you have to focus on scholarly, academic or peer-reviewed resources in your literature review. The most commonly peer-reviewed resources are journals and conference papers, where submissions are reviewed by subject experts, to determine their quality and contribution to the field. A scholarly journal article includes a list of references to show that the author has consulted the writings of other scholars and set their own work within the context of a larger body of research. For many academic conferences, the papers submitted are also peer-reviewed before they are accepted for presentation at the conference and subsequently published within the conference proceedings.

Creating a search strategy

When you commence any type of research, you should have a question in mind that will serve as the basis and foundation on which to work. This question may change since the more you find out, the more you can focus your research. Even if you are just starting out with a topic in mind, a question will help you to find information containing the answers that you require. It may be that you have a number of research questions or that your topic can be divided into smaller parts or sub-questions. Make sure that you do not have too many questions, as this could over-complicate your research. It is advisable to check with your supervisor as to the number and nature of your research questions.

Having established your questions, you need to consider the level of detail needed, which can vary according to the scholarship level at which you are practising (for example, undergraduate, graduate, doctoral, etc.) and the purpose of the research (for example, essay, term paper, dissertation, article, etc.). If you have a specific deadline then you need to factor in how much time you can devote to the literature search and what level of detail you can achieve. If a topic has been under investigation for many years, you may need to identify key standard texts while still retaining a current perspective. For a more up-to-date topic, you may struggle to find many academic journal articles and have to rely more on recent reports published online.

Next, take your research question and turn it into keywords. These will be used to search library catalogues, the Internet and indexes, whether they are at the back of a book or part of a database to help you find journal articles and reports. Keywords need to describe your topic in a succinct way. They should make sense, whether standing alone or combined with other subject terms. When choosing keywords, consider:

- different spellings – remember that some words have different spellings, for example, *counselling* (UK) and *counseling* (USA)
- alternative terminology – you may describe young people as *youths* but someone else may use *teenagers*
- singular or plural – many resources, whether electronic or print, may not differentiate but test your online search with both singular and plural forms to confirm
- abbreviations and acronyms – you may be accustomed to describing something in its abbreviated format but that is not necessarily what all writers have chosen to do
- synonyms – what you describe as *leadership* may have been called *management* or *administration* by someone else.

When you are using Internet search engines and databases, there are techniques, known as truncation and wild cards, which you can employ to help overcome these keyword conundrums. If you add a truncation symbol, such as an asterisk or question mark, to the stem of a word, you will retrieve that stem plus anything that follows. For example, *teen** will provide references that include *teen*, *teens* and *teenagers*. Wildcards will help overcome variations in spellings since the use of the symbol within a word indicates that any letter can take the place of that symbol, for example *wom?n* will produce references for *woman* and *women*. The symbols used for truncation and wildcards may differ between databases or search engines. Check the Help function of whichever electronic resource you are searching for their precise usage. Sometimes, one keyword or phrase can describe your subject adequately to retrieve references. However, it is more likely that you will need to combine keywords using the connector AND to narrow the focus and provide you with a more manageable set of results. Alternatively, if you are not finding sufficient references, you can broaden your search by trying some synonyms or alternative terminology connecting your keywords with OR.

Some of the databases used to find journal articles and conference papers may also provide you with ideas for alternative terminology and synonyms. Look at the subject headings and keywords that have been used to describe relevant articles or check the database's thesaurus, if it has one. Other features within a database that may help to refine your search strategy would be a date limiter and restricting your search to a certain type of literature, such as empirical studies.

Finding background information

While it may be tempting to start your search for background information with Wikipedia, it is not the source that your research supervisor will want to see in your reference list. The Wikipedia entry may contain some good information but their own disclaimer states that 'Wikipedia makes no guarantee of validity' (Wikipedia, 2010).

When you start a research topic about which you know very little, or you have terminology that you do not understand, it is advisable to consult reference books. A subject dictionary focusing on education would be an excellent source from which you could obtain detailed definitions of words and phrases. Similarly, a subject encyclopaedia could provide excellent summaries of topics relevant to the field of education. Most academic libraries supporting schools of education will stock relevant subject dictionaries and encyclopaedia, as will larger public libraries.

Once you have established your basic understanding of a subject and its terminology, you can move on to gather general information from books within education or a related area, such as psychology or management. Use your well-defined keywords to search a library's catalogue or an online bookshop but keep your keywords simple since library catalogues are not always clever enough to deal with truncation and wildcards!

When searching a library catalogue, you may find a bibliography relevant to your research. This type of resource can be helpful since it is the product of someone else's research on a subject where they list all books, journal articles and reports that they were able to find at the time of writing. However, *time* is the operative word since you would need to ensure that your own literature search continues from the date that the author's listing left off. You should check the date of all the literature that you use to ensure that it is not so old as to render it irrelevant to your research topic.

An increasing number of books are becoming available online with some being free and others accessible as rental or download purchases. You may find that an academic library has an electronic version of a key text available to access through an institutional authentication system. Google Books has an ever-growing supply of free electronic texts where you may be able to view the full text or a summary.

Using databases to find articles, reports, conference papers, theses, and more

When searching for journal articles, research reports and conference papers, the most effective method is to use electronic databases. These databases are usually subscription-based and you will be allowed access by virtue of your membership of a library. Databases index articles, reports and conference papers using keywords to describe the content. Often they provide an abstract summarising the information and some may even provide the full text of the item. If the database itself does not provide full text, then it is possible that your library may have linked the database to other sources, which can provide you with the full text either electronically or in print. There are hundreds of different databases, covering many subjects, and the ones most relevant to education are listed below:

1 *British Education Index (BEI)* – This index covers around 350 education and related journals published in Europe with a specific British focus. It also provides subject and author indexes for conferences and some online documents. It covers from 1976 to the present, with its Thesis Index going back to 1950.

2 *Educational Resources Information Center (ERIC)* – ERIC indexes over 775 journals and, within over a million records, it also lists numerous books, conference papers, research reports and policy papers. It covers from 1966 onwards and is produced by the US Department of Education.

3 *Australian Education Index (AEI)* – This is smaller than its British and American counterparts, indexing just over 100 journals in detail. However, it is useful for an Australian perspective, with some international journals. It covers from 1979 onwards.

The topic that you are researching may be one that borders on subjects related to education. There are many other subject databases and it is advisable to consult a librarian about the best choice. Some that you may encounter are:

1 *PsycINFO* – This covers subjects related to psychology, including counselling. It is international with coverage beginning in 1984 but some libraries may have an historic archive going back to 1887.

2 *ISI Web of Science* – This is the generic name for a database that includes citation indexes for Arts and Humanities, Science and the Social Sciences Citation Index with references back to 1970. It also has access to a Conference Proceedings Citation Index for the Social Sciences and Humanities.

In some instances, it may be possible to run your search in two or more databases simultaneously when the databases are hosted by the same commercial vendor. This is possible within *Web of Science* and through the host providers of *ERIC/PsycINFO*.

If you do not have access to library databases, then you may be interested in what has been published in open-source journals, many of which are scholarly. While open-source journals only make up a small proportion of the total of journals published worldwide, and are sometimes poorly indexed, they do have the advantage of being freely available. Some collections of open-source journals can be found at:

Directory of Open Access Journals (www.doaj.org) – This website provides links to over 400 international education journals and many others in the social sciences.

Education Research Global Observatory (www.ergobservatory.info/ejdirectory. html) – This lists open-access peer-reviewed journals in education within its Directory of Open Access Scholarly Journals in Education.

Newspapers are not considered to be a scholarly source but they can serve as a primary source and sometimes provide a local perspective on an issue. Many larger academic and public libraries are likely to have backfiles of newspapers on microfilm dating from the nineteenth century or earlier. Two of the more common newspaper databases are listed below but other generic databases can provide good coverage:

1 *Nexis* (also known as *LexisNexis*) – This is a comprehensive database providing full-text access to most national, some regional British newspapers and a few international newspapers.

2 *NewsBank* (also known as *Access World News*) – This database covers a large number of international newspapers with a focus on North America. Like *Nexis*, it is full text and updated daily.

For many educational topics, you will find excellent information in the *Times Educational Supplement* and the *Times Higher Educational Supplement*, both of which can be searched online retrospectively.

While conference papers are indexed by the major educational databases, they can also be found in specific conference databases, such as *Zetoc*. This database covers over 16,000 worldwide conference proceedings and another 20,000 journals held by the British Library. Generally, it is only the national libraries, such as the British Library and the American Library of Congress, which retain large collections of conference proceedings. For many conference papers, you will need to rely on an interlibrary loans service to supply you with a copy of a paper or the whole conference proceedings.

Occasionally, you may find that a doctoral thesis or dissertation has been written on your topic. It is possible to search for details of theses that have been published in the UK using the *British Library's Index to Theses*, available online through many academic libraries. Alternatively, if you have a more worldwide focus, you could search *Dissertation Abstracts International*. While a thesis submitted to a British university is likely to be available via interlibrary loan through the British Library or from the awarding institution, international dissertations may only be available for a fee through *Dissertation Abstracts International*, supplied by a company called ProQuest.

Effective Internet searching

When you search the Internet for research information, you should always start with Google Scholar because its resources generally come from academic publishers, professional bodies and online university repositories. Google Scholar will not necessarily supply you with the full text of a document but it should give you sufficient information so that you can find it within a library's resources or via interlibrary loan. Some libraries link their electronic resources to Google Scholar so that you can retrieve the full-text document online after passing through an institutional authentication system. You can also make your Internet search more effective by using the Advanced Search function, combining your keywords with date, publication or format limiters. If you do not have access to an academic library, then Google Scholar will often lead you to publishers' websites where you can pay to download items.

Internet gateways or portals have been created by librarians or indexers and serve as a guide to other websites already evaluated for their quality of information. Some gateways worth investigating are:

> *BUBL* (http://bubl.ac.uk) – This covers all subject areas including educational policy, assessment, technology and research. It is hosted by Strathclyde University in Scotland.

> *Intute* (www.intute.ac.uk) – This gateway contains resources selected by subject specialists across a range of British universities and has excellent coverage for education. Unfortunately, it stopped being updated in 2011 since it lost its source of government funding but provides an excellent archive.

> *ipl2 (Internet Public Library)* (www.ipl.org/) – This is produced by Drexel University in Philadelphia, in association with other American colleges. It lists over 340 education websites with an international focus.

Google Scholar may direct you to institutional repositories or you could check whether a university to which you are affiliated has one. Online repositories contain conference papers, journal articles, theses, dissertations and book chapters authored by members of the institution. At the time of writing, there were over 2000 online repositories worldwide including disciplinary repositories, many of which are listed in *The Registry of Open Access Repositories* (http://roar.eprints.org/). Through Google Scholar, you may also find relevant pre-prints, working papers and technical reports, which would not have been so easy to retrieve before the advent of the World Wide Web.

Specialist data

Depending on the nature of your research topic, you may need to obtain information published in sources that are updated annually or are more random in their publication cycle.

In the UK, the Office for National Statistics is a government body responsible for collecting, collating and disseminating statistics in many different areas, including education and training. PDFs of annual statistical reports are available from its website (www.statistics.gov.uk). The statistics relate to a variety of regions and topics, such as examinations, qualifications, educational establishments, the curriculum, expenditure, etc. A comparable source in the USA is the annual Statistical Abstract, produced by the US Census Bureau (www.census.gov/compendia/statab/brief.html). There is also the National Center for Education Statistics (NCES), which collects data related to the USA and other countries, under the auspices of the US Department of Education, Institute of Education Sciences (www.nces.ed.gov).

There are many relevant government publications available, such as Acts of Parliament (for example, Children, Schools and Families Act 2010), Statutory Instruments, bills and papers arising from parliamentary committees. The National Archives is the British government body responsible for making this information, dating from 1267, available via its website (www.legislation.gov.uk). In the USA, you will find the Government Printing Office's Federal Digital System (www.gpo.gov/fdsys/search/home.action) to be the most accessible source for information emanating from the three branches of the federal government: legislative, judicial and executive. It is worth searching on government websites in other countries for their equivalent information archives.

Evaluating what you find

The Internet makes it much simpler to gather information quickly and easily. 'The challenge is to find quality information' (McMillan and Schumacher, 2006: 100). If you have collected your references using Google Scholar, or by selecting the option for peer-reviewed journals in a database, you can be more confident that you have found scholarly resources. If not then you need to evaluate your sources using criteria such as:

- Bias – suggestions of bias could come from the use of emotional language, a particular funding source or the author's affiliation (Mertens, 1998). If you suspect bias, you can ensure that you include facts that balance the argument, incorporating information produced by someone with a differing viewpoint.

- Currency – just because a web page exists, it does not mean that it is updated regularly. Check to see when the information was last updated. With Google Scholar, you can choose to retrieve articles published between specific dates.

- Reliability – is the author known to you, as a writer of other scholarly works, or affiliated with an academic or reputable research organisation? If your source is not scholarly, can you vouch for its reliability in another way? Is the writer providing a balanced argument backed up by data and evidence from other reliable sources?

- Verifiability – if your topic is controversial or involves numbers, see if you can find another source with similar evidence or the same numbers.

Systematic review

Evidence-based practice is a systematic review technique that has long been accepted in the field of medicine but has raised some questions when applied to education (Thomas and Pring, 2004). A systematic review 'uses explicit, systematic and clearly identified methods to try to reach an unbiased conclusion' (Hek and Moule, 2006: 37). The following of strict search criteria and the provision of a critical appraisal for each source are key features of systematic reviews. The Institute of Education in London has an established Evidence for Policy and Practice Information and Co-ordinating Centre (EPPI-Centre) as part of its Social Science Research Unit. The Centre hosts an online Evidence Library (http://eppi.ioe.ac.uk/cms/Default.aspx?tabid=56&language=en-US) containing reviews across many topics in education, including initial teacher education, early years care, gifted children, literacy and health education. If there is a review already produced on your topic, then it will greatly assist your research since many of the steps mentioned in this chapter will have been completed by experts in the field. However, as with a bibliography, you will need to ensure that your own systematic review of the literature continues from the date of publication of the review contained in the Evidence Library. There have also been some concerns expressed as to whether the reviews included are as exhaustive as they should be (MacLure, 2005), so this should not be used as a substitute for your own comprehensive survey of the literature.

Obtaining resources both in print and electronically

If you are registered with a higher education library, then it is possible to access up to 80 per cent of the scholarly resources that you need for an undergraduate or masters degree. If you are working at a doctoral level, then you will be using more specialised sources, which may necessitate going outside your home institution.

Most academic libraries will provide you with access to thousands of journals online enabling you to conduct the majority of your research from wherever you have Internet access. Occasionally, a library may only have print copies of certain journals, in which case you will need to visit, or you could check if they have a postal service for students studying at a distance. As mentioned previously, many of the library databases may include the full text of the article that you require. However, just because it is not in one database, it does not mean that the library does not own it. You need to get into the habit of searching your library's complete journal holdings online. This will also be useful when you need to track down journal articles that have been cited in another article or book chapter. When you search for journal articles in this way, remember that your first point of reference is the title of the journal and not the title of the article.

If a book or journal article is not available at your own library, or you do not live close to the university at which you are registered, check whether your library has any reciprocal borrowing agreements with other academic libraries. The largest reciprocal borrowing programme in the UK is the SCONUL Access Scheme (www.access.sconul.ac.uk/), which allows students registered on postgraduate, part-time and distance-learning courses to borrow books from over 170 member institutions.

If you find that your most convenient library cannot provide access to the resource that you require, then you can make use of the interlibrary loans service, for which you may be charged. The possibility that you may need to rely on interlibrary loans is one of the many good reasons to begin your research as soon as possible since items can take up to two weeks to be supplied to you. Check with your library for more details of charges and approximate delivery times.

Managing information

As important as it is to conduct your literature search in a systematic fashion, it is also vital to take an organised approach to the management of your retrieved information. 'It cannot be over-emphasized that strict management of the search is an essential part of the search for literature relevant to your topic. Keeping *accurate*, *consistent* and *correct* records is the basis of good project management' (Hart, 2001: 36). As you proceed through the research steps outlined in this chapter, take time to record:

- your research question(s) and keywords
- the combinations of keywords that work best
- the catalogues, databases, search engines and portals that you search
- how many references you find in different databases.

Most importantly, record the details of every piece of information to which you are making reference, including page numbers, if you are using a direct quotation. By taking a systematic approach to the management of your information, you will be saving yourself time in the long term. When you are at the writing-up stage, and especially when you come to list your works cited, you do not want to be held back by having to start a search all over again because you did not record the volume, issue number or page numbers of a journal article.

Fortunately, there are some online tools that can assist you with the management of your references. If you are affiliated with a university then you may be able to obtain a free, or low-priced, copy of a software programme, such as Reference Manager or Endnote. There is also a range of free software, such as Zotero (www.zotero.org). Reference management software allows you to create a database of everything that you have found that could be relevant to your current or any future research topic. With many packages, you can import references from database and Internet searches and then export the references into bibliographies formatted in one of many different referencing styles.

Keeping up-to-date

Once you have started on the research path, there are numerous ways in which you can maintain research currency and be alerted to developments in your field. Many commercial databases incorporate a current awareness service where you can save your successful searches to your own account or profile and set a regular time frame for the search to be re-run and the results emailed to you. Alternatively, if you have a favourite journal, you can arrange through a database or the journal's website to have the table of contents emailed to you every time a new issue is published. If you are registered with a British academic library, then you may want to consider setting up a (free) account with the Zetoc Alert service (http://zetoc.mimas.ac.uk/alertguide.html) provided by the British Library. You can receive email alerts matching your specified search criteria such as journal titles, authors or keywords from articles and papers.

Some databases or websites will allow you to set up an RSS feed to keep up-to-date with changes. You could also register with a free web service such as ChangeDetection (www.changedetection.com), which emails you every time there is a change to a website that you specify. You may want to use change detection or an RSS feed to alert you if someone has posted to a blog that you follow. There are many active researchers who create blogs to alert the world to new developments and publications in their field. 'Perhaps the most revolutionary aspect of the Internet is its ability to connect people with shared interests' (McMillan and Schumacher, 2006: 104).

Another way to keep up-to-date and to link with other researchers or workers is to join a relevant discussion list. In the UK, the best source for discussion lists is JISCMail (www.jiscmail.ac.uk/), which is the Joint Information Systems

Committee's (JISC) National Academic Mailing Service. JISCMail is primarily for those working in further and higher education but many list managers will accept applications from other interested researchers or people who have a valid reason for wishing to join. Many researchers have used the JISCMail service in order to conduct surveys or ask questions of people with a similar academic interest. The discussion lists can also alert you to conferences and new publications in your area of research.

Ethical use of information

Once you have gathered information, you need to ensure that you are using it ethically. The ethical use of information means respecting authorship and not trying to pass off someone else's words, thoughts, ideas or products as your own. In addition, when you create a reference list, you are showing the person for whom you are writing that you have used authoritative sources and not just made up the facts!

Technology has made it easy to copy and paste large chunks of text from online documents but if you do so without acknowledging the source then you are guilty of plagiarism. Be careful when you take notes from your readings to differentiate between your own paraphrasing and direct quotations so as not to get confused later (Bell, 2010). If you are paraphrasing someone else's words, then you need to ensure that you give them an in-text reference and full details of the source in your reference list. If you are using the exact words of someone else, whether you copy them from a book, article or website, you must use quotation marks and cite the page number alongside the in-text citation. If you are uncertain whether what you are doing could be construed as plagiarism, check with your tutor or a librarian. Most academic institutions will give you a copy of their plagiarism policy or make it available online. They may even provide you with a guide or an Internet tutorial on how to avoid plagiarism.

One way to avoid plagiarism is to ensure that you adopt the practice of citing your references in an approved referencing style at an early stage. As previously mentioned, reference management software can help you organise your references following one of many different styles, such as Harvard, Numeric, the American Psychological Association (APA) or Modern Language Association (MLA). There are websites that will outline the requirements of each of these styles but it is always best to check with the person for whom you are writing to see if they have a required or preferred system.

All work, whether available in print or online, is protected by copyright and subject to the copyright laws of the country in which it was created. Copyright is essentially a property right intended to protect the rights of creators from exploitation of their works by others (Cornish, 2009). Just because someone has made their work freely available on the Internet, it does not mean that you can use it without due acknowledgment or, in some cases, express permission.

Obtaining help and guidance

If you are affiliated with a higher education library, then it is a good idea to make your subject librarian your best friend! They can help you throughout the process with advice and guidance on which databases, portals and other online sources to use. Many academic libraries provide online research guides, which are usually freely available whether you are a registered student or not.

Many of the commercial databases and search engines have Help pages and sections where they may include online tutorials to guide you through effective search processes. YouTube contains short videos, which have been produced by libraries, on many of the different literature searching methods that have been described in this chapter. If you are new to literature searching, it would be worthwhile spending time reviewing the Internet for Education tutorial (http://www.vtstutorials.co.uk/tutorial/education/?sid= 2232085&itemid=12021), which is part of the JISC Virtual Training Suite, created by librarians and lecturers in the UK.

The open access movement is one of the fastest growing areas for scholarly research, which means that some of the resources mentioned in this chapter can rapidly become out of date and replaced by the latest digital publications. However, the 'old chestnuts', such as the British Education Index and ERIC, will be with us for many years to come and should always be an early 'port of call' for the educational researcher. An even earlier call, whether in person, by telephone or online, should be to an education subject librarian whose job it is to keep up-to-date with all resources in this area.

Key points

- Take time to plan your research strategy.
- Use a wide variety of information resources to balance your arguments.
- Evaluate your sources and be prepared to modify your search strategy.
- Maintain records of your search process and items found.
- Start as soon as possible!

Questions and reflections

1 Consider your research questions and how these may be broken down into keywords.
2 Is your topic recent or one with an historical perspective?
3 How can you ensure that your review of the literature is systematic?
4 What evaluative criteria have been applied to your chosen resources?

Recommended further reading

Badke, W. (2011) *Research Strategies: Finding Your Way Through the Information Fog*. Bloomington, IN: iUniverse.

Written by an American librarian, this is a clear and simple guide on how to undertake the research process, from selecting a topic through to finishing the written work.

Cohen, L., Manion, L. and Morrison, K. (2011) *Research Methods in Education* (7th edn). London: Routledge.

Now in its 7th edition, this book has been used by many educational researchers over the years. This latest edition includes useful additional information on literature searching.

George, M.W. (2008) *The Elements of Library Research: What Every Student Needs to Know*. Princeton, NJ: Princeton University Press.

This guide is aimed at undergraduate students but provides many practical tips and guidelines that are helpful to all students and especially those returning to learning.

Ridley, D. (2008) *The Literature Review: A Step-by-step Guide for Students*. London: Sage Publications.

This book focuses on the literature review process and would make an excellent 'guide on the side' providing much more detail on topics covered in this chapter.

References

Bell, J. (2010) *Doing Your Research Project: A Guide for First-time Researchers in Education, Health and Social Sciences* (5th edn). Maidenhead: Open University Press.

Cornish, G.P. (2009) *Copyright: Interpreting the Law for Libraries, Archives and Information Services* (5th edn). London: Facet Publishing.

Hart, C. (2001) *Doing a Literature Search: A Comprehensive Guide for the Social Sciences*. London: Sage.

Hek, G. and Moule, P. (2006) *Making Sense of Research: An Introduction for Health and Social Care Practitioners*. London: Sage.

Keeble, P. and Kirk, R. (2007) Exploring the existing body of research, in Coleman, M. and Briggs, A.R.J. (eds) *Research Methods in Educational Leadership and Management* (2nd edn). London: Sage.

MacLure, M. (2005) 'Clarity bordering on stupidity': Where's the quality in systematic review? *Journal of Education Policy* 20(4): 393–416.

McMillan, J.H. and Schumacher, S. (2006) *Research in Education: Evidence-based Inquiry* (6th edn). Boston, MA: Pearson Education.

Mertens, D.M. (1998) *Research Methods in Education and Psychology: Integrating Diversity with Quantitative and Qualitative Approaches*. London: Sage.

Thomas, G. and Pring, R. (2004) *Evidence-based Practice in Education*. Maidenhead: Open University Press.

Wikipedia (2010) *Wikipedia General Disclaimer*. Retrieved from Wikipedia: http://en.wikipedia.org/wiki/Wikipedia:General_disclaimer

CHAPTER 6

Authenticity in Research: Reliability, Validity and Triangulation

Tony Bush

Chapter objectives

The purpose of this chapter is to examine different ways in which the authenticity and quality of educational research may be assessed. The specific objectives are:

- To explain what is meant by authentic research.
- To discuss the concept of reliability and how it can be applied to quantitative and qualitative research.
- To discuss the concept of validity and how it can be applied to quantitative and qualitative research.
- To explain methodological and respondent triangulation and how they apply to educational research.

Introduction

Assessing quality and authenticity, or 'truth' (Scott, 2007), is important for researchers of educational leadership and management for two reasons:

- It helps in assessing the quality of studies undertaken by other researchers.
- It helps in determining their research approach and methodology.

Although research methods should be determined largely by the aims and context of the research, they should also have regard to quality criteria. This enables the researcher to respond with confidence when explaining methodology at a conference, seminar or viva voce examination. This notion of scrutiny is important: can the researcher defend and explain decisions about methodology to peers, professionals and examiners? This concept may be particularly important for research on school leadership and management. Given the global significance of this field, and the strong belief in the role of leadership in determining institutional and student outcomes, there is a temptation for researchers to place the best possible gloss on their findings. A full and open explanation of the methods used by researchers is essential if their results and interpretations are to be accepted by policy makers, practitioners, journal editors and other researchers.

The authenticity and quality of educational and social research can be judged by the procedures used to address reliability, validity and triangulation. These are all important and complex terms whose meaning and salience vary according to the stance of the researcher. These concepts were originally developed for use in positivist, or quantitative, research (see Chapter 2). However, Yildirim (2010: 79) stresses that these concepts may be employed in qualitative research, while Brock-Utne (1996) asserts that they are equally important in both traditions:

> The questions of validity and reliability within research are just as important within qualitative as within quantitative methods though they may have to be treated somewhat differently. The commonly held assumption that qualitative methods pay attention to validity and not to reliability is false. (Brock-Utne, 1996: 612)

Reliability

Definition

There is wide support for the view that reliability relates to the probability that repeating a research procedure or method would produce identical or similar results. It provides a degree of confidence that replicating the process would ensure consistency. These notions underpin definitions of this concept:

> A measure is reliable if it provides the same results on two or more occasions, when the assumption is made that the object being measured has not changed ... if a measure, or indeed a series of measures when repeated give a similar result, it is possible to say that it has high reliability. (Scott and Morrison, 2006: 208)

> Reliability refers to the consistency and stability of a measurement, and is concerned with whether the results of a study are replicable. (Hartas, 2010: 71)

Reliability in surveys

A survey aims to collect a substantial amount of data in order to draw conclusions about the phenomenon under investigation (see Chapter 10 for further discussion of surveys). Johnson (1994: 13) describes it as 'eliciting equivalent information from an identified population'. Fogelman and Comber (2007: 126) stress that surveys are a research *approach*, not a research *method*. They cite Cohen et al.'s (2000: 169) definition:

> Surveys gather data at a particular point in time with the intention of describing the nature of existing conditions, or identifying standards against which existing conditions can be compared, or determining the relationships that exist between specific events.

Reliability in survey research requires standard instruments, such as questionnaires and structured interviews, and meticulous instrument design and testing, for example through piloting. One of the main ways of assessing reliability is through the 'test–retest' procedure. A reliable instrument should give more or less the same results each time it is used with the same person or group. 'When tests are developed, they are typically tested for reliability by giving them to a group of people then calling back those same people a week later to take the test again' (Bernard, 2000: 49).

Youngman (1994: 263) refers to the notion of reliability in questionnaire research and suggests three ways in which it might be checked:

- Comparing findings with other sources, such as school records. This links to the notion of methodological triangulation, which is discussed later in this chapter.

- Cross-checking findings with the pilot study. Bell (2007: 232) stresses the need for questionnaires to be piloted, to be confident that the instrument is appropriate for its intended purposes.

- Direct questioning of respondents to see if personal responses match previous answers. This might occur through interviewing a sample of those surveyed by questionnaire and repeating certain questions. In the author's research on black and minority ethnic leaders in England (Bush et al., 2006b), many of those responding to the research team's e-survey were also interviewed to obtain more depth and detail. This provided a helpful reliability check.

Wragg (2002: 156) asks two important questions in applying the concept of reliability to interviews:

- Would two interviewers using the same schedule or procedure get similar results?

- Would an interviewer obtain a similar picture using the procedures on different occasions?

Fowler (1993) emphasises the need to ensure that all interviewees are asked the same questions in the same way if the procedure is to be reliable. This can work only if the interview schedule is tightly structured, with the properties of a questionnaire.

> A survey data collection is an interaction between a researcher and a respondent. In a self-administered survey, the researcher speaks directly to the respondent through a written questionnaire. In other surveys, an interviewer *reads* the researcher's words to the respondent. In either case, the questionnaire is the protocol for one side of the interaction. (Fowler, 1993: 71; emphasis added)

Of course, in single-handed research such as postgraduate dissertations and theses, the interviewer and the researcher are the same person but the key point is that reliability depends on a highly structured instrument. When the researcher wants to modify the instrument to probe or prompt respondents, using a semi-structured approach, reliability may be compromised. Cohen et al. (2000) express reservations about an over-emphasis on reliability for interviews because this may have implications for validity. Because reliability requires a standardised approach, it may limit validity. Validity is likely to require a friendly, human approach that allows respondents to answer in their own way, expressing their thoughts and feelings, and not to be restricted by the artificiality of a standard instrument. 'Where increased reliability of the interview is brought about by greater control of its elements, this is achieved ... at the cost of reduced validity' (Cohen and Manion, 1994: 282). (For further discussion of reliability in interviews, see Chapter 17 of this volume.)

This argument goes to the heart of the earlier discussion about research paradigms. Structured interviews are similar to questionnaires in their design and both may be regarded as methods within the positivist tradition. They both provide potential for 'reliability'. However, unstructured or semi-structured interviews are often used by interpretive researchers and assume greater diversity in both the design and use of the research instrument and in the nature of responses from participants. This may limit the scope for relia-bility while enhancing validity. We shall return to this debate later.

Reliability in case study research

Johnson (1994: 20) defines a case study as 'an enquiry which uses multiple sources of evidence. It investigates a contemporary phenomenon within its real-life context when the boundaries between phenomenon and context are not clearly evident'. (For further discussion of case studies, see Chapter 11 of this volume.)

Yin applies the concept of reliability to case study research:

> The objective is to be sure that, if a later investigator followed exactly the same procedures as described by an earlier investigator and conducted the same case study all over again, the later investigator should arrive at

the same findings and conclusions ... The goal of reliability is to minimise the errors and biases in a study. One prerequisite ... is the need to document the procedures followed in the earlier case ... The general way of approaching the reliability problem is to conduct research as if someone were always looking over your shoulder. (1994: 146)

Case study research usually involves several different methods. The main approaches are interviews, observation and documentary analysis (Bassey, 1999: 81). We shall examine reliability issues in relation to each of these methods.

Interviews

Cohen et al. (2000: 268) suggest that 'the interview ... may be used as the principal means of gathering information having direct bearing on the research objectives'. Increasingly, interviews may be conducted by telephone, Skype or email, as well as face to face. The nature and applicability of reliability procedures depend on the type of interview utilised by the researcher. In structured interviews, where the questions are predetermined, the approach to reliability is similar to that of a questionnaire survey. When interviews are undertaken as part of case study research, they may be semi-structured or unstructured, allowing each participant to respond in their own way. Such interviews differ from the structured approach in that the interviewee contributes to shaping the conversation. What they want to say becomes as important as what the researcher wants to ask. As we noted earlier, it is more difficult to ensure reliability using unstructured or semi-structured interviews because of the deliberate strategy of treating each participant as a potentially unique respondent.

The increasing recognition that each school provides a distinctive context for practising school leadership increases the difficulties involved in seeking reliability in interview research. The author's evaluation of the *New Visions: Induction to Headship* programme (Bush and Glover, 2005; Bush et al., 2006a), for the English National College, illustrates this point. The research involved interviewing a large number of new headteachers about their experience of the programme, and about its in-school effects. The evaluation team's semi-structured interviews covered the common experience of the participants, with some scope for reliability, but the application of the programme's ideas within schools inevitably varied significantly, leading to a response shaped by the unique context of the school. In this dimension of the research, reliability was unattainable and may not have been desirable.

Observation

Observation can be powerful, flexible and 'real' (Moyles, 2007: 237). It may be the basic tool in classroom research and can also be significant for studies of leadership and management issues, notably in observing meetings. The author's research on high-performing leadership teams, for the National College (Bush et al., 2011; Bush and Glover, 2012), involved observation of SLT meetings designed to assess how these teams operated, and to see what features contributed to the team's success.

Brock-Utne (1996) applies the concept of reliability to participant observation and asks three questions 'of great relevance':

- Would we have seen the same and interpreted what we saw in the same way if we had happened to have made the observation at a different time? This question deals with the stability of the observations.

- Would we have seen the same and interpreted what we saw in the same way if we had happened to pay attention to other phenomena during observation? We may here speak of parallel form reliability.

- Would a second observer with the same theoretical framework have seen and interpreted the observations in the same way? We may speak here of objectivity or intra-judge subjectivity. (Brock-Utne, 1996: 614–15)

These questions illustrate in stark form the difficulties involved in achieving reliability in observational research. If the observation had been made at a different time, the phenomenon itself would have changed. Different people may be present, there may be an alternative agenda, and participants may bring different thoughts and feelings to the meeting. Predetermining the purpose and focus of the observation helps to avoid being distracted by other phenomena but this can only be partly successful.

Moyles (2007: 250) explains that reliability in observational research depends on the quality of the research instrument, and the number of observations undertaken. She also advocates piloting the observations, and seeking inter-rater reliability, described as inter-observer reliability by Scott and Morrison (2006: 208). In the author's evaluation of the 'New Visions' programme (Bush et al., 2006a), programme events were observed by two or more researchers who recorded events separately, using the same structured framework. The researchers' independent records of the event were compared and an overview report prepared. Although most events were identified by both observers, a few points were noted by one researcher and missed or omitted by the other(s). This example illustrates the precarious nature of reliability in observational research, even where procedures are specifically adopted to address this issue. (For further discussion of participant observation, see Chapter 14 of this volume.)

Documentary analysis

Documentary analysis is an indispensable element in most case studies. Bush et al.'s (2011) evaluation of South Africa's pilot Advanced Certificate programme, for principals and other senior leaders, involved scrutiny of course modules, student portfolios and school policy documents, as well as interviews with participants and their colleagues, as part of 27 school-based case studies.

The concept of reliability can be applied to documentary analysis. Fitzgerald (2007: 287) identifies 'Is this document reliable?' as one of eight questions to be asked when undertaking documentary research. Reliability is easier to address when the approach is based on content analysis, a method which often involves counting words or terms found in the text (Cohen and Manion, 1994: 55). Robson (1994: 243) regards reliability as one of the advantages of content analysis using documents: 'The data are in permanent form and hence can be subject to re-analysis, allowing reliability checks and replication studies.' He recommends that two people are involved in coding text to improve reliability, although this is difficult for single-handed researchers such as postgraduate students. (For further discussion of documentary analysis, see Chapter 20 of this volume.)

It is evident from this brief account that applying the concept of reliability to case study research is problematic, notably in semi-structured or unstructured interviews and in observation. This is unsurprising as reliability is a notion associated with positivist rather than interpretive research. This leads Bassey (1999) to dismiss it for case studies and to substitute the concept of 'trustworthiness' put forward by Lincoln and Guba (1985).

Reliability and validity

Aspinwall et al. (1994) regard reliability, along with validity and relevance, as one of the key tests in judging the adequacy of research:

> Is it reliable? Would similar conclusions be drawn if the information was obtained by somebody else or by some other method? This is a tricky area. Again, quantitative indicators are often more reliable than more qualitative ones [but] their reliability may be bought at the expense of their validity. Where reliability is a problem, there is advantage in using more than one kind or source of data in relation to a particular criterion: [i.e.] triangulation. (Aspinwall et al., 1994: 218)

Scott and Morrison (2006: 208) note that a research finding might be reliable but not valid and 'thus of no worth to the researcher'. The tension between reliability and validity in qualitative research is noted by Hartas (2010: 74): 'In many ways, establishing the validity is more important than achieving reliability, in that the results of a study may be reliable but not valid, making the entire research exercise worthless'.

As we noted earlier, reliability may be achieved only by reducing validity. We turn now to consider this latter concept.

Validity

Definition

The concept of validity is used to judge whether the research accurately describes the phenomenon that it is intended to describe. The research design, the methodology and the conclusions of the research all need to have regard to the validity of the process:

> Validity ... tells us whether an item measures or describes what it is supposed to measure or describe. If an item is unreliable, then it must also lack validity, but a reliable item is not necessarily also valid. It could produce the same or similar responses on all occasions, but not be measuring what it is supposed to measure. (Bell, 1999: 104)

Validity, like reliability, is a notion primarily associated with positivist research and has been questioned by those who favour qualitative, or interpretive, approaches. Denzin and Lincoln (1998) emphasise the central importance of validity within positivist paradigms and claim that it is inappropriate for other perspectives. Kincheloe and McLaren (1998) reject 'traditional' validity as unhelpful for 'critical' qualitative research and join Bassey (1999) in advocating the alternative concept of 'trustworthiness':

> Where traditional verifiability rests on a rational proof built upon literal intended meaning, a critical qualitative perspective always involves a less certain approach characterised by participant reaction and emotional involvement. Some analysts argue that validity may be an inappropriate term in a critical research context, as it simply reflects a concern for acceptance within a positivist concept of research rigour ... Trustworthiness ... is a more appropriate word to use in the context of critical research. (Kincheloe and McLaren, 1998: 287)

Despite this negative view, several writers regard validity as wholly appropriate for both quantitative and qualitative research. Hartas's (2010: 451) definition links validity to trustworthiness: validity is 'a criterion for the integrity of a study in terms of accuracy of inferences and the trustworthiness of results'.

Types of validity

Several different types of validity have been identified by writers on research methods in education (Cohen and Manion, 1994; Cohen et al., 2000; Hartas, 2010). The main distinction is between internal and external validity. *Internal* validity relates to the extent that research findings accurately represent the phenomenon under investigation, as the following definitions suggest:

> The degree to which findings correctly map the phenomenon in question. (Denzin and Lincoln, 1998: 186)

> The accuracy or authenticity of the description being made ... [it is] a measure of accuracy and whether it matches reality. (Scott and Morrison, 2006: 253)

Cohen and Manion (1994: 99–101) apply the notion of internal validity to several different research methods. In relation to survey research, they point to two potential causes of invalidity:

- Respondents may not complete questionnaires accurately. They suggest that validity may be checked by interviewing respondents. This is an example of methodological triangulation.

- Those who fail to return questionnaires might have responded differently to those who did so. They suggest follow-up contact with non-respondents by trained interviewers to establish their views. This is an expensive strategy, which is likely to be prohibitive for many single-handed researchers, including postgraduate students. Validity is enhanced if the survey produces a substantial response. The greater the response rate, the smaller the risk of invalidity.

The main potential source of invalidity in interviews is bias: 'The sources of bias are the characteristics of the interviewer, the characteristics of the respondent, and the substantive content of the questions' (Cohen and Manion, 1994: 282). They suggest careful formulation of questions and interviewer training as possible solutions but bias is likely to be endemic, particularly in semi-structured and unstructured interviews, and is difficult to eliminate.

The risk of bias may be reduced through respondent validation (Scott and Morrison, 2006: 252), where transcripts or the researcher's notes are returned to the interviewee for confirmation or amendment. The author consistently uses this approach following interviews (see, for example, Bush, 2011; Bush et al., 2006a, 2006b).

Similar problems arise in participant observation, where there may be 'observer bias' (Moyles, 2007: 250), and the researcher's 'judgement [may] be affected by their close involvement in the group' (Cohen and Manion, 1994: 111). As we noted earlier, the concept of validity may be rejected as a positivist construct, which cannot easily be applied to qualitative methods, including observation and most types of interview.

Silverman (2000: 176–7) refers to another problem, which may compromise validity in qualitative research. He says that researchers must avoid the 'special temptation' of 'anecdotalism', where 'a few well-chosen examples' are used to illustrate the findings. He argues that triangulation provides a way of addressing this problem (see below).

External validity relates to the extent that findings may be generalised to the wider population, which the sample represents, or to other similar settings:

External validity ... is a measure of generalisability. (Scott and Morrison, 2006: 253)

External validity refers to our ability to generalise the results beyond the context of a specific study. (Hartas, 2010: 76)

Brock-Utne (1996: 617) notes that external validity is usually applied in positivist research and she is sceptical about applying this notion to qualitative methods. Case study research, for example, may be criticised because it does not match the survey approach in terms of generalisation. Indeed, Yin

(1994: 147) claims that the unique case often provides the rationale for single case studies. Here, the potential for generalisation is necessarily limited.

Bassey (1999) addresses this issue by distinguishing between statistical and 'fuzzy' generalisations and linking these notions to quantitative and qualitative approaches:

> The statistical generalisation arises from samples of populations and typically claims that there is an *x* per cent or *y* per cent chance that what was found in the sample will also be found throughout the population: it is a quantitative measure. The fuzzy generalisation arises from studies of singularities and typically claims that it is possible, or likely, or unlikely, that what was found in the singularity will be found in similar situations elsewhere: it is a qualitative measure. (Bassey, 1999: 12)

Bassey (1999) refers to 'singularities' but generalisation may become less 'fuzzy' if several similar case studies are undertaken. Yin (1994) says that the problem of generalisation can be minimised by replicating the study in another similar setting. This process should lead to wider acceptance of the external validity of the findings:

> The investigator is striving to generalise a particular set of results to some broader theory ... the theory that led to a case study in the first place is the same theory that will help to identify the other cases to which the results are generalisable ... A theory must be tested through replication of the findings in a second or even third [case], where the theory has specified that the same results should occur. Once such replication has been made, the results might be accepted for a larger number of similar [cases], even though further replications have not been performed. (Yin, 1994: 145)

In the author's research on the South African pilot programme for school principals (Bush et al., 2011), there were 27 case studies of programme participants. There were several similar findings in respect of teaching, course materials, mentoring, networking and site-based assessment, enabling the research team to make well-founded generalisations about the programme.

Triangulation

Triangulation means comparing many sources of evidence in order to determine the accuracy of information or phenomena. It is essentially a means of cross-checking data to establish its validity:

> The principle of triangulation rests on the assumption that particular events are being investigated and that, if they can be investigated in a number of different ways and those different ways concur, then the researcher may then believe that their account is a truer account of those events. (Scott, 2007: 11)

Triangulation may be defined as the use of two or more methods of data collection in the study of some aspect of human behaviour ... The use of multiple methods, or the multi-method approach, as it is sometimes called, contrasts with the ubiquitous but generally more vulnerable single-method approach that characterises so much of research in the social sciences ... triangular techniques in the social sciences attempt to map out, or explain more fully, the richness and complexity of human behaviour by studying it from more than one standpoint. (Cohen and Manion, 1994: 233)

This latter definition links the notion of triangulation to a multi-methods approach. This is known as *methodological triangulation*, using several methods to explore the same issue. An alternative, or additional, approach is *respondent triangulation*, asking the same questions of many different participants (McFee, 1992). Scott (2007: 11–13) extends this discussion by identifying four types of triangulation:

1 Data triangulation; different data sets are collected at different times. Respondent triangulation can be seen as one type of data triangulation.

2 Investigator triangulation; where more than one data collector/analyst is used to confirm or disconfirm the findings of the research.

3 Theoretical triangulation; where more than one theoretical position is used in interpreting data.

4 Methodological triangulation; where strategies or methods are mixed to corroborate one against the other.

The author's research into management development and governor training in the Gauteng province of South Africa (Bush and Heystek, 2006) adopted both methodological and respondent triangulation. A 100 per cent sample survey of all principals was complemented by case studies of 30 schools identified by stratified sampling (methodological triangulation). Within each case study school, interviews were held with up to six different individuals: the principal, the chairperson of the school governing body (SGB), a teacher governor, a teacher who was not a member of the SGB, a non-teaching staff member and, in secondary schools, a student governor (respondent triangulation). A similar approach was adopted when evaluating the English Succession Planning programme for the National College, when two surveys were conducted and there were also 12 case studies involving interviews with several participants (Bush, 2011). In both these examples, data were checked across different methods and sources.

Cohen et al. (2000: 113) say that triangulation may be used in either positivist or interpretive research but it is particularly valuable in case study research when multiple methods are often employed (Bassey, 1999: 81). In policy-related research, for example, the aims of the policy may be stated in documents. Interviews and/or observation may then be undertaken to establish whether these aims were realised or if the policy has had certain unintended consequences. Conducting such interviews with different user groups (for example, teachers and school leaders) may lead to the conclusion that the policy impacted differentially on each group. Robson (2002) points to the value of using interviews and observations for triangulation in a study primarily based on content analysis of documents:

> The documents have been written for some purpose other than for the research, and it is difficult or impossible to allow for the biases or distortions that this introduces ... [There is a] need for triangulation with other accounts [and] data sources to address this problem. (Robson, 2002: 358)

Triangulation is fundamentally a device for improving validity by checking data, either by using mixed methods or by involving a range of participants. While contributing to validity, its use is not a panacea. Scott (2007: 14) argues that 'triangulation as a device cannot deliver what it promises'. The assumption that 'true' fixes on 'reality' can be obtained separately from different ways of looking at it (Silverman, 2000: 177) may also be incompatible with certain approaches to qualitative research that value and celebrate individual or subjective ways of seeing and interpreting phenomena.

Conclusion

Research has the potential to influence policy and practice and its importance for educational leadership and management has grown since the inception of the English National College, which strongly emphasises practitioner research as well as funding about half of all school leadership research in England (Weindling, 2004). Both new and experienced researchers need to ensure that research findings are authentic. Reliability and validity are the two main issues to address when seeking to ensure authenticity while triangulation is one important way in which validity may be sought.

We noted earlier that reliability and validity may be regarded as constructs within the positivist research tradition. However, authenticity remains an important issue for qualitative researchers. It may be achieved through alternative concepts such as trustworthiness (Lincoln and Guba, 1985), or truth (Scott, 2007), or through a modification of the positivist concepts to enhance their applicability to interpretive, or phenomenological, research.

Lincoln and Denzin (1998) go beyond the debate about positivist and interpretive research to point out that validity is not an absolute concept:

> Validity represents the always just out of reach, but answerable, claim a text makes for its own authority ... the research could always have been better grounded, the subjects more representative, the researcher more knowledgeable, the research instruments better formulated, and so on ... validity is the researcher's mask of authority, which allows a particular regime of truth ... to work its way on the world. (Lincoln and Denzin, 1998: 415)

Authenticity may be an elusive target, but it is an important objective for educational leadership and management researchers. While there is no perfect truth, a focus on reliability, validity and triangulation should contribute to an acceptable level of authenticity sufficient to satisfy both researcher and reader that the study is meaningful and worthwhile.

Key points

Key points to consider when planning and executing research:

- Trying to ensure that your research is reliable and valid.
- Asking if your instruments measure what they are supposed to measure (validity).
- Addressing whether or not you are seeking generalisation and, if so, what strategies should be adopted to maximise the prospect of achieving this.
- Considering whether to repeat procedures to see if they produce the same results.
- Deciding whether to use different methods, and generate different data sets, to enhance triangulation.
- Considering whether you would be able to defend the authenticity of your research to a knowledgeable audience.

Questions and reflections

1 How will you ensure that your research is reliable and valid?
2 How will you ensure that your research instruments measure what they are supposed to measure?
3 How will you maximise the validity of your research by adopting methodological and/or respondent triangulation?
4 Would you be able to defend the authenticity of your research at a seminar or conference?

Recommended further reading

Denzin, N.K. and Lincoln, Y.S. (1998) *The Landscape of Qualitative Research*. Thousand Oaks, CA: Sage.

This book provides a helpful overview of validity in qualitative research.

Hartas, D. (2010) *Educational Research and Enquiry: Qualitative and Quantitative Approaches*. London: Continuum.

This book provides definitions of the key terms discussed in this chapter and also addresses the tensions between reliability and validity.

Scott, D. (2007) Resolving the Quantitative–Qualitative Dilemma: a Critical Realist Approach. *International Journal of Research and Method in Education* 30 (1): 3–17.

This article provides a helpful discussion of different types of triangulation.

Silverman, D. (2000) *Doing Qualitative Research: A Practical Handbook.* London: Sage.

This book offers a valuable perspective on validity in qualitative research and also raises important questions about triangulation.

References

Aspinwall, K., Simkins, T., Wilkinson, J. and McCauley, J. (eds) (1994) Using success criteria, in Bennett, N., Glatter, R. and Levačić, R. (eds) *Improving Educational Management through Research and Consultancy.* London: Paul Chapman.

Bassey, M. (1999) *Case Study Research in Educational Settings.* Buckingham: Open University Press.

Bell, J. (1999) *Doing Your Research Project.* Buckingham: Open University Press.

Bell, J. (2007) The trouble with questionnaires, in Briggs, A.R.J. and Coleman, M. (eds), *Research Methods in Educational Leadership and Management* (2nd edn). London: Sage.

Bernard, H. (2000) *Social Research Methods: Qualitative and Quantitative Approaches.* Thousand Oaks, CA: Sage.

Brock-Utne, B. (1996) Reliability and validity in qualitative research within education in Africa. *International Review of Education* 42(6): 605–21.

Bush, T. (2011) Succession planning in England: new leaders and new forms of leadership. *School Leadership and Management* 31(3): 181–98.

Bush, T. and Glover, D. (2005) Leadership for early headship: the New Visions experience. *School Leadership and Management* 25(3): 217–39.

Bush, T. and Glover, D. (2012) Distributed leadership in action: high performing leadership teams in English schools. *School Leadership and Management* 32(1): 21–36.

Bush, T. and Heystek, J. (2006) School leadership and management in South Africa: principals' perceptions. *International Studies in Educational Administration*, 34(3): 63–76.

Bush, T., Briggs, A.R.J. and Middlewood, D. (2006a) The impact of school leadership development: evidence from the 'New Visions' programme for early headship. *Journal of In-service Education* 32(2): 185–200.

Bush, T., Glover, D. and Sood, K. (2006b) Black and minority ethnic leaders in England: a portrait. *School Leadership and Management* 26(4): 289–305.

Bush, T., Kiggundu, E. and Moorosi, P. (2011) Preparing new principals in South Africa: the ACE: School Leadership programme. *South African Journal of Education* 31(1): 31–43.

Cohen, L. and Manion, L. (1994) *Research Methods in Education.* London: Routledge.

Cohen, L., Manion, L. and Morrison, K. (2000) *Research Methods in Education* (5th edn). London: Routledge.

Denzin, N.K. and Lincoln, Y.S. (1998) *The Landscape of Qualitative Research.* Thousand Oaks, CA: Sage.

Fitzgerald, T. (2007) Documents and documentary analysis: reading between the lines, in Briggs, A.R.J and Coleman, M. (eds). *Research Methods in Educational Leadership and Management* (2nd edn). London: Sage.

Fogelman, K. and Comber, C. (2007) Surveys and sampling, in Briggs, A.R.J. and Coleman, M. (eds), *Research Methods in Educational Leadership and Management* (2nd edn). London: Sage.

Fowler, F. (1993) *Survey Research Methods*. Newbury Park, CA: Sage.

Hartas, D. (2010) *Educational Research and Enquiry: Qualitative and Quantitative Approaches*. London: Continuum.

Johnson, D. (1994) *Research Methods in Educational Management*. Harlow: Longman.

Kincheloe, J. and McLaren, P. (1998) Rethinking critical theory and qualitative research, in Denzin, N. and Lincoln, Y. (eds), *The Landscape of Qualitative Research*. Thousand Oaks, CA: Sage.

Lincoln, Y.S. and Denzin, N.K. (1998) The fifth moment, in Denzin, N. and Lincoln, Y. (eds), *The Landscape of Qualitative Research*. Thousand Oaks, CA: Sage.

Lincoln, Y.S. and Guba, E.G. (1985) *Naturalistic Inquiry*. Newbury Park, CA: Sage.

McFee, G. (1992) Triangulation in research: two confusions. *Educational Research* 34(3): 215–19.

Moyles, J. (2007) Observation as a research tool, in Briggs, A.R.J. and Coleman, M. (eds), *Research Methods in Educational Leadership and Management* (2nd edn). London: Sage.

Robson, C. (1994) Analysing documents and records, in Bennett, N., Glatter, R. and Levačić, R. (eds), *Improving Educational Management through Research and Consultancy*. London: Paul Chapman.

Robson, C. (2002) *Real World Research* (2nd edn). Oxford: Blackwell.

Scott, D. (2007) Resolving the quantitative–qualitative dilemma: a critical realist approach. *International Journal of Research and Method in Education* 30(1): 3–17.

Scott, D. and Morrison, M. (2006) *Key Ideas in Educational Research*. London: Continuum.

Silverman, D. (2000) *Doing Qualitative Research: A Practical Handbook*. London: Sage.

Weindling, D. (2004) *Funding for Research in School Leadership*. Nottingham: NCSL.

Wragg, E. (2002) Interviewing, in Coleman, M. and Briggs, A.R.J. (eds), *Research Methods in Educational Leadership and Management*. London: Paul Chapman.

Yildirim, K. (2010) Raising the quality in qualitative research. *Elementary Education Online* 9(1): 79–92.

Yin, R.K. (1994) Designing single and multiple case studies, in Bennett, N. Glatter, R. and Levačić, R. (eds), *Improving Educational Management through Research and Consultancy*. London: Paul Chapman with the Open University.

Youngman, M. (1994) Designing and using questionnaires, in Bennett, N., Glatter. R. and Levačić R. (eds), *Improving Educational Management through Research and Consultancy*. London: Paul Chapman.

CHAPTER 7

The Ethical Framework of Research Practice

Hugh Busher and Nalita James

Chapter objectives

This chapter discusses:

- How ethical research practices in educational leadership are based on value-driven research processes.
- How ethical research practices in educational leadership reflect and articulate with key aspects of educational organisations – power, culture, decision making, construction of identity, learning communities, policy contexts.
- Particularly problematic areas of insider or practitioner research.
- How an explicitly ethical framework of research helps research projects to:

  - Construct collaborative cultures.
  - Gain trustworthy knowledge to benefit a range of communities.
  - Gain and maintain participants' informed consent.
  - Protect participants and their institutions from harm by preserving their anonymity and privacy.
  - Create a secure curation and publication of data.

What do we tell our students?

In the social sciences, the ethics of research are closely linked to constructing collaborative communities in which researchers act as hosts (Derrida, 2000) for their research projects, inducting new participants into them. Part of this social construction is clarifying the rules of engagement with participants, whether it is an online or onsite research project (James and Busher, 2009), so the research is carried out in a respectful manner (British Educational Research Association [BERA], 2004). These rules are intended to help keep participants safe from harm, build trust with participants and ensure trustworthy outcomes from the research which will benefit society. 'Research should be conducted so as to ensure the professional integrity of its design, the generation and analysis of data, and the publication of results' (Economic and Social Research Council [ESRC], 2005: 23). However, researchers can only achieve this with 'the direct and indirect contributions of colleagues, collaborators and others' (2005: 23) which should also be acknowledged.

Leading research projects is a collaborative and value-laden practice (Fullan, 2003; Starratt, 2007). Researchers have to consider the ethics of how they conduct research and their responsibilities within the research process (Knobel, 2005) for constructing 'respect for the person (participants, researchers, and people in situations in which the research is carried out), knowledge, democratic values, the quality of educational research, academic freedom' (BERA, 2004, para. 6). For example, researchers cannot tell senior staff in a school the views offered by participants in a project, even if the senior staff as gatekeepers to the institution – see below – think it would benefit the management of the school. To do so would breach ethical agreements with participants to preserve their anonymity and protect them from potential harm.

Research is intended to be of reciprocal or mutual benefit to researchers, participants and society. Researchers should make clear to participants at the start of a project how they and other people might benefit from the research (Robson and Robson, 2002). For example, studying the decision-making processes of school subject areas should give insights into how relationships between staff contribute to the success of a department. The executive summary report of the project would explain this to all interested parties.

Research projects as value-driven learning communities

The ethics of research are intimately intertwined with constructing purposeful collaborative learning communities, called research projects, based on trust and respect amongst its members working together for a purpose. Every participant in a project learns, as well as helping to construct knowledge to achieve a research project's purposes. Through their participation, participants come to (re)define some aspects of their identities in relation to the shared practices of a particular community, such as a research project. They use symbolic markers to reify boundaries between themselves and other people (Williams, 2006).

This has implications for research project leaders. For example, potential participants in a project or gatekeepers guarding access to a research site, expect a researcher to use socially appropriate communications to show respect for them when explaining the reason for studying a specific topic or phenomenon, the potential value of the findings, the part participants will play in a project and what that involves in terms of time and activity, the potential ethical risks in the study (Sikes, 2006) and how the researchers will address these issues (James and Busher, 2006). These perspectives are inscribed and sustained in the developing community of a new research project through the value-laden actions of the researcher(s)/leaders. Understanding these aspects helps participants, whether students or staff in a school or parents of a school, to gain a sense of ownership of the research and give their informed consent for their involvement at the start of a project and throughout its life. In addition, online researchers show respect for online community members by participating in the community being studied for an extended period before any data collection takes place (Knobel, 2005). Madge and O'Connor (2005) argue that researchers should declare themselves as such from the start of their contact with an online community.

Learning communities (Bolam et al., 2005; Busher et al., 2007; Stoll and Louis, 2007; Hord et al., 2010), like research projects, depend for their success on developing successful collaborative interpersonal relationships between members to achieve identified purposes. However, these will be influenced by the visible social characteristics (age, race, gender and organisational status) of researchers and participants because of the culturally developed interpretations people hold, and may affect the outcomes of research conversations or observations, i.e. affect its authenticity and credibility (Lincoln and Guba, 1985).

Lack of visible social characteristics in online research only changes the problem. The invisibility of participants and researchers from each other in online interactions may make it more difficult for researchers to know with whom they are talking, raising 'new problems in judging what is authentic' (Hine, 2000: 118), or whether their modes of communicating are socially appropriate 'because cyberspace is not always a harmonious cultural sphere' (Knobel, 2005: 158) and participants and researchers are located 'within a complex web or context of enacting particular identit[ies] online' (Knobel, 2005: 159). However, the extent to which researchers and participants in online research construct credible and consistent stories through their text-based exchanges (Lee, 2006), which is what people do in face-to-face conversations, helps to give authenticity to a conversation. Further, these conversations can be triangulated with other sources of evidence. For example, in a research project on the construction of collaborative cultures in a school, information given by one member of staff can be cross-referenced to that of other project members or to school documents to establish its probable credibility. Sometimes the domain name of a participant's email will indicate the institution in which a project participant works, although this could jeopardise participants' privacy.

Constructing ethical collaborative cultures amongst research project participants

Researchers have a duty of care (Glenn, 2000) to participants who join their projects as well as for those whose environments are affected by their research, especially when participants might be deemed 'vulnerable' (ESRC, 2005: 8;

see also Ess and the Association of Internet Researchers [AoIR], 2002), or when research might be deemed to generate greater risk of harm to participants (see Table 7.1).

Table 7.1   Research likely to cause greater risk of harm to participants

Vulnerable groups – for example, children and young people, those with a learning disability or cognitive impairment, or individuals in a dependent relationship

Sensitive topics – for example, participants' illegal or political behaviour (for example, underage smoking or sex), their experience of violence (for example, bullying), their abuse or exploitation, their mental health, their gender or ethnic status

A gatekeeper normally permits initial access to members – for example, ethnic or cultural groups, students or teachers in school or college, or inmates and other members of custodial or health and welfare institutions

Deception or research conducted without participants' full and informed consent at the time the study is started

Access to records of personal or confidential information, such as students' school or college records, whether of personal or academic performance, including genetic or other biological information, such as doctors' records

Inducing psychological stress, anxiety or humiliation or causing more than minimal pain, such as taking non-physical performance tests, or making unusual presentations to colleagues, or undertaking activities with which participants are normally unfamiliar, for example, taking photographs round a school or college of the sites where they interact with other people for various reasons

Intrusive interventions – for example, the administration of drugs or other substances, vigorous physical exercise, that participants would not normally encounter in their everyday life

Source: Adapted from ESRC, 2005: 8

Participants can be made vulnerable by particular types of research design (ESRC, 2005) or studies focusing on particular sensitive topics which, for example, require access to records of personal or confidential information (see Table 7.1). For example, where a study induces psychological stress, perhaps because a researcher wants to video-record teachers and students interacting in a classroom, researchers should be prepared to support any participants who are distressed by this. Where deception is an essential part of the research design, perhaps through staff or students taking apparently high-stakes tests when a researcher actually wants to study participants' attitudes to different types of assessment, researchers are expected to make participants aware of what procedures have taken place immediately after the research has finished (BERA, 2004; see also British Sociological Association [BSA], 2002). Where research is onsite in the school context, it is important that it does not distract from the everyday practices of working with teachers and children. Such issues need to be covered when seeking access and consent from principals or school leaders.

The rapid growth of research using computer-mediated communication (CMC) such as email, chat rooms, discussion boards and wikis to examine, for example, the impact of the Internet on students' learning or teachers' (pedagogic) practices or the micro-political processes in a school presents researchers with the challenge of how to protect research participants' vulnerabilities in the online environment. Further, it raises specific questions about what ethical research practice online particularly entails (James and Busher, 2006). This issue is further amplified for educational researchers engaged in online research as there can be a wide range of people investing directly or indirectly in the project who need to be taken into account, be they parents, students, teachers or educational leaders.

Privileging human rights: the impact of context on research project cultures

The need for researchers to gain participants' informed consent to join a research project arises from fundamental democratic rights to freedom and self-determination, including choosing to join or not to join a project free from coercion or bribery (ESRC, 2005: 7) and having the right to withdraw at any time from it. Research with children and young people and people in institutions poses a particular concern for researchers. BERA (2004) requires its members to comply with Articles 3 and 12 of the United Nations Convention on the Rights of the Child (1989) when working with children and with the spirit of these articles when working with vulnerable adults. Members of both groups may be less able to grasp the advantages and costs of taking part in a research project because they lack either the language or the conceptual understanding to make sense of what researchers might tell them about a project before they join it. Or they may think they have no choice but to take part because an authoritative person such as a teacher or care home manager has asked them to do so. With such people, researchers have to explain the purposes, processes and part to be played by participants, as well as the voluntary nature of participation in the project, in language that the participants can understand before asking them to give their informed and, usually, written consent. However, 'there is no simple rule for getting right the balance between potential risks to participants and benefits of the research to a wider community' (ESRC, 2005: 25).

This deontological (human rights) stance to research ethics, emphasising the rights of participants in research who are likely to be in a less powerful position than researchers to shape the research process, is held in member states of the European Union (Capurro and Pingel, 2002: 193). In the USA, a utilitarian view is held (Ess and the Association of Internet Researchers [AoIR], 2002: 20), allowing research to be carried out if, on balance, it does more good to society than harm, even if it risks causing harm to participants.

The rights of research participants are also affected by legislation in many countries on the use of electronic data, including research data, that is collected and stored. For example, in Britain researchers must comply with legal requirements for the storage and use of personal data as set down by the Data Protection Act (1998) and amended by the Data Protection Act (2003). People are entitled to know how and why their personal data is being stored, to what uses it is being put and to whom it may be made available (BERA, 2004, para. 24). Consequently, researchers have to take 'appropriate measures ... to store research data in a secure manner' BSA, 2002, para. 36). In many countries, national governments or their agencies exercise surveillance of CMC (James and Busher, 2009). Given the 'ethical pluralism' of the world, researchers who carry out research across international boundaries or with people from more than one country have to cope with participants' rights in different contexts and cultures.

Insufficient consideration is often given to the appropriateness of the context or site in which research is to be conducted (Walford, 2001). Such social, economic and policy contexts, be they those for online communities or for physical sites such as educational institutions, have implications for participants in and the outcomes of research. The communities that participants inhabit shape how research and researchers are perceived and how participants may respond to invitations to take part in research or may be perceived by others when taking part in research (Benjamin, 2002). For example, Shah (2004) points out that when an interviewer is a member of the opposite sex to the participants or of a different ethnic group or cultural community, this may make interviewing or observation more problematic, since such attributes may make some of the participants feel uncomfortable and unwilling to share their views openly. (For further discussion of cross-cultural research, see Chapter 4 of this volume.) Clearly demarcated social and power differentials between researchers and participants, such as that between children and adults, or between adults of different formal status in a school or college, has a similar impact.

Constructing cultures in research projects (and in educational institutions)

Research project cultures are social constructs (Giddens, 1984) based on participants' values, interests and lived experiences in various communities, and their cultural and social capital (Bourdieu, 1986). Although people's social relationships are tied to the social frameworks from which they come (Giddens, 1991), researchers can respect participants' cultural plurality by structuring research projects to take account of participants' cultural preferences. For example, a researcher can take care to meet participants at times convenient to them or to meet them online asynchronously. The language used in research projects contributes to the construction of cultural meanings (Knobel, 2005). How research project members address each other and talk about the project, through the respectfulness with which they treat each other, also develops the culture of the research project.

These research project cultures, like those of subject areas in educational institutions (Busher et al., 2007), are constructed in the interstices, or third spaces (Bhabha, 1994), of people's other social and institutional interactions. In and through the third spaces of research conversations, people from different backgrounds create a hybrid culture that is neither entirely theirs nor entirely that of the others in the developing community. In these third spaces, members of a research community 'elaborate strategies of selfhood – singular or communal – that initiate new signs of identity ... in the act of defining the idea of society itself' (Bhabha, 1994: 2). Members of online communities in one study talked about their cultural spaces in essentialist terms (Williams, 2006) to give their community a sense of identity because Internet technologies and globalisation have blurred senses of space that previously helped to map cultures. These cultures link participants' practice in a research project to wider constellations (Wenger, 1998) of academic norms and practices.

For research project communities to work, members have to perceive collectively and individually the worth and symbolic value of continuing to participate in them (Williams 2006: 174), in order to achieve perceived benefits whether shared or not, or experienced personally or altruistically. For example, teachers may choose to be involved in a research project because they think it will benefit students' learning, whether or not they personally gain anything from taking part in that project.

Constructing trust and ownership in a research project

The construction of trust between researchers and participants, whether online or onsite, is an important element in building the culture of a research project. Trust is closely related to a sense of ownership of a research project and a belief that participants are respected and able to influence the trajectory of the project.

One aspect of constructing trust is creating a safe environment in which to work. Researchers using online sites need to ensure that electronic data curation (storage) is sufficiently safe for the purposes of their research project. Projects dealing with everyday matters may not need a very secure environment, but those dealing with sensitive topics or vulnerable people will. This is because of the legal and less legal means of scrutiny to which their participants' communications might be subjected by governmental or commercial agencies.

Another aspect is researchers ensuring that CMC is respectful. Onsite, ethical self-reflection can ensure that researchers avoid interjections when observing teachers and students. Online, researchers need to take care that 'the anonymity of the Internet does not lead them to dominate the interactional space' (Knobel, 2005: 157). One way to do this is to acknowledge participants' ownership of their interview and visual data and the right to decide whether the text/speech accounts of their research conversations should be published.

Researchers need to negotiate clearly with participants as to how their findings will be used and for what purposes during and after the research project. To safeguard how participants are (re)presented in and through a research project and avoid breaching their or others' privacy or confidentiality, researchers may allow participants to edit their conversations before they are published in a public domain. In online research, many members of online communities believe that their communications are private dialogues, even when they are communicating to an internationally based community. So they are loath to have their perceived private conversations made public through the publication of research (Madge and O'Connor, 2005).

The ethics of power: researchers as leaders of research project communities

Constructing and sustaining rules and social structures

As core members of research project communities (Wenger, 1998), researchers play a central part in constructing their cultures and processes to achieve trustworthy outcomes to benefit society, as well as the participants in it. Oakley (1981) suggests that the culture most likely to generate successful research projects, especially for those using interpretative and critical ontologies, might be described as collaborative or participatory, following the literature of teacher leadership (Muijs and Harris, 2003), democratic leadership (Harris, 2004) and moral leadership (Fullan, 2003; Starratt, 2007). It reflects the culture found in successful learning communities in or of schools and colleges. An important initial step in building this culture is explaining a project's purposes to participants, potential participants and gatekeepers – see below – what part they are being asked to play in it and at what cost to themselves, how it will be managed and the intended social and interpersonal values enshrined within it. The purposes and processes of a research project are sometimes clarified to potential participants in it by constructing a rubric for a project (James and Busher, 2009) (see Table 7.2). Similar explanations of a project usually accompany the consent forms, required for projects carried out under the guidelines of the ESRC (2005) given to participants, when they are first asked to join a project.

Full membership of a research project community does not occur immediately an individual joins it. Membership is constructed slowly as people are inducted into it by 'old hands' (Lave and Wenger, 1991) or project leaders (Wenger, 1998) and gradually choose to engage and disclose themselves more fully (Lee, 2006), learning a community's norms of behaviour and practice. However, this is also likely to lead to a sense of tension between what they wish to disclose and to whom (Williams, 2006).

As well as constructing the internal process of a research project community, researchers have to negotiate with its external contexts, such as the schools or colleges or education systems in which it is located, to gain resources for its purposes and support from the gatekeepers to these sites, such as school principals. If the site for research is an online community, then permissions need to be asked of the website moderator and/or community elders to conduct research in that space (Kim, 2000, cited in Bishop, 2006). To succeed, researchers need to make clear the benefits of the research to the gatekeepers institutionally or personally and explain how their institutions will be protected from harm. In such contexts, researchers should not compromise their integrity or the credibility of the study by pretending to be someone they are not.

Table 7.2 Rubric for conducting interviews with psychology lecturers

A little while ago you completed a questionnaire, which focused upon professional identity, how it is managed within the professional environment and whether it is possible to generate a common sense of identity across the psychology profession. You agreed to take part in an email interview, which will address the issues raised in that questionnaire. Please read the following guidelines and if you are still happy to take part in the interview, please reply to this email and I shall send you the first question. The email interviews will consider the issues that arose in the questionnaire in more depth. The data gathered through the email interviews will provide a transcript of your account. These accounts will be used to inform the research study.

In undertaking the email interview, please note the following guidelines:

i If you are still willing to take part in this study, please reply to this email straight away.

ii The interviews will be conducted in strictest confidence and your anonymity will be assured.

Throughout the research project:

iii You will be asked 11 substantive questions.

iv These questions will be sent to you one at a time. Please respond to the question by email. Each question may be followed up by supplementary questions.

v It is anticipated that an ongoing dialogue will occur. In order to achieve this, please ensure that you answer on top of the message and question sent to you. PLEASE DO NOT ANSWER AT THE BOTTOM OF IT. This will ensure the sequence of questions and answers is not broken.

vi Please do not delete any part of the email dialogue. This will be our record of the conversation.

vii Please reply to each email question within three working days if possible. I will also try to reply to your response within that timescale.

viii It is anticipated that the email dialogue will be completed within 10 weeks.

ix Once the dialogue is complete, you will be asked to authenticate your account.

x The completed dialogue may be followed up by further email discussion.

Source: James and Busher, 2009: 44

Creating a secure environment for research

Creating a secure environment includes ensuring that research conversations and other information are recorded and stored/curated securely during and after the end of a research project. Recording participants' conversations in locations where they are unlikely to be overheard by other people helps to protect them from harm. Being respectful of how participants prefer to record information, takes account of participants' cultural contexts where there is suspicion about how electronic recordings might be used (James and Busher, 2009) or taboos about who or what may be photographed or video-recorded. When working with children or vulnerable people, researchers have to be particularly careful to ensure that their privacy and dignity are not impaired as participants may have given their consent to a project without fully realising its implications. 'In some cases it may be necessary to decide whether it is proper or appropriate even to record certain kinds of sensitive information' (BSA, 2002, para. 34), such as information that is detrimental to, or unsupported opinion about, the character of other participants in a study or the institution in which a research project is sited.

Curating data has to avoid the possibility of harm being done to research participants (ESRC, 2005). Personal information about participants should not normally be stored mechanically or electronically with research information from them. And all information, especially textual or visual information, has to be rendered anonymous when storing it as it can be migrated very easily outside the research project community. Consequently, only data relevant to the specific purposes of a research project should be collected and stored (ESRC, 2005). Statistical outcomes of research also have to be presented ethically in ways that are not misleading and are comprehensible to people who are unfamiliar with statistical procedures. For example, the publication of raw score data on students' academic attainments is probably unethical since it is open to misinterpretation as a measure of school performance, as compared to individual students' performances, when not set in the contexts of other indicators of students' achievements in and outside a school and the social and economic environment of a school and its individual students and staff.

When storing online data, complete anonymity is almost impossible to guarantee, as information about the origin of a computer-transmitted message will be difficult to remove (Stewart and Williams, 2005). Researchers have to comply with two frameworks when storing research data electronically. One is the ethical codes that constrain their work. The other is the law of whichever nation state in which researchers are based – see above.

'The form of any publication, including publication on the Internet [should] not directly or indirectly lead to a breach of confidentiality and anonymity' (BERA, 2004, para. 26). When writing up the outcomes of a project, data collected for it can only be used in ways that are compatible 'with the original purpose of the project' (Elgesem, 2002: 201). For example, it is unethical to use extracts from project data for teaching purposes, especially if not properly anonymised, or to share it with other people salaciously, if participants have not given their express permission for that. This is because people's conversations in written or electronic form or their visual social artefacts are *their* social products, not those of the researchers. This constraint includes any agreements with third parties, such as principals or other gatekeepers to a research site, about the terms under which researchers are allowed access to data.

Going solo: undertaking practitioner research

Participating in any research involves risk to the individuals concerned. Inviting individuals to participate in research means that the researcher is also agreeing to protect participants from harm and violation of their privacy. The sovereignty of the individual is critical in research that involves gathering data about personal experiences, whether research is conducted onsite or online.

Practitioner or insider researcher is particularly problematic in this respect. As a practitioner in a school or college, researchers cannot be sure to what extent their practitioner roles influence the choice of people to participate or not in a project and the way participants shape the information they give them. Gaining informed consent or protecting participants' anonymity can be difficult, not least because, unintentionally or not, practitioners' influence constitutes a form of coercion on potential participants, which is unethical. This breaches one of the key principles for engaging participants with research (ESRC, 2005) and threatens the construction of trust with participants that is essential to a successful research project. Participants are likely to perceive a practitioner carrying out research as having particular agendas or interests (Ball, 1987) related to practice in a school as well as to research, especially if the researcher occupies a powerful formal role in a school, whether as a senior member of staff or as a teacher carrying out research with students, or has other means in the formal and informal organisation of a school for projecting power and influence (Busher, 2006).

This threatens the credibility of a study, since the authenticity of participants' texts and observed actions is more difficult to establish. However, developing the collaborative approaches to research discussed above and involving participants in the construction of the research project rather than merely supplying it with information is likely to strengthen this authenticity. (For further discussion of practitioner research, see Chapter 12 of this volume.)

A practitioner in a school or college may have the advantage of already being known to his or her participants, have inside perspectives and the support of important gatekeepers in an institution. Although this may help her/him understand more thoroughly the contexts in and of which participants are talking (Benjamin, 2002), it is also likely to affect the way in which participants feel comfortable to talk with researchers. Further, a practitioner, as an insider to an institution's processes, not only has to be sensitive to issues such as taking up the time of their colleagues in the research process, but will also have difficulty in guaranteeing participants' anonymity and confidentiality to protect them from harm, since what is told to the practitioner in the context of a research project is also told to the same person who occupies another and possibly more powerful role formally in a school or college, particularly in a small institution.

Constraining research project data so that it does not influence other aspects of researchers' and participants' working in a school is particularly difficult for practitioner researchers, especially if senior managers wish to use the research data for micro-political ends, or participants wish to manipulate the data for their own use. The curation of data is particularly problematic since it is very easy for information collected as research data to 'leak out' into the everyday interactions between a researcher and participants and a researcher and their peers and colleagues. In particular, where this information may alter the way in which particular participants are perceived by others, this 'leakage' could be perceived as breaching confidentiality, if not actually causing them harm in some way, and so constitute a breach of ethical practice.

Key points

Every research project has to negotiate its own agreed norms between researchers and participants to establish an ethical framework of process. This negotiation is central to persuading participants that they are protected from intentional or unintentional harm and so free to (re)present themselves truthfully. Such a framework from the outset should include an 'ethics of care' that at the very least involves a respect for the interests and values of those who participate in online research (Capurro and Pingel, 2002: 194). It must also make clear whether or not the environment in which the discussions are conducted is secure so that participants are aware of the risks they might be facing. Secure environments ensure that the risk to participants' privacy is minimised. Participants must be made fully aware of the risks involved so that they can freely choose whether or not they want to take part. In seeking to protect participants from harm, online research is no different from face-to-face research projects, but with the advent of CMC it has become more difficult to make sure texts, sounds and pictures are used ethically.

Questions and reflections

1 In what ways might the construction of collaborative cultures in research projects improve the trustworthiness of outcomes?

2 In what ways do researchers act as leaders of research projects, even when they are the sole researcher?

3 What are the main ethical issues facing insider researchers, and how might these be resolved?

Recommended further reading

James, N. and Busher, H. (2009) *Online Interviewing*. London: Sage.

This book focuses on the processes of using an online environment to carry out qualitative research. It is intended for an audience of knowledgeable beginners who want to develop work in this area when already familiar with some of the basics of carrying out qualitative research.

Madge, C. (2007) Developing a geographers' agenda for online research ethics. *Progress in Human Geography* 31: 654–74.

Obviously, many ethical issues of onsite research are directly translatable to the online context. However, this paper proposes that given the recent increased formal regulation and research governance over research ethics in many countries, it is important that discussion of such issues continues as an embedded part of professional self-regulation and that procedural ethical guidelines are used as creative forums for reflexive debate.

Sheehy, K., Nind, M., Rix, J. and Simmons, K. (2005) *Ethics and Research in Inclusive Education: Values into Practice*. London: RoutledgeFalmer/Open University Press.

The recent move towards inclusive education increases the importance of people being more aware of the critical legal and ethical responsibilities that arise from this. This edited collection of readings, written from the standpoint of inclusive education rather than 'special education', will develop people's ability to identify and respond to ethical dilemmas that occur within particular research methodologies and settings. The contributions draw upon examples of inclusive practices from around the world.

References

Ball, S.J. (1987) *The Micro-politics of the School*. London: Methuen.
Benjamin, S. (2002) *The Micro-politics of Inclusive Education*. Buckingham: Open University Press.
Bhabha, H. (1994) *The Location of Culture*. London: Routledge.
Bishop, J. (2006) Increasing participation in online communities: a framework for human–computer interaction. *Computers in Human Behavior* 23(4): 1881–93.
Bolam, R., McMahon, A., Stoll, L., Thomas, S. and Wallace, M. (2005) *Creating and Sustaining Effective Professional Learning Communities: Research Report 637*. London: DfES and University of Bristol.
Bourdieu, P. (1986) Forms of capital, in Richardson, J.G. (ed.) *Handbook of Theory and Research for the Sociology of Education*. New York: Greenwood Press, pp. 241–58.
British Educational Research Association (BERA) (2004) *Revised Ethical Guidelines for Educational Research*. Southwell: BERA.
British Sociological Association (BSA) (2002) Statement of Ethical Practice for the British Sociological Association. Available at: www.britsoc.co.uk/equality/Statement+Ethical+Practice.htm (accessed 13 July 2011).
Busher, H. (2006) *Understanding Educational Leadership: People, Power and Culture*. Maidenhead: Open University Press/McGraw-Hill.
Busher, H., Hammersley-Fletcher, L., and Turner, C. (2007) Making sense of middle leadership: community, power and practice. *School Leadership and Management* 27 (5): 405–22.
Capurro, R. and Pingel, C. (2002) Ethical issues of online communication research. *Ethics and Information Technology* 4: 189–94.
Derrida, J. (2000) *Of Hospitality*. Stanford, CA: Stanford University Press.
Economic and Social Research Council (ESRC) (2005) *Research Ethics Framework*. Swindon: ESRC.
Elgesem, D. (2002) What is special about the ethical issues in online research? *Ethics and Information Technology* 4: 195–203.

Ess, C. and the Association of Internet Researchers (AoIR) (2002) Ethical decision-making and Internet research. Available at: http://aoir.org/reports/ethics.pdf (accessed 13 July 2011).

Fullan, M. (2003) *The Moral Imperative of School Leadership*. Thousand Oaks, CA: Corwin Press.

Giddens, A. (1984) *The Constitution of Society*. Berkeley, CA: University of California Press.

Giddens, A. (1991) *Modernity and Self-identity*. Cambridge: Polity Press.

Glenn, S. (2000) The darkside of purity or the virtues of double-mindedness, in Simons, H. and Usher, R. (eds) *Situated Ethics in Educational Research*. London: RoutledgeFalmer.

Harris, A. (2004) Democratic leadership for school improvement in challenging contexts, in Macbeath, J. and Moos, L. (eds) *Democratic Learning: The Challenge to School Effectiveness*. London: RoutledgeFalmer. pp. 164–77.

Hine, C. (2000) *Virtual Ethnography*. London: Sage.

Hord, S., Roussin, J. and Sommers, W. (2010) *Guiding Professional Learning Communities: Inspiration, Challenge, Surprise, and Meaning*. Thousand Oaks, CA: Corwin.

James, N. and Busher, H. (2006) Credibility, authenticity and voice: dilemmas in online interviewing. *Qualitative Research* 6(3): 403–20.

James, N. and Busher, H. (2009) *Online Interviewing*. London: Sage.

Knobel, M. (2005) Rants, ratings and representation: ethical issues in researching online social practices, in Sheehy, K., Nind, M., Rix, J. and Simmons, K.(eds) *Ethics and Research in Inclusive Education: Values into Practice*. London: RoutledgeFalmer/ Open University Press.

Lave, J. and Wenger, E. (1991) *Situated Learning: Legitimate Peripheral Participation*. Cambridge: Cambridge University Press.

Lee, H. (2006) Privacy, publicity and accountability of self-presentation in an online discussion group. *Sociological Inquiry* 76(1): 1–22.

Lincoln, Y.S. and Guba, E.G. (1985) *Naturalistic Inquiry*. Beverly Hills, CA: Sage.

Madge, C. and O'Connor, H. (2005) Mothers in the making? Exploring notions of liminality in hybrid cyberspace. *Transactions of the Institute of British Geographers* 3 (1): 83–97.

Muijs, D. and Harris, A. (2003) Teacher leadership – Improvement through empowerment? An overview of the literature. *Educational Management Administration and Leadership* 31(4): 437–48.

Oakley, A. (1981) Interviewing women: a contradiction in terms, in Roberts, H. (ed.) *Doing Feminist Research*. London: Routledge. pp. 30–61.

Robson, K. and Robson, M. (2002) Your place or mine? Ethics, the researcher and the Internet, in Welland, T. and Pigsley, L. (eds) *Ethical Dilemmas in Qualitative Research*. London: Ashgate.

Shah, S. (2004) The researcher/interviewer in intercultural context: a social intruder! *British Educational Research Journal* 30(4): 549–75.

Sikes, P. (2006) On dodgy ground? Problematics and ethics in educational research. *International Journal of Research & Method in Education* 29(1): 105–17.

Starratt, R. (2007) Leading a community of learners. *Educational Management Administration and Leadership* 35(2): 165–83.

Stewart, K. and Williams, M. (2005) Researching online populations: the use of online focus groups for social research. *Qualitative Research* 5(4): 395–416.

Stoll, L. and Seashore Louis, K. (2007) *Professional Learning Communities: Divergence, Depth and Dilemmas*. McGraw-Hill Education: Open University Press.

United Nations (1989) *Convention on the Rights of the Child*. New York: United Nations.

Walford, G. (2001) Site selection within comparative case study and ethnographic research. *Compare* 31(2): 151–64.

Wenger, E. (1998) *Communities of Practice: Learning, Meaning, and Identity*. New York: Cambridge University Press.

Williams, J.P. (2006) Authentic identities: straightedge subculture, music and the internet. *Journal of Contemporary Ethnography* 35(2): 173–200.

Part B

Approaches to Research

CHAPTER 8

Research Design: Frameworks, Strategies, Methods and Technologies

David Scott

Chapter objectives

- To determine the characteristics of an appropriate research design for the field of educational leadership and management.
- To characterise a research design as a set of relationships between ontological and epistemological standpoints, research strategies and data-collection methods.
- To give an account of alternative relationships between ontological and epistemological perspectives, research strategies and data-collection methods.
- To give an account of alternative ontological and epistemological frameworks.
- To present a series of alternative research strategies and methods.
- To offer a series of illustrative case studies/scenarios and examples drawn from the field of educational management and leadership.
- To surface those issues relating to the design of research projects in educational management and leadership that are relevant to online research.
- To address the relationship between theory and practice in relation to the design of research projects.

Introduction

This chapter will address a range of issues relating to the design of research projects in the field of educational leadership and management. It will focus on those ontological and epistemological frameworks that position the researcher and the research in the field, those strategies chosen by the researcher that fit with these ontological and epistemological frameworks, and the methods, approaches and technologies used by the researcher to collect and analyse the data, which have emerged from prior considerations given to these frameworks and strategies. It will also attempt to characterise the types of representations made by researchers depending on the frameworks, strategies and methods they have chosen to use.

A research design refers to the schema or plan that constitutes the research study. It is the means by which the objectives or aims of the study are fulfilled. However, the shape or form that the research design takes is dependent on paradigms or viewpoints about two important matters. The first of these is ontological and this refers to relationships, structures, mechanisms, events, happenings and behaviours in the world which have an objective existence, and on which the researcher focuses their attention. These are the objects of research. The second matter is epistemological and this refers to how the researcher or observer can know or come to understand them.

The different paradigms reflect different views on the nature of reality and thus can be characterised along a continuum with, at one end, a belief in the existence of a real world, regardless of any attempts to know it, and, at the other end, a view that our efforts to know the world are always mediated through paradigms, worldviews and ways of understanding, in short, they are theory-dependent and there is no sense that we can give to the notion of an independent reality, separate from our attempts to know it. Thus, there are no facts about the world which are not in some sense socially produced or dependent on conventions agreed in society. In between these two positions are a range of viewpoints, such as Searle's (1995) position, in which he distinguishes between brute and social facts, with the latter being characterised as temporarily, ontologically and logically dependent on brute facts and the former representing the world as it is presently constituted. The different paradigms also reflect different views on how we can know this reality and, therefore, in like fashion, can be characterised along a continuum with, at one end, a belief that, in principle at least, this reality can be adequately represented in language if the correct procedures are followed, and, at the other end, a belief that there is no Archimedean standpoint and that we can only see the world through a particular lens, formed and developed in society.

Positivism/empiricism

An example of one such lens is representational realism, a framework that is presupposed by positivism and the practices of empiricist research. Whilst philosophically there are many variants of realism, there are certain common features. The best-known variant could be characterised simply as common sense expressed in philosophical language, and this suggests that the world exists independently of our lives and socio-cultural practices, including the practice of research: the world is 'real' and it exists around us 'out there', indifferent to our hopes, beliefs and desires at any particular moment. The nature of the world out there is something about which we can make discoveries through research, and our knowledge increases with every discovery. Thus, research in the scientific mode brings us closer to true descriptions of the world in the form of theories that express these truths. The independent existence of the world is the essence of the view of objectivity shared by common sense, and some naive scientific viewpoints. Truth is achieved through applying appropriate rationally grounded techniques. For any field of understanding, there will be one true description of the world, and this description must command universal assent, since once a truth is established it is unassailable; it has a cognitive authority which makes it irrational not to assent to it.

The classical form that empiricism usually takes is that all knowledge is derived from experience. There are two variants of this. The first is that all knowledge causally originates from experience, and the second is less dogmatic and suggests only that all knowledge is justified by experience. In the first case, an assumption is made that the human psyche has a tabula rasa form on which experience leaves its mark. There are, therefore, no innate ideas. This view is problematic, in that it is unable to explain notions such as time and necessity as these cannot be directly observed; indeed, it is hard to understand how these could be construed as observable phenomena. Thus, the second and weaker variant – knowledge that can be believed is justified only through experience – is considered to be more credible.

Positivism has its origins in the classical theory of empiricism, and indeed borrowed from empiricism the idea that knowledge has its foundation in sense data. The principal problem that it encountered relates to the impossibility of accessing data through the senses without some prior theory to make sense of it. In short, observations are concept-dependent. This has to be distinguished from concept determination, because this implies that theories developed about reality are observation-neutral. There would be no need to make observations if theory development was always prior to the making of observations.

The rejection of the radical separation of facts from values has led to the development of alternative methodologies, such as critical theory and postmodernism, where assumptions are made that theory, and indeed a system of value, is prior to and underpins the collection of data. However, this does not necessarily lead to the conclusion that since data and therefore facts are inevitably informed by values of one type or another, there is no point in empirically examining the world. Observations may be concept-dependent but they are not concept-determined. An alternative to the extremes of positivism/empiricism and radical relativism is critical realism which, in the first place, is based on a critique and rejection of empiricism. For empiricists, what is given to the senses constitutes the world as it is. It is possible to accurately describe that world, a world of sense impressions, if the correct procedures are followed, and these correct procedures comprise the observer or researcher bracketing out their own preconceptions of the world and making an objective assessment of it. Language can therefore act as a neutral medium for describing the world. For Bhaskar (1989), there is a major problem. This relates to the way cause and effect are treated as 'the constant conjunction of atomistic events or states of affairs, interpreted as the objects of actual or possible experience' (Bhaskar, 1989: 158). What is being conflated here is epistemology (how we can know reality) and ontology (reality itself). He describes this as the ontic fallacy. This means that a successionist rather then generative view of causation is being proposed. Bhaskar (1989) distinguishes between structures that generate and have the potential to generate occurrences and the atomistic viewpoint adopted by empiricists, where reality consists of these constant conjunctions of experiences.

On the other hand, critical realism also seeks to distance itself from radical relativism. Whereas with empiricism, descriptions of the world are collapsed into sense data, radical relativists working from a different perspective, sever the link between text and reality so that only texts have epistemological significance, and these only make reference to other texts and not to any underlying reality. In short, radical relativists are anti-realist. Bhaskar (1989), as a realist, though not of a naïve kind, identifies three domains: the real, consisting of mechanisms; the actual, consisting of events; and the empirical, consisting of experiences. Events can happen in the world without them being observed. Mechanisms can neutralise other mechanisms so that nothing changes in life that can be directly observed; indeed, mechanisms can retain their potentiality for influencing the world, without them actually doing so. What this suggests is that these mechanisms are relatively enduring, whereas our capacity and our procedures for knowing them change and are determined by social and political arrangements, in the present and stretching back in time.

Critical realism has certain implications for educational research. For example, educational researchers frequently collect data in mathematical form that allows them to identify associations or correlations between variables. It is assumed that these associations or correlations correctly describe reality and that cause–effect relations can be inferred from them. Critical realists suggest that the identification of causal relations is a much more complex affair and that conflating associations or correlations with causes may lead to a mistaken view of reality. A belief in one of these paradigms or viewpoints (i.e. positivism/empiricism, radical relativism and critical realism) has implications for the actual practices that constitute the research process, and thus depending on which one is chosen, particular strategies and methods are discarded or adopted.

Characteristics of research design

Some theorists have suggested that concerns about ontological and epistemological matters are not relevant to the collection and analysis of data, which constitutes the essence of any research design. For example, Harden and Thomas argue that:

When reading some texts on research methodology for education, for example, one might expect each report of primary research to begin with an exposition of its epistemological and ontological foundations since this would appear to be a prerequisite of all education research. However, when reporting empirical research, most authors go straight into the background of their study and a description of the phenomenon under investigation – assuming both that the phenomenon under investigation exists and that it is possible to study it. (Harden and Thomas, 2005: 265)

The argument suggested here is flawed for a number of reasons. First, though many researchers believe that they operate pragmatically, that is, they do not make epistemological and ontological claims, in fact this is exactly what they do in claiming that the phenomena to be investigated do exist and that it is possible to study them. Second, in making this claim they are making a number of implicit connections between ontological and epistemological frameworks *and* those strategies and methodologies that researchers adopt at the more practical level of research design. If, and this is not accepted by everyone, it is possible to develop a language and practice of research that can operate outside the value-laden practices of everyday life, an extraordinary value-free universal means of expression, then it follows that the first task of the researcher is to seek out such a method and apply it in full measure. Third, pragmatic (in a non-philosophical sense) viewpoints ignore those epistemic frameworks, which underpin all research practices. For example, the issue of the degree or level of participation by the researcher in the research setting is underpinned on both sides by a number of assumptions about the researcher–research participant relationship (whether the relationship should be independent and detached or dialectical), about the nature of truth statements that emerge (whether they should be nomothetic or ideographic) and about how the data should be inscribed in the research report (adopting a representational realist approach or adopting a narrative and reflexive account of the phenomena).

What this implies is that there are philosophical questions which have to be answered prior to the decisions researchers have to make about the strategy and methods that they adopt. Empiricists believe that there is mind-independent reality waiting to be discovered, and that social reality consists of the constant conjunction of atomistic events or state of affairs (ontology). They further believe that these atomistic events can be known through the observations of researchers, who behave in an objective fashion and do not bring their own conceptions and preconceptions to the act of observation (epistemology); indeed, that to entangle them with the values of the researcher would not allow a truthful picture to emerge. The next level is the strategic level, and a further argument is made to the effect that these constant conjunctions of events or objects are similar enough to allow precise quantification. Finally, at the level of method, an instrument is chosen which conforms to the researcher's ontological, epistemological and strategic frameworks, which allow data to be collected and analysed.

However, it is likely that, if a different decision had been made at the onto-logical level, then this would have led to different decisions being made at the other levels. So, for example, if a depth ontology is subscribed to where reality is understood as stratified along the lines of the empirical consisting of expe-riences, the actual consisting of events and the real consisting of underlying mechanisms, and, furthermore, this is underpinned by a belief that this level cannot be directly observed and does not influence events and experiences in a mechanical way, then this has implications for the decisions that the researcher makes at the levels of epistemology, strategy and method.

Strategies

At the strategic level of research design, in conformity with the epistemo-logical and ontological perspectives of the researcher, there are a number of different approaches. In summary these are: *experiments*, *survey* work (see also Chapter 10), *action research* (see also Chapter 12), *case study* (see also Chapter 11), *interview studies* (see also Chapter 17) and *observational* enquiries, with some but not all of them co-existing within the same research design. Though suc-cessful *experiments* in the field of education and education management are rare, quasi-experiments which do not meet the rigorous requirements of the experimental method are commonplace. The experimental method requires the researcher to intervene in the natural setting and control a number of variables to determine a causal relationship between two or more properties of an individual or unit. A true experiment builds in both pre- and post-tests *and* experimental and control groups. Further to this, a process of randomisa-tion is applied to the selection of the control and experimental groups to ensure that members of the two groups are alike in their skills and capacities before the intervention takes place. More complicated designs are also possible where two or more interventions are made to a variety of different groups; or where a series of interventions are contrasted (over time) with a series of non-interventions; or where a number of experimental treatments are compared using an appropriate number of groups over a number of different time periods. All of these designs involve variable analysis, and controlling for different influences that might or might not contribute to the effects of an intervention (see Case study 1).

Case study 1: Randomised experiments

In 1985, Tennessee initiated a longitudinal class size reduction experiment. The experiment, titled Project STAR (Student/Teacher Achievement Ratio), randomly assigned over 6,000 young children to one of three within-school experimental

(Continued)

(Continued)

groups: a small class with 13 children, a large class with 26 children with a single teacher, or a large class with a teacher and an aide. At the end of the study period, the achievements of children in the small classes were almost one month ahead of the achievements of children in the other two classes. After four years, children who attended the small classes were 5.4 months ahead in reading and 3.1 months ahead in mathematics of the other two classes. These positive effects may have even extended into high school. Compared with students who had experienced large class sizes, children in small classes achieved higher high-school grades, and were more likely to complete advanced academic classes, take college admissions tests and ultimately graduate (Krueger and Whitmore, 2001).

Survey researchers collect data about larger populations than experimental researchers. Surveys may lead to simple frequency counts or to more complicated relational analysis. In educational research, there are two important types. The first is correlational research, in which, through the use of various statistical devices, relationships between phenomena are identified and a calculation of the probability of those relationships occurring in other settings is made. The second is ex-post facto research, in which the researcher searches for causal relationships among phenomena by retrospectively reconstructing what happened. Data are collected in a variety of ways, and their collection typically involves structured interviews, postal questionnaires, standardised tests of performance or the use of attitude inventories. Surveys have one principal advantage and this is that data are collected from a large number of respondents. In order to do this, the method, usually in the form of a questionnaire, is standardised. This means that respondents are expected to understand each question in the same way (see Case study 2).

Case study 2: Surveys

Zepp and Hong (2007: 12) in a research project attempted to answer two questions:

1 'Do teachers' perceptions of the traits and behaviours of good and bad leaders vary across cultures?
2 If so, are differences in the perceptions of the relevant importance of various leadership traits and behaviours related to a model of cultural categories?'

They developed a questionnaire to enable them to examine cultural differences. The questionnaire was piloted and the authors came up with eight good traits of educational leaders, eight bad traits, eight good behaviours and eight bad behaviours. These 32 items were put into a single questionnaire, in which subjects were asked to rank in importance their top three choices for the most important items in each of the four groups of eight items. The questionnaire was administered to approximately 100 teachers in each of seven different countries: Cambodia, Hong Kong, Pakistan, Qatar, Taiwan, Uganda and the USA. In each case, questionnaires were given to a wide variety of schools – rural, urban, private, public, primary and secondary.

A third educational research strategy is *action research*. This is a process which helps practitioners to investigate an aspect of their practice with a view to solving problems and improving it. Practitioners themselves identify the area to be researched, selecting the research techniques best suited to help them investigate the problem and find appropriate solutions. Partly because of the close links between the research and the action, the process is cyclical rather than linear. In other words, the experience of applying research to improve practice may be continuous, as new understandings are reached and new goals identified (see Case study 3).

Case study 3: Action research

Booth and Segon (2009) undertook a piece of action research to determine the nature of leadership and management development for participants and the research facilitator in applying a cooperative inquiry approach that supported the following:

1 'Greater decision making of course content processes and context by programme participants;
2 Application of reflection on practice as a key assessment and development characteristic of the programme;
3 Development of soft skills to support leadership and management practices'. (2009 : 33)

The action research cycles followed participants' journeys and insights from learning situations in the programme. This included participants' reflections on action and research on practice going through the programme, and interviews with participants who had completed the programme to plot changes to leadership and management practices resulting from the programme. These descriptions, together with supporting diary records of learning sessions (see also Chapter 22), participant and researcher conversations and emails, informed the process and provided support for the changes in leadership and management practice experienced by participants during the programme.

A fourth research strategy is case study, and this can be understood in two different and incommensurable ways: either as a set of procedures integral to all types of research; or as a paradigmatically separate form of research. In each, the concept of the case is treated differently. Ethnographers, for example, choose to study particular segments of social life that are naturally occurring and that seem to have clearly defined boundaries, such as activities within a school over a definite time period. Though social actors within these boundaries also have experiences outside them, the boundaries are well enough understood to constitute the object of enquiry as a case (see also Chapter 14). Ethnographers therefore argue that the detailed description of the case that emerges can be complemented by examination of other cases that seem to have similar properties, such as other schools of a similar nature. Theory development is either cumulative, in that as a greater number of cases is studied, the database becomes more extensive and rich and the findings more reliable, enabling the researcher to generalise to larger populations; or theory developed from one or more cases can then be tested by examining further cases.

Survey researchers, on the other hand, understand the case in a different way, by focusing initially on a specified population; that is, they choose to concentrate on a group of seemingly like cases – for example, all secondary schools in a locality or country – and work backwards so that the case is defined by the characteristics of the parent population as it is currently understood. Because the emphasis is placed on the examination of a large number of cases, each of them has to be conceptualised in a particular way; that is, the variables associated with them have to be understood in a similar fashion by participants and the assumption is made that these understandings apply to all the cases. Furthermore, because the design focuses on a large number of cases and because survey researchers wish to compare such cases, then mathematical models are considered appropriate and these variables have to be expressed so that they conform to the principles of additivity, linearity and proportional variation. The implication of this is that different methods are appropriate in survey research because researchers have to handle a large number of cases which, for the sake of comparison, have to be expressed in a standardised way (see Case study 4).

Case study 4: Case studies

Bush et al. (2005) conducted an evaluation of 'How Teams Make a Difference: The Impact of Team Working'. The evaluation focused on the impact of two National College for Leadership in Schools (NCSL) programmes, 'Working Together for Success' (WTfS) and 'Developing Capacity for Sustained Improvement' (DCSI). The main research questions were:

- What experiences are needed to bring about improvement in team working?
- Is there a shift towards more effective team working?
- What difference does team work make?

- Is there a more effective senior leadership team and better relationships with middle leaders?
- Is there improved development planning with a long-term perspective, greater coherence and more control of the agenda for change?
- Is there a determined and systematic focus on learning?
- Is there a sustained commitment to a programme of professional development beyond participants' involvement in the programme?
- Do the programmes provide a similar methodology of, and approach to, effective team work or are there differences between them? If the latter, what are the implications for the NCSL?

The evaluation comprised 10 case studies of schools which had completed, or embarked upon, one of these programmes.

Interview studies are a strategy used by researchers either on their own or as part of another strategy such as case study. A range of interview approaches from structured to life-history interviews have been developed. A survey researcher, for example, gathers information about respondents' views on a number of different issues, but the method is pre-set; and it involves the asking of precisely similar questions to large numbers of respondents. At the other extreme are semi-structured interviews in which respondents are encouraged to set the agenda of the interview, though the presence of an interviewer and other forms of control exerted by them means that the respondent never has full control of the setting. The interviewer sets up the interview, is involved in the negotiation of place, purpose and agenda at the initial stages, and, unless they remain silent throughout the interview, asks questions, prompts answers and elicits responses. Respondents provide answers and give accounts of their lives in terms of their understanding of the settings in which they are located. Thus, gender, race, class and other types of power relations are conveyed by the researcher and form an essential backdrop to the answers that respondents provide. The relationship between the giver and reader of those codes is never straightforward. The setting in which the interview takes place is a depository of available meanings from which the interviewee draws in giving their answers. However, what a face-to-face encounter does is to allow the interviewer to make a judgement about how those signs are being read and thus to locate their data in the contexts in which they were collected (see Case study 4).

A final strategy developed by educational researchers is observation. Observational techniques are much used in educational research, either on their own or to complement other strategies. A number of dimensions structure the different approaches to the collection of observational data. The first of these dimensions concerns the role of the researcher. Participant observers argue that it is the task of the social scientist to interpret the meanings and experiences of social actors, a task that can only be achieved through working closely and directly with the individuals involved. This means that the observer's account, though still a perspective on events that she did not initiate, has an added dimension: direct experience of the activities under investigation. This involves an act of imagination or identification which allows the observer 'to grasp the psychological state (i.e. motivation, belief, intention or the like) of an individual actor' (Schwandt, 2005: 120).

The other end of the spectrum comprises a purely observational role in which observers seek to detach themselves from the social setting being investigated. Here, the intention is to behave as a fly on the wall and not disturb or change what is being studied. Except for the purposes of gaining access, the researcher interacts as little as possible with participants in the research. There are three reasons for this. First, this detached stance allows observers to gain a more comprehensive view of what is being observed; they are less likely to be influenced by the agendas of participants. Second, this stance allows observers to become more detached from their own specific agendas and from the way they are positioned (i.e. in terms of age, sex and ethnicity) in relation to the subjects of their research. Third, it allows them to gain a more objective view of the reality being investigated. As with any instrument, there are epistemological assumptions underlying its use. These assumptions comprise a belief that the preconceptions and viewpoints of the observers should not play a part in the particular construction of reality. Researchers are able to bracket out their own values and represent a reality which is not dependent on them as researchers. They merely act as conduits. Representation therefore becomes a relatively straightforward act (though various devices are set in place to check the reliability of the data collected, or to put it another way, to check that researcher bias does not enter into the research act). If, however, the research act is understood in Gadamerian terms, as a 'fusion of horizons' (Gadamer, 2004) in which the observer and the observed fuse their different versions of the world, then such a detached stance is considered inappropriate (see Case study 5).

Case study 5: Observational studies

Graham et al. (2011) researched leadership in post-compulsory settings, using ethnographic methods. The work was an observational study and can be contrasted with quasi-experimental quantitative strategies where leadership is understood as a variable and other variables are controlled for. In contrast, this study developed understandings of leadership by pointing to examples of what leaders actually did as they went about their everyday work. Instead of seeing leaders as charismatic heroes, the study investigated a number of routine aspects of the work of principals, how leadership was being performed, the everyday management of organisational personnel in meetings and how success and failure were defined and understood by the principals themselves. Over a period of time, educational leaders were observed in their natural environments.

Method

The fourth level of research design refers to the tools or techniques used to collect, analyse and interpret data in education research. Commonly, methods are described in terms of quantitative techniques such as the making of statistical calculations or qualitative techniques such as interviews, naturalistic and systematic observation, document analysis (see also Chapter 20) and focus groups, for example. Methods also constitute the procedures and, as importantly, the procedural rules that enable education researchers to confirm that the knowledge they have created has reliability and validity (see also Chapter 6). Methods can be further categorised in terms of three types of rule-focused procedures. The first refers to the rules for establishing the key elements of the study, such as hypotheses, theories and concepts. The second refers to the rules for collecting the data, and the third to the rules for analysing and interpreting the data. A further issue in relation to method concerns the setting in which data collection takes place, and how the method is employed – whether, for example, an interview is conducted face to face or online. The mode of online data collection, for example, has epistemological and ontological implications. Questions asked online allow respondents to reflect, temporally sequence and cross-reference their answers, either to other texts or to their own experiences and understandings. This means that the data which are collected are both quantitatively and qualitatively different from those collected in face-to-face settings. Methods then, such as interviews, are the means by which strategies are fulfilled.

Conclusions

The contention in this chapter is that the design of any research study has to be conceptualised at four levels: ontology, epistemology, strategy and method; and that further to this, those levels are logically, temporally and causally dependent on the level from which they emerged. These are horizontal relations in designing research projects. There are also vertical relations and examples of these are ethical and pedagogical concerns, which cut across the different levels of research design and complement horizontal relations (also discussed, for example, in Chapter 7 in terms of ethics). Finally, the relationship between theory and practice in relation to the design of research projects needs to be addressed. This chapter has presented an account, at a theoretical and abstract level, of those ontological, epistemological, strategic and methodological concerns that pertain to and impact on the collection and analysis of data and subsequently to the representations of reality that the researcher wants to make. However, research at the empirical level always has to take account of the contingencies and occurrences of everyday life, and thus inevitably research practices reflect these as much as they reflect theoretically ideal models of good practice.

Key points

- The four levels of research design are ontology, epistemology, strategy and method.
- Choice of strategy and method is always determined by positions taken by the researcher with regards to ontology and epistemology.
- These frameworks may be placed on a continuum with empiricism/positivism at one end and radical relativism/post-modernism at the other. At various points on the continuum are: critical realism, interpretivism, pragmatism, ethnomethodology, phenomenology and various forms of neo-realism.
- Research always has pragmatic elements; however, it is a mistake to believe that this accounts for all the elements of a research study.
- Since research in the field involves human activities, ethics are central to the way the researcher behaves.
- Research strategies comprise: experimentation, quasi-experimentation, survey work, case study, action research, interview studies, observation studies and documentary analysis.
- Research methods always need to fit with research strategies, and they refer to: interview data, observations, survey data, documents, secondary data analysis, literature reviews, test data and experiential data.
- The chosen research design always determines the type of data that is collected, and indeed its development precedes data collection.
- Finding out about the world has undeniable social and political elements, and these need to be surfaced in accounts that are made of it.

Questions and reflections

1. What are you trying to find out?
2. What is an appropriate design for your research study?
3. What is your chosen ontological stance and what are your reasons for choosing it?
4. What is your chosen epistemological stance and what are your reasons for choosing it?
5. What is the relationship between the data you are collecting and the object of your research?
6. How do you understand the relationship between yourself as the data-collector and the data you are collecting?
7. What value perspective is interpolated into your study and in what way?
8. What is your ethical stance and why have you chosen this stance?
9. What is your chosen strategy and why have you chosen this strategy?
10. How does your chosen strategy align with your epistemological and ontological perspective?

11 What is your preferred approach to the use of quantitative and/or qualitative approaches and what are your reasons for employing either one of these or a combination of the two?
12 What methods have you chosen to use and why have you chosen these methods?

Recommended further reading

The literature on research design is extensive and the following list is only a small proportion of that literature. It is offered here as a guide to some of the issues discussed in this chapter:

Bartlett, D. and Payne, S. (1997) Grounded Theory – Its Basis, Rationale and Procedures, in McKenzie, G., Powell, J. and Usher, R. (eds) *Understanding Social Research: Perspectives on Methodology and Practice*. Lewes: Falmer Press.

Bassey, M. (1999) *Case Study in Educational Settings*. Buckingham: Open University Press.

Bhaskar, R. (1998) *The Possibility of Naturalism*. London and New York: Routledge.

Blaikie, N. (2007) *Approaches to Social Enquiry*. Cambridge: Polity Press.

Blumer, H. (1969) *Symbolic Interactionism*. Englewood Cliffs, NJ: Prentice-Hall.

Bogden, R. and Biklen, S. (1982) *Qualitative Research for Education*. Boston: Allyn and Bacon.

Bohman, J. (2000) *New Philosophy of Social Science*. Cambrige. MA: MIT.

Bryman, A. (1988) *Quality and Quantity in Social Research*. London: Unwin and Hyman.

Burton, D. (2000) *Research Training for Social Scientists*. London: Sage.

Campbell, D.T. and Stanley, J.C. (1963) Experimental and Quasi-experimental Designs for Research on Teaching, in Gage, N. (ed.) *Handbook of Research on Teaching*. Chicago: Rand McNally.

Carr, W. and Kemmis, S. (1986) *Becoming Critical: Education, Knowledge and Action Research*. Lewes: Falmer Press.

Corbin, J. and Strauss, A. (2007) *Basics of Qualitative Research: Techniques and Procedures for Developing Grounded Theory*. London: Sage.

Creswell, J.W. (1998) *Qualitative Inquiry and Research Design: Choosing among Five Traditions*. Thousand Oaks, CA: Sage.

Denscombe, M. (1998) *The Good Research Guide to Small-Scale Research Projects*. Buckingham: Open University Press.

Denzin, N. and Lincoln, Y. (eds) (2005) *Handbook of Qualitative Research*. London: Sage.

Elliott, J. (1991) *Action Research for Educational Change*. Buckingham: Open University Press.

Erben, M. (1996) The Purposes and Processes of Biographical Method, in Scott, D. and Usher, R. (eds) *Understanding Educational Research*. London: Routledge.

Gillham, B. (2000) *The Research Interview*. London: Continuum.

Glaser, B.G. and Strauss, A.L. (1967) *The Discovery of Grounded Theory: Strategies for Qualitative Research*. Chicago: Aldine.

Gomm, R., Hammersley, M. and Foster, P. (eds) (2000) *Case Study Method: Key Issues, Key Texts*. London: Sage.

Hammersley, M. (1992) *What's Wrong with Ethnography?* London: Routledge.

Hammersley, M. and Atkinson, P. (2007) *Ethnography: Principles in Practice*. London and New York: Routledge.

Harre, R. (2011) *Theories and Things*. London: Sheed and Ward.

Hitchcock, G. and Hughes, D. (1995) *Research and the Teacher: A Qualitative Introduction to School-based Research*. London: Routledge.

Lather, P. (1991) *Getting Smart: Feminist Research and Pedagogy with/in the Postmodern*. New York: Routledge.

Layder, D. (1993) *New Strategies in Social Research*. Cambridge: Polity Press.

Lincoln, Y. and Guba, E.G. (2000) The Only Generalization is: There is No Generalization, in Gomm, R., Hammersley, M. and Foster, P. (eds) *Case Study Method: Key Issues, Key Texts*. London: Sage.

Lofland, J., Snow, D., Anderson, L. and Lofland, L. (2004) *Analysing Social Settings: A Guide to Qualitative Observation and Analysis*. Belmont, CA: Wadsworth.

Lomax, P. (2002) Action Research, in Coleman, M. and Briggs, A. (eds) *Research Methods in Educational Leadership and Management*. London: Paul Chapman Publishing.

May, T. (1993) *Social Research: Issues, Methods, and Process*. Bury St Edmunds: St Edmundsbury Press for The Open University.

Miles, M.B. and Huberman, A.M. (2007) *Qualitative Data Analysis: An Expanded Source Book*. London: Sage.

Morrison, M. (2002) What do we Mean by Educational Research?, in Coleman, M. and Briggs, A. (eds) *Research Methods in Educational Leadership and Management*. London: Paul Chapman Publishing.

Outhwaite, W. (1987) *New Philosophies of Social Science: Realism, Hermeneutics and Critical Theory*. London: Macmillan.

Pawson, R. and Tilley, N. (1997) *Realistic Evaluation*. London: Sage.

Pole, C. and Lampard, R. (2002) *Practical Social Investigation: Qualitative and Quantitative Methods in Social Research*. Harlow: Pearson Education for Prentice Hall.

Pole, C. and Morrison, M. (2003) *Ethnography for Education*. Buckingham: Open University Press.

Robson, C. (2002) *Real World Research: A Resource for Social Scientists and Practitioner-Researchers*. Oxford: Blackwell.

Sayer, A. (1992) *Method in Social Science: A Realist Approach*. London: Routledge.

Scott, D. (2000) *Realism and Educational Research: New Perspectives and Possibilities*. London: RoutledgeFalmer.

Scott, D. and Usher, R. (2011) *Researching Education: Data, Methods and Theory in Educational Enquiry*. London: Cassell.

Silverman, D. (2001) *Interpreting Qualitative Data: Methods for Analyzing Talk, Texts, and Interaction* (2nd edn). London: Sage.

Usher, R. (1996) A Critique of the Neglected Assumptions of Educational Research, in Scott, D. and Usher, R. (eds) *Understanding Educational Research*. London: Routledge.

Usher, R. (1997) Telling a Story about Research and Research as Story-telling: Postmodern Approaches to Social Research, in McKenzie, G., Powell, J. and Usher, R. (eds) *Understanding Social Research: Perspectives on Methodology and Practice*. London: Falmer Press.

Van Maanen, J. (1988) *Tales of the Field: On Writing Ethnography*. Chicago: Chicago University Press.

Winch, P. (2007) *The Idea of a Social Science and its Relation to Philosophy*. London: Routledge.

Yin, R.K. (1994) *Case Study Research: Design and Methods* (2nd edn). Thousand Oaks, CA: Sage.

References

Bhaskar, R. (1989) *Reclaiming Reality*. London: Verso.

Booth, C. and Segon, M. (2009) Leadership and Management Development: An Action Research Project. *International Review of Business Research Papers* 5(2): 19–41.

Bush, T., Scott, D., Morrison, M. and Middlewood, D. (2005) *Final Report – Team-Building (An Evaluation of WTfS and DCSI)*. Nottingham: National College for School Leadership, pp.1–102.

Gadamer, H-G. (2004) *Truth and Method*. London: Continuum.

Graham, C., Iszatt-White, M., Kelly, S., Randall, D. and Rouncefield, M. (2011) *Leadership in Post-Compulsory Education*. London: Continuum.

Harden, A. and Thomas, J. (2005) Methodological Issues in Combining Diverse Study Types in Systematic Reviews. *International Journal of Social Research Methodology* 8(3): 257–71.

Krueger, A. and Whitmore, D. (2001) The Effect of Attending a Small Class in the Early Grades on College Test Taking and Middle School Test Results: Evidence from Project STAR. *Economic Journal* 111: 1–28.

Schwandt, T. (2005) Constructivist, Interpretivist Approaches to Human Inquiry, in Denzin, N. and Lincoln, Y. (eds) *Handbook of Qualitative Research*. London: Sage, pp. 118–37.

Searle, J. (1995) *The Construction of Social Reality*. London and New York: Free Press/ Simon and Schuster.

Zepp, R. and Hong, H. (2007) *Perceptions of Leadership in Three Professions: Studies in Cambodian Leadership*. Battambang, Cambodia: Australian Centre for Development.

CHAPTER 9

Mixed Methods Research

Mary F. Hibberts and R. Burke Johnson

Chapter objectives

This chapter is concerned with mixed methods research and is underpinned by a number of learning objectives. By the end of the chapter, readers will be able to:

- List the strengths and weaknesses of quantitative research.
- List the strengths and weaknesses of qualitative research.
- Define mixed research.
- Explain how to use the notational system used to depict mixed research designs.
- Compare and contrast the nine mixed methods research designs.
- List and explain Greene, Caracelli and Graham's (1989) five rationales for conducting mixed research.
- List and describe the eight steps in conducting mixed research.
- Explain the strengths and weakness of mixed research.

Introduction

In our view, the three major research or methodological paradigms in educational leadership and management are quantitative research, qualitative research and mixed research. Mixed research is the paradigm that systematically combines aspects of quantitative and qualitative research methods into a single study to take advantage of each paradigm's strengths. By the way, you should know that mixed research is also commonly referred to as *mixed methods research, multiple research approaches, mixed methodology, multimethod* and *multiplism*. All of these terms appear in mixed research literature and can be used as approximate synonyms. Because mixed research is often about more than just methods, we prefer the term 'mixed research' to 'mixed methods research' and we will use the term mixed research in this chapter. We define *mixed research* as the broad type of research in which elements or approaches from quantitative and qualitative research are combined or mixed in a research study.[1]

The advantages and disadvantages of using quantitative and qualitative approaches have led a growing number of researchers to study the effects of integrating both into single research studies. An important concept shared by proponents of mixed research is *the compatibility thesis* that says quantitative and qualitative methods can be used together *as long as the assumptions of both paradigms are respected* and the approaches are thoughtfully combined to complement each other for specific research purposes. Further, mixed researchers believe that mixing research assumptions, methods and approaches helps improve the overall quality of research. It is important to note that a higher quality design is not guaranteed from simply mixing approaches. Rather, the benefits are a function of how well the researcher understands the characteristics of each paradigm *and* how well the researcher strategically chooses and mixes paradigm characteristics and methods to answer the specific research questions. Here is a key point: *if you want to make educated mixing decisions about your designs, you need to be knowledgeable about the strengths and limitations of quantitative and qualitative research.* Therefore, we begin by reviewing some strengths and weakness associated with quantitative and qualitative research shown in Tables 9.1 and 9.2.

Table 9.1   Strengths and weaknesses of quantitative research

Strengths

- Researchers can test and validate theories.
- Random samples, when used, allow statistical generalisation.
- It is strong on internal (causal) validity, and replication is used to increase external (generalising) validity.
- Nomothetic causation (i.e. scientific laws, general causal relationships) is demonstrated.
- Experimental manipulation and control provides strong internal validity.
- Laboratory experiments can be conducted and analysed quickly.
- It produces standardised measures of relationship (for example, statistical significance, effect size).
- It is useful when studying large groups of people and providing the etic (i.e. 'objective outsider') perspective.
- Administrators, politicians and other stakeholders traditionally view quantitative results as more credible than qualitative results.

Weaknesses

- The categories of meaning and theories used by the researcher might differ from those used and accepted by local constituencies.
- Researchers sometimes exhibit tunnel (narrow) vision and confirmation bias.
- General research findings might not apply well for particular local contexts and particular individuals and might, in particular circumstances, be considered potentially superficial.

Table 9.2   Strengths and weaknesses of qualitative research

Strengths

- Data preserve meaning and language used by participants.
- Enables in-depth study of selected cases and description of complex phenomena in local contexts.
- It can allow for cross-case comparisons.
- It can explicate insiders' perspectives (i.e. the emic viewpoint) with authenticity.
- It can identify contextual and situational factors.
- It studies dynamic processes allowing researchers to identify and document patterns, sequences and change.
- Grounded explanatory theories can be generated.
- Data are typically collected in naturalistic settings and are not 'artificial'.
- Idiographic causation (i.e. causation that we observe, purposively produce or experience in our lives) can be documented.

Weaknesses

- It is difficult to generalize findings to different people, contexts and situations.
- Testing hypotheses and theories can be cumbersome.
- Some administrators, programmes and stakeholders might perceive qualitative research as less credible.
- Data collection and analysis is often time consuming.
- Qualitative results are more prone to researcher biases, errors and idiosyncrasies than quantitative data analysis.

As you can see, both quantitative and qualitative research have many strengths and some limitations. For example, quantitative research is useful for identifying cause-and-effect relationships when experimental designs with random assignment are used, and it is useful for making generalisations from samples to populations when random sampling is used. However, it is difficult to explore new phenomena in depth or investigate participants' inside perspectives using quantitative methods. Fortunately, qualitative methods are especially useful in providing detailed information about particular groups' and individuals' lives, perspectives and beliefs. On the other hand, the in-depth study of particular groups and individuals usually relies on small non-random samples that are not statistically generalisable to other populations. Understanding these and other methodological characteristics will help you to design quality mixed research to better answer your research questions.

Pragmatism is a popular philosophy in mixed research. This means you should mix research components in ways that you believe will work for your research problem, question and circumstances. While some researchers value only quantitative or only qualitative research, pragmatists use whatever combinations should help to achieve the epistemological justificatory status that John Dewey called *warranted assertability* (Dewey, 1998/1938: 161). That is, as mixed researchers, our goal is to provide very good evidence to support our research claims. We are not searching for absolute/eternal truths in educational leadership research. Rather, we are using combinations of available research tools to gather strong evidence to support or warrant our claims and produce provisional truths and perspectival truths in order to improve understandings and to guide future practice. Some general characteristics of pragmatism are presented in Table 9.3.

Table 9.3   General characteristics of pragmatism

Pragmatism:

- Attempts to find the middle ground between philosophical dualisms.
- Views knowledge as both a human construction and a product of the reality of the world we live in.
- Endorses fallibilism and rejects absolute truth as flowing from empirical research.
- Views justification in terms of what Dewey called 'warranted assertability'.
- Endorses pluralism (for example, different, even conflicting, theories and perspectives can be useful and true).
- Endorses methodological eclecticism and pluralism to gain knowledge.
- Holds that truth (i.e. absolute Truth) is 'the opinion which is fated to be ultimately agreed to by all who investigate' (Peirce, 1992/1878: 139). The 'final interpretant ... is that which would finally be decided to be the true interpretation if consideration of the matter were carried so far that an ultimate opinion were reached' (Peirce, 1998/1909: 96). In contrast, day-to-day experience and 'experimenting' only provide lowercase 't' truths (i.e. instrumental and provisional truths); these are the truths we live by in the meantime.
- Endorses an explicitly value-oriented approach to research, advocating shared values such as democracy, freedom, equality and progress.
- Views organisms as continually adapting to their worlds. The present is always an opportunity to improve understandings in a way that fits and works in our physical, social and psychological environments.

The pragmatic philosophy and the concept of warranted assertability complement a cardinal rule of virtually all scientific research which says to use information from multiple sources to help warrant or justify your claim. It is the thoughtful, purposive and appropriate mixing of logics and methods that enhances warranted assertability in mixed research designs. According to the fundamental principle of mixed research, researchers should strategically mix methods, approaches and concepts in a way that produces an overall design with complementary strengths (broadly viewed, including both divergence/ expansion and convergence of insights/perspectives) and non-overlapping weaknesses (Brewer and Hunter, 1989; Johnson and Turner, 2003; Webb et al., 1981). You can view this principle as offering a 'logic' for deciding how to mix approaches to answer your research question(s). A list of strengths and weaknesses of mixed research is provided in Table 9.4.

Table 9.4   Strengths and weaknesses of mixed research

Strengths

- Words, pictures, and narrative can be used to add meaning to numbers.
- Numbers can be used to add precision to words, pictures and narrative.
- Researchers can generate *and* test a mixed-methods grounded theory.
- A researcher is not confined to a single method or approach.
- It can provide fuller, deeper, more meaningful answers to a single research question.
- It can concurrently study and link nomothetic (general) *and* idiographic (particularistic) causation.
- It can link theory and practice to generate 'practical theory'.
- The strengths of an additional method can be used to overcome the weaknesses in another method by using both.
- Convergence and corroboration of findings can enhance evidence of a particular claim (called triangulation).
- Divergence and additional findings can add insights and broader understanding that will be missed when only a single method is used.
- Qualitative data can identify quantitative measurement problems.
- Qualitative components can insert an exploratory and feedback loop into otherwise quantitative studies.
- Quantitative sampling approaches can be used to increase the generalisability of qualitative results.
- Combining quantitative and qualitative research produces integrated, mixed or multiple knowledge.

Weaknesses

- It is difficult for a single researcher to understand and conduct both quantitative and qualitative research; it might require a research team.
- The researcher must understand multiple methods and approaches and how to appropriately mix them.
- Methodological 'purists' contend that one should always work within a single paradigm.
- It is more expensive and time consuming.
- There are challenges in balancing/assessing the outcomes of qualitative and quantitative data analysis at the interpretation and theorisation stages.

The research continuum

Mixed research provides a framework for combining quantitative and qualitative research approaches. Mixed researchers systematically use elements from both paradigms to collect, analyse, validate and interpret data. Mixed research is also flexible in that some study modifications are sometimes needed even after the research has begun. As shown in Figure 9.1, mixed research takes up the majority of the research continuum that varies from

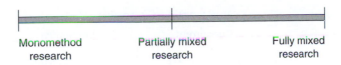

Figure 9.1 The research continuum

monomethod at the far left (i.e. a strictly quantitative or strictly qualitative study) to *fully* mixed research at the far right of the continuum (i.e. research that incorporates quantitative and qualitative methods with equal emphasis throughout the study). Research can be considered minimally mixed if it includes only a small degree of mixing (such as one open-ended question at the end of a quantitative questionnaire). As more and more of both types of research components are integrated in the research, the mixed designs move along the continuum towards the right from being partially mixed towards fully mixed research.

At a minimum, researchers should *always* combine and integrate the results from quantitative and qualitative methods during the interpretation stage. Interpreting results together allows you to view the 'bigger picture' and construct *meta-inferences*. A meta-inference is an interpretation drawn from multiple methods and sources that integrates the findings from the separate quantitative and qualitative data. We next introduce you to some specific mixed research designs.

Types of mixed research design

Mixed research is still an emerging field and thus designs are continually being developed and explored. Our typology for classifying mixed research designs described below is a starting point for thinking about designs. If you are interested in other mixed research typologies, we suggest you look at those provided by Creswell and Plano Clark (2011), Greene (2007), and Teddlie and Tashakkori (2009).

We categorize mixed research designs according to two dimensions: time orientation and paradigm emphasis. *Time orientation* refers to *when* researchers incorporate methods/strands from quantitative and qualitative research into their mixed design. Researchers can either use methods from each paradigm concurrently (i.e. at roughly the same time) or sequentially (i.e. one approach follows the other over the course of the study). *Paradigm emphasis* refers to the type of mixing of quantitative and qualitative methods and epistemological/paradigmatic assumptions. Designs are considered of equal status when the methods receive equal weight or the epistemologies are treated equally. Dominant status (qualitative dominant or quantitative dominant) occurs when one method or paradigmatic logic drives the research and the other approach is 'added on' to the study.

Time Order Decision

		Concurrent	Sequential
Paradigm Emphasis Decision	**Equal Status**	QUAL + QUAN	QUAL → QUAN QUAN → QUAL
	Dominant Status	QUAL + quan + QUAN + qual	QUAL → quan qual → QUAN QUAN → qual quan → QUAL

The research designs are shown in the
four cells

Figure 9.2   Mixed methods design matrix

Crossing the dimensions results in a 2 (time orientation: concurrent versus sequential) by 2 (paradigm emphasis: equal versus dominant status) *research design matrix* (see Figure 9.2). To understand this matrix, you need to become familiar with a commonly used mixed research symbol system. The basic notation works like this:

- QUAL or qual stands for qualitative research.
- QUAN or quan stands for quantitative research.
- Capital letters denote dominance or increased weight.
- Lower case letters denote lower dominance or weight.
- A plus sign (+) represents concurrent data collection.
- An arrow (→) represents sequential data collection.

For example, the symbol combination qual → QUAN indicates a design in which a quantitative paradigm is dominant (QUAN is in capital letters and qual is lower case) and the qualitative part precedes the quantitative part (the → indicates a sequential design). Let's try another one. Suppose the research design is represented as QUAN + QUAL. This combination indicates an equal status of quantitative and qualitative methods (both are in capital letters) and the quantitative and qualitative parts occur at approximately the same time (the + indicates concurrent methods).

To take an example, let's say you want to conduct a mixed study in which you predominantly collect qualitative data and generally emphasise the logic of that type of research. During your study, you take notes while observing participants' behaviour in the field, you conduct one-on-one depth interviews with multiple participants, and you record and transcribe discussions occurring in three focus groups. At the very end of the study, you ask participants to fill out a short structured questionnaire consisting of 10 attitudinal items using quantitative rating scales (for example, 1 – *strongly disagree*, 2 – *disagree*, 3 – *agree*, 4 – *strongly agree*) providing some quantitative data. How would you symbolise your research design? Think about how the research approaches are incorporated over time and how much emphasis each paradigm received. The research design is qualitative dominant, sequential design, symbolised like this: QUAL → quan.

Let's examine a published example of a mixed research study, and determine its design.

Ivankova, Creswell and Stick (2006) were interested in doctoral students' persistence in an online educational leadership programme. First, they collected quantitative survey data with current and former students and identified variables that predicted persistence (external factors, self-motivation, a sense of virtual community). Second, they conducted a qualitative phase to dig deeper into the nature of the predictive factors. They selected four individuals and collected extensive qualitative data. They used depth interviews, open-ended questionnaires, archival class participation information and elicitation materials including photos, objects and other personal items related to persistence. The data from the second (qualitative) phase were used to understand the predictive factors identified in the first (quantitative) phase. The authors stated that they gave primary emphasis to the qualitative data. We would therefore call this a *qualitative-dominant sequential design* (quan → QUAL). The authors added 'explanatory' to their design name to mean that the qualitative data were used to help them explain the quantitative data.

Stages of the mixed research process

The mixed research process generally includes eight steps:

1 Determine whether a mixed design is appropriate.
2 Determine the rationale for using a mixed design.
3 Select or construct a mixed research design and mixed sampling design.
4 Collect the data.
5 Analyse the data.
6 Continually validate the data.
7 Continually interpret the data.
8 Write the research report.

The mixed research design process begins with careful deliberation about the appropriateness of using mixed methods. Once a decision is made to use a mixed design, researchers move through the steps in the order that suits their research situation. Researchers can move back and forth between steps for many reasons (for example, revisit previous decisions, revise research strategies, questions or objectives, explore methods and data in different ways, continually interpret and validate findings, and write parts of the research report throughout the process). In other words, the eight steps are not necessarily linear or sequential.

Step 1. Determine whether a mixed design is appropriate

Empirical research begins with a researcher selecting a research topic, determining the research problem/purpose, and developing a set of specific research questions. In quantitative studies, it is also customary to develop a set of research hypotheses. Concurrently, you will identify your research objective(s). Some popular research objectives are to explore, predict, describe, explain or determine the influence of one or more factors on an important outcome (such as learning, leading).

Your research objectives, purpose and questions will often (but not always) suggest that you should use a mixed research design. For example, you might want to explore the culture of a particular group of people and, using this information, develop a culturally appropriate questionnaire to measure some characteristics of that type of group. Or you might want to use findings from a quantitative questionnaire to help develop a qualitative interview protocol. You must also consider the feasibility/logistics involved in conducting your study. Although mixed research can increase the quality of most designs, it is more time-consuming, expensive and complex than monomethod research. You need to consider your resources and constraints before investing in a mixed study.

Step 2. Determine the rationale for using a mixed design

If you decide a mixed design is appropriate for your research, you should identify the rationale for your mixed design. You should consider Greene, et al.'s (1989) five broad rationales for conducting a mixed study and identify your purpose for mixing: triangulation, complementarity, development, initiation and expansion (Greene, 2007). You also can combine two or more of these, or construct a new one as needed.

Triangulation is a rationale for using a mixed design when a researcher is interested in studying a particular phenomenon with multiple methods and is hoping for converging results. For example, in a study conducted to investigate leadership practice and time allocation of principals, Camburn et al. (2010) collected multiple kinds of data and compared results across methods. Specifically, workplace observations were used to confirm the accuracy of daily logs completed by principals (Camburn et al., 2010). Corroboration of results from multiple methods (if it occurs) adds credibility to findings and increases confidence about inferences drawn from the data. *Complementarity* is the term used when a researcher wants to tap into multiple facets or dimensions of a single complex phenomenon; the strategy is to use widely different methods to elaborate, deepen, enhance and broaden your view, inferences and interpretations. *Development* is used when a researcher wishes to use one method to help inform the other method. For example, you might collect qualitative data to identify important categories and use those categories to develop a questionnaire. *Initiation* is the most generative term and is used when you seek discovery of paradox, contradiction or new perspectives about a single complex phenomenon; the strategy is to select very different methods to help make initiation likely; the researcher hopes for dissonance or divergence. Last, *expansion* is the rationale when a researcher seeks to extend the scope and range of enquiry by using multiple methods to learn about different phenomena examined in a study.

Step 3. Select or construct mixed research design and mixed sampling design

You should thoughtfully and creatively combine methods, strategies and basic designs in a way that specifically suits your research question(s). You can start with our basic design typology by answering two critical questions: (1) Will methods and ideas from one paradigm be given priority, or will they have equal status? (2) Should quantitative and qualitative strands or phases occur concurrently or sequentially? Your answers will allow you to identify a design within our typology according to two dimensions (Figure 9.2). If your design is more complex than the designs in our matrix, you should use ours only as a starting point and add features and components as needed. For example, your research questions might require a design that is predominantly quantitative and includes qualitative methods at the beginning and end of your study. In this case, you would use a qual → QUAN → qual design.

There are many design possibilities in mixed research. In addition to our two dimensions (paradigm emphasis and timing), you can vary the number of phases, number and combination of methodological approaches, stage of integration, function of the research, kinds of phenomena to be examined, and theoretical or ideological perspective (Greene, 2007: 118; Teddlie and Tashakkori, 2009: 141). As a result, mixed research provides an opportunity for you to be creative, develop designs that work and customise your research design to best suit your investigation. Remember, however, that you must always be able to justify your design.

The design phase also involves decisions about sample selection. We recommend the mixed sampling framework provided by Onwuegbuzie and Collins (2007). Mixed sampling designs are classified according to two dimensions: (a) time orientation of the sampling methods and (b) the relationship between the quantitative and qualitative samples (i.e. sample relationship). The time orientation is the same as earlier. You determine whether the data will be collected from the quantitative and qualitative phases sequentially or collected from both phases at the same time (i.e. concurrently).

The sample relationship is classified as one of four types: identical, parallel, nested or multilevel. An *identical* sample relation means that the same participants participate in both the qualitative and quantitative parts of the study. A *parallel* relation means that different people participate in the qualitative and quantitative phases but both samples are drawn from the same population. A *nested* relationship means that the sample from one phase uses a sub-sample of participants in the other phase of the study. Last, a *multilevel* relation involves quantitative and qualitative samples that come from different levels of a multilevel population. For example, you might collect a survey from a sample of children at an elementary school (obtaining quantitative data) and conduct depth interviews with teachers from the school (obtaining qualitative data).

Combining these two sampling dimensions (time orientation and sample relationship) produces eight 'mixed sampling designs': (1) identical-concurrent, (2) identical-sequential, (3) parallel-concurrent, (4) parallel-sequential, (5) nested-concurrent, (6) nested-sequential, (7) multilevel-concurrent and (8) multilevel-parallel. For example, using a *nested-sequential sampling design*, San Antonio and Gamage (2007) investigated empowerment among educational stake-holders via questionnaires and then selected a sub-sample from the original stakeholder sample to participate in an in-depth interview phase. The researchers collected quantitative data in the first phase and qualitative data in the second (i.e. sequentially) and used a *nested* sample relationship because the second sample was selected from the original sample.

After you choose your mixed sampling design, you must determine the quantitative and qualitative sampling methods for your study. For the quantitative part, will you use random or non-random sampling? For the qualitative part, will you use random sampling or one of the distinctive qualitative sampling approaches (for example, homogeneous selection, extreme case selection, critical case selection, opportunistic sampling)? How many participants should you include in each sample? As you can see, research and sampling designs are usually developed together during the research planning process.

Step 4. Collect the data

Next, you have to decide how you will collect your data. Mixed researchers have many *data collection methods* at their disposal and should identify the most appropriate combination to use. There are six *major* methods of data collection in educational research (and many minor methods). The major data collection methods are tests, questionnaires, focus groups, observations, interviews and secondary or existing data. You can use a mixed version of one of these (*intra*-method mixing) such as a mixed questionnaire, or you might use a combination of two or more methods of data collection (*inter*-method mixing).

Muijs et al. (2006) used inter-method mixing to investigate the relationship between leadership development and actual leadership behaviour in highly successful organisations. They conducted a sector-wide survey to collect quantitative data and then purposively selected senior managers, middle managers and first-line organisational managers to participate in focus groups and in-depth bibliographical interviews. This inter-method mixing (question-naires and focus groups) allowed them to collect survey data from a broader cross-section of the staff and focus groups and interviews to explore deeper underlying motivations of leaders. Whatever you choose to investigate, your research questions, objective(s) and rationale for using a mixed design should guide your decisions about what data collection methods to use and how to mix them appropriately.

Step 5. Analyse the data

When analysing quantitative and qualitative data, mixed researchers can select from the full range of analysis techniques. Your research objective(s), purpose, questions/hypotheses and the type of data collected will drive your decisions about what analysis techniques are appropriate. You start by analysing your quantitative data using quantitative techniques and analysing your qualitative data using qualitative techniques. Sometimes data are also analysed with the other analytic approach. For example, *quantitising* refers to conversion or coding of qualitative data into numbers or symbols that provide quantitative information. Quantitised data will often be combined with the quantitative data and analysed using quantitative techniques.

For example, a researcher observing leadership within work teams in an organization might videotape group interaction during a work challenge and count the number of times participants use words such as *I*, *we*, *them* and *us*. The researcher could then create frequency distributions to illustrate the number of times the words were used; the researcher could also search for trends in the characteristics of individuals frequently using particular words. In a grounded theory study, Schulte et al. (2010) used qualitative methods and identified themes in the reported characteristics of effective school principals (for example, leader, organised, flexible, being visible, professional). After identifying the qualitative themes, they converted them into numbers (i.e. quantitised) and formed a matrix consisting of 1s and 0s. This allowed these researchers to statistically analyse whether participants' themes varied as a function of sex, ethnicity and college status.

Mixed researchers can also *qualitise* data; this involves converting quantitative data into qualitative data. Often, qualitising data involves creating profiles for particular result patterns or average profiles to group individuals into more meaningful categories. Narrative profiles constructed from numerical data might help the researcher during data interpretation or might be more meaningful to invested stakeholders. Naming or labelling factors in factor analysis is another example of qualitising. The key idea is that numbers can be converted into words, themes or narrative profiles to provide qualitative information or be analysed using qualitative methods.

Mixed data analysis can be classified into four types. You will need to provide answers to these two questions: What type(s) of data do you have? And how many data analysis approaches will you use? Data can be either quantitative or qualitative. If you decide to use only one type of data in your study, then you have *mono*data. If both quantitative and qualitative data are used, you have *multi*data. Next, determine how many analysis techniques you will use. If you analyse your data using only one type of analysis (only quantitative analysis or only qualitative analysis), then it is called *mono*analysis. If you use both types of data analysis, then it is called *multi*analysis.

Answers to those two questions can result in four types of mixed analysis: monodata–monoanalysis (this is actually not a type of mixed analysis), monodata–multianalysis (this requires quantitising or qualitising your data), multidata–monoanalysis (this approach should be avoided) and multidata – multianalysis. We recommend using multidata–multianalysis in mixed research. This means you have both types of data (quantitative and qualitative) and use both types of analysis (qualitative and quantitative analysis). This provides a more thorough analysis of your data and better enables the making of meta-inferences.

Step 6. Continually validate the data

Onwuegbuzie and Johnson (2006) outlined nine key types of validity or legitimation in mixed research. The first is called *sample integration validity* and is based on the extent to which appropriate claims are made from the quantitative and the qualitative samples to yield quality meta-inferences. Second, *inside-out validity* refers to the extent that a researcher understands, interprets and presents the subjective 'insider' or emic viewpoint *and* the researcher's 'objective outsider' or etic perspective. Third, *weakness minimisation validity* is the extent to which the weakness(es) of one approach is compensated for by the strengths from another. *Sequential validity* is present to the degree that the researcher addresses possible order or sequencing effects that might occur in sequential designs. *Conversion validity* refers to the degree to which quantitising or qualitising data yields quality meta-inferences.

Mixed researchers should also be clear about their paradigmatic beliefs and knowledge of quantitative and qualitative principles when conducting and reporting mixed research. When researchers demonstrate a deep understanding and make their epistemological and methodological beliefs clear, they have *paradigmatic mixing validity*. *Commensurability mixing validity* refers to the degree to which a researcher is able to conduct and interpret research as a quantitative researcher, as a qualitative researcher and as a mixed researcher. If done by a single researcher, he/she must learn how to shift back and forth between perspectives. If you are unable to make this kind of Gestalt switching, you can use a research team with both quantitative and qualitative expertise. The mixed researcher should listen to both sides, mediate and integrate findings of the team into quality meta-inferences that reflect a broader mixed methods view of the phenomenon. *Political validity* refers to a mixed researcher's ability to address the interests and viewpoints of multiple stakeholders in the research process; one must be especially careful to include viewpoints of those with little power.

Finally, *multiple validities* in mixed research refers to the degree to which the researcher addresses *all* relevant validity issues. That is, in addition to the nine validities discussed here, mixed researchers must also address and resolve validity issues associated with quantitative research (i.e. internal, external, construct and statistical conclusion validity) and qualitative research (for example, descriptive, interpretative and theoretical validity)! This is difficult but very important.

Step 7. Continually interpret the data

Like validation, data interpretation is also a continual process. Interpretation begins when the first data are collected and continues throughout the process to the formal interpretation phase after all the data have been collected, analysed, and validated. In sequential mixed designs, researchers analyse and interpret the data from the first phase before moving on to the second phase of the study. For example, interpretations from the first phase might influence the specific questions, methods or rationale used in the second phase (for example, development, explanation or elaboration of some data collected during phase one).

Quantitative and qualitative data from concurrent mixed designs can be interpreted separately or together. At a minimum, mixed researchers integrate, combine and/or compare quantitative and qualitative results during interpretation. Also, quantitative and qualitative data can and often should be integrated during analysis to make a combined analysis possible. Such processes are challenging, not least when analysing and interpreting data that are different in scale and depth. Synthesising data during analysis and interpretation allows you to make more insightful interpretations or meta-inferences. Integrating data and/or results helps you to incorporate multiple sources of information, identify trends, make comparisons and identify contradictions or inconsistencies within your data.

Step 8. Write the research report

As a starting point, you can structure your mixed report around the sections typical of most research reports (i.e. abstract, introduction, method, results, discussion and references). The primary change in mixed research reporting is the organization of quantitative, qualitative and mixed elements within one or more of these sections. There is no single writing technique or organization strategy that is appropriate for all mixed reports. Therefore, as long as you clearly address all of your research questions and provide defensible evidence to justify your claims, you can be creative about your personal presentation style. One writing technique is to organize some sections of your report by research paradigm (quantitative, qualitative and mixed). For example, the results section might begin with a description of only the quantitative results, followed by a section of only qualitative results, and then a discussion of the integrated mixed results. Another style is to organise your results by research questions and include the viewpoints and results for each approach.

No matter how you choose to organise the quantitative, qualitative and mixed elements in your report, the most important thing is to know your audience and write in a way that clearly communicates your research findings. Within your report, you should explain your personal mixed philosophy and incorporate multiple perspectives about the phenomenon under investigation. As a mixed researcher, you must respect the thinking styles of each approach while writing and integrating them into your report. This is especially important when you present integrative conclusions (i.e. meta-inferences) driven by qualitative and quantitative data, findings and perspectives. When writing your report, the key is to clearly address your research questions, to make your report descriptive and readable, and to provide your readers with justifiable and convincing evidence for each of your research findings.

Key points

Mixed research is still a youthful methodological paradigm. As mixed research continues to emerge and acceptance increases, new designs, and information about the merit of these designs, will come. In our opinion, students and professors should explore the many possibilities of mixed research, and over time, mixed research will perhaps become the dominant research or methodological paradigm. The strengths of mixed research are provided in Table 9.4. Additional points made in this chapter include the following:

- Mixed researchers systematically combine aspects of quantitative and qualitative research in a way that produces an overall design with complementary strengths (broadly viewed) and non-overlapping weaknesses.

- Mixed researchers often adhere to the philosophy of pragmatism, which says to use combinations of methods or research approaches that work best in addressing your research question(s).

- The typology of mixed research designs (shown in Figure 9.2) is based on two major dimensions: time orientation (i.e. concurrent vs. sequential) and paradigm emphasis (i.e. equal status vs. dominant status). Crossing these into a matrix yields nine distinct mixed research designs that can be represented symbolically.

- There are eight (often non-linear) steps in the mixed research process: determine whether a mixed design is appropriate; determine the rationale for using a mixed design; select or construct a mixed research design and mixed sampling design; collect the data; analyse the data; continually validate the data; continually interpret the data; and write the research report.

- Mixed researchers often move back and forth among the eight research steps during the research process. In particular, mixed researchers tend to move back and forth during data analysis, data validation, interpretation and report writing.

- You should be aware of the limitations associated with mixed research, especially those that pertain to time, expertise, resources, training and effort expended.

- Mixing approaches in educational research has the potential to increase diversity and collaboration among researchers, increase confidence in results, increase conclusion validity, yield more insightful understandings of phenomena, promote more creative designs and data collection, and increase synthesis of theories. Therefore, the limitations of mixed research should be weighed against the numerous potential benefits of this approach.

Questions and reflections

1 Which of the following do you tend to like the best: qualitative research, quantitative research or mixed research? Why?

2 Design a mixed research study that employs quantitative and qualitative methods sequentially and with equal paradigm status. Discuss and provide a rationale for why the phases are ordered in the way that you propose.

3 Which of the rationales for conducting mixed research do you think is the most important in the area of research that is important to you (triangulation, complementarity, development, initiation or expansion)? Why?

4 Try to think of a hypothetical study design that includes quantitative and qualitative components. What would you call the design?

Recommended further reading

Creswell, J. W. and Plano Clark, V. L. (2011) *Designing and Conducting Mixed Methods Research*. Los Angeles, CA: Sage.

This is the new edition of one of the leading textbooks on mixed methods research. The chapter on designs provides a popular design typology, and the following chapter shows published examples using the different designs. The authors provide a useful explanation of how to produce a visual representation of the design of any mixed study. The writing style is simple and clear.

Greene, J. C. (2007) *Mixed Methods in Social Inquiry*. San Francisco, CA: Jossey-Bass.

This is one of the leading textbooks on mixed methods research by one of its founders. The author integrates a lot of important literature and provides the best explanation of the 'dialectical approach' to mixed research.

Hesse-Biber, S. N. (2010) *Mixed Methods Research: Merging Theory with Practice*. New York: Guilford.

This is one of the newest textbooks on mixed methods research. The author emphasises the connection of theory and practice, and that the research design should follow one's research questions, not vice versa.

Johnson, R. B., Onwuegbuzie, A. J. and Turner, L. A. (2007) Toward a definition of mixed methods research. *Journal of Mixed Methods Research* 1(2): 1–22.

This article surveys definitions provided by 21 well-known authors. The differences among three major types or branches of mixed research are also explained: qualitative-dominant, quantitative-dominant and equal-status mixed research.

Tashakkori, A. and Teddlie, C. (eds) (2010) *Handbook of Mixed Methods in Social and Behavioral Research.* Thousand Oaks, CA: Sage.

This is the second edition of the Handbook. It offers an outstanding line-up of articles about most aspects of mixed research, including philosophy/theory, methodological/ practical issues and applications in multiple fields.

Teddlie, C. and Tashakkori, A. (2009) *Foundations of Mixed Methods Research: Integrating Quantitative and Qualitative Techniques in the Social and Behavioral Sciences.* Thousand Oaks, CA: Sage.

This is one of the leading textbooks on mixed methods research. The authors provide a very useful discussion of the history of mixed research, offer excellent chapters on design, sampling and analysis, and include a glossary.

Note

1　Although the definition of mixed research given here is the authors' definition, it is typical of the 19 definitions of mixed methods research found in a survey of multiple leaders in the field (see Johnson et al., 2007).

References

Brewer, J. and Hunter, A. (1989) *Multimethod Research: A Synthesis of Styles.* Newbury Park, CA: Sage.

Camburn, E. M., Spillane, J. P. and Sebastian, J. (2010) Assessing the utility of a daily log for measuring principal leadership practice. *Educational Administration Quarterly* 46: 707–37.

Creswell, J. W. and Plano Clark, V. L. (2011) *Designing and Conducting Mixed Methods Research.* Los Angeles, CA: Sage.

Dewey, J. (1998/1938). The problem of logical subject-matter. In. Hickman, L. A and Alexander, T. M. *The Essential Dewey, Volume 2: Ethics, Logic, Psychology.* Bloomington, IN: Indiana University Press.

Greene, J. C. (2007) *Mixed Methods in Social Inquiry.* San Francisco, CA: Jossey-Bass.

Greene, J. C., Caracelli, V. J. and Graham, W. F. (1989) Toward a conceptual framework for mixed-method evaluation designs. *Educational Evaluation and Policy Analysis* 11: 255–74.

Ivankova, N. V., Creswell, J. W. and Stick, S. L. (2006) Using mixed-methods sequential explanatory design: From theory to practice. *Field Methods* 18: 3–31.

Johnson, R. B., Onwuegbuzie, A. J. and Turner, L. A. (2007) Toward a definition of mixed methods research. *Journal of Mixed Methods Research* 1(2): 1–22.

Johnson, R. B. and Turner, L. A. (2003) Data collection strategies in mixed methods research. In Tashakkori, A. and Teddlie, C. (eds) *Handbook of Mixed Methods in Social and Behavioral Research* (pp. 297–319). Thousand Oaks, CA: Sage.

Muijs, D., Harris, A., Lumby, J., Morrison, M. and Sood, K. (2006) Leadership and leadership development in highly effective further education providers. Is there a relationship? *Journal of Further and Higher Education* 30: 87–106.

Onwuegbuzie, A. J. and Collins, K.M.T. (2007) A typology of mixed methods sampling designs in social science research. *The Qualitative Report* 12(2): 281–316.

Onwuegbuzie, A. J. and Johnson, R.B. (2006) The validity issue in mixed research. *Research in the Schools* 13(1): 48–63.

Peirce, C. S. (1992/1878) How to make our ideas clear, in Houser, N. and Kloesel, C. (eds) *The Essential Peirce: Selected Philosophical Writings, Volume 1, 1867 to 1893* (pp. 124–41). Bloomington, IN: Indiana University Press.

Peirce, C. S. (1998/1909) Excerpts from letters to William James. In the Peirce edition Project, *The Essential Peirce: Selected Philosophical Writings, Volume 2, 1893 to 1913* (pp. 492–502). Bloomington, IN: Indiana University Press.

San Antonio, D. M. and Gamage, D. T. (2007) PSALM for empowering educational stakeholders: Participatory school administration, leadership, and management. *International Journal of Educational Management* 21: 254–65.

Schulte, D. P., Slate, J. R. and Onwuegbuzie, A. J. (2010) Characteristics of effective school principals: A mixed-research study. *Alberta Journal of Educational Research* 56: 172–95.

Teddlie, C. and Tashakkori, A. (2009) *Foundations of Mixed Methods Research: Integrating Quantitative and Qualitative Techniques in the Social and Behavioral Sciences*. Thousand Oaks, CA: Sage.

Webb, E. J., Campbell, D. T., Schwartz, R. D., Sechrest, L. and Grove, J. B. (1981) *Nonreactive Measures in the Social Sciences* (2nd edn). Boston: Houghton Mifflin.

CHAPTER 10

Surveys and Sampling

Daniel Muijs

Chapter objectives

Survey research is one of the most widely used research methods in the field of educational leadership, and certainly the most used quantitative approach. As we will see, this is because of its flexibility and the ease of gathering a large amount of data relatively cheaply compared to many other methods. In this chapter, we will discuss:

- The characteristics of survey research.
- Its advantages and disadvantages in the context of research on leadership.
- The practicalities of developing valid and reliable survey studies.

What is a survey?

Survey research is a method of collecting standardised data from a large number of respondents. Survey research designs are characterised by the collection of data using standard questionnaire forms. The key element of survey research is standardisation. In a survey, we will ask the same questions to all respondents. Survey research, if the sampling framework is appropriate, also allows us to collect data that we can *generalise* to a population. We will discuss this further in the section on sampling. Most of us are familiar with survey research – if not as researchers ourselves, we will almost certainly have taken part in various surveys over the years. This ubiquity can breed contempt in respondents and an overly casual attitude to design in developers, but, as we will see below, there are some good reasons for the popularity of this method (Buckingham and Saunders, 2004).

Why (not to) use survey research?

Survey research has a number of advantages that have made it one of the most popular forms of research in the social sciences. First of all, survey research is highly flexible. It is possible to study a wide range of research questions using survey methods. You can describe a situation, study relationships between variables, and so on. Because survey research does not set up an artificial situation like an experiment, it is easier to generalise findings to real-world settings, as this is where the research takes place. Survey studies are also efficient in terms of our being able to gather large amounts of data at reasonably low cost and effort compared to other methods like observation. It is also easy to guarantee respondents' anonymity, which may lead to more candid answers than less anonymous methods like interviews. Survey research is therefore particularly suited for canvassing opinions and feelings about particular issues. The use of standardised questions allows for easy comparability between respondents and groups of respondents (differences between men and women, for example).

Obviously, surveys do not allow the researcher to control the environment, and are therefore less suited to answering questions of causality than experimental designs. Nevertheless, by collecting data on as many relevant variables as possible, using longitudinal designs and careful statistical modelling, it is sometimes possible to tentatively reach a view on cause and effect, although it will never be as clear-cut as in an experiment. A further limitation is that it is difficult to come to a deeper understanding of processes and contextual differences through questionnaires, which are standardised and by their nature limited in length and depth of responses. A combination of survey and qualitative methods can help here. Finally, while questionnaires are highly suited to gathering information on respondents' perceptions and opinions of a situation, gathering information on respondent behaviours can be problematic as self-reports are not always reliable in this respect (see Muijs et al., 2006). The study we report as an example below shows that responses to questions about leadership may show significant biases both with regards to reporting on one's own and others' behaviours, with leaders seeing their own leadership as transformational, but that of their line manager as transactional (Muijs, 2010).

The key question is then when or when not to use survey research. This will largely depend on the research question we want to answer. Survey research is particularly suited for asking research questions about issues relating to:

- quantity (for example, how many headteachers have a doctoral degree?)
- opinions and attitudes (for example, how effective do headteachers feel leadership preparation programmes are?)
- relationships between variables (for example, are female teachers more likely to value distributed leadership?)
- perceived behaviours (for example, how many hours a month do headteachers spend on instructional leadership-related activities?).

An example of survey research in educational leadership

An example of survey research in leadership is a study carried out by Muijs et al. (2006) into leadership in post-compulsory further education (FE) in England. The project focused in particular on the relationship between leadership styles and leadership development in effective FE institutions. Purposive sampling was used to select organisations rated as highly effective on a range of performance indicators, including attainment and inspection data. Ten sites were selected on this basis.

A survey was sent out to all members of staff in the organisations. A total of over 1500 surveys were returned. Respondents had the option to complete the survey either electronically or by pencil and paper. The survey was designed to measure leadership styles of respondents and their line managers, using scales for transformational, transactional and distributed leadership. Leadership development was measured using items based on Frearson's (2002) categorisation of leadership development activities in the sector. The survey was completed by staff at all levels of the organisation, including senior managers, middle managers and non-management staff.

Results showed that transformational leadership seemed well supported in these organisations, but that distributed leadership received far less support from respondents, both with regards to its perceived effectiveness and to its application. The findings also suggested that there is a relationship between leadership development and leadership behaviours, with the type of leadership development experienced being related to respondents' views of leadership. Experiential leadership development (such as mentoring and shadowing) appears to be related to positive views of transformational leadership, course-based leadership development (such as university courses) to distributive leadership and individual-based leadership development (such as online distance learning) to transactional leadership. While we found a relationship, this does not in itself, of course, prove causality. However, this study is suggestive of the possible utility of leadership development in shaping leadership and therefore in influencing the effectiveness of the organisation. These findings also put into question certain strongly held views of the overall effectiveness of particular forms of leadership development, different forms of leadership development being related to different leadership styles.

The epistemological foundations of survey research

The choice to conduct survey research is not unrelated to one's epistemological position. While survey research is, as we have seen, a broad and flexible methodology, it does fit more within realist epistemological paradigms. The use of standardised questions (the same questions for all respondents) by definition limits the extent to which a survey can address individual circumstances and contexts. This means that a constructivist or objectivist epistemology, which champions the individual construction of meaning, would not lead one to use survey research which tends, to a certain extent, to impose standard definitions of the meaning of what is being researched. Survey research would therefore fit more naturally with one of the three main realist epistemologies in leadership research: positivism, post-positivism and pragmatism (Muijs, 2010). (For further discussion of the relationship between positivism and quantitative research, see Chapter 2 of this volume.)

Sampling

Once we have decided to use survey research, one of the first decisions we need to take is what our *population* and our *sample* will be. The population, in statistical terms, is the group of people or things we want to reach a conclusion about. For example, when taking an opinion poll of voting intentions, the pollsters are not interested in just how the 2000 or so sampled respondents are likely to vote, but want to reach a view on the likely voting intentions of all voters. The population here is therefore all people who are likely to vote in the elections. Similarly, we may wish to say something in general on the relationship between gender and leadership, but it would be impractical and expensive to survey all headteachers in the UK.

Because of the practical difficulties involved in surveying whole populations, we will in most cases need to take a *sample* of the population. There are many possible ways of doing this, the most common being probability and non-probability sampling.

In order for us to be able to generalise, we need to have an *unbiased* sample of the population, which means that we want our sample to be representative of the population we are studying, and not skewed towards one group or another. If we were trying to generalise to all 10-year-olds, for example, we wouldn't want to sample only all-girls schools. The best way of ensuring that our sample is unbiased is by using *probability sampling methods*.

Random sampling

The most well-known of these is *simple random sampling*. Typical of a simple random sample is that everyone in the population has exactly the same chance of being included in the sample. This is because the sample is drawn at random from the population (for example, by putting names in a hat, or more typically nowadays, by using random number generators). That makes it the most unbiased form of sampling, and this is the method used to draw lottery numbers, for example. Saying that this is the most unbiased sampling method would suggest that it is a good idea to attempt to use simple random sampling at all times. However, when one looks at actual educational research, it is clear that the majority of studies do not in fact use this method. Why is this? There are a number of reasons, some good, some less so. One good reason is that while simple random samples are excellent for generalising to the population as a whole, we might in some cases want to generalise to a specific sub-population that is too small to be reliably picked up in any but the largest of samples. We might, for example, want to compare the well-being of students in private and state-run schools. Taking a random sample of 1000 pupils may leave us with only a very small group of students in private schools. Therefore, to ensure a suitably large number in both, we might want to use *stratified random sampling*. Doing this involves first dividing the population into the groups we want to study, in this case private and state-school attendees, and then randomly sampling from each group separately, so we would obtain a sample of 500 pupils in private and 500 in state-run schools.

Quota sampling

In some cases, we may want to ensure that different subgroups are represented in our sample in accordance with their presence in the population. Again, unless you take a very large sample, this will be difficult to achieve for small subgroups. Therefore, we sometimes specify in advance what proportion of those groups we want to have in our sample, and sample until that quota is fulfilled. For example, we may have a population in which 10 per cent of pupils are of Afro-Caribbean descent. In *quota sampling*, as this method is called, we will sample Afro-Caribbeans until we have reached our quota, in this case 10 per cent of 1000, or 100 Afro-Caribbeans.

Cluster sampling and multi-stage sampling

Another reason not to use simple random sampling lies in the problem of being able to draw conclusions about sites in which members of the population are nested. For example, in leadership research we are often interested in whether or not particular forms of school leadership may impact on student outcomes. Leadership in schools is, however, a school-level variable (leadership happens at the whole-school level), while pupil outcomes happen at the individual pupil level. Saying anything about school effects would be difficult if we used simple random sampling. Even if we were to have a large sample of 1000 students, the likelihood would be that they would be spread over a large number of schools (900, say), meaning that in most cases we would have one pupil or maybe two in a given school. Obviously, it would be nonsensical to extrapolate effects of school leadership on outcomes from findings on one pupil in that school! Therefore, when we want to look at school effects we will usually sample schools randomly, and then survey all pupils in that school. More generally, using *cluster sampling* we will randomly sample higher-level sites in which members of the population are clustered, and then survey all respondents in those sites. A related method is *multistage sampling* in which we first sample higher level sites (for example, school districts) at random, then randomly sample a lower stage (for example, schools in those school districts), and then randomly sample members of the population in that stage (for example, pupils within school). This can be done for any number of stages, the three given here being just an example. A problem with cluster and multistage sampling methods is that they are no longer purely random. This is because, generally speaking, people who are clustered within a site (for example, pupils in a school) are more similar than they are across sites. If we think about schools, we know that within schools pupils are likely to be more homogeneous with respect to social background (due to catchment-area effects) than the population of pupils as a whole. Also, the very fact of being within a site, such as a school, will tend to make people more similar, as they are subject to the same peer group effects and culture of the organisation. This leads to problems when we are doing statistical analyses, in that we will need to use methods that have been designed especially for this type of sample.

Volunteer sampling

The above are all probability sampling methods, and if used properly we can be reasonably confident that we have an unbiased approximation of the population. Probability sampling methods are not necessarily the most common sampling methods in educational research, though. Two other sampling methods appear to be particularly frequent. One popular method is *volunteer sampling*. Volunteer sampling occurs when we ask people to volunteer to take part in our research, through an advertisement in a local paper or professional publication, a notice on a university campus, etc. This method has the obvious advantage of being easy and cheap, but is highly problematic from the point of view of obtaining an unbiased sample. People who volunteer to take part in survey research are often untypical. They are likely to be those people who have particularly strong views on the research subject or have a lot of time on their hands. Often, volunteering is encouraged by giving a (financial) reward to participants. This can help alleviate bias to some extent, but unless the reward is substantial this is unlikely to attract respondents who enjoy a good income. Bias is therefore a serious problem with this sampling method.

Convenience sampling

Probably the most common sampling method in educational studies at present is *convenience sampling*. This occurs where the researcher has easy access to particular sites, such as headteachers she has worked with before, or pupils in her own school, and uses those people in her research. This method has obvious advantages in terms of cost and convenience, but suffers from serious problems of bias, as the sites one has easy access to may not be representative of the population. If one works in a rural school, for example, pupils will differ in many respects to those in an inner-city environment. This limits the generalisability of results to those areas that are similar, remembering that geographic area may also be a factor that differentiates pupils (Munn and Drever, 1999).

Designing survey research

The following stages are typically followed when designing a survey study:

1 Define research objectives and overall design

As with any other type of research, we start by defining our research objectives. A wide variety of research questions can be studied using survey methods, as we mentioned above.

Research designs should be realistic and feasible. In survey research in particular, the temptation is to specify a research design which attempts to capture the full complexity of the world through a very extensive research design. Often, it will not be possible to collect data on all the variables we might want to include because of financial and time constraints, and we may have to settle for a sample that is a bit smaller than we would have liked. Where this is the case, the key is to select those variables that we think are most likely to affect our outcomes.

Once we have defined our research objectives, we can proceed to the research design, which will be dependent on those objectives. For example, if we wanted to look at how leadership styles change over time, we would have to do a *longitudinal* study, surveying leaders over a number of years. If we wanted to find out about headteachers' opinions on a new policy initiative by the Department for Education, a *cross-sectional study* where you would just survey them once would suffice. If we wanted to survey whether headteachers' opinions had changed following an intervention, pre- and post-surveys would be suitable. We might also want to mix different methods, for example a large-scale survey followed by in-depth interviews of a small sub-sample. A range of options is possible, depending on research objectives and, not least, research budgets.

2 Formulate hypotheses

While in experimental designs it is common to develop and test hypotheses in all cases, this is not necessarily so in survey designs. In some cases, we will want to make specific predictions about relationships between variables in the form of hypotheses (for example, 'there is a relationship between leadership styles and organisational performance'). Generally speaking, the flexibility of survey research means that these can be wide-ranging and complex (for example, 'the relationship between leadership styles and organisational performance will depend on the prior effectiveness of the organisation'). Not all survey studies test specific hypotheses, however. Some survey studies can be purely descriptive. For example, one common use of survey studies is looking at voting intentions. Researchers do not start from specific hypotheses (for example, 'The Democratic share of the vote is hypothesised to be more than .40'), but merely wish to test what intentions are. Therefore, whether one wants to test specific hypotheses or conduct a more descriptive study (for example, 'what percentage of teachers has engaged in professional development activities over the past year?') will depend on your research question.

3 Define what information you need

Once research questions and, where necessary, hypotheses have been decided on, you need to think about what information is needed to answer these research questions. If your research objectives suggest that a survey study would be a suitable method, you need to decide what information you will need to collect through your survey study. This will involve deciding what questions to ask, whether to use pre-published scales, how long to make your survey, and so on. We will look at a number of these issues later on in this chapter.

4 Collect survey data

Data collection is the next phase, and another one where problems can occur in survey studies. Data can be collected through pencil-and-paper questionnaires, telephone or face-to-face interviews and online methods such as web-based questionnaires.

Traditionally, the most common method in educational research has been the use of the *pencil-and-paper questionnaire*. The main advantage of this method is its familiarity to users, the fact that it allows users to complete the questionnaire at their own convenience, and the fact that it allows them some time to think about their answers. Disadvantages are often low response rates and time-consuming follow-up and data entry.

Nowadays, questionnaires are increasingly produced *online*. In essence, these are similar to pencil-and-paper questionnaires, with the advantage that answers can be directly stored in a database and that many online systems allow simple analyses to take place, which saves a lot of time (and therefore money) by eliminating data input. It is also easy to make these questionnaires adaptive, in that one can vary questions based on previous responses. Technophobia or a lack of access to the Internet may be problems in some populations or countries.

Telephone interviews allow the interviewer to continue until the target sample size is met, and are better suited to quota sampling methods than pencil-and-paper questionnaires. They often allow input of answers to a computer system, saving valuable data input time. Like online question-naires, they can be made adaptive. However, bias can occur in telephone interviews. While in Western countries most people are connected to the telephone system, some are not listed in telephone directories, a problem that is increasing as more people are relying exclusively on mobile phones and no longer use landlines. Also, many people find telephone question-naires intrusive, and will refuse to participate. There is also little time for respondents to think over answers. When doing telephone interviews, it is important to ensure that phone calls are made at a time when respondents are available.

Face-to-face interviews again allow the interviewer to reach sample-size tar-gets and quotas and can be adaptive, but like phone interviews can be seen as intrusive and therefore induce non-cooperation. The place that is chosen to conduct face-to-face interviews can introduce bias, as in the practice of inter-viewing in shopping malls during the day, where one is unlikely to reach those who are working during that time. Face-to-face interviews will involve as much data input as pencil-and-paper questionnaires.

Whatever sampling method we use, we will have to confront the problem of non-response to the survey. Non-response in online and pencil-and-paper surveys can be very substantial, many questionnaires receiving response rates well below 50 per cent, and virtually none (save small-scale questionnaires completed involuntarily, such as compulsory student feedback) receiving a 100 per cent response rate. This non-response wouldn't matter if we could be certain that those that do not respond are very similar to respondents on all relevant variables, and therefore would have answered the survey similarly if they had taken part. However, this is by no means certain, and in many cases we can be sure that this is not the case. Generally, people who feel more strongly or have a particular axe to grind about the subject are more likely to respond, as are people with an interest in research more generally. Also, people with more time on their hands tend to respond more readily to questionnaires. Low-response rates obviously make our final sample smaller, which means we have less 'statistical power' to test our hypotheses. Therefore, we need to try and maximise our response rates. There are a number of things we can do to help:

- Keep the questionnaire sufficiently short (30 minutes maximum) and attractive.
- Minimise cost and effort to respondents.
- Promise (and provide!) respondents who complete and return the questionnaire feedback on the research project.
- Provide a reward for completion. Book tokens, vouchers, etc. are usually appreciated.
- Follow-up phone calls and visits to participants may help improve response rates quite considerably.

Non-response takes on slightly different forms in telephone and face-to-face formats, in that it is always possible to continue phoning or interviewing new respondents until a certain target response number has been reached. This does not solve the problem of non-participants (those people that have refused to take part) being in some way different from those that have agreed to participate, however, and the same issues as with online and pencil-and-paper survey research remain. Therefore, it is again best to try and maximise initial response rates and minimise the number of non-respondents. The methods we can use to help us achieve this are similar to those mentioned with respect to online and pencil-and-paper questionnaires.

None of these methods will totally eradicate non-response, and we therefore need to carefully consider what factors can lead to non-response and how we can correct for differences between non-respondents and respondents.

Designing survey items

There are a number of question types we can include in a survey instrument. The first distinction to make is that between *open-ended* and *closed* questions.

Open-ended questions allow the respondent to formulate her own answer, whereas closed questions make the respondent choose between answers provided by the researcher.

An example of an open-ended question is:

What teaching method do you think is best for teaching reading?

....
....
....
....

An example of a closed question would be:

Which method do you think is best for teaching reading? Choose one answer only:

Analytic phonics

Systematic phonics

A balanced approach

A whole language approach

You will not be surprised to hear that both have advantages and disadvantages. Open-ended questions have the advantage of allowing the respondent to freely formulate an answer. This can be important, as it allows you as a researcher to discover opinions or answers that you had not thought about before. In closed questions, answers are limited to those you have formulated at the start, with no room for surprises. Inclusion of an 'other' category will only remedy this to a limited extent, as the respondent will be influenced by the answers presented to her/him in the preceding categories and will be less likely to choose this option. However, open-ended questions are more difficult and time-consuming to work with, as the answers will first need to be coded and quantified using some form of content analysis. There is also a loss of standardisation and comparability of answers across respondents. Finally, open-ended questions are more time-consuming for respondents, who will, as a result, be more inclined not to answer this type of question than closed questions.

The category of closed questions is itself quite broad, encompassing a range of question types. A first type is the *yes/no* question (for example, do you agree with the government's policy on classroom assistants? Yes or no). This is obviously an easy form for respondents, but on the other hand does not provide a lot of subtlety in responses. You might, for example, want to know to what extent respondents agree with government policies. In that case, it is better to use some form of *rating scale*. Rating scales allow the respondent to choose one of several options indicating level of agreement or opinion on an item. Rating scales can take on a number of forms, and can have a differing number of response categories. For example:

Rating Scale Example 1

I think all headteachers in this state should receive a $10,000 pay rise (please choose one answer):

Strongly agree   Agree   Disagree   Strongly disagree   Don't know

Rating Scale Example 2

I think all headteachers in this state should receive a $10,000 pay rise (please rate your agreement on the 10-point scale, with 10 being agree strongly, and 0 being disagree strongly):

Agree strongly   10 9 8 7 6 5 4 3 2 1 0   Disagree strongly

A contested question is whether or not to include a middle, neutral category (neither true nor untrue). A reason for not doing so is that answers to this category are often difficult to interpret, as some respondents who do not understand the question or don't have an opinion choose this option. In that case, you are left to wonder what a response in this category means: an actual 'neither true nor untrue of me', a 'don't know', or a 'don't understand the question'? This problem can be at least partly alleviated by including a 'don't know' category at the end of the scale (never in the middle, otherwise you will be causing the same confusion). Another problem can be that including the middle category can encourage respondents to 'sit on the fence', which some respondents do very frequently. This is called the *central tendency* problem, and is most likely to occur with more sensitive or controversial questions. To avoid this, we can choose not to use a middle category. On the other hand, some respondents may be genuinely neutral, and by not offering a middle category we might be misrepresenting their views.

A problem that can occur in questionnaires is that of *positive response bias*. This mainly occurs if respondents are asked about their views on a number of desirable or popular alternatives. Respondents may rate all of these equally favourably, making it difficult to see which option they would really prefer. Take, for example, the following possible goals of education:

- Academic achievement.
- A caring environment.
- Developing positive attitudes to learning.
- A student-centred environment.
- Developing enterprising citizens.
- Enhancing pupils' self-esteem.

If we asked respondents (headteachers in this case) to rate individual items using rating scales, we are likely to find that all are rated highly. That would not give us a good indication of which element they really find the most important. To remedy this, we would need to use some sort of forced-choice format, by either asking them to rank the choices from 1 to 6 in order of importance (Example 3) or by forcing them to choose between two options (Example 4). If we use enough choices, we can again calculate rankings.

Rating Scale Example 3

Please rank the following goals in order of importance for your school from first to sixth, with 1 indicating the most important goal, 2 the second most important goal, and so on:

... High academic achievement
... Providing a caring environment
... Providing a student-centred environment
... Developing positive attitudes to learning
... Developing enterprising citizens
... Enhancing pupils' self-esteem

Rating Scale Example 4

Please indicate which of the following two goals you think is most important:

High academic achievement

OR

Providing a caring environment

Quality assurance in survey research

As we have mentioned above, if we want reliable and valid responses, we need to ensure quality in our survey designs. There are a number of factors to take into account when developing a questionnaire:

- Keep it brief. The first element of good questionnaires, whatever way they are administered, is that they are not too long. This is because lengthy questionnaires will annoy respondents, leading to higher levels of non-response or to respondents getting bored and not completing the questionnaire accurately. There is a slight conflict here with the imperative to try and collect as much data as possible, but it must be remembered that if the data you have collected is inaccurate, it doesn't help you to have loads of it! Four sides of A4 is a good rule of thumb for maximum questionnaire length.

- Keep your questions clear and simple. Ambiguously worded questions will lead to ambiguous responses, so it is important to phrase questions in such a way that they are understandable to all respondents. It is best to err on the side of caution here, and to remember that what may be clear to you as a researcher may not be clear to respondents. Use of acronyms is to be avoided, and where technical terms are used it is good practice to explain them.

- Consider the order of questions. Usually in a survey we will want to collect some data on respondent characteristics such as age, experience, gender and social background (for example, occupation). Not all respondents enjoy answering this kind of question, and some will refuse to do so. It is therefore good practice to put this type of question at the end rather than, as is common, at the beginning of the questionnaire. This is because if you annoy respondents at the start, they are unlikely to complete your questionnaire.

- Include a 'don't know' category in rating scales to give respondents who do not have an answer or an opinion a chance to make this choice. This is particularly important if you are using rating scales with a neutral mid-point, otherwise those respondents who wish to answer 'don't know' are likely to choose this mid-point, making their answer hard to interpret.

- Avoid double negatives (if you don't disagree …) in questionnaires, as they lead to confusion among respondents, who have to do an extra cognitive action to interpret the question.

- Ask only one question in any item. This seems obvious, but is in practice often forgotten. It is easy to succumb to the temptation of putting two questions into one item, such as 'Do you think Reading Recovery is an effective and efficient way of improving reading scores of low-achieving readers?' The issue here is that both you and the respondent will have problems interpreting this question and the answers. A respondent may think Reading Recovery is effective, but not efficient in terms of cost or time. What does she answer? Likewise, when you receive responses to this question, how do you interpret them? Does a negative response mean the respondent thinks the programme is both ineffective and inefficient? Or just ineffective?

- Take into account cultural differences. It is important to make sure your instruments are culturally sensitive. Avoid items or wordings that may be unclear or offensive to different cultures, such as asking respondents for their 'Christian name' (Muijs, 2010).

(For further discussion of reliability and validity in survey research, see Chapter 6 of this volume.)

Piloting and testing

The single most effective strategy to minimise problems is to make sure you *pilot* your instruments. Piloting has a number of distinct phases.

First, it is a good idea to ask a group of experts in the field to have a look at your questionnaire and make any comments as to whether items are appropriate, or could be worded better or replaced.

When you have revised your survey instrument based on these comments, it is a good idea to pilot the instrument. To pilot an instrument, you need to sample a small group of respondents from the population you are interested in, and administer the survey to them. The quality of the instrument can be determined in two ways: statistically you can look for any anomalous answer patterns that suggest that questions haven't been properly understood, for example a large number of non-responses to a particular question. It is also a good idea to ask the respondents to complete an additional short survey on what they think of the questions, whether they understood them clearly and what changes they might suggest. Alternatively, you could interview them about this.

You will then need to revise the survey instrument based on the results of the pilot. In this way, you will have ensured that the survey is likely to be relevant to and understood by your respondents when you take the full sample and administer the survey.

Key points

- Survey research is one of the most widely used research methods in the field of educational leadership, and certainly the most used quantitative approach. This is because of its flexibility and the ease of gathering a large amount of data relatively cheaply compared to many other methods.

- Survey research is particularly suited for asking research questions about issues relating to quantity, opinions and attitudes, relationships between variables and perceived behaviours. Survey research is less suited to looking at questions relating to processes or in-depth understanding of meaning.

- Once we have decided to use survey research, one of the first decisions we need to take is what our *population* and our *sample* will be. The population, in statistical terms, is the group of people or things we want to reach a conclusion about. The sample is the group we are actually surveying. We need to try and make sure our sample is as unbiased as possible. This is best done by using probability sampling methods.

- If we want reliable and valid responses, we need to ensure quality in our survey designs. To do this, we need to follow best practice in designing survey items, and pilot any instrument before using it with our final sample.

Questions and reflections

1   Think of a survey you have recently completed. What do you think of it in relation to the quality issues we have discussed above? What would you do to improve this survey?

2 As we mentioned earlier, survey research is one of the most widely used methods in leadership research. Do you think it is overused? Why/why not?

3 Do you think it is possible to design a constructivist survey? If yes, how would you do this?

Recommended further reading

Buckingham, A. and Saunders, P. (2004) *The Survey Methods Workbook: From Design to Analysis*. Cambridge: Polity Press.

This is a general overview of the practicalities of doing survey research, with a lot of useful exercises.

Fink, A. (2002) *The Survey Kit*. Newbury Park, CA: Sage.

This is probably the most comprehensive set of books on survey design, interesting mainly if you want to engage in a lot of survey research.

Munn, P. and Drever, E. (1999) *Using Questionnaires in Small Scale Research*. Edinburgh: Scottish Council for Research in Education.

This is an excellent guide to practical survey design, written for the busy education practitioner.

References

Buckingham, A. and Saunders, P. (2004) *The Survey Methods Workbook: From Design to Analysis*. Cambridge: Polity Press.

Frearson, M. (2002) *Tomorrow's Learning Leaders*: *Developing Leadership and Management for Post-Compulsory Learning Survey Report*. London: Learning and Skills Development Agency.

Muijs, D. (2010) *Doing Quantitative Research in Education* (2nd edn). London: Sage.

Muijs, D., Harris, A., Lumby, J., Morrison, M. and Sood, K. (2006) Leadership and Leadership Development in Highly Effective Further Education Providers: Is there a Relationship? *Journal of Further and Higher Education* 30(1): 87–106.

Munn, P. and Drever, E. (1999) *Using Questionnaires in Small Scale Research*. Edinburgh: Scottish Council for Research in Education.

CHAPTER 11

Case Studies

Michael Bassey

Chapter objective

To show how case study, as an investigation of a singularity, can be a valid and useful form of research in education that may lead to greater understanding and enhancement of practice.

Introduction

I once heard an American educational researcher start a lecture by saying, 'There are three kinds of researcher: those that count things and those that don't'. She paused, we waited. She continued: 'I do not belong to the first kind'; laughter slowly moved around the hall. Her lecture was based on qualitative research. Case study is usually a form of qualitative research – and so often doesn't involve counting!

Because this book is for educational managers and students, I must make clear that I am writing about case study as a form of enquiry and not as a learning tool in the form that often features in management classes. It is, of course, true that cases used as teaching materials in classes have arisen from systematic and thorough enquiry, but they are usually written up with pedagogic intentions rather than with research criteria in mind.

A prescriptive definition of research case study

Several years ago, I had the opportunity of carefully examining the concept of case study as a research approach (Bassey, 1999), and I came to the conclusion that it needed pulling into shape! Figure 11.1 presents a definition that I believe gives a useful prescriptive account of what constitutes a worthwhile educational case study. Others provide different definitions and different ways of categorising case studies: Gillham (2000), Hamel et al. (1993), Hancock and Algozzine (2006), Simons (2009), Stake (1995), Yin (1994, 2003); see also Stake in Denzin and Lincoln (2000). If you have the time, patience and a dissertation supervisor demanding a literature survey, dip into these, but I think you will do much better to get stuck into investigating your chosen case!

An educational case study is an empirical enquiry which is:

- conducted within a localised boundary of space and time (i.e. a singularity)
- into *interesting* aspects of an educational activity, programme, institution, system or work of an individual
- mainly in its natural context and within an ethic of respect for persons
- in order to inform the judgements and decisions of practitioners or policy makers
- or of theoreticians who are working to these ends, and
- such that sufficient data are collected for the researcher to be able to:

  (a) explore *significant* features of the case
  (b) create *plausible* interpretations of what is found
  (c) test for the trustworthiness of these interpretations
  (d) construct a *worthwhile* argument or story
  (e) relate the argument or story to any relevant research in the literature
  (f) convey *convincingly* to an audience this argument or story
  (g) provide an audit trail by which other researchers may validate or challenge the findings, or construct alternative arguments.

Figure 11.1   Prescriptive definition of research case study

The terms in italics in Figure 11.1 inevitably entail value judgements being made by the researcher. It is worth elaborating on some of the terms contained in this description of educational case study.

An educational case study ...

'Educational' locates this in the field of educational research (including educational leadership and management research). I define educational research as critical enquiry aimed at informing educational judgements and decisions in order to improve educational action.

... an empirical enquiry ...

This means that the starting point is the collection of data – usually by asking (and listening to the answers of) questions, observing actions or extracting evidence from documents.

... conducted within a localised boundary of space and time ...

Most writers agree about this. When the report of the case study is written, it focuses on a location and a defined period of time.

... (i.e. a singularity) ...

This is a term meaning that a particular set of events, or programme, institution, classroom, or the work of a person, etc. is the focus of the case study research.

... into _interesting_ aspects ...

Why spend time on it if the subject is not interesting? There should be something about the set of events, or programme, institution, classroom, person, etc. that is judged worth systematically describing to others, or there should be some feature or issue of it that deserves to be explored in order to try to understand what is happening.

... mainly in its natural context ...

This is one of the strengths of case study research, and again is something on which most writers agree. Case study research entails being where the action is, taking testimony from and observing the actors first hand.

... and within an ethic of respect for persons ...

Research bodies such as the British Educational Research Association (BERA) insist that all educational research should be conducted within an ethic of respect for persons (and of respect for truth and for democratic values) (see also Chapter 7 for a discussion of research ethics). The closer one comes to the people being studied, the more important it is to ensure that they are willing to be studied, and that what they say or do is reported in such a way that it is not prejudicial to their best interests. (Remember that the philosopher Schopenhauer [1788–1860] warned that people can be like porcupines – the closer they get to each other, the more they prick each other.)

... in order to inform the judgements and decisions of practitioners or policy makers ...

Case study is arduous and demanding of both researchers and researched. It should not be wasted on trivial pursuits, but should aim to contribute to understanding in greater depth than hitherto some aspect of what educationalists (in the widest sense) actually do.

... or of theoreticians who are working to these ends ...

We should not expect that all educational research will immediately inform the concerns of practitioners or policy makers. It is essential that researchers also build scaffolds for other researchers to climb – with the hope that ultimately the climbers will be able to inform those who follow them. Case study research can contribute to this.

... in such a way that sufficient data are collected ...

Case study means that researchers need to collect sufficient data to allow them to explore features, create interpretations and test for trustworthiness. But 'sufficient' is a two-edged word meaning 'not too little, not too much'. There is no point in the case study researcher collecting more data than can be handled successfully in the time available – and that entails exercising considerable insight and judgement.

... to explore <u>significant</u> features of the case and to create plausible interpretations of what is found ...

It is only of limited value for a researcher to conclude 'if teachers do x then y may happen'. It is much better to go beyond this and try to discover why y may happen, for this may contribute to a theoretical understanding that illuminates other events.

... to test for the trustworthiness of these interpretations ...

The critical approach should be ubiquitous in research. The question 'Does this really mean what we claim it means?' should always be borne in mind. Some tests of trustworthiness are given at the end of this chapter. In common with some other writers on case study, I prefer the term 'trustworthiness' to the terms 'validity' and 'reliability' (for an elaboration of this concept, see Lincoln and Guba [1985: 218]). 'Reliability' is an impractical concept for case study since by its nature a case study is a one-off event and therefore not open to exact replication. (For further discussion of these terms, see also Chapter 7.)

... to relate the argument or story to any relevant research in the literature ...

If research is compared to a giant jigsaw puzzle, then finding a new piece of the puzzle is of limited value unless it can be fitted into an area of the picture or at least stored with related pieces of the picture, ready to be slotted into it. The 'conceptual background' is an important section of most research papers, but the literature cited should be rigorously restricted to items judged pertinent to the enquiry. (Don't fall into the academic trap of thinking that the longer the list of references the better the paper!)

... to construct a <u>worthwhile</u> argument or story and to convey convincingly to an audience this argument or story ...

Unless research outcomes are expressed in a readable way for the intended audience they are likely to be ignored and the enterprise wasted. This is a particular problem for case study researchers for their accounts, in trying to do justice to their data, tend to be lengthy. Some answers to this are given later.

... to provide an audit trail by which other researchers may validate or challenge the findings, or construct alternative arguments

This idea is not widely practised today but I commend it. The audit trail is a flow chart of the data, and of its analysis and interpretation, which enables others to examine the evidence for the trustworthiness of the study and also enables them to exercise their own creativity in finding alternative interpretations. The idea is to invite a colleague to conduct an audit of one's research and to comment on its perceived trustworthiness.

Different end-points for research case study

The comedian Peter Cook, playing a clergyman in the pulpit, told how he left the railway station by 'the way you're meant to go in and was hailed by a railwayman. "Hey, mate! Where do you think you are going?" – or at least that was the gist of his remark.' He went on: 'But I was grateful to that man, for he put me in mind of the kind of question that I want to ask you, "Where do you think you are going?"' As researchers, you must ask yourselves the same question.

In my attempt to reconstruct the concept of case study (Bassey, 1999), I identified at least three different end-points, as shown in Figure 11.2.

- Story-telling and picture-drawing case study
- Evaluative case study
- Theory-seeking and theory-testing case study linked to fuzzy general predictions.

Figure 11.2   Three different end-points for case study research

Story-telling and picture-drawing case studies

Story-telling and picture-drawing case studies are both analytical accounts of educational events, projects, programmes or systems aimed at illuminating theory.

Story-telling is predominantly a *narrative account* of the exploration and analysis of the case, with a strong sense of a time line. For example, a story-telling case study might be an account of how a particular school responded over a period of time to the introduction of school development planning.

Picture-drawing is predominantly a *descriptive account*, drawing together the results of the exploration and analysis of the case. For example, a picture-drawing case study might be an account of the system of school development planning operating in a particular school at a point in time. In both of these examples, the research expectation would be that a case study attempted to contribute to theoretical ideas about school development planning. Often this entails the bringing together of a number of case studies, as will shortly be illustrated.

An example of a story-telling case study is one that I wrote of events that took place over 10 years earlier: 'The Nottinghamshire staff development project 1985–1987' (Bassey, 1999). It is a 21-page account that draws on the 250-page case record prepared at the time. Drawing on interviews, questionnaires, documents and transcripts of group discussions, it describes how the project started and what steps I took to find out what was happening in my role as an illuminative evaluator to the project. It shows how I tried to tease out the ideology of the project, then tested it (I later found that the project sponsors did not accept that they had an ideology!). I interviewed people who were heavily involved in the project and others who only knew of it at second or third hand. Eventually, I was able to describe the enthusiasm that the project generated in its key participants, but also to show that the less people were involved in it, the more they were inclined to treat it with cynicism. I finished this story-telling case study with this somewhat polemical statement:

> Perhaps the story has not ended yet. There are important messages for the national government ... classrooms are being seen as units of production and teachers as technicians carrying out tightly defined functions. I believe it is time that the banner be raised again to assert the essentiality of teachers being recognised as professionals, fundamentally working for the effective education of young people, and striving to enhance their practice through the shared process of structured reflective action. Only when they are free to exercise their own judgements and make their own decisions can they provide that enthusiasm, insight and enlightenment [that] young people need from their teachers if they are to grow up responding creatively and happily to a changing and challenging world. (Bassey, 1999: 115)

McMahon et al. (1997) provide an example of a picture-drawing case study:

> This is a study of a primary school in Bristol, a school which has a vibrant, exciting atmosphere, where pupils and teachers work hard and effectively. A school described by governors, parents and teachers as 'marvellous', 'absolutely brilliant', 'exciting', 'inviting' and about which the chair of governors said 'it's all buzzing in the school now'. The classrooms and corridors are filled with displays of children's work, there is a school choir which has sung in Bristol Cathedral, children study the violin, participate in workshops with artists in residence, enter and win competitions, put on excellent, high-standard performances for their parents at Christmas, look after an area of woodland as part of an environmental project, enjoy and experience success with their academic work and above all are valued as individuals.

> Teachers in schools like this can be justifiably proud of their work, but the achievements here are greater, since this is a school that can accurately be described as one which is succeeding against the odds. (McMahon et al., 1997: 271)

This case study is based on interviews with governors, the headteacher, teachers and parents, observation and study of school documents. The case study is largely descriptive, but clearly, throughout the data collection, the researchers have kept asking the question: 'How has this school been transformed from one that was struggling?'
They offer this explanation:

> ... hard work must be seen as a major explanatory variable. However, it is also important to note that this work and effort has had a clear focus and has been carefully planned by the headteacher in consultation with her

staff … The headteacher has been able to build her staff into a strong team, help them develop a clear sense of direction and purpose, and together they have turned the school around. It is for these reasons that the school is succeeding against the odds. (McMahon et al., 1997: 280)

Theory-seeking and theory-testing case studies leading to fuzzy general predictions

This type of case study is best described by an example. MacGilchrist et al. (1997) carried out nine picture-drawing case studies in primary schools in England in the mid-1990s of systems of school development planning. They looked at questions such as: 'Who participates in preparing the plan?', 'Who acts on it?' and 'How is its success monitored?' Analysis of this data led them to ask further questions such as: 'Who has ownership of the plan, and how broad are its purposes?' They were seeking a theoretical structure and they discovered that their findings could be interpreted in terms of four types of school development planning, which they termed the rhetorical plan, the singular plan, the co-operative plan and the corporate plan. Using their data, they put to the test the

assumption, made particularly by policy-makers, that school development plans (SDPs) will improve schools, [that] they are the answer to self-management and as such will make schools more effective.

We can categorise their work in the nine schools as a multi-site theory-testing case study. They expressed the outcome as what I have called a 'fuzzy prediction'. It is 'fuzzy' (Bassey, 2001) because, instead of trying to state 'what works', it states 'what may work': in other words, it has built-in tentativeness or fuzziness (for an account of the concept of fuzziness in logical systems, see Kosko [1994]). MacGilchrist et al. said:

This study … has shown that school development planning can be used as a school improvement strategy … Of the four types identified, only one [the corporate plan] was found to have a positive impact on student, teacher and school-wide improvements. (MacGilchrist et al., 1997: 246)

Evaluative case studies

These are enquiries which set out to explore some educational programme, system, project or event in order to focus on its worthwhileness. The case may be tightly structured as an examination of the extent to which the programme's stated objectives have been achieved, or it may be illuminative in the phrase coined by Parlett and Hamilton (1977). It may be formative (in helping the development of the programme) or summative (in assessing it after the event). It draws on theoretical notions but is not necessarily intended to contribute to the development of theory – and in that sense is different from the other kinds of educational case study described above.

Multiple-site case studies

As noted, the study described above by MacGilchrist et al. (1997) illustrates the idea of multiple-site case studies. According to how the study is viewed this was either nine case studies in nine primary schools (each conducted along the same lines of enquiry into their development planning), or one case study into school development planning, carried out on nine sites. The distinction is, of course, unimportant. But the reason for the nine studies is very significant. These researchers were trying to say something significant about development planning and in order to do this they cast their net widely. As a result they came up with a four-fold typology. Perhaps they might have added to their typology had they studied more schools – but there is always a limit to what is possible. It is important to realise that in such a study there is an attempt to include as many varieties of practice as can be found, but no attempt to quantify them. If we wanted to know how prevalent these types of planning are, survey techniques would be needed. In this way sometimes case study and survey methods work in tandem, the case study informing the design of the survey.

Stages in conducting case study research

It is helpful to see the conduct of case study research as a stage-by-stage process (see Figure 11.3), but the reader must recognise that the procedures described here will only rarely be in complete accord with the processes of actual studies. Research is a creative activity and every enquiry has its own unique character. (See also Chapter 8 for further discussion of research design.)

Stage 1: Identifying the research purpose

Going back to first principles, the purpose of research is trying to make a claim to knowledge, or wisdom, on the basis of systematic, creative and critical enquiry. It is about trying to discover something that was not known before and then communicating that finding to others. A helpful way of

---

Stage 1: Identifying the research purpose
Stage 2: Asking research questions
Stage 3: Drawing up ethical guidelines
Stage 4: Collecting and storing data
Stage 5: Generating and testing analytical statements
Stage 6: Interpreting or explaining the analytical statements
Stage 7: Deciding on the outcome and writing the case report (publishing)

Figure 11.3   Possible stages in conducting case study

thinking about that 'something' is to see it as a research hypothesis to be tested, or as a research problem to be tackled, or as a research issue to be explored. Deciding initially on one of these provides a platform for asking research questions.

This is not a rigid classification. Often a research purpose can be expressed under more than one of these headings. Although one of the three may be judged to be the most suitable way of describing the research at a particular stage of enquiry, this may change and another of the three headings may be seen as a more apt way of describing the purpose of the research.

A *research hypothesis* is a tentative statement or conjecture that is in a form which can be tested. For example:

> That the introduction of performance management in this school will within three years have made a step-change in our examination results.

It enables clear research questions to be asked which should provide evidence that either supports the hypothesis or refutes it. The research purpose is to test the hypothesis.

A *research problem* identifies a difficulty which can often be expressed as a contradiction between what is happening and what someone would like to happen. For example:

> The introduction of performance management in this school is welcomed by the senior management team (SMT) as a means of raising standards in examinations, but most staff believe it will damage senior/junior staff relationships and hence have a deleterious effect on results.

The popular idea that where there is a problem the job of the researcher is to find a solution, is usually unrealistic. The research is more likely to formulate and try out ways in which the problem may be better understood and so be alleviated or the difficulty reduced, and it is to this end that appropriate research questions need to be asked.

A *research issue* is the least defined purpose of research. It describes an area for enquiry where no problems or hypotheses have yet been clearly expressed that can direct the enquiry. For example:

> How will the introduction of performance management affect our school?

The research in this case will strive to focus the issue through asking pertinent research questions. Later, the research can be reformulated as a problem or a hypothesis.

Early on in a research programme, the question should be asked: 'What kind of report is it envisaged will eventually be written?' Will it, for example, be a story-telling or picture-drawing study, or an evaluative study, or a theory-seeking/theory-testing study? The last of these obviously links with the idea of a hypothesis, while story-telling, picture-drawing and evaluation tend to be linked to either issues or problems.

As an example, consider an investigation pursuing the above research issue. Suppose that it is refocused as an over-arching question:

What are the current perceptions of performance management of school staff?

This is the question that defines the claim to knowledge the enquiry is intended to make when the first stage of the research is done, and hopefully will lead to a more focused enquiry that endeavours to move the school forward. It is not a research question in a technical sense because it does not set the agenda for data collection and analysis. The end-point of this stage of the research is likely to be a picture-drawing case study.

Stage 2: Asking research questions

Research questions drive enquiry. They should be formulated in a way that:

- sets the immediate agenda for research
- establishes how data are to be collected
- limits the boundaries of space and time within which it will operate
- facilitates the drawing up of ethical guidelines and
- suggests how analysis can start.

Thus, in terms of the above example, these might be posed as research questions:

- What documents have come into school that influence staff perceptions? (Collect documents and news cuttings.)
- What is the understanding and expectation of each member of the school management team (SMT) of performance management? (Conduct 10-minute interviews based on four main questions.)
- What is the understanding and expectation of a 10 per cent sample of non-SMT teaching staff of performance management? (Conduct 10-minute interviews based on the same four main questions.)

It will next be necessary, of course, to decide what the 'four main questions' are. Interview time is limited in recognition of the fact that everybody concerned is very busy and may well see the conduct of this research as unnecessary.

Stage 3: Drawing up ethical guidelines

Parallel to devising research questions should be the drawing up of ethical guidelines for the project (see also Chapter 7 of this volume). In the above example, the researcher and head (as senior member of the school) may agree the following guidelines:

- Interviews will not be digitally recorded but notes will be made and written up as brief reports. These will be shown to the interviewees as soon as possible after the events and will only be included in the *case record* in a form agreed by the interviewees, and with pseudonyms. Inclusion in the 'case record' (see below) will mean that the researcher may cite the evidence in the case report.

- Any *case reports* will require the agreement of the headteacher before being made available to school staff.

- Any *case reports* will not be published outside the school unless permission is given by the headteacher and chair of governors.

Stage 4: Collecting and storing data

Case study research has no unique methods of data collection or of analysis. Perhaps it is worth stating two rules which, although superficially obvious, are ones that from time to time we all fail to observe. First, be systematic in recording data by, for example, noting date and time and place of collection, and keeping back-up files. Second, do not collect more data than you have the time and energy to analyse. If possible, it is best to analyse data as it arises, rather than waiting until all is collected.

As part of a systematic approach, it can be valuable to number each piece of data as it is stored, for ease of future reference. For example, each interview report may be given a reference number, with decimal points for answers to each of the key questions. (See also Chapter 25 for further discussion on the handling and storage of data.)

I commend the following terminology for data storage and data processing:

- The *archive* is the total collection of rough notes, tidied-up notes and draft reports. It needs a running index and probably resides in computer files, cardboard boxes or the drawer of a filing cabinet. Ideally, a date for its destruction (to protect confidentiality) is part of the ethical statement.

- The *case record* includes agreed interview transcripts and agreed observation reports, the final versions of analytical statements, the interpretive writings and the day-by-day journal of the research, and other documents. These are the papers, polished in format, that will eventually be approved for potential public access, but which are likely to be too voluminous for the sustained attention of all but the most dedicated reader. They are the researcher's source for the writing of the case report and are likely to be stored electronically for as long as the researcher chooses.

- The *case report* – the end-point (perhaps one of several) of the case study – is written in one of the formats described earlier, drawing on the case record and citing it systematically as the source of data. A website is a good place to make it generally available – provided this has been agreed by those involved.

One essential feature of ethical research is the application of a system for ensuring that in terms of data taken from people, only those data which have been agreed in terms of the ethical guidelines are transferred from the archive to the case record.

The idea of *annotations* to data as they are stored can be helpful. Ideas often begin to develop during data handling and it is worthwhile having a systematic procedure for recording these changes – perhaps by using a different font on the computer. (See also Chapter 25 for a discussion of annotating qualitative data.)

It is helpful to keep on the computer a *day-by-day journal* of the researcher's activities – with entries showing who was seen, when, where and why, and recording when analytical work was done, etc. Unless you have a brilliant memory, this is invaluable for checking on what has been done and monitoring progress.

Stage 5: Generating and testing analytical statements

Case study work usually produces a great deal of data and analysis is needed to condense everything collected into meaningful statements. These analytical statements need to be firmly based on the data and indeed may suggest the need for more specific data to be collected.

For example, a concise answer to the research question:

What is the understanding and expectation of a 10 per cent sample of non-SMT teaching staff of performance management?

will require careful re-reading of the interview notes, the formulation of draft statements (that is to say, hypotheses) and the systematic testing of these (and amendment where necessary) against the data. The outcome should be one or more statements which are in accord with the data.

When this has been done for the other research questions, it may be appropriate to look for deeper analytical statements. They will arise from reading and reflecting on the first round of statements, and going back to the data: they may be stimulated by the annotations that have been made. For example, it could be that this analytical statement is posited:

In this school, the less staff know about how performance management will operate, the stronger are their objections to it.

The result of testing analytical statements is that some of them stand and some need modifying, while others lack verity and are rejected. Analysis and data testing is an iterative process which continues until the researcher feels confident that the analytical statements he/she produces are trustworthy.

It is quite possible that the first round of enquiry will stop at this point and the central purpose of the research be refocused. Thus, if the analytical statement above is thought to be trustworthy, the next move should be a management imperative, such as:

Spend a training day briefing everybody about management performance.

In a large school, this might be a useful outcome from a research case study – but we might hope that not too much time has been invested in producing it. What would be much more deserving of time would be a case study investigation into how performance management could enhance student achievements – an enquiry that might need research on a departmental basis.

Stage 6: Interpreting or explaining the analytical statements

This is where 'How?' and 'Why?' questions are brought to bear on the analytical statements in an attempt to provide understanding of the way things are. Interpretations tend to be associated with particular individuals or groups of people, while explanations tend to be attempts at expressing cause-and-effect relationships, within the boundary of the study.

Stage 7: Deciding on the outcome and writing the case report (publishing)

Before deciding that work on a case study is finished, it is worth getting a colleague, as a critical friend, to conduct an audit; in other words, ask your colleague to read through the data and its analysis and judge whether your understanding of what has been found is reasonable.

It may be that publication amounts to no more than distributing a few sheets of report reproduced on a photocopier, or speaking about the case at a staff meeting. If your research has wider implications, it may be appropriate to put it up on the school or college website; in this event it may be possible to link the case report in the form of a narrative story or descriptive picture with a fuzzy prediction of what may be found elsewhere. (For further discussion of dissemination, see Chapter 26.)

Tests of probity

It is important for any form of research to be subject to tests of probity. In terms of the ethics of respect for truth and respect for persons, I find the 12 tests listed in Figure 11.4 helpful.

Key points

Case study research into issues of educational leadership and management is vitally needed today because of the intense political scrutiny to which educational leaders are subjected. For example, we need studies that highlight the impossible: cases where, however good the leader is, other factors prevent the national 'expected' level of achievement being reached (and so where sacking the leader is both unjust and a stupid waste). We need case studies of good practice and bad, of the competent and the mediocre – not simply of the story-telling or picture-drawing kind, but theory-seeking/theory-testing studies which try to tease out why a situation is good, bad or mediocre. This is the contribution case study can make to educational leadership, which surveys cannot touch.

Tests of trustworthiness

- Has there been prolonged engagement with data sources?
- Has there been persistent observation of emerging issues?
- Have data been adequately checked with their sources?
- Has there been sufficient triangulation of data leading to analytical statements?
- Has the working hypothesis, or evaluation, or emerging story been systematically tested against the analytical statements?
- Has a critical friend tried to challenge your findings thoroughly?
- Is the account of the research sufficiently detailed to give the reader confidence?
- Does the case record provide an adequate audit trail?

Tests of respect for persons

- Initially has permission been given to you by an appropriate manager to conduct the research in terms of the identification of an issue, problem or hypothesis, in this particular setting?
- What arrangements have been agreed for transferring the ownership of the record of utterances and actions to the researcher, thus enabling the latter to use them in compiling the case record?
- What arrangements have been agreed for either identifying or concealing the contributing individuals and the particular setting of the research in the case report?
- What arrangements have been agreed for giving permission to publish the case report and in what form?

Figure 11.4   Tests of probity in case study research

Questions and reflections

1 Why undertake case study? What special phenomenon are you trying to investigate?

2 How will you design your study to capture *interesting* aspects of the case?

3 How will you disseminate your findings whilst retaining confidentiality?

Further recommended reading

Foremost, I recommend reading your own field notes, in order to create intelligent analytical statements. But if you need more help, try the following :

Bassey, M. (1999) *Case Study Research in Educational Settings*. Buckingham: Open University Press.

This covers in greater depth the ideas expressed in this chapter and gives more examples of case study writing.

Simons, H. (2009) *Case Study Research in Practice*. London: Sage.

This is a comprehensive, well-written account by a very experienced case study researcher which sometimes puts a different slant on issues to mine. In the first three weeks of your research, read one of her 20 Case Study Memos just before you go to bed – or first thing in the morning if they keep you awake. They are excellent!

Envoi

Get to it. Good luck.

References

Bassey, M. (1999) *Case Study Research in Educational Settings*. Buckingham: Open University Press.

Bassey, M. (2001) A solution to the problem of generalisation in educational research: fuzzy prediction. *Oxford Review of Education* 27(1): 5–22.

Denzin, N.K. and Lincoln, Y.S. (eds) (2000) *Handbook of Qualitative Research* (2nd edn). London: Sage.

Gillham, B. (2000) *Case Study Research Methods*. London: Continuum.

Hamel, J. with Dufour S. and Fortin D. (1993) *Case Study Methods*. Thousand Oaks, CA: Sage.

Hancock, D.R. and Algozzine, B. (2006) *Doing Case Study Research*. New York: Teachers College Press.

Kosko, B. (1994) *Fuzzy Thinking: The New Science of Fuzzy Logic*. London: HarperCollins.

Lincoln, Y.S. and Guba, E.G. (1985) *Naturalistic Inquiry*. Newbury Park, CA: Sage.

MacGilchrist, B., Mortimore, P., Savage, J. and Beresford, C. (1997) The impact of development planning in primary schools, in Preedy, M., Glatter, R. and Levačić, R. (eds) *Educational Management: Strategy, Quality and Resources*. Buckingham: Open University Press.

McMahon, A., Bishop, J., Carroll, R. and McInally, B. (1997) Fair Furlong Primary School, in Harris, A., Bennett, N. and Preedy, M. (eds) *Organisational Effectiveness and Improvement in Education*. Buckingham: Open University Press.

Parlett, M. and Hamilton, D. (1977) Evaluation as illumination: a new approach to the study of innovatory programmes, in Hamilton, D., Jenkins, D., King, C., McDonald, B. and Parlett, M. (eds) *Beyond the Numbers Game: A Reader in Educational Evaluation*. London: Macmillan.

Simons, H. (2009) *Case Study Research in Practice*. London: Sage.

Stake, R.E. (1995) *The Art of Case Study Research*. London: Sage.

Stake, R.E. (2000) Case studies, in Denzin, N.K. and Lincoln, Y.S. (eds) *Handbook of Qualitative Research* (2nd edn). London: Sage.

Yin, R.K. (1994) *Case Study Research*. London: Sage.

Yin, R.K. (2003) *Case Study Research* (3rd edn). London: Sage.

CHAPTER 12

Practitioner Research

Rachel Lofthouse, Elaine Hall and Kate Wall

Chapter objectives

In this chapter, we explore the possibilities for practitioners researching their educational leadership practice and contexts. We will:

- Give introductory guidance about the use of approaches – particularly action research – which are often used to support enquiry processes.
- Focus on the ways in which interrogation of data that are routinely collected in schools can be combined with traditional and innovative research methods.
- Look at the way in which practitioner research can be an integral part of school improvement in its broadest sense.

We will make clear the underlying assumptions of practitioner enquiry and what the implications of engaging in enquiry are for individual teachers, groups of colleagues and institutions. Since practitioner enquiry can be carried out by an individual working alone, by a small team of mutually supportive colleagues or through a systematic institution-wide approach to professional learning and the improvement of standards, we have intentionally focused on these three levels (Figure 12.1). We believe that an institutional approach incorporating practitioner enquiry at these levels will raise standards of teaching and learning and generate the best possible outcomes for learners in a learning community where the development and retention of staff and the sharing of professional expertise are the bedrock of the process.

Practitioner enquiry in school improvement and developing learning communities

In most political systems, whether they are local or national, there is a drive for school improvement. The improvement agenda can become all-consuming,

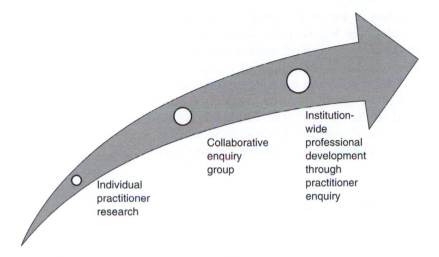

Figure 12.1 Different levels of practitioner enquiry

particularly when it involves meeting challenging targets on many fronts. For example, a school may be focusing on improving attendance levels, persuading pupils to engage in healthy lifestyles, altering the curriculum to enable greater engagement, or working towards improved literacy outcomes in response to national targets in order to improve the country's Programme for International Student Assessment (PISA) rankings. In many countries, the dominance of this culture of performativity leads to school leaders scanning the horizons for the next set of targets, while expecting their school staff to provide evidence that the current targets are being met. However, this outwardly focused environment may not be conducive to professional learning or sustained school improvement.

If, as demonstrated by Barber and Mourshed (2007), the significant factor in pupils' academic success is teacher quality, then it makes sense that gains in teachers' own learning and development are a critical component in raising pupils' achievement and attainment. This does not mean, however, that all professional development programmes have an impact on either teacher or pupil learning. It is important to question how teachers address their own or their organisation's development needs. From an English perspective, Pedder and MacBeath (2008) found that most teachers' continuing professional development was passive, not well situated in their work contexts and rarely collaborative or informed by research. This contrasts with Webster-Wright's (2009) concept of 'authentic professional learning', by which she suggests a 'focus on [teacher] learning with a shift of emphasis from passive development to active learning' (p. 713). Practitioner enquiry offers one model of active teacher engagement in their own learning through which organisational improvement may be effected. It offers opportunities for professional learning which can be 'congruent with professionals' authentic experiences of learning yet cognisant of the realities of the workplace with respect to professional responsibilities' (Webster-Wright, 2009: 727). Timperley (2009) identified the characteristics of the professional learning environment likely to impact on student outcomes. She found evidence that teachers need recurring opportunities to develop a working understanding of the integration of knowledge and skills related to teaching and learning, and multiple opportunities to apply this in practice. In addition, she found evidence of positive outcomes when the professional learning experience forced teachers to question their beliefs and challenge their assumptions. Practitioner enquiry, especially when supported in collaborative groups, in which teachers can process their new learning in a professional community, can provide such conditions.

What is practitioner research?

Many different terms are used to describe the process of people looking in a systematic way at what is going on in their practice. This first section will provide a way of talking about this process that clarifies some of the theoretical complexity so that we can understand what the parameters of practitioner research are in action. We cannot do without the theoretical complexity (Elliott, 2001; Stenhouse, 1981), since it provides a way of taking our individual experience of engaging *in* research and offers a common language so that we can engage *with* others' research (Hall, 2009). This reflexive process of engaging in and with research allows us to take part in the debate about the nature of learning and our role within it. As we explore this debate, we have found it helpful to engage with the vocabulary of the nature of knowledge and to recognise the potential impact of underpinning ideas on the choices we make in research. The pathway we describe is only one of many potential approaches. We begin with beliefs about how things are – *ontology* – and what can be known about them – *epistemology*. (For a full discussion of these concepts, see Chapter 2.) The underpinning ideas of practitioner research are that we have an impact on the

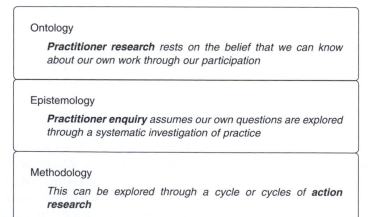

Figure 12.2   Knowledge and approaches to knowledge in practitioner research

world around us that can be observed in a number of ways; that the actions we take are intentional and that we can explore the effects of our actions against those intentions as a way of judging their success or failure (see Figure 12.2).

So what can be known? We recognise that the systems within which we act are complex and the relationships between cause and effect are difficult to track, but fundamentally we believe that we need to explore these relationships, so that the value of our practice is maximised. We do not expect to 'solve' the big questions of learning and teaching, but we do expect to collect data that are meaningful to us and to those who share our contexts, data that will give us the warrant to continue with current practice, to scrap something that no longer works or to introduce something new (Dewey, 1922/2008). As already stated, evidence from large-scale meta-analysis suggests that what teachers do is a significant factor in learner outcomes (Hattie, 2009), so we have an ethical duty, at the very least, to reflect on our practice (Schön, 1983). How much more effective could we be if that reflection were directed, systematic and communicated to our colleagues (Stenhouse, 1983)?

The development of the practitioner enquiry is fundamentally shaped by three key ethical considerations:

- The allegiance of the practitioner to the current cohort of learners, their needs and priorities.
- The belief of the reflective practitioner that practice can always be improved.
- The recognition of the strategic priorities of the institution.

In a practitioner enquiry, therefore, we 'own' the question because it has been generated by what is currently going on in our practice which is causing some sort of disturbance: something is not working or is working better than we had expected; there is something that we don't understand that bothers or excites us; something new has entered our context (a new policy, a shift in curriculum, a learner with a particular set of needs). These ideas or hunches can be expressed in a number of ways (see Figure 12.3) and can relate to student learning, professional learning or organisational learning.

> *I would like to improve ...*
>
> *I want to change ... because*
>
> *I am perplexed by ...*
>
> *Some people are unhappy about ...*
>
> *I'm really curious about ...*
>
> *I want to learn more about ...*
>
> *An idea I would like to try out in my class is ...*
>
> *I think ... would really make a difference to ...*

Figure 12.3   Some starting points

The ownership of the enquiry however is shared: we do not undertake an enquiry on a whim but because the problem is right there in front of us, driven by our context and our learners and intimately bound up with their needs. This means that we have a series of ethical commitments bound up in the *purpose* of our research (Groundwater-Smith and Mockler, 2007). If we are clear about what it is that we are trying to achieve, both in our own minds and in how we talk to others, then the approaches that we use, the way in which we recruit people to our study and the ways in which we collect data will be constantly under ethical scrutiny. This might mean that some of our 'normal practice' is questioned, perhaps because we have got into the habit of assuming that our students consent to filling in questionnaires or that our colleagues are happy to provide face-to-face feedback, even though we might be in a position of authority. Although these are uncomfortable reflections, they are another benefit of the enquiry process, which encourages us to examine the taken-for-granted as well as the new. (Chapter 7 of this volume offers a detailed consideration of the ethical issues facing the practitioner-researcher.)

This clarity of purpose will help us to share findings with colleagues, within and potentially beyond the institution; if we find that something does (or equally crucially does *not*) seem to work in the classroom, then that is useful information for other practitioners, whether they work in the classroom next door, in another department, or, given the potential of the Internet to disseminate our work, in another school or indeed in another country.

Action research

If practitioner enquiry is considered to be an epistemology, then a common associated approach (or *methodology*) – though by no means the only one available – is that of action research, in which we can gather data or make an intervention based on an enquiry question, using a range of tools to collect information, then evaluate the evidence gathered and generate strategies for action or modified enquiry questions for another cycle (Figure 12.4). The action research cycle is one that fits into leaders' and teachers' accustomed professional practice, since the process of 'plan, do, review' is at the bedrock of the routines and development of curriculum, pedagogy and assessment. What distinguishes action research from normal practice is the intentional use of a range of tools that will give the teacher data that would not usually arise from teaching and learning or that would not be analysed in a systematic way. Action research is frequently criticised for being less reliable and systematic than other research approaches. However, this is not an inherent problem with action research but arises from the tendency of action researchers to be less than clear about how they have chosen and used their research tools and how the elements being enquired into have been separated out from the many factors in each classroom or institution.

The detail of the methods within action research is very much the choice of the individual practitioner, since they need to answer a particular enquiry

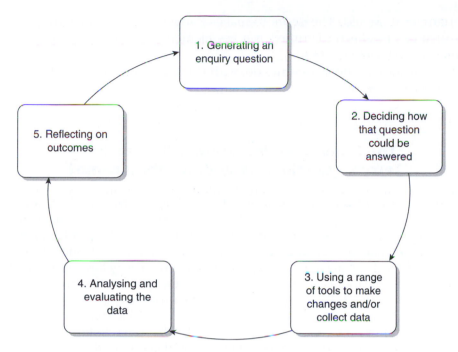

Figure 12.4 Elements of the action research cycle

question in a particular context. There is no assumption that each action research will necessarily follow a particular qualitative or quantitative pattern, though we note that in our professional lives we both count things and tell stories about them, which implies that we make meaning through a combination of both elements and that reliable and valid research might therefore be supported by a range of data. In this chapter, we have drawn on our work with leaders and teachers in schools, colleges and universities to describe what practitioner research actually looks like on the ground, rather than to engage with the debate around what it 'should' be like.

Ways to undertake a practitioner enquiry

In this next section, we focus on the key lessons we have drawn from our work with practitioners undertaking research in their own contexts: that the enquiry question must fit the context; that the process of clarifying the question helps us to choose how to answer it, and that there are a range of approaches to gathering data.

Generating and developing an enquiry question

Most practitioner enquiries start with a hunch about how something new or improved could be incorporated into practice or a sense that something is not working as it should. The desire to make changes, the pull towards 'positive dissonance', has been identified as a key element that keeps teachers in the profession (Day et al., 2006).

We will start, as most enquiries do, with the germ of an idea and the example of Terry's question.

The Individual Practitioner Researcher – Terry's question: 'Why don't they come?'

Terry is Head of Mathematics in a large 11–18 school, in the outskirts of a city. Some of the families are relatively affluent, some more disadvantaged and the cultural and ethnic mix of the area is diverse. Twice a year, Terry's school holds Parent Consultation Evenings, with the aim of passing backwards and forwards information about student progress. These evenings are very busy for the staff and it is a couple of years before Terry realises that he is only getting to see some of the parents. The same families turn up each time, engaged, interested, sometimes demanding. Where are the others? One of his more experienced colleagues offers the view that it is the parents who 'can't be bothered' who don't come, or the parents whose children aren't doing so well. Terry is aware that there is research that shows that parents can make a difference to their children's schooling by showing support and interest, but he also knows that he's never met the parents of some of his real 'high fliers'. Terry isn't sure, but he'd like to find out lots of things: who does and doesn't come, whether this is connected to children's performance in mathematics and school in general, the reasons why parents don't come, and whether anything could be done to change it.

As practitioner-researchers, our starting point needs to be turned into a question that is answerable and manageable (Baumfield et al., 2008). Broadly, there are two types of enquiry question: 'What's going on?' and 'What happens if?' A practitioner-enquirer needs to decide whether they are investigating an existing phenomenon (what's going on) or whether they are going to instigate a change and explore the impact (what happens if). Either type of question is equally valid, but the distinction is important as it will influence the kind of answer that you are looking for and therefore the process that is undertaken. Once this decision is made, then the next stage is to think about the aspect of practice that you are interested in and how it could be measured or observed (the evidence you might collect). This information can then be combined to form a question. This process is exemplified in Figure 12.5, which looks at Terry's enquiry question.

Enquiry questions in real life

When researching real life, we have to accept complexity. It is not possible to transfer a teacher and class into a research laboratory to create experimental

Why do some parents come to meetings and some don't?	
What's going on?	**What happens if?**
Aspect of practice	Who came or didn't come to the last meeting?	I target those parents I've never seen by writing or emailing them directly?
	What do I already know about their children's performance?	What information would they like from me about their children?
Measure	Attendance lists and class lists	Response rate to letters and/or emails
	School held data on attendance, behaviour and attainment	Analysis of the responses and the reactions to what I feed back
Enquiry question	Is there any connection between attending parent consultation evenings and how students do in my school?	Can I improve communication with the parents who don't come to consultation evenings?

Figure 12.5 Moving to an enquiry question

conditions: even if we could, this would not iron out the complexities of what each individual brings to the lab from their previous experiences. With each starting point, there is likely to be a range of possible factors that might be explored and a number of measures that could be used. The place that any enquiry starts from can only be a best guess: there are always unexpected and unknown factors which impact on the situation we are exploring. This means that the enquirer needs to work through a number of choices in deciding on the most appropriate question for their study. These choices depend on what makes most sense (to the individual researcher and to the context), what is practical within the organisation (some changes might be impossible to measure and some data might be overwhelming to collect) and who the audience is for the research (will our audience be more convinced by stories, graphs or a combination of the two?). There is no right or wrong pathway through this process, but we must be clear about the decisions we have made and why. A colleague reading our work needs to understand the link we have made between the outcome and the measure, so we need to present our thinking in a transparent way, acknowledging the variables that might be an influence (see Figure 12.6).

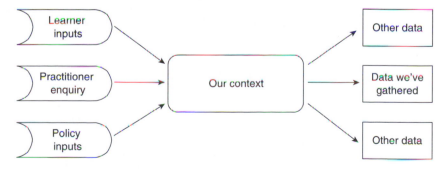

Figure 12.6 Acknowledging the complexity of data in schools and colleges

Once we arrive at a question for enquiry, an essential stage is checking how realistic the question is. First, we need to consider the manageability: thinking about the constraints of context and the number of different priorities and how an enquiry fits in with these wider responsibilities. Practitioner-enquirers tend to be busy people and so adding research into their workload is a burden. Therefore, ensuring that a question has good overlap with an enquirer's normal duties is imperative. To increase manageability, it helps if the research and teaching and learning processes are not compartmentalised: the question needs to be embedded in practice and not be additional. We need to think creatively about how our enquiry can fulfil multiple agendas and different aspects of our responsibilities. So, for example, a school development aim may be to improve the quantity and quality of boys' writing. While we are interested in ability grouping, these aspects could combine to become a question: does within-class ability grouping impact on boys' attainment in writing? If both the teacher and the organisation have an interest in the outcomes, this helps to support the enquiry, since the teacher remains motivated to explore and the organisation keen to support the enquiry process.

An aspect of manageability is the precision of the research question. This means wording the question in a way that is unambiguous (for example, instead of saying *'improve attainment'*, use *'raise marks from a mean of 65–80 per cent in end-of-module tests'*) and reasonable (is an increase of 65–80 per cent realistic, either within the timescale set or given other learners' attainment in the same test?). We also need to ensure that we are only asking one question, or at least that we have unpacked the elements within our question. This is illustrated with another example of an enquiry question in Figure 12.7.

Choosing the tools to answer an enquiry question

Once the question is clear, then we need to think about the types of evidence we are going to be collecting to answer it. It is helpful to think quite flexibly

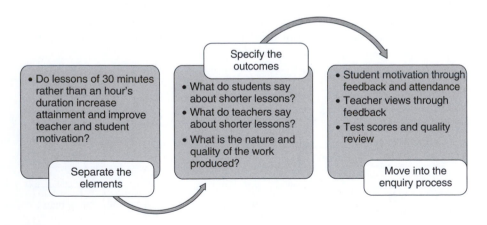

Figure 12.7 Unpacking the elements in an enquiry question

about what might constitute data within a practitioner enquiry, in that it needs to be pragmatic to fit around other aspects of our work. One of the key practical messages is that ideally evidence should be collected, where possible, to fulfil more than one purpose. This helps with the manageability of the research process. So, if the register is being taken at the start of a class every session in a post-compulsory college, then the register data can be used in your research to explore whether student motivation to turn up to new and improved lessons has manifested in better attendance. If learners are completing logs or reflective diaries to aid their reflection across subjects, then you can ask them if it is OK to look through and identify whether their perceptions mirror or challenge your own.

Anything we might collect can fall into one of the following four categories (Baumfield et al., 2008):

Data collected normally in schools

Schools are data-rich environments: information is being collected every day at individual pupil/teacher level, at class level and at school level all the time: for example, special needs records, attendance, behaviour records and test scores. This type of data represents large and consistent data sets and does not add much to our workload to collect it.

Data collection that can be incorporated into the school routine

In that accountability and self-evaluation are current themes within education, there are various techniques which can be built into this framework and can be part of our research while also fulfilling other elements of a teacher's job. For example, teachers' peer observations can be focused around research-based observation schedules and the student council and community organisations can be used to survey opinion of the student body, parents and families.

Data arising from teaching and learning activities

The products of teaching and learning can be research data: for example, work samples and learning logs can be used to tell the story of an individual's or a group's learning over a term or school year. The best outcome is where we can find a tool that gives us effective feedback in the classroom – improving our practice – as well as contributing to our enquiry question.

Traditional research methods

This category includes interviews, questionnaires and observations, all of which are extremely useful in both a quantitative or qualitative research strategy. These are necessary when the data and tools that naturally occur in our institutions fall short of answering our enquiry questions.

Maria's example that follows is a good example of a project that is dependent upon the energy and motivation of an individual, one that might, on the surface, seem less easy to explore using naturally occurring data.

> ### The Collaborative Enquiry Group – Maria's question: 'How can I motivate my colleagues to talk to one another about learning?'
>
> Maria is the Head of the English Department in a vocational college, serving learners from 14 years old through adulthood. Her staff provide basic education to adults, literacy support for students taking vocational courses, and literature courses for public examinations for young people and adults up to university-access level. The range of experience and practice is very wide and she is aware that there are barriers between the staff, some of which are based on the status of their courses and some on the different terms of employment that they have. Maria's personal performance target is to re-organise and re-vitalise the continuing professional development programme for her team. Currently, certain generic training experiences in classroom management, assessment and the use of new technology are offered and the feedback from staff is lukewarm. Having just completed her own Masters degree with a practitioner enquiry focus, she is enthusiastic about the potential for enquiry to change the culture of the department, both in terms of allowing teachers to focus on and improve their own practice but also to get them talking to one another about their own and their students' learning. Maria's long-term goal is to create an enquiry group but she realises that she first needs to explore why staff are not engaging fully in professional learning opportunities. She hopes that she can then work on supporting her colleagues in becoming comfortable with talking together about effective learning.

Maria's enquiry therefore uses the 'What's going on round here?' approach for her first cycle and 'What happens if I?' for her second (see Figure 12.8). The findings from the first cycle will influence her choice of intervention for the second cycle.

Practitioner-researchers need to be pragmatic in matching research questions with the evidence that is available and easy to collect. At the same time, we recognise that learning and teaching are complex and interrelated and that cause and effect are hard to isolate. Therefore, a multi-method approach can be helpful with different kinds of tools and data working together to answer a research question and different perspectives strengthening, or problematising the 'case'. In particular, using a combination of qualitative and quantitative data is useful; as a broad rule, the quantitative data tells you what happened and to what extent, while the qualitative data explores why it happened and how it was perceived by everyone involved. It is useful to consider different perspectives on the same phenomenon (there is little point implementing something the students love if the teachers cannot stand it) and to think about the difference that might be apparent between declarative beliefs and behaviours (the interviews with students might be very positive, but they are not turning up to the lesson which indicates they are not so keen).

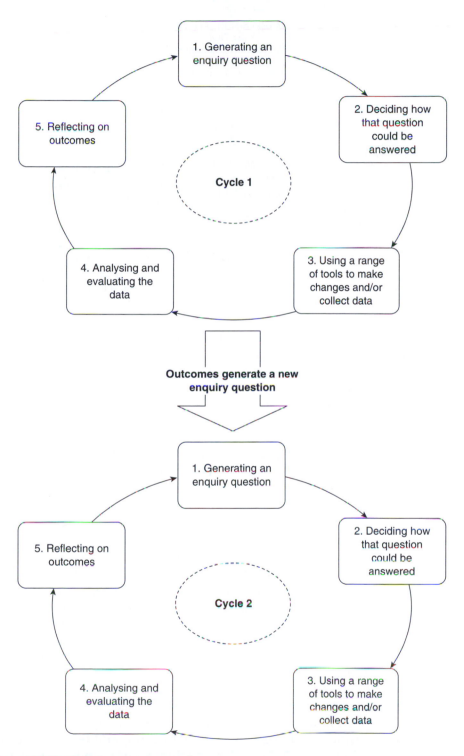

Figure 12.8 Enquiry over two cycles

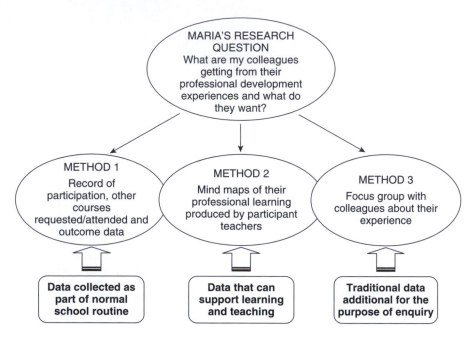

Figure 12.9 How multiple methods can address a research question

(adapted from Baumfield et al., 2008: Maria's cycle 1)

At first, collecting more than one kind of data can seem demanding, but when we keep in mind the categories of research evidence outlined above then this can become more manageable. In many of our practitioner research projects, people have found it useful to collect at least three different types of data (Figure 12.9), two of which are either collected anyway in school, or support teaching and learning by giving immediate feedback to the teacher.

Only one data collection method comes from outside practice, perhaps a more traditional research method like an interview or questionnaire. Maria's research question is addressed using three different methods; however the first is simply the normal record-keeping that goes on in the college (which tells Maria about participation and impact), the second is the natural product of the teachers' learning and completed as part of their own record-keeping (these mind maps tell Maria about the nature and quality of teachers' current experience) and only the third is additional (needed in order for Maria to find out more about the 'why'). The focus group will therefore need to be carefully added into the research plan and Maria will need to consider how to incentivise colleagues to participate.

In this example, Maria's first practitioner enquiry cycle supported her hunch about practitioner enquiry: the courses her colleagues have attended have been highly technical and curriculum-focused but their mind maps reveal a desire to explore pedagogy and the interactions and relationships in their classrooms. The focus group confirmed her analysis and brought forward their explanations for this mismatch: financial and policy pressures and, perhaps most crucially, their reluctance to try out enquiries without the explicit permission to experiment from the college management. Reflecting on this, Maria decides that the only way she can show her colleagues that permission is by being a co-enquirer. She therefore sets up her second cycle with the question 'How can a group of colleagues provide support and challenge for each other's enquiries?' This is illustrated in Figure 12.10.

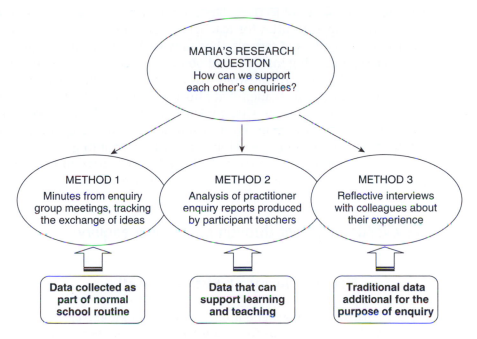

Figure 12.10 How multiple methods can address a research question

(adapted from Baumfield et al. 2008: Maria's cycle 2)

Effective leadership is critical in the development and sustainability of such a learning community, but as Maria's example demonstrates, as a leader, active participation rather than simply managing others may be our most useful role. School leaders who model and engage in practitioner research reinforce the learning culture and establish that the organisation is open to the outcomes of enquiries.

Practitioner enquiry as a collaborative activity

Maria's enquiry trajectory exemplifies how practitioner enquiry can be incorporated into professional learning activities in an organisation, but completing enquiry as part of a supportive network is almost as important as undertaking the enquiry process itself. It is important that the findings from enquiry are shared, i.e. made public (Stenhouse, 1981). Engaging in a community where the process and outcomes of enquiry are the focus of conversations facilitates an ethos of reflective and strategic thinking (Moseley et al., 2005) which will support school improvement. This leads us to our final example of practitioner enquiry that explores an institution-wide initiative.

An educational leader or leadership team will tend to promote, permit or limit the opportunities for teachers to undertake practitioner enquiry, and it is worth noting that this might be either deliberate or inadvertent. Where there is a deliberate facilitation of practitioner research, it is common for there to be at least two stated objectives. First, the leadership team will intend to provide enhanced opportunities for teachers to develop their own professional knowledge and skills, and second, they may wish to focus the enquiries to support progress in meeting institutional objectives, usually closely related to specific learner outcomes. To illustrate these principles, we draw on the experiences of teachers at The Academy at Shotton Hall School which serves a relatively deprived community in County Durham, England. Lesley Powell, the headteacher, strategically reviewed and remodelled the programme for teachers' continuing professional development (CPD), enabling more than 20 teachers to join a university-accredited Master's level programme which was taught at the school and was based on practitioner research.

Institution-wide development through practitioner enquiry

The Academy at Shotton Hall

'It is very clear that simply throwing out huge amounts of information on one CPD day to very busy staff is a recipe for failure. Like other professionals teachers need time to think, practise, reflect and share ideas if they are to embed change' (Powell cited in McGrane and Lofthouse, 2010: 158). This was the starting point for the development of Masters accredited practitioner enquiry as an approach to school improvement. An initial focus on developing teaching thinking and an enquiry-based curriculum were selected to correspond with the recognised needs of both pupils and staff, to support the development of independent learning skills. There was a strong intention that the action research group would naturally form a community of enquiry of a critical mass of staff, which would develop a shared enquiry focus and could reach out to the wider school community beyond the sessions. The teachers undertook individual enquiries which related to their own teaching within the institution-wide context. The enquiries have provided an opportunity for teachers to discuss teaching and learning in an environment in which the questioning of established practices is encouraged, and have allowed initiatives to be developed and tested across subject areas and year groups. Teachers have become more comfortable dealing with dissonance, challenging assumptions and research evidence, and draw on a range of influences to direct and reflect upon their professional learning. Practitioner enquiry focused on the needs of the students has supported the school in moving from 'Satisfactory' to 'Outstanding' in almost every category in three years. Some of the participating teachers now lead teaching and learning development work for the wider staff body. Growing staff confidence has led them to contribute articles and case studies to various publications, and the school will be working towards new national status which will allow it to take a lead role in initial and continuing professional development.

In developing practitioner enquiry as a collaborative approach, it is possible to bring together both like-minded colleagues and partners with different perspectives; as such a community of critical friends can be formed. Within this community, the enquiry focus allows teachers to use their professional curiosity to enter into dialogue with others and seek out expertise. Ideally, such conditions will trigger experimentation and innovation which is then monitored and assessed using rich data sources and multiple perspectives. The collaborative group can ensure that the teachers' activities are channelled through a disciplined, robust and shared enquiry process.

Key points

The process of practitioner enquiry provides opportunities for experimentation, self-evaluation and reflection that retain a focus on pupil outcomes. However, leadership, working at all levels, is important in creating a professional learning environment in which these aspects of practice are supported and promoted in order for developments in teaching and learning to become embedded and sustained. In the absence of such a culture, the changes that have been desired and invested in all too easily 'decay and disappear' (James and McCormick, 2009: 982).

School leaders may model practitioner enquiry, by involving themselves in teacher development programmes that are based on enquiry cycles, or even by using practitioner enquiry as a means to develop leadership practices in the school. In doing so, they provide a warrant for change and development which can filter through the teaching community.

Where practitioner enquiry is located within both school and individual development priorities, and as such where the ownership of the enquiry is not removed from the participants, the shared intent can be a strong motivational factor in helping to sustain professional learning through several cycles of activity.

Schools that adopt formal enquiry approaches to development often do so in a culture in which collaborative practice, coaching and self-evaluation are seen as formative and progressive rather than as part of performance-based routines. This challenges many of the adopted practices and cultures in schools, and our experience from a range of projects indicates that enquiry-based cultures can be difficult to sustain when key teaching or leadership staff leave the school, or when external pressures cause a sudden shift in emphasis for school improvement.

School-based practitioner research can provide a new momentum for school leadership, drawing out the motivations, expertise and professionalism of the school community, providing a real opportunity for long-term school improvement, succession planning and a broader appreciation of the achievements of learners.

Questions and reflections

1   How does practitioner enquiry fit into a wider process of school improvement?

2   Practitioner enquiry is all about researching pedagogic practice – how can the competing demands of research and practice be best managed?

3   What structures and opportunities already exist for collaborative CPD, and could these be developed to incorporate practitioner enquiry?

Recommended further reading

Baumfield, V., Hall, E. and Wall, K. (2008) *Action Research in the Classroom*. London: Sage.

This is a good overview of the enquiry process with a lot of practical examples.

Groundwater-Smith, S. and Mockler, N. (2007) Ethics in practitioner research: an issue of quality. *Research Papers in Education* 22(2): 199–211.

This paper sets out the key ethical questions which underpin good quality research.

Hall, E. (2009) Engaging in and engaging with research: teacher enquiry and development. *Teachers and Teaching: Theory and Practice* 15(6): 669–82.

This paper explores the role of enquiry in professional practice. It unpicks the relationship between a practitioner who is engaged in the process of research and the teacher who is engaged with the research field: is one mutually exclusive of the other or is there a facilitatory interaction?

Stenhouse, L. (1981) What counts as research? *British Journal of Education Studies* 29(2): 103–14.

This paper gives a compelling argument for the role of the teacher in research.

Timperley, H. (2009) *Teacher Professional Learning and Development* (Educational Practices Series). Available at: www.educationcounts.govt.nz/themes/BES

This report looks at the benefits and impacts of teachers' professional learning, including through enquiry.

References

Barber, M. and Mourshed, M. (2007) *How the Best Performing School Systems Come Out on Top*. McKinsey & Company. Available at: www.closingtheachievementgap.org/cs/ctag/download/resources/111/Barber_worlds_schools.pdf?x-r=pcfile_d

Baumfield, V., Hall, E. and Wall, K. (2008) *Action Research in the Classroom*. London: Sage.

Day, C., Stobart, G., Sammons, P. and Kington, A. (2006) Variants in the work and levels of teachers: relative and relational effectiveness. *Teachers and Teaching: Theory and Practice* 12: 169–92.

Dewey, J. (1922/2008) Education as Engineering. Reproduced in *Journal of Curriculum Studies* 41(1): 1–5.

Elliott, J. (2001) Making evidence-based practice educational. *British Education Research Journal* 27(5): 555–74.

Groundwater-Smith, S. and Mockler, N. (2007) Ethics in practitioner research: an issue of quality. *Research Papers in Education* 22(2):199–211.

Hall, E. (2009) Engaging in and engaging with research: teacher enquiry and development. *Teachers and Teaching: Theory and Practice* 15(6): 669–82.

Hattie, J. (2009) *Visible Learning: A Synthesis of Over 800 Meta-analyses Relating to Achievement*. London: Routledge.

James, M. and McCormick, R. (2009) Teachers learning how to learn. *Teaching and Teacher Education* 25(7): 973–82.

McGrane, J. and Lofthouse, R. (2010) *Developing Outstanding Teaching and Learning: Creating a Culture of Professional Development to Improve Outcomes*. Milton Keynes: Optimus Education.

Moseley, D. V., Baumfield, V., Elliott, J., Gregson, M., Higgins, S. R., Miller, J. and Newton, D.P. (2005) *Frameworks for Thinking: A Handbook for Teachers and Learners*. Cambridge: Cambridge University Press.

Pedder, D. and MacBeath, J. (2008) Organisational learning approaches to school leadership and management: teachers' values and perceptions of practice. *School Effectiveness and School Improvement* 19(2): 207–24.

Schön, D. (1983) *The Reflective Practitioner: How Professionals Think in Action*. London: Temple Smith.

Stenhouse, L. (1981) What counts as research? *British Journal of Education Studies* 29(2): 103–14.

Stenhouse, L. (1983) Research as a basis for teaching. Inaugural lecture from University of East Anglia, in Stenhouse, L. (ed.) *Authority, Education and Emancipation*. London: Heinemann.

Timperley, H. (2009) *Teacher Professional Learning and Development* (Educational Practices Series). Available at: www.educationcounts.govt.nz/themes/BES

Webster-Wright, A. (2009) Reframing professional development through understanding authentic professional learning. *Review of Educational Research* 79(2): 702–73.

CHAPTER 13

Grounded Theory Research

Clive Dimmock and Martha Lam

Chapter objectives

This chapter has two main objectives:

- To sketch a theoretical and methodological background to grounded theory (GT).
- To exemplify each stage of the systematic processes that a postgraduate or teacher would use in applying GT methodology, from initial problem identification to final outcome.

The chapter has two sections: the first is structured around a number of key questions relating to the theoretical background to GT. The second section follows the design features of a GT study (which are generic) through its stages and sequences from problem identification, literature review, data collection and analysis, trustworthiness, and finally, to findings and their transferability. Each of the key stages in the second section is exemplified by reference to an actual grounded theory doctoral thesis on how successful women academics managed their careers.

Theoretical background to grounded theory

What is grounded theory?

Grounded theory is a research approach and methodology, employing a combination of inductive and deductive methods, falling within the interpretive paradigm, relying on conventional qualitative methods of data collection, and a unique system of coding in data analysis. Creswell (2005: 396) defines it as a 'systematic, qualitative procedure used to generate a theory that explains, at a broad conceptual level, a process, an action, or interaction about a substantive topic'. He continues: 'this theory is a "process" theory – it explains an educational process of events, activities, actions, and interactions that occur over time. Also, grounded theorists proceed through systematic procedures of collecting data, identifying categories (or themes), connecting these categories, and forming a theory that explains the process' (Creswell, 2005: 396).

GT is distinct from other qualitative methods that collect primary empirical data, as revealed in this chapter. It is much more than a way of capturing how participants think, feel or behave; consequently it is not, as some mistakenly think, synonymous with empiricism. Rather, GT involves a discrete set of systematic and analytical methodological processes that mark it apart from other qualitative approaches (Creswell, 2007; 2009).

When is grounded theory appropriate to adopt?

As a methodology, GT is well suited to studies in educational leadership. This is because of its ability to offer a theory or explanation of complex interactive situations involving human beings in their natural or organisational settings, such as schools or universities. GT is particularly attractive in the following situations. First, it is an appropriate methodology when no previous existing theories exist to explain the problem under investigation. The theory so generated is new and grounded in the data that are collected – whether the context is a class, a school or a group of teachers or principals. Second, it is especially apt when a study involves a complex process, such as how a principal manages a group of troublesome teachers; or how teachers manage badly behaved students in their class (see for example, O'Donoghue and Chalmers, 2000). It is also suited to explaining leadership practices and actions in certain school or university events – such as how school leaders support professional learning communities or teacher professional development activities. A further example is the use of GT to study a group of individuals to see how they each managed their career development – as exemplified in the second section of this chapter. Third, a major purpose and outcome of GT is to generate a typology – in this case, of leaders, teachers or students. If the key aim of a study is to differentiate participants by categorising or forming a typology, then GT meets these aims admirably. Fourth, it is a helpful methodology for inexperienced qualitative researchers since it requires strict application of a systematic set of procedures for collecting and analysing data. Fifth, postgraduate students and teachers may see advantages in GT in enabling them to handle large amounts of qualitative data. This it does through the use of coding and abstraction; a code, concept or construct is an economic and efficient descriptor for an otherwise lengthy and complex set of data. In this respect too, it is a valid methodology for doctoral studies, which are normally expected to make a contribution to theory; in the case of GT, a new theory is generated. For the above reasons, GT demands strong cognitive skills of conceptualising and abstracting.

The purpose and outcome of GT is thus to build a theory about the phenomenon being studied. It is possible to build a theory about even the smallest group of teachers, students or school leaders, and the interactions between them. In framing the research, it is imperative for the researcher to ask – what is the problem of practice that I wish to understand, or manage? The next question to ask is – what are the aims and purposes of the study that derive from the problems of practice? And then – what are my research questions? By addressing these issues sequentially, the basis of the research design is already beginning to form.

In every case, the theory that results from a GT study can only strictly be applied within the confines of the sample chosen. Thus, if the sample is a particular class, or group of teachers or school leaders, then the theory is bounded or restricted to them. However, theoretical explanations and implications may be transferable to other classes, teachers or school leaders in similar situations.

What are the differences between three grounded theory designs?

There are three different types of GT designs, as recognised by Creswell (2005):

1 The *systematic* design – associated with Strauss and Corbin (1990), which is more structured and tends still to be the version of GT most favoured by research students, who need to get proposals accepted and studies completed within time frames; this type allows research questions, literature searches and heuristic frameworks to be considered before data collection.

2 The *emerging* design – associated with Glaser (1992) – who advocates a 'purer', more anthropological approach, where research questions emerge as the research is under way, and where no preconceived theories or frameworks are endorsed; the literature review is done after data collection.

3 The *constructivist* design – associated with Charmaz (2006), who argues that the more systematic GT procedures of Strauss and Corbin (1990) detract from GT and place the researcher in too powerful a position. Rather, Charmaz advocates more flexible guidelines for GT, while still keeping some of the conventional systematic principles, such as theoretical sampling. In addition, she stresses a more proactive, interpretative role taken by the researcher, who she sees as interacting with the participants and the data to an extent that leads both parties to *co-construct* the theory (as opposed to Strauss and Corbin [1990] and Glaser [1992] who tend to see theory 'emerging' from the data).

What methodological assumptions does grounded theory make?

Grounded theory falls within the interpretivist paradigm. It assumes that reality is subjective and is formed from the experienced life of individuals in social situations (see Chapter 2). This perspective is aligned to symbolic interactionism, which holds that human beings act on the basis of the meaning of phenomena, which they define and re-define through interaction with others in social situations (Blumer, 1969).

Designing and implementing a research study using GT

In the following discussion, the procedural principles and examples assume that of the three approaches to GT outlined above, the more systematic GT approach associated with Strauss and Corbin (1990) is adopted.

Research problem, research aims and research questions in grounded theory

Deciding the research problem is the first step in the design. What types of research problem are suitable for GT? How can the problem be made researchable? And where do we look for problems? Undoubtedly, the best researchable problems are experienced first hand in schools. But problems may be sourced from journals, books and leader and teacher colleagues. In some ways, the more complex and multi-dimensional the problem, the more researchable it is; such problems are often described as 'messy' or 'swampy'. Leadership problems may stem, for example, from the underachievement of goals and tasks, or conflict in relationships between staff, or from a lack of resources. A different kind of problem is the relative absence of women in senior educational or academic positions. Once the problem is identified, it needs to be conceptualised to make it researchable. This is achieved by expressing the problem using appropriate concepts drawn from relevant disciplines.

After the research problem is conceptualised, the research aims need to be decided. In a GT study, the aim will ultimately be to develop a substantive theory about a central phenomenon lying at the heart of a problem or an issue. In educational leadership, a typical aim might seek greater understanding of how and why leaders adopt certain processes and behaviours in their work lives, or why they act in the way they do to achieve certain outcomes or overcome specific challenges.

Once the research aims are identified, the research questions are framed to address the problem. Research question(s) should be phrased to give flexibility to explore the phenomenon in depth. The uniqueness of context in educational leadership means that it is unlikely that the relationships have been studied previously in the specific environment envisaged. The initial research question is often broad, but becomes more focused as research proceeds, and is often broken into specific research questions (SRQs) to make it more researchable. Grounded theory requires research questions that are *action- and process-orientated*, typically involving interactive and interpersonal processes related to individual and organisational behaviour in schools and universities. For example, RQs might centre on how individuals or members of an organisation cope with, or manage, the processes involved in a particular challenge, change or difficulty. This requirement of GT makes it an ideal approach for research in educational leadership and management, which are also primarily about processes. Typically in GT, research questions are framed in terms such as:

'How do principals (and/or teachers) manage, handle or cope with, problem X?' The following are two examples:

  i How do principals (or middle-level leaders) manage novice teachers in primary schools in city Y?

  ii What strategies are used by department heads (or principals) to distribute leadership to teachers in secondary schools?

Example from a Hong Kong doctoral thesis on careers of successful women academics

The following is a more detailed example to illustrate the above concepts taken from a GT doctoral thesis on how successful women academics in Hong Kong managed their careers (Lam, 2006).

Research problem

The phenomenon of the under-representation of women in senior academic positions was the research problem. Specifically, the problem focused on the dearth of women academics in Hong Kong universities occupying senior academic positions. The study defined 'successful women academics' as those in senior positions at professorial level or above. It was based on participants' perspectives and accounts of the meaningful experiences and events in their lives, particularly those they perceived as impacting on their academic careers.

Research aims

Paradoxically, the GT study reported here did not set out to explore the veracity of the so-called 'pipeline theories'; nor did it set out to establish the existence of a supposed 'glass ceiling' for female academics in higher education in Hong Kong. Rather, it sought to examine and analyse the life events, experiences and career pathways of a cohort of outstanding female academics in Hong Kong, thereby contributing to the existing body of knowledge of what is required of women who aspire and succeed to senior positions in academia. It was also hoped that senior female academics in the study could serve as occupational role models for future generations of female academics in Hong Kong because the experiences of these successful women offer valuable insights for those who might aspire to similar positions in future.

Research questions

The main research question was: 'What, in the life histories of particular senior female academics in Hong Kong, has contributed to their career success?'

  This main question was fractured into specific research questions to make it more researchable:

- How did their childhood and education affect their careers?
- What life events and relationships helped to lay the foundation for the development of their careers?

- What experiences, attitudes and skills were deemed to have been critical?
- What strategies, if any, did they use to attain senior positions?
- What factors were perceived to have affected the advancement of their careers?
- How did they manage multiple roles?
- What kinds of support did they deem to be necessary?
- What advice would they give to women who aspire to senior academic positions?

The place of the literature review in grounded theory

Since we are adopting the Strauss and Corbin (1990) systematic approach to GT, the literature review is more conventional; that is, it comes *early* in the study and assists in refining the research questions. The interplay between the research questions and the literature review is often iterative, being a two-way influence process. The literature review may also provide some early concepts and heuristic frameworks that are useful for developing instruments of data collection, such as interview schedules and observation checklists, and for data analysis.

Example from Hong Kong doctoral thesis on careers of successful women academics

The literature review initially focused on the careers of successful women, with a particular focus on female academics in Hong Kong. A dearth of such literature, particularly from a life history and grounded theory perspective, became apparent, as was the fact that no single concept – such as a 'glass ceiling' or a 'pipeline effect' – would be comprehensive enough to account for the complexities of women's career development. Nonetheless, the review provided valuable background knowledge for the study (such as the fact that most of the existing literature adopted a feminist perspective) and confirmed the appropriateness of approaching this topic differently, that is, from a combination of a life history and a grounded theory perspective; it also helped to refine the research questions.

The interplay between the research questions and the literature review continued later in the research analysis process. Meanwhile, the researcher finally settled on presenting the literature review in four broad categories: (1) 'gender gap' in higher education, (2) career aspirations and pathways of female academics, (3) life experiences and situations that had contributed to career success for such women, and (4) necessary and desirable attitudes and skills required of successful female academics.

Data collection

GT applies the same methods of data collection as other qualitative methods, namely, interviewing, observation and documentary sources. Of these three, interviews (especially semi-structured interviews) are the most commonly used. However, some studies combine two or even all three methods of data collection. Adopting multiple methods of data collection is encouraged as it is a way of improving the triangulation and trustworthiness of the data. More educational leadership studies should adopt observation and documentary sources to complement interviews. In regard to the interview schedule, the researcher must justify the reason for including each of the interview questions and note from where they were derived. Interview questions need to be aligned to the research questions, and may be sourced from the literature review, and from preliminary fieldwork (or previous studies if they exist).

Data collection and analysis are undertaken simultaneously; that is, the researcher may collect data from a few participants, then undertake analysis; the results of that analysis may lead the researcher to re-focus questions for the next round of data collection, the results of which are then analysed; and so the process continues until no new information is being gathered from additional participants. Data (and the categories formed from them) are then deemed to be 'saturated'.

Example from Hong Kong doctoral thesis on careers of successful women academics

Data collection in the study involved initial documentary analysis of the biographies of participants, followed by in-depth semi-structured interviews. Professional profiles of the respondents – website résumés, media reports and profile information available through the institutions and the media – were collected and analysed before the interviews. Semi-structured interviewing provided structure for common themes to be addressed while allowing sufficient freedom to explore particular issues of concern to individual interviewees. A minimum of two face-to-face interviews were requested of each respondent; the duration of each interview ranged from 1½ to 2 hours. These were supplemented with email conversations and some documentary analysis, as appropriate, before and after the interviews. Data analysis began shortly after the first two rounds of interviews, and then continued concurrently with subsequent interviews.

An interview schedule, or 'aide-memoire' (Burgess, 1984), was developed on the basis of a list of topics and questions generated from the main research question. This 'aide-memoire' was intended to serve as a reminder to the researcher of what to ask in line with the project's objectives. Not all of the questions were asked in every interview and the question sequence and order also varied. The website materials, at http://www.sagepub.co.uk/briggs. Supplementary Figures 13.1 and 13.2 present the initial aide-memoires that were developed for the two interviews.

Sampling

The criteria used for sampling in GT studies is as critical as random sampling is in quantitative methods, since it is obvious that the nature and form of data collected depends on who was actually sampled!

Sampling for the GT researcher is a two-element process: first, there are 15 different types of purposive sampling (see Gall et al., 2007). In helping to choose one from among them, or combinations of them (since a combination of two or more purposive sampling methods may be appropriate to use), one needs to refer back to the aims of the research, and the research questions. For example, if the aim is to study exceptionality, then atypical purposive sampling would be most appropriate. On the other hand, if the aim and research questions presume some kind of representativeness of a norm or average, then typical case purposive sampling would be most appropriate. The aim of GT studies is often to generate a theory that applies to the broadest range of leaders, teachers or students. By so doing, the theory generated has greater coverage and hence applicability. This means that given the smallness of sample sizes (see next paragraph), researchers try to look for the greatest variation among participants' behaviours, practices and processes. This is called maximum variation sampling and constitutes one form of purposive sampling. The second element of GT sampling is the most cited, and is known as theoretical sampling, the aim of which is to choose participants according to their potential to add value to the theory being developed. Thus, the researcher typically begins interviewing with a few participants and then deliberately seeks out those most likely to enrich and inform the formation of the theory. 'Saturation' is reached when new participants offer no new angles, views or perspectives. Theoretical sampling may best be seen as running alongside and even as integrated with maximum variation sampling. Lastly, research involves compromises. Occasionally, insurmountable obstacles to meeting these principles of sampling are encountered. In such cases, the researcher may have to resort to opportunity and convenience sampling, which tend to be regarded as weaker and less rigorous forms of sampling. In such cases, it is often decided that it is better to have some research on the phenomenon, even with convenience sampling, than have no study at all.

A key feature of GT studies is their strong emphasis on comprehensive, in-depth data. To compensate for the volume of data, sample sizes are small – for doctoral study, often between 10 and 25 participants. This range of sample size usually offers a satisfactory compromise between achieving reasonably good theoretical sampling that comes close to saturation level, while generating a volume of data that is still manageable.

Example from Hong Kong doctoral thesis on careers of successful women academics

Purposive (criterion) sampling was employed in the open-coding and axial-coding stages to ensure the inclusion of senior female academics from different disciplines and from the eight universities in Hong Kong, and with different personal characteristics. Certain broad criteria were first determined – such as seniority/rank, ethnicity and tertiary background. Gaining access to suitable respondents was a significant problem. Senior female academics were still in a small minority in Hong Kong, and the population from which to select a suitable sample was therefore limited.

At later stages of coding (axial- and selective-coding stages), theoretical sampling became more directed, and the researcher chose people and documents with a view to verifying the storyline. To ensure theoretical density (Strauss and Corbin, 1990), the 11 senior female academics included in the study were from diverse backgrounds in terms of academic interests, teaching experience, roles within their institutions and family backgrounds.

Memos, field notes and diagrams

GT researchers normally make heavy use of memos throughout the entire research process (memos can be theoretical, methodological or substantive), as well as field notes and diagrams, as techniques to aid the collection and analysis of data and assist the theorising process.

Example from Hong Kong doctoral thesis on careers of successful women academics

Figure 13.1 is an example of how diagrams were used in the analysis of data and to assist the theorising process. The first diagram shows the relationships between dominant attributes, career orientations, career strategies and career outcomes.

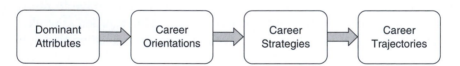

Figure 13.1   Relationships between dominant attributes, career orientations, career strategies and career trajectories

Since the dominant attributes of the respondents were continuously influenced by various factors, including attribute properties such as the personal, social and institutional factors that emerged in the women's socialisation experiences, these factors modified the effect of attributes on career trajectory. Figure 13.2 further develops Figure 13.1; it helps explain the differences in the career decisions made by the respondents, and thus accounts for: (1) the emergence of the typology; and (2) individual differences among respondents of the same type.

Data analysis

GT is most distinct from other qualitative approaches in its processes of data analysis. The first step entails raw data (usually text and interview

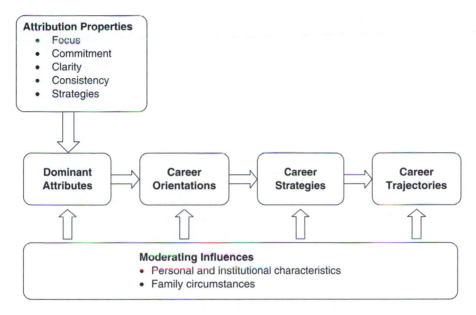

Figure 13.2   Moderating influences on the effect of attributes on career trajectory

transcripts) being divided into meaningful units (sentences or paragraphs) and coded in the margins of the transcript. A code is a label for a concept that captures the essence of the meaning extracted from each sentence or paragraph. Hundreds of codes may be generated from transcripts. Rules and procedures apply in lending rigour to the process: coding systematically records and allocates incidents, events and experiences captured in the data. The second step involves the formation of related codes into categories, and the comparison of each new code with existing categories to decide the category into which it fits (or whether it should start a new category). As more details of the process, experience or practice emerge, each category is built up by adding to its properties (qualitative features), each of which may have dimensions (the quantitative characteristics for each property).

Both of the above steps are termed *open coding*, and are used by qualitative researchers in general (see Chapter 23). Incidents and practices are coded and compared and placed in homogeneous categories. Each category can be further fractured into more detailed elements (properties and their dimensions).

Grounded theory involves two further types of coding, each representing a successively higher level of abstraction; these are *axial* and *selective* coding, and they give grounded theory its uniqueness. Both are based on exploring the relationships and interrelationships between categories, with the latter distinguishing a core category (a kind of common denominator) to underpin all categories.

In *axial coding*, the data are re-assembled in new ways after open coding. A coding paradigm or visual model is drawn by the researcher who identifies a *central phenomenon,* then goes on to explore *causal conditions* that lead to the central phenomenon, then *specific strategies, actions or practices* adopted to manage the phenomenon, within *specific contextual* and *intervening conditions*, before finally delineating the *consequences or outcomes* of the strategies. If the data collected to date do not allow for categories to form in the above italicized areas (that is, questions were not included from the beginning) then the researcher must go back into the field to collect the data needed to gather the missing information to allow the completion of axial coding.

In *selective coding*, a *core category* is selected to which the other categories can be related and conceptualised in a supporting and associative relationship. The core category then becomes the central phenomenon in which all other categories are integrated. It becomes the basis of the newly constructed substantive theory.

Example from Hong Kong doctoral thesis on careers of successful women academics

Data analysis involved all three steps of coding – open coding, axial coding and selective coding.

Open coding

To generate concepts, the early interviews were coded on a line-by-line basis and, if appropriate, on a word-by-word basis. As some concepts and categories emerged repeatedly, certain sections of the later interviews were coded paragraph-by-paragraph to identify the similar categories. Throughout the coding process, code notes and memos were maintained with regard to: (i) the questions asked of the data; and (ii) the relationships among concepts and categories that emerged. Supplementary Figure 13.3 (see companion website) provides an example of an open-coded transcript from the first interview of the first round of semi-structured interviews.

Axial coding

Axial coding was used to make connections among the categories and their sub-categories, as identified in the open-coding stage. Hypotheses were proposed with respect to these relationships, and the hypotheses were then tested against existing and new data as they became available. Code notes and memos were maintained with respect to the relationships among categories and their sub-categories in accordance with the model proposed by Strauss and Corbin (1990: 99), as illustrated below:

(A) CAUSAL CONDITIONS → (B) PHENOMENON →
(C) CONTEXT → (D) INTERVENING CONDITIONS →
(E) ACTION/INTERACTION STRATEGIES →
(F) CONSEQUENCES

Supplementary Figure 13.4 (see companion website) provides an example of an axial coding theoretical memo on a category (mission search).

Selective coding

Supplementary Figure 13.5 (see companion website) is an example of a selective coding theoretical memo on the core category (dominant attributes).

The outcome: a grounded theory, typology and propositions

In achieving the main objective of GT research, namely the construction of the actual grounded theory, a storyline or general descriptive view explaining the whole data set and its empirical grounding, is explicated. The theory is normally based on a typology of participants, and propositions about each of the types in relation to the core category and supporting categories. Hence, if a study had, say, 20 participants, and their responses were each tracked through the various categories and relationships between categories (especially axial coding), it is normally possible to discern common patterns of practice sufficient to group participants into distinct types. For example, the 20 participants might fall into three or four types, with each type displaying different patterns of experiences, reactions, feelings, behaviours and practices from the other types. Propositions then help the researcher tell the story and provide an explanation of how each type responds (in different ways) to the same central phenomenon and under what conditions.

Example from Hong Kong doctoral thesis on careers of successful women academics

Substantive theory of selective attribution in career trajectory

The major outcome of the study was the emergence and construction of a grounded theory that described how the 11 senior female Hong Kong academics perceived their socialisation experiences and attributes, and how they had used these effectively to achieve success in their academic lives. This was entitled the 'theory of selective attribution in career trajectory'. The fundamental conceptual framework underpinning the theory was a reciprocal relationship between an individual's attributes (personal, social and academic) their socialisation processes and their resultant career trajectory. The following sections illustrate theory construction, from the extrication of a storyline to the development of propositions and a typology of senior female academics.

The storyline

The 'storyline' described how the senior female academics made selective use of their attributes to build successful careers in higher education. The pertinent features of their life histories demonstrate that many of the desirable 'success attributes' that they possess were formed and nurtured through various socialisation experiences, particularly in the early stages of their lives. At different stages of their careers, the interplay of their dominant attributes and their personal and professional socialisation experiences affected their construction (and subsequent redefinition) of their personal orientations – thus producing variations among individuals in their career orientations, strategies and pathways. According to the selective use of various attributes by the individual women, different clusters of dominant attributes were formed. It was thus possible to construct a typology of the women academics to describe and explain how they used their attributes selectively to achieve career success.

The main propositions

The 'theory of selective attribution in career trajectory' can be presented as two related sets of propositions: (1) propositions relating to the overall theory of how the female academics selectively used their attributes to determine their career trajectories; and (2) propositions relating to a typology of the senior female academics.

1 Propositions relating to the overall theory

   i Career plans and dominant attributes

     Few of the participating academics began their academic lives with a clear career plan. Most began to examine their career options and strategies seriously after they had been in their jobs for a few years. Once they had identified their preferred roles, they were able – through a self-evaluation process – to make best use of their dominant attributes to enhance their career trajectories.

   ii Modification of attributes by socialisation

     The women's attributes were continuously modified by socialisation experiences – such as family requirements, work situations, significant relationships and critical life events.

   iii Subsequent career trajectories

     The interplay of attributes and socialisation experiences influenced the women's career trajectories; and their careers had a reciprocal influence on the women's attributes and socialisation experiences. These interactions account for variations in their career orientations, strategies and pathways.

Figure 13.3 illustrates the interrelationship of attributes, socialisation processes and career trajectory.

2 Propositions relating to the typology of the senior female academics

   Three divergent patterns of attributes became apparent in the coding process and these led to three types of senior female academics being identified ('career academics', career educators' and 'career opportunists'). Although all three types shared some common attributes, the most influential attributes in terms of their career trajectories were sufficiently distinctive to differentiate them. Table 13.1 provides a comparative analysis of the dominant attributes of the three types.

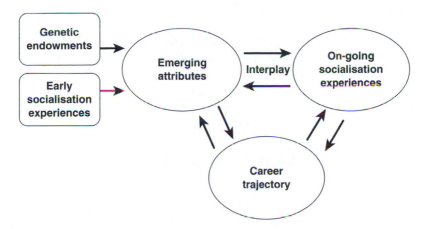

Figure 13.3   Impact of interplay of attributes and socialisation experiences on career trajectory

Table 13.1   Dominant attributes of the typology

	Career Academics	Career Educators	Career Opportunists
Personal Characteristics	*Attributes in common:* independent, intelligent, perseverant, resilient, committed to work, diligent, receptive, reflective, highly energetic, positive		
	Visionary, investigative, self-disciplined, research-oriented	Easy-going, people-oriented, caring, humanitarian, student-oriented	Flexible, versatile, politically astute, opportunistic, people-oriented
Personal Identities	Scholar, researcher	Educator, teacher, administrator	Educator, teacher, administrator, project manager
Missions and Core Values	To contribute to knowledge development	To educate and to serve	To bring about change to improve the quality of teaching and student education
	Passion for knowledge	Passion for education	Passion for innovation
	Driving force: achieve breakthroughs in research; inspire students	Driving force: see improvements in students and courses	Driving force: achieve self-satisfaction, see improvements in students and courses
	Pleasure: discovery of new knowledge	Pleasure: student and department recognition	Pleasure: new projects and leading effective teams

Trustworthiness

Ensuring trustworthiness (equivalent to validity and reliability) is essential in GT studies. Lincoln and Guba (1985) identify four main criteria for trustworthiness: credibility, dependability, transferability and confirmability. Triangulation of data collection, member checking and the keeping of an audit trail are three powerful and common ways of ensuring trustworthiness is met. (See also Chapters 6 and 11 of this volume.)

Example from Hong Kong doctoral thesis on careers of successful women academics

Multiple methods of data collection and prolonged engagements of the researcher with the respondents were used in the study to enhance credibility. During the data collection and analysis phases, the researcher engaged in sessions of 'peer debriefing' (Lincoln and Guba, 1985: 308) with a colleague who had expressed interest in the study. To ensure 'referential adequacy' (Lincoln and Guba, 1985: 313), the interviews were recorded, transcribed and stored to provide a referential benchmark against which later data analyses and interpretations could be compared for adequacy. 'Member checks' (Lincoln and Guba, 1985: 316) were performed by asking the respondents to verify the content of the transcripts and summaries of interpretations of the interviews.

A detailed record of interview schedules, recorded tapes, supplementary documents, field notes and coding notes was kept to ensure the stability and 'trackability' of data and theory development in the study. In addition, documentary analysis pertaining to the respondents and issues relevant to the study was maintained throughout the process of data collection and analysis, and this served as a means of 'triangulation'.

'Transferability' rather than 'generalisability'

Transferability rather than 'generalisability' is the more apt term in GT; it invites readers to draw inferences from the study after applying the findings to their own situations. GT does not aim to generalise to larger samples or populations, hence random sampling is not applicable or appropriate; rather, it seeks to build theory that is bounded by the cases and individuals studied, rather than test application to other contexts. Hence, securing a sample of participants who together present a *range* of perspectives or practices or who conform to specified, relevant criteria is more important than sheer numbers of participants. However, by judiciously selecting the sampling strategy – say typical case sampling – the applicability or transferability of the findings from a particular study may be enhanced. Additionally, in-depth detailed description of the context of the central phenomenon allows others to compare context and conditions in the study with their own, thus enabling the transferability process. Moreover, a GT theory generated for a small number of leaders or teachers may subsequently be tested using large-scale quantitative surveys in similar or different contexts.

Example from Hong Kong doctoral thesis on careers of successful women academics

The aim was not to generalise the theory to all senior women academics in Hong Kong, but rather to understand the processes that had enabled a select group of women academics to achieve successful careers (judged by promotion and seniority) through their own perspectives of their lives and professional experiences, and then develop an explanatory theory of how they managed to achieve senior positions.

The extent of transferability of the theory depends upon the degree of similarity between the women participants and the Hong Kong context, and women academics in other contexts. While the 'theory of selective attribution in career trajectory' is more transferable to female academics in similar situations to those of the cohort of senior female academics studied, the theory may help other women academics to reflect on their own life goals and experiences, as a way of gaining new insights into the meanings of their own lived experiences.

Key points

In considering the contribution of grounded theory to research in educational leadership, this chapter has presented grounded theory research as:

- well suited to investigating problems and challenges faced by educational leaders in schools and higher education
- concerned with how people (leaders) manage or cope with challenging situations (in and out of school or university)
- enabling the building of theories (such as that of educational leadership) where none previously existed, using inductive and deductive processes
- a qualitative research approach with rigorous, distinct and systematic procedures, especially in coding at the data analysis stage
- using small samples, but collecting comprehensive, in-depth data about a problematic phenomenon in order to better understand it
- a research approach that highlights the importance of sampling strategy, since the sample determines the nature and content of the data collected; other crucial procedures include open, axial and selective coding
- an approach which identifies typologies and propositions that explain how individual leaders and groups or types of leaders manage and lead in particular situations and contexts.

Questions and reflections

1 How would you decide whether grounded theory is suitable as an approach for a particular research project you have in mind?

2 What are the sequential stages, and the procedures associated with each stage, in a grounded theory you are designing?

3 What makes grounded theory distinct from other qualitative research methods?

4 What purpose does abstraction and conceptualisation serve in grounded theory?

Recommended further reading

Charmaz, K. (2006) *Constructing Grounded Theory*. Thousand Oaks, CA: Sage.

A slightly different approach emphasising the co-construction of theory between participants and researcher.

Punch, K.F. (2005) *Introduction to Social Research: Quantitative and Qualitative Approaches* (2nd ed.). London: Sage.

A good general introduction to data analysis and coding in GT.

Strauss, A. and Corbin, J. (1990) *Basics of Qualitative Research: Grounded Theory Procedures and Techniques*. Newbury Park, CA: Sage.

The 'Bible' in terms of GT methods, written by one of the founding GT researchers – clearly written and easy to read.

References

Blumer, H. (1969) *Symbolic Interaction: Perspective and Method*. Berkeley, CA: University of California Press.

Burgess, R.G. (1984) *In the Field: An Introduction to Field Research*. London: Allen & Unwin.

Charmaz, K. (2006) *Constructing Grounded Theory*. Thousand Oaks, CA: Sage.

Creswell, J.W. (2005) *Research Design: Qualitative, Quantitative and Mixed Methods Approaches* (2nd edn). Thousand Oaks, CA: Sage.

Creswell, J.W. (2007) *Qualitative Inquiry and Research Design: Choosing Among Five Approaches* (3rd edn). Thousand Oaks, CA: Sage.

Creswell, J.W. (2009) *Research Design: Qualitative, Quantitative and Mixed Methods Approaches* (3rd edn). Thousand Oaks, CA: Sage.

Gall, M.D., Gall, J.P. and Borg, W. (2007) *Educational Research: An Introduction*. Boston, MA: Allyn and Bacon.

Glaser, B.G. (1992) *Basics of Grounded Theory Analysis*. Mill Valley, CA: Sociology Press.

Lam, M.P.H. (2006) Senior women academics in Hong Kong: A life history approach. Unpublished doctoral thesis, University of Leicester.

Lincoln, Y.S. and Guba, E.G. (1985) *Naturalistic Inquiry*. Beverly Hills, CA: Sage.

O'Donoghue, T. and Chalmers, R. (2000) How teachers manage their work in inclusive classrooms. *Teaching and Teacher Education* 16(8): 889–904.

Strauss, A. and Corbin, J. (1990) *Basics of Qualitative Research: Grounded Theory Procedures and Techniques*. Newbury Park, CA: Sage.

CHAPTER 14

Ethnography

Marlene Morrison

Chapter objectives

Using examples, this chapter:

- Introduces ethnography as process and product.
- Considers its main characteristics.
- Confronts and responds to criticisms of its strengths and weaknesses.
- Summarises key methods, notably 'participant' observation.
- Examines recent developments in virtual ethnography.
- Recommends a resurgence of interest.

Introduction

Both ethnography and empirical studies of education leadership and management are at 'crossroads' moments in their development. The core intentions of this chapter are therefore, first, to highlight ethnography's potential for the research and practice of leadership, and second, to demonstrate how new forms of ethnography – virtual, visual, Internet, *Netnography* – can extend studies beyond specific locations towards wider configurations of leadership and management, those described, for example, as *distributed, system, collaborative, inter-service* and/or *inter-professional* (Morrison and Arthur, forthcoming; Morrison and Glenny, 2011). Discussion extends to research about leadership learning, since increasingly this includes *informal, online* and *distance* as well as other forms of computer mediated communication (CMC) and practice communities of leaders, teachers and learners.

History

Ethnography has its roots in social science, specifically the traditions of social anthropology of the nineteenth and twentieth centuries; Malinowski, Evans-Pritchard and Radcliffe Brown were deeply influential in the study of cultures, events, locations and situations which were 'exotic' and distant from research-ers' own. Equally influential is research by Robert Park and Ernest Burgess in Chicago of the 1930s. Their 'social mosaic' approach (Bulmer, 1984) and intention to participate in the lives of participants who were the focus of their studies, brought 'participant observation' to prominence. As ethnographers began to focus on situations that were neither remote nor unusual, 'making the familiar strange' became equally important. From the middle of the twen-tieth century, ethnography produced detailed accounts of educational lives and experiences which:

> whilst grounded in the ... circumstances of the discrete location, event, or setting, were nevertheless illustrative of wider ... processes. Moreover, analysis ... yielded *conceptually grounded accounts* (Glaser and Strauss, 1967) which challenged the validity of positivist research. (Pole and Morrison, 2003: 14, emphasis added)

Ethnography and leadership

Ethnographic studies have been more numerous in sociological studies of education than studies of leadership. The former derive from seminal studies of life and work in schools (Ball, 1981; Burgess, 1983; Lacey, 1970; Wolcott, 2003). Since the 1960s, publications about ethnography as method and meth-odology have been prolific, not least about what is 'right' and 'wrong' with it (Brewer, 2000; Coffey, 1999; Hammersley, 1992; Hammersley and Atkinson, 1995). Ethnography is often included in texts about doing research (Denzin and Lincoln, 1998; Pole and Lampard, 2002), most notably in relation to qualitative research design and analysis (Dey, 1993; Glaser and Strauss, 1967; Silverman, 2001). This applies equally to education (Pole and Morrison, 2003; Scott and Morrison, 2007) and to organisational sociology (Fine et al., 2008). In the leadership field, with notable exceptions, its use remains peripheral. A number of reasons might be suggested.

First, whilst ethnography has gained 'respectability', the technical, meth-odological and logistical demands of immersion in field research may have deterred sponsors of short-run leadership research and small-scale researchers.

Second, definitions of ethnography are not without ambiguity, even among ethnographers. In extremis, ethnography is sometimes viewed as all that a large-scale quantitative survey is not (Pole and Morrison, 2003: 2).

Third, when ethnographers are '*the* essential research instrument' (LeCompte and Preissle [1993: 91–2], emphasis added), levels of engagement may be too daunting for practitioner researchers. Its 'impression management' aspects, which also involve a juggling of multiple identities, is not for the faint-hearted (Coffey, 1999; Hammersley and Atkinson, 1995). Moreover, when some ethnographies have taken an autobiographical turn, for example where researchers are themselves the leaders of educational organisations under ethnographic scrutiny, findings have sometimes been read as 'borderline self-indulgence' or 'narcissistic' (Lofland and Lofland, 1995: 14).

Finally, and perhaps most significantly, ethnographies that foreground persons of power and influence have, unsurprisingly, been resisted most strongly by those with most of both. This occurs when leaders limit research access to self-report interviews and/or minimal observation. In which case, research becomes less amenable to the intensive, interrogative 'gaze' that ethnography claims as a core strength.

Yet, albeit in increasingly adaptive forms, ethnography is valued for the deep, critical insights it provides into organisational life, and, it follows, leadership. In organizational sociology, for example, Fine et al. (2008: 2) highlight six key contributions to: 'the elaboration of informal relations', 'organisations as systems of meaning', 'organisations and their environments', 'organisational change', 'ethics and normative behaviour', and 'power, politics, and control'. Whilst this resonates with claims made in this chapter about ethnography's contribution to leadership studies, it is recognised that its 'unique contributions' create some 'trade-offs' (p. 3), not least in terms of what ethnography can legitimately claim to represent and/or make generalisations about.

Characteristics, methodology and method

Pole and Morrison (2003) identify the main characteristics in terms of processes (*doing* ethnography) and outcomes (*producing* ethnographies). Emphases are upon:

- discrete event(s) or setting(s);
- concern for the full range of behaviours within the event or setting;
- research methods which may combine qualitative and quantitative approaches but where the emphasis is upon understanding behaviours from inside the discrete event or setting;
- data collection and analysis which moves from detailed description to the identification of concepts and theories which are grounded in the data collected;
- rigorous and thorough research, where the complexities of the event or setting are of greater importance than overarching trends or generalizations. (p. 3)

Requirements are for 'contextualised description', 'insiders' perspectives' and the final 'construction of an account ... which is grounded in the collected data and ... incorporates a conceptual framework that facilitates understanding of social action at both an empirical and theoretical level' (p. 4). Elsewhere, Brewer (2000) refers to ethnography as *Method,* that is, the tools used to collect data and the techniques for analysing them, and as *Methodology* – 'the broad theoretical and philosophical framework into which these procedural rules fit' (p. 2).

Methodology

In epistemological terms, ethnography is located within 'a theoretical tradition which [gives] ... primacy ... [to] the importance of situated meaning and contextualised experience as the basis for understanding social behaviour' (Pole and Morrison, 2003: 5). The traditions of naturalism (O'Connell-Davidson and Layder, 1994), 'Verstehen' (Weber, 1949) and interpretative analysis are, therefore, deeply implicated. Insiders' accounts are not construed as distanced, objective accounts of the worlds they inhabit, but as subjective accounts by insiders and others of their experiences. These are not reduced to 'opinion, dogma, or journalism' (Pole and Morrison, 2003: 5). On the contrary, they are located within 'the structures which shape, limit, and in some cases, define social action' and are 'central to the explanation and understanding of that action' *(2003: 5).*

Method

Traditionally, ethnographers have prioritised methods in which 'there is direct contact between researchers and the research' (Pole and Morrison, 2003: 7). However, this definition, even in its 'purest' form, does not really allow for the innovative forms that 'contact' increasingly takes in multi-modal worlds. Nonetheless, a general distinction is being made here between the use of research tools which are most commonly aligned with qualitative approaches, notably, participant observation and unstructured interviewing, and a more inclusive range that includes, for example, questionnaires and surveys.

Taking an inclusive approach, most research methods might be seen as potentially 'ethnographic'. However, ethnographers (2003: 7) are keen not to be identified with an 'anything goes' attitude to the use of methods. Instead, advocacy is for a pluralism of method (*not* methodologies) where ethnographers are required to think creatively about the methods they use, whilst always privileging 'a detailed insider's view' (p. 8) over that of outsiders. 'Inclusive' ethnography might include quantitative methods, for example, 'as long as [such methods] adhere to the epistemological principles of naturalism, in seeking to gather data with as little disturbance to the ... every day rhythms of the location as possible' (p. 9) and where such data are most likely to be useful in providing evidence about the wider context within which the specific event, location and actions occur.

Ethnography's requirement for 'deep involvement in individual settings' (Pole and Morrison, 2003: 10) has also been subject to a range of interpretations. Weick (1985: 568) characterised ethnography as 'sustained, explicit, methodical observation and paraphrasing of social situations in relation to their naturally occurring contexts'. Fine et al.'s (2008) subsequent interpretation of this definition is to *exclude* as ethnographic fieldwork in which 'the fieldworker does not remain in the field (for months … even years) to become "saturated" with first-hand knowledge of the setting' (p. 2). Yet, recent trends, notably in education, towards 'compressed' (Jeffrey and Troman, 2004: 538) or 'blitzkrieg' ethnography (Rist, 1980) are increasingly seen as pragmatic responses to situations where sponsors fund shorter-run research rather than lengthy immersions.

Other debates focus on the extent to which ethnographic research is or ought to be 'applied'. Again, Fine et al. (2008: 2–3) *exclude* as ethnographic, 'field studies where the primary goal is not to describe and interpret the experiences of organizational members, but to produce critical interventions into organizational functioning'. From this perspective, action research and ethnography appear almost antithetical. Yet, this strict dichotomy between knowledge creation and application is not routinely accepted; for example, Pole and Morrison argue that the importance of ethnographic research is not only to create 'knowledge for knowledge sake' (Brewer, 2000) but also 'to contribute to educational policy and practical action' (Pole and Morrison, 2003: 127). For others, the debate relates primarily to where the 'intervention' emphasis is placed, since most ethnographers stress its potential to improve 'human life worlds' (Fine et al., 2008: 26) whether this influence is 'indirect and general' or 'direct and specific' (Hammersley, 1992: 151).

Controversies

Ethnography has been subject to sustained critique, as much from within the field of qualitative research as without. Awareness of such critiques enables researchers/readers to make decisions not only about whether ethnography *is* the most appropriate approach for addressing their research questions, but also to defend their ethnographic stance by addressing relevant criticisms appropriately, and discarding irrelevant ones, without recourse to defensiveness. Some criticisms are easily countered, for example the tendency to describe and characterise events and people rather than quantify them, the latter being a characteristic to which ethnography does not necessarily aspire. Other criticisms are more difficult to counter: sloppy forms of imprecise writing and opaque analysis unaccompanied by audit trails to explain how ethnographic data were collected and analysed have been rightly condemned. Referring to the 'gold standards' of research, Silverman (2001: 189) notes that all research 'requires affirmative answers to two questions: Have … researchers demonstrated successfully why we should believe them? And, does the research problem tackled have theoretical and/or practical significance?'

Here, I draw readers' attention to three challenges. The first concerns issues of 'pretend' ethnography; the second and third relate to issues of representation and generalisability.

'Pretend' ethnography

Ethnographers' core tasks are to research social action within discrete locations from first-hand experience. A primary objective is to collect data that convey the subjective reality of those who work, study and/or live in those locations. The underpinning question is 'What is going on here?' 'Here' might relate to the school, college, university, senior management team, principal's office, department or classroom, and means 'getting up close' to a range of situations, events and people.

However, a tendency in many leadership studies is to report only/mainly leaders' 'words', especially in interviews, as if they were either untainted truths or sufficient explanations of leadership activities. A limitation is the failure to recognise the problematic status of interview data as situated accounts. More than this, it reports 'what is going on here' from single perspectives *and* a lack of depth of engagement, and then describes the approach as ethnographic when it is not. Whilst the so-called 'authentic' perspectives of leaders might constitute a form of qualitative enquiry, such findings cannot constitute *ethnographic* research. The issue is less about the need for evidence triangulation (important though this is), and more about ethnography's core focus upon the *multiplicity* of voices and actions needed to analyse leadership. In this sense, ethnography is always concerned with the detailed, multiple interrogations of 'talk, text, and interactions' (Silverman, 2001) in ways that 'pretend ethnography' seems not to be. This requires:

> a presence of mind described by Fielding (1993: 157) as 'rolling with the punches', and 'effort to "think" oneself into the multiple perspective of [informants] – the introspective, empathetic process Weber called "verstehen"'. (Pole and Morrison, 2003: 18)

Representation

Ethnographic research emphasizes its claims to represent the 'nature' of social reality, commonly through transcript analysis of actors' words. Such 'realistic' conceptions have been challenged as naïve (Hammersley, 1992) and/or misguided (Silverman, 2001) if they fail to recognise the ethnographer's role in interpreting that 'nature'. The ethnographer is 'not merely a conduit for data collection and the emergence of convincing accounts' (Pole and Morrison, 2003: 130), whether this is about leadership, school improvement, power relations, and so on, but is also an active participant in the research account. Seriously implicated here is the role of researcher and research as *reflexive* and *constructive*. The intellectual and practical act of representation not only gives careful consideration to detailed data collection and analysis, but also recognises the importance of ethnographers' skills as inscribers, transcribers and, ultimately, as participants and interpreters. Ethnography's distinctive contribution relies on the *centrality* of the researcher: 'This sets it apart from ... approaches which see the unearthing of knowledge about [educational] life untainted by the researcher as achievable, or something to be striven for' (Pole and Morrison, 2003: 131).

Generalizability

Ethnography has been used mainly to investigate the single, the local and the small-scale; generalisability might neither be sought nor claimed. However, a core question asked of all research endeavours is 'So what?'. Gubrium (1988) evoked typologies of ethnography as 'structural' (what is going on here?) and 'articulative' (how is it understood, and by whom?). When ethnographers move beyond knowledge and understanding to ask 'What do we need to do to make the situation or activities of people better?', their accounts have been described as 'practical' ethnography (Gubrium, 1988). Such approaches have brought praise and approbation in equal measure. Yet, utilitarian and evaluative ethnographies of the single instance, event or location have retained their popularity, especially in informing policy and practice. A key issue remains the rigour of data collection and analysis, and the application of 'grounded' data to establish conceptual and theoretical frameworks.

The possibility of utility or generalizability beyond the single or few cases has been debated. Yin (1994) argued that the inferences and generalisations drawn from small-scale ethnographic scrutiny are different in type from those that might derive from the large-scale, or quantitatively. For Stake (1978), what mattered was the use that researchers made of ethnographies to develop 'naturalistic generalizations'; others still continued to emphasise 'fitness for purpose' and 'transferability' (Guba and Lincoln, 1989).

More recent debates about generalisability have been influenced by Bassey (1999), who referred to the potential for ethnographic case studies to provide 'fuzzy generalizations', noting 'that something has happened in one place and ... may happen elsewhere' (p. 52). Subsequently, Hammersley (2001) argued that generalisations from all research approaches are matters of degree, and that, far from being unique to ethnography, 'fuzzy generalizations' feature in all research, not least when researchers predict what is likely to happen sometime or somewhere else, and/or to others on the basis of the evidence gained (p. 224).

Earlier, Hammersley (1992: Ch. 5) also distinguished between 'empirical' and 'theoretical' generalisations. In the former, he proposed that claims for generalisability might be improved when: ethnographers assessed their own findings in relation to wider sets of research about the same phenomena; researchers considered ethnographic approaches in tandem with other complementary approaches, and/or ethnographers produced multi-site case studies (pp. 89–90). In relation to 'theoretical' generalisation, Hammersley considered the relative strengths of ethnography in developing theory and conceptual insights rather than establishing or confirming universal laws of truth or falsity (pp. 89–90).

In summary, what seems central to ethnographic research as process and product is the relationship between the researcher as ethnographer, the data s/he collects, the way the researcher chooses to fashion the account, and the clarity in which claims for transferability and/or generalisation, empirical or theoretical, are made.

In the next section, different methods for collecting data are introduced. Those discussed in other chapters are not pursued in depth. However, participant observation is considered more fully, and illustrated in the research examples that follow.

Primary and secondary data

Ethnography lends itself to a variety of data collection methods. Introduced here are methods often referred to as *primary*, that is, based on 'first hand experience' (Pole and Morrison, 2003) and 'active' rather than 'passive' (Pole and Lampard, 2002). These are distinct from *secondary* data, that are collected from sources where 'there may not be the immediacy of contact between researcher and the researched' (Pole and Morrison, 2003: 47). Primary methods most commonly associated with ethnographic research are participant observation, ethnographic interviewing, case study, life history, focus group and drama work. Ethnographic interviews are commonly (but not exclusively) relatively unstructured (rather than unsystematic), and more likely viewed as constructions by interviewer and interviewee, and where 'the respondent is encouraged to answer the question in her or his own terms' (May, 1993).

The appeal of secondary data is in understanding the wider context in which multiple individual actions might be understood, not least in relation to social structures. Existing data can be used for purposes that differ, perhaps, from those for which they were originally collected; these include published surveys, documents, official statistics, art and artefacts. Located between the primary and secondary, and dependent upon the purposes for which they are used, are diaries (see also Chapter 22), photographs, drawings and paintings (Pink, 2001). Photographs, for example, are seen as 'a heuristic device which the ethnographer can use to pose ... questions about the school ... [or the senior management team], but also as a valuable resource ... which can be ... analysed in the same way as textual data' (Pole and Morrison, 2003: 65). In combination, it is important to reiterate that 'it isn't the data on their own that make a piece of research ethnographic, but it is their particular approaches to analysis and issues relating to representation' (Pole and Morrison, 2003: 65).

Careful *analysis* of the data collected is a key aspect of ethnographic research and is detailed in full elsewhere (Brewer, 2000; Pole and Morrison, 2003) and in Part D of this book, especially Chapter 25. Its centrality links both to the technical challenges created by the sheer volume of data collected, most frequently though not exclusively in textual forms, and the epistemological challenges of the range of meanings and interpretations that are applied. Again, following Pole and Morrison (2003: 109–10), it is important for ethnographers to demonstrate that final accounts drawn from systematically collected and analysed data contain most if not all of the following features:

1   Tell readers what the 'story' is about.
2   Give readers a clear sense of context.

3 Enable the reader to trace and track the history and progress of the ethnographic research.

4 Illustrate how and why key concepts emerged.

5 Provide data clearly.

6 Provide conclusions which show clear connective links to the educational worlds in which the research operated.

Participant observation

Most people have a sense of what observation is. Ethnography provides the opportunity to listen, watch, record and share with participants what they say and do. There are important differences between what 'watchers' observe, and what ethnographers do. As Silverman (2001: 45) comments: 'Ethnography puts together two different words, "ethno" means "folks", while "graphy" stems from "writing"'. As Pole and Morrison (2003: 20) insist, 'the ethnographer is the writer about "folks" *par excellence*'. Ethnography takes observation a step further. A key feature is the ethnographer's participation in the setting being studied: 'among the "folks" of interest are ourselves' and 'a challenging feature of "taking part" and "being there" is the extent to which the ethnographer writes her/himself into the script' (2003: 20). In ethnographic observation, there is a progressive focusing and 'funnelling' (Hammersley and Atkinson, 1995) of 'data towards conceptual and theoretical frameworks ... in the sense that categories generated in the early stages of observation are "saturated" (Glaser and Strauss, 1967) through more observation and/or triangulation with multiple methods in order to provide analytical frameworks' (Pole and Morrison, 2003: 21–2).

Participation makes many demands, not least in relation to the level of participation that might be adopted. These have been considered fully elsewhere (Gold, 1958) and are not rehearsed here except to note that all research observations have important implications, whether in terms of researcher access, role maintenance and impression management, relationships with gatekeepers, skills of and opportunities for note taking, and exit strategies.

In the following sections, examples of the ethnographic approach are drawn from leadership research. Readers might like to consider which 'kinds' of ethnography are being described, and with which implications, not least whether an ethnographic orientation has the potential to produce more than what Bryman (1996: 288) described as a proliferation of 'essentially hagiographic pen portraits of successful leaders from whom "lessons" can be learned'.

Ethnographic orientations to leadership for diversity

This section derives from research about diversity in leadership in UK Further Education (Lumby et al., 2007). The specific interest for this chapter lies in the methodological opportunities to observe leadership behaviours in 'sensitive' contexts of diversity (Morrison and Lumby, 2009). The research, directed by Lumby, investigated how and why some leaders were included and excluded from organisational influence. It sought responses to challenging questions about individual and collective leadership identities that were also embedded in equality and social justice agendas. Whether the research undertaken *did* constitute ethnography is open to discussion. Jeffrey and Troman (2004: 538) have described similar kinds of ethnographic orientations as 'compressed' ethnography. In this sense, whilst a seven-month project, in five case study institutions, comprising a two-person team in each case study location, and covering 15 leadership meeting observations, and at least 10 interviews in each of the five sites, might match Jeffrey and Troman's description, it differed markedly from the seminal work of Wolcott (2003), for example, conducted in one school over two years. Yet:

> Some features ... would be recognisable to ethnographers working ... in longer time frames. For example, the researchers entered the field with some over-arching themes for investigation, and through iterative engagement with the data, others emerged ... A proliferation of observations and interviews also led to the use of *synecdoche*, a well-known approach in Ethnography (Burgess and Morrison, 1998). Such portrayals were not 'just' to provide 'textual' pictures ... but were also used to meet ... ethical obligations not to present case studies as 'wholes', thus seeking to protect the identity of individuals who were either discussing sensitive issues about personal or 'racial' characteristics ... or making reference to those upon which their future careers and promotions might ultimately depend ... [T]he approach was ... context and data-led, and ... constituted documentary, observational, and interview material. (Morrison and Lumby, 2009: 67, emphasis added)

Interview and observation

Participant interviews were considered crucial in developing understandings about what diversity and/or diverse leadership meant to participants in terms of the contexts in which they worked. But, to understand how leaders acted, observations of meetings with leadership groups operating at different levels of power and influence within the colleges were also undertaken. The meetings were 'potential theatres of performance' (Morrison and Lumby, 2009: 73) in which the most overt forms of leadership might be investigated through talk, interaction, conversational flow and directed activity planning. An observational framework was developed to collect:

> *Contextual* data about the aims and purposes of the meeting ... visible characteristics of attendees if apparent, a spatial map of the meeting ... whether chaired or not, degrees of formality, minutes taken and by whom.

Content and focus data about the substantive focus ... the allocation of time for specific items ...

Patterns of interaction data about who spoke first, most, least, how, why, and about what; whether interaction was primarily through the chair ... from one to many ... or in particular sub-groups ...

Emotional flow data about whether emotional displays were evident or not ... what kinds of reactions they evoked.

Decision-taking and making data about whether decisions were taken at the meeting, by whom, about what ... and to whom responsibility was allocated for taking action. (pp. 73–4)

This framework gives readers some sense of the demands made upon the research team not only in planning observations, but also in collecting and analysing data. Ultimately, vignettes provided critical insights into how leaders and leadership teams functioned, and were used to illuminate core findings, for example about how some leaders, who espoused an ethic of distributed leadership, applied that ethic in mythical or symbolic (Samier, 1997) rather than real terms. Others suggested how and why leaders might be adept at stalling some kinds of change, by resisting the challenges that arose from divergent perspectives. Overall, through an ethnographic orientation, the research team were able to understand at first hand: how organisational values, belief systems and ideologies of leadership were demonstrated in group encounters; the structures, functions, discrepancies and contradictions of leadership in organizations as described by participants; and aspects of organisational life observed as leadership in action.

New directions

There are recent emerging concerns about whether 'conventional' ethnography seems rather dated, 'small' even, in terms of the increasing 'bigness' of local, regional, national and global 'worlds', suggesting the need for a re-configuration of ethnography beyond the site-centric. For example, Eisenhart (2001: 16, 19) asks: 'How should we adjust our conceptual orientations and methodological priorities to take into account apparently changing human experiences and priorities?' And, relatedly: 'How can we conscientiously encourage more ethnography, even use it as a standard bearer of good qualitative research, if its methods no longer fit the life and experiences of those we are trying to understand?' Recent directions in education leadership are illustrative, where there is growing preoccupation with system, collaborative and/or inter-service and inter-professional leadership. Leaders' (and researchers') attention is extended beyond single sites to wider, multiple locations. New reference points are identifiable: first, the study of school cultures may be in need of reassessment as boundaries between cultures experienced within and beyond school become permeable and more diverse. Second, if educational experiences of leaders, teachers and students are no longer confined to single locations or to traditional temporal patterns and sequences, then it is timely to consider new conceptions of boundedness and sequence (Eisenhart, 2001; Nespor, 1997). Third, once education is experienced as intersections between multiple networks, ethnographers need to make sense of these 'tangled up' (Nespor, 1997) interactions innovatively, and as sources of power, conflict, diversity and identity.

Ethnographic research does not cease to map the local and the specific; rather, ethnographic forms are needed to move beyond:

> treating the school as a container filled with teacher cultures, student subgroups, classroom instruction, and administrative micro-politics ... to see school as an intersection in social space, a knot in a web of practices that stretch into complex systems beginning and ending outside the school. (Nespor, 1997: xii)

Such interests incline some ethnographers towards virtual environments, and an interest in researching multi-modal educational worlds.

Virtual ethnography

Ethnography's influence has mainly related to face-to-face interactions among individuals and groups. The Internet provides ways of transmitting information between researchers and participants in the absence of close physical contact. CMC is 'a catch-all term' (Pole and Morrison, 2003: 123) to describe:

> the kinds of communication that occur when teachers, learners, and educationalists communicate with one another across computer networks. Such communication can be synchronous (both parties are present simultaneously) or asynchronous (parties need not be); interaction can be one to one, one to many, and many to many; the communication can be text-based or video or audio transmitted.

This opens up the possibility of moving ethnography into virtual settings, including the activities of leadership development and administration. Iszatt White et al. (2006), for example, have interrogated how 'everyday' leadership work is accomplished through the use of information and communications technology (ICT). In their ethnomethodologically centred ethnography of leadership in Further Education, they point to:

> the use of mundane information systems such as email, spread sheets, presentation packages, desk-top publishing ... diary systems and so on ... Observations reveal ... that much of what we might characterise as leadership work, presenting and enforcing decisions, ensuring compliance, managing disputes etc is carried out through the use of email – and that in increasingly distributed educational organizations management by 'walking about' has been supplemented by 'sitting down and emailing'. (p. 14)

As CMC becomes more commonplace, researchers argue that it no longer makes sense to describe online and off-line worlds as if they were separate facets of daily experience (Garcia et al., 2009). Whilst there is a plethora of research about the Internet and CMC, ethnographies to demonstrate the integrated experiences of people off-line and online are still less common (but see Hine, 2000; Kendall, 2004; Kozinets, 2002; Leung, 2005). Indeed, understanding some individuals' lack of access to both kinds of experience also allows ethnographers to consider the 'real' consequences – educationally, politically and socially – for those excluded as leaders and/or learners from both or either 'worlds'.

A quest for 'rich description' is also a feature of *Netnography* which draws mainly upon the techniques and traditions of cultural anthropology to investigate instances where communities are formed through CMC, and do not exist off-line. To date, this has been applied mainly to marketing and consumer research (Kozinets and Handleman, 1998). Here, the data collected are mainly text-based, and combine netnographers' 'field notes' with data, for example, from newsgroup postings, transcripts from MUD (multi-user dungeons), Internet chat sessions and email (Beckmann and Langer, 2005).

A realignment of ethnography to accommodate technologically mediated phenomena has implications for ethnographers' use of research tools (Hine, 2000). Garcia et al. (2009) draw attention to procedures for approaching and interacting with research subjects, especially the need to develop analytical skills with textual and visual data without the co-presence of researcher and researched; to learn 'impression management' via CMC modalities such as email, chat rooms and instant messaging; and to reconsider and apply ethical principles of human subject protection in 'new' environments. Such issues are likely to proliferate if ethnographers increasingly focus their attention, for example, upon online communities of leadership practice, leadership development programmes using off-line and online learning, and, as importantly, leadership forms in which direction and influence extend beyond single sites to multiple arenas, time zones and contexts.

Participant experience

Participant observation and interviewing change when they occur online; the participant observer becomes 'the participant-experiencer' (Walstrom, 2004) who watches text and images on an online screen rather than face-to-face. The term 'experiencer ... captur[es] what it is like to participate in the group by reading and posting messages' (Garcia et al., 2009: 58). Garcia et al. note not only opportunities for 'unobtrusive observation' or 'lurking', but, in relation to the latter, a variety of positions taken by online ethnographers about its advisability. Whilst some ethnographers have advocated 'lurking' as a preliminary tactic to gain access or devise questions, others view 'lurking' as the antithesis of ethnography, not least because the latter is both an ethical and dialogic process of at least two-way communications, in contrast to 'lurking' which is not (Garcia et al., 2009).

The nature of the data affects the kind of data obtained; this is more than a matter of the medium, but also relates to the way different groups use specific 'emoticons' to express physicality, emotion or locality, and where the vernacular poses 'interpretive puzzles' for the ethnographer. Moreover, 'a print out of a chat room conversation is not a substitute for observing the interactional and sequential processes that produced them' (p. 62). Whereas in off-line ethnographies, researchers observe body language, movements and interactions, in online ethnography, the use of pictures, images, colours, graphic design and/or page layout is of greater significance. These include avatars or visual representations of participants' characters, as well as webcams or video recordings, sounds and movements.

As in the ethnographies discussed earlier, online interviewing is also a data source; interviews tend to be asynchronous, as through discussion boards and 'blogging', but are increasingly synchronous, sometimes involving video conferencing or webcams. In combination, approaches evoke new considerations about how ethnographers present themselves, and deal with ethical issues, not least when the 'boundaries between public and private spaces' (Garcia et al., 2009) may be drawn differently in online environments.

Overall, whilst this introduction to virtual ethnography suggests that many challenges faced in terms of data collection, analysis and interpretation are not markedly at odds with those faced by all ethnographers, it is the different ways in which methods are used and understood in virtual environments that marks out its distinctive aspects and ethical requirements.

Summary

In 2012, localized settings still provide access points for studying and capturing vicarious experience. But as Eisenhart (2001: 24) has noted:

> What's different now is that everyday life, including life in schools, seems to be faster paced, more diverse, more complicated, more entangled than before. The kinds of personal and social relationships, exchanges, and networks we participate in seem to be taking new forms, tying together otherwise disparate people ... We need Ethnography to help us grasp these new forms, but we need also to move beyond conventional methods to meet the challenges these new forms ... present.

As the leadership field becomes more outward-facing in terms of collaborations, networks and federations, so ethnography is looking innovatively towards researching both the local and the discrete and broader multi-modal networks of relationships and cultures. This suggests that for ethnographies of leadership at least, a renaissance in use is overdue. This might allow ethnographers not only to research the everyday *and* changing realities of leadership but, as Waite (2000) has suggested, to 'unsettle' its current formulations in ways highlighted by Geertz (2000: 64) when he suggested that ethnography's role was 'to keep the world off-balance … setting off firecrackers'. Not all forms of 'unsettling' are necessarily dramatic. As Iszatt White et al. (2006) contend, much of what *is* leadership work gets missed in research 'that avoids the actual and see-able business of doing leadership work' in favour of producing 'docile matri[ces] for exercising … theoretical will'. Methodological tendencies to avoid ethnography have also been noted not just on technical grounds but also because the career risk to self that arises from ethnographic multi-perspectives is considered too great.

For policy makers and professional practitioners, 'new' themes of leadership and management increasingly evoke inter-organization and intra-organization collaboration. Ethnographic research offers the potential for productive methodological and substantive convergence in order to understand and, as importantly, to critically assess the experiences and meanings evoked in interactions within organisations where 'distributed', 'system', 'diverse', 'collaborative' and other forms of leadership are espoused.

Key points

An enduring legacy of ethnography is its capacity to mount data-rich challenges to purportedly detached, objective and value-free orientations to the conduct of empirical research in educational settings. This chapter has hopefully provided a platform of ideas, concepts, methods and examples to encourage researchers in the leadership field to consider ethnography as method and methodology, and as frameworks for analyses to 'think with'. Like all researchers, ethnographers do not necessarily agree about which aspects of their work are or, indeed, ought to be most significant. Yet, their research provides one of the few opportunities for the detailed examination of leadership work. As such, it might be expected to have impacted much more upon the training and development of leaders than it has to date. Its strength remains its potential to provide deep and rich accounts not in isolation but through connections with the broader structures and systems of which leaders and leadership work are part.

Questions and reflections

1   You are a primary/secondary school lead practitioner. Your school has recently been twinned 'online' with a school in South Africa. Think about the purposes of such arrangements and how its processes and outcomes might be researched. What might be ethnography's contribution? What methods could be applied, and why?

2   You are a university academic. The university in which you work is undergoing major reorganisation. How and why could ethnographic study allow you to focus upon the management of change? What might be its strengths and weaknesses, and from which/whose perspectives?

3   You are a member of a senior management team in a school which has recently become part of a federated arrangement with several other schools. How and why could ethnographic research allow you to interrogate the benefits for all/some students' learning? Which methods might seem appropriate?

Recommended further reading

Brewer, J. (2000) *Ethnography.* Buckingham: Open University Press.

This provides readers with a broad yet incisive examination of ethnography's purposes and uses across the social sciences.

Morrison, M. and Lumby, J. (2009) Is leadership observable? Qualitative orientations to leadership for diversity: a case from FE. *Ethnography and Education* 4(1): 65–82.

Readers might find it helpful to read this example of how an ethnographic orientation was applied to a short-run funded research project about leadership and diversity.

Pole, C. and Morrison, M. (2003) *Ethnography for Education.* Maidenhead: Open University Press.

This book features definitions of ethnography, its uses, a discussion of data analysis and representation, and an assessment of the challenges facing ethnography, all of which draw upon educational examples from actual research.

References

Ball, S.J. (1981) *Beachside Comprehensive: A Case Study of Schooling.* Cambridge: Cambridge University Press.

Bassey, M. (1999) *Case Study Research in Educational Settings*. Buckingham: Buckingham University Press.

Beckmann, S.C. and Langer, R. (2005) Netnography: rich insights from online research, accessed at http://frontpage.cbs.dk/insights/670005.shtml on 18 February 2011.

Brewer, J. (2000) *Ethnography.* Buckingham: Open University Press.

Bryman, A. (1996) Leadership in organizations, in Clegg, S., Hardy, C. and Nord, W. (eds) *Managing Organizations: Current Issues.* Thousand Oaks, CA: Sage.

Bulmer, M. (1984) *The Chicago School of Sociology, Institutionalization, Diversity and the Rise of Sociological Research.* Chicago: University of Chicago Press.

Burgess, R.G. (1983) *Experiencing Comprehensive Education: A Study of Bishop McGregor School.* London: Methuen.

Burgess, R.G. and Morrison, M. (1998) Ethnographies of eating in an urban primary school, in A. Murcott (ed.) *The Nation's Diet: The Social Science of Food Choice.* London: Longman.

Coffey, A. (1999) *The Ethnographic Self: Fieldwork and the Representation of Identity.* London: Sage.

Denzin, N.K. and Lincoln, Y.S. (1998) Entering the field of qualitative research, in Denzin, N. and Lincoln, Y. (eds) *Strategies of Qualitative Inquiry* (2nd edn). London: Sage.

Dey, I. (1993) *Qualitative Data Analysis: A User Friendly Guide for Social Scientists*. London: Routledge.

Eisenhart, M. (2001) Educational ethnography, past, present, and future: ideas to think with. *Educational Researcher* 30(8): 16–27.

Fielding, N. (1993) Ethnography, in Gilbert, N. (ed.) *Researching Social Life*. London: Sage.

Fine, G.A., Morrill, C. and Surianarain, S. (2008) Ethnography in organizational settings, accessed at www.law.berkeley.edu/centers/cslc/conferences/Fine, Morrill and Surianarain-Org Ethnography(2008).pdf on 18 April 2011.

Garcia, A.C., Standlee, A.I., Bechkoff, J. and Cui, Y. (2009) Ethnographic approaches to the Internet and Computer-Mediated Communication. *Journal of Contemporary Ethnography* 38(1): 52–84.

Geertz, C. (2000) *Available Light: Anthropological Reflections on Philosophical Topics*. Princeton, NJ: Princeton University Press.

Glaser, B. and Strauss, A.L. (1967) *The Discovery of Grounded Theory*. Chicago: Aldine.

Gold, R. (1958) Roles in sociological field observation. *Social Forces* 36(3): 217–23.

Guba, E. and Lincoln, Y.S. (1989) *Fourth Generation Evaluation*. Newbury Park, CA: Sage.

Gubrium, J. (1988) *Analysing Field Reality*. London: Sage.

Hammersley, M. (1992) *What's Wrong with Ethnography?* London: Routledge.

Hammersley, M. (2001) On Michael Bassey's concept of fuzzy generalization. *Oxford Review of Education* 27(2): 219–25.

Hammersley, M. and Atkinson, P. (1995) *Ethnography: Principles and Practice* (2nd edn). London: Routledge.

Hine, C. (2000) *Virtual Ethnography*. London: Sage.

Iszatt White, M., Kelly, S. and Rouncefield, M. (2006) 'Ethnography and Leadership', presented at the Liverpool Ethnography Conference, 13–14 September, Liverpool.

Jeffrey, B. and Troman, G. (2004) Time for Ethnography. *British Educational Research Journal* 30(4): 535–48.

Kendall, L. (2004) Participants and observers in online ethnography: five stories about identity, in Johns, M. D., Chen, S-L. S. and Hall, G. J. (eds) *Online Social Research: Methods, Issues & Ethics*. New York: Peter Lang.

Kozinets, R.V. (2002) The field behind the screen: using netnography for marketing research in online communities. *Journal of Marketing Research* 399(1): 61–72.

Kozinets, R.V. and Handleman, J. (1998) Ensouling consumption: a netnographic exploration of the meaning of boycotting behaviour. *Advances in Consumer Research* 39(1): 36–72.

Lacey, C. (1970) *Hightown Grammar*. Manchester: Manchester University Press.

LeCompte, M.D. and Preissle, J. (with R.Tesch) (1993) *Ethnography and Qualitative Design in Educational Research*. San Diego, CA: Academic Press.

Leung, L. (2005) *Virtual Ethnicity: Race, Resistance and the World Wide Web*. Burlington, VT: Ashgate Publishing.

Lofland, J. and Lofland, L.H. (1995) *Analysing Social Settings: A Guide for Qualitative Observation and Analysis*. Belmont, CA: Wadsworth.

Lumby, J., Bhopal, K., Dyke, M., Maringe, F. and Morrison, M. (2007) *Integrating Diversity in Leadership in Further Education. A Research Report*. Lancaster: Centre for Excellence in Leadership.

May, T. (1993) *Social Research. Issues, Methods, and Process*. Buckingham: Open University Press.

Morrison, M. and Arthur, L. (forthcoming) Leadership for inter-service practice: collaborative leadership lost in translation? *Educational Management Administration and Leadership*.

Morrison, M. and Glenny, G. (2011) Collaborative inter-professional policy and practice: in search of evidence. *Journal of Educational Policy* 41(3).

Morrison, M. and Lumby, J. (2009) Is leadership observable? Qualitative orientations to leadership for diversity: a case for FE. *Ethnography and Education* 4(1): 65–82.

Nespor, J. (1997) *Tangled-Up in School: Politics, Space, Bodies, and Signs in the Educational Process*. Mahwah, NJ: Lawrence Erlbaum.

O'Connell-Davidson, J. and Layder, D. (1994) *Methods, Sex, and Madness*. London: Routledge.

Pink, S. (2001) *Doing Visual Ethnography*. London: Sage.

Pole, C. and Lampard, R. (2002) *Practical Social Investigation: Qualitative and Quantitative Methods in Social Research*. Harlow: Pearson Education for Prentice Hall.

Pole, C. and Morrison, M. (2003) *Ethnography for Education*. Maidenhead: Open University Press.

Rist, R.C. (1980) Blitzkrieg ethnography: on the transformation of a method into a movement. *Educational Researcher* 9(2): 8–10.

Samier, E. (1997) Administrative ritual and ceremony: social aesthetics, myth, and language use in the rituals of everyday organizational life. *Educational Management Administration and Leadership* 25(4): 417–36.

Scott, D. and Morrison, M. (2007) *Key Ideas in Educational Research*. London: Continuum.

Silverman, S. (2001) *Interpreting Qualitative Data: Methods for Analysing Talk, Text, and Interactions*. London: Sage.

Stake, R.E. (1978) The case study in social inquiry. *Educational Researcher*, 7 February: 5–8.

Waite, D. (2000) Critical, new directions in educational leadership. *Investigation Administrava* 29(66): 1–3. Accessed at www.132.248.9.118991/herila/Investigacio Administrava/2000/vol29/no86/4pdf

Walstrom, M.K. (2004) Ethics and engagement in communication scholarship: analysing public online support groups as researcher/participant experiencer, in E.A. Buchanan (ed.) *Virtual Research Ethics: Issues and Controversies*. Hershey, PA: Information Science Publishing.

Weber, M. (1949) *The Methodology of the Social Sciences*. New York: Free Press.

Weick, K.E. (1985) Systematic observational methods, in Lindzey, G. and Aronson, E. (eds) *The Handbook of Social Psychology* (3rd edn). New York: Random House.

Wolcott, H. (2003) *The Man in the Principal's Office* (5th edn). Walnut Creek, CA: Altimira Press.

Yin, R.K. (1994) *Case Study Research: Design and Methods* (2nd edn). Thousand Oaks, CA: Sage.

CHAPTER 15

Narrative and Life History

Alan Floyd

Chapter objectives

After reading this chapter, you should:

- Understand narrative and life history in its history and background.
- Be aware of some strategies for collecting and analysing narrative and life history data.
- Appreciate some of the ethical issues involved with this type of research.

The purpose of this chapter is to explore some of the key issues surrounding narrative enquiry and life history in educational leadership and management research. While not claiming to be comprehensive, it is hoped that it will act as a starting point for the researcher who feels that their research question lends itself to such an approach. The further reading list and references at the end of the chapter provide readers with the opportunity to investigate the approach further and explore the issues raised here in more depth.

Introduction: Why narrative and life history?

A few years ago, while working as a lecturer in a UK university, I became interested in finding out why academics took on leadership and management positions and hearing about their experiences once they were in these roles. In short, I was interested in their career stories. This interest led me to begin my doctoral studies investigating academic career trajectories (Floyd, 2009), the main results of which have been published in two subsequent papers (see Floyd, 2012; Floyd and Dimmock, 2011). As I was particularly interested in finding out how individuals perceived and described their experiences of being in a leadership role, I adopted the interpretive paradigm but, like many novice researchers, I found that defining and developing the exact methodological approach for my study proved difficult because of the differing viewpoints of established researchers on qualitative research traditions (Gall et al., 2007).

After reading about, and reflecting on, which approach to use, I began to be influenced by writers who recognise that in any study of complex social situations, biography, history and contexts are inextricably linked and the interaction between researcher and informant is a crucial part of the research process (see, for example, Bozionelos, 2004; Clandinin and Connelly, 2000; Goodson and Sikes, 2001; Hollway and Jefferson, 2000; Josselson and Lieblich, 1993, 1995; Sparkes, 1994). These writers argue the need for narrative enquiry to help explain the complexities of certain social situations, such as the inter-relationships between career trajectory, socialisation and identity investigated in my study. Therefore, in order to answer my doctoral research question, I used a narrative approach as broadly defined by Chase (2005):

> Contemporary narrative inquiry can be characterised as an amalgam of interdisciplinary analytic lenses, diverse disciplinary approaches, and both traditional and innovative methods – all revolving around an interest in biographical particulars as narrated by the ones who live them. (p. 651)

Narrative enquiry is a developing field (Clandinin et al., 2007) and is concerned with personal perspectives of people's experiences of an event or series of events (Newby, 2010). Therefore, the approach is particularly suited to studies whose research questions are based around exploring perceived, subjective experiences of individuals or groups of individuals. There are a variety of forms of narrative research practices including autobiography – when the narrative is constructed by the researcher; oral history – when individuals or groups of individuals reflect on events; and life history – when a person's entire life is narrated (Creswell, 2007).

For my doctoral study, I used a life history approach. Life history research 'emphasises the inner experience of individuals and its connections with changing events and phases throughout the life course' (Bryman, 2008: 695) and this is normally achieved through a one-to-one interview process (Goodson and Sikes, 2001). Such interviews differ from unstructured interviews in that life history interviews explicitly acknowledge the historical influence that a person's biography has on their current experiences and perceptions, as Goodson and Sikes (2001: 2) explain:

1 It explicitly recognizes that lives are not hermetically compartmentalized into, for example, the person we are at work (the professional self) and who we are at home (parent/child/partner selves), and that, consequently, anything which happens to us in one area of our lives potentially impacts upon and has implications for other areas too.

2 It acknowledges that there is a crucial interactive relationship between individuals' lives, their perceptions and experiences, and historical and social contexts and events.

The above key assumptions tied in very well with the main aim of my doctoral study, as I soon realised that in order to understand people's career trajectories and lived experiences of being in a leadership and management position more fully, it was important to appreciate that they could not be explained in isolation but needed to be understood with reference to wider biographical influences. Thus began my interest in using the narrative approach, specifically the use of life history, to help understand research problems based around educational careers and individuals' experiences of being in a leadership role.

Life history research has been around in sociological research since the turn of the 20th century (Goodson, 2001). The approach experienced a rapid rise in popularity with sociologists in the 1920s and 1930s until around 1940 when it fell from favour as an approach in social sciences as more quantitative, statistical approaches began to dominate (Frazier, 1978). More recently, there has been a resurgence in the use of the life history approach (Dhunpath, 2000), particularly when examining teachers' lives and careers (examples include Ball and Goodson, 1985; Kelchtermans, 1993; Sparkes, 1994; Wedgwood, 2005; Woods, 1993). Specific examples of educational leadership and management research projects which have used a narrative/life history approach include Rayner and Ribbins (1999) who investigated the professional lives of headteachers in special education in the UK, and more recently, Moorosi (2010) who studied South African female principals' career paths where 'female principals were asked to narrate their detailed experiences on their career path leading to the principalship' (p. 550).

The approach is not without its critics, with one of the main criticisms being that the data are too subjective, difficult to validate and not generalisable (Bryman, 2008). However, this empiricist view fails to acknowledge that 'the focus is not on the factual accuracy of the story constructed, but on the meaning it has for the respondent' (Dhunpath, 2000: 545) and that attempting to generalise from such data would go against the key assumptions of qualitative research (Lichtman, 2010). Rather, the narrative approach aims to illuminate a person's lived experiences and 'can give a uniquely rich and subtle understanding of life situations' (Punch, 2009: 191). This argument will be developed towards the end of this chapter.

In the following sections, by drawing on my own experiences, appropriate literature and other suitable research examples, I outline some of the key issues that researchers need to think through when undertaking their own research studies if using a narrative or life history approach.

Collecting the data

Once a suitable setting has been identified in relation to your research question, and ethics approval has been granted, the tasks of choosing, contacting and interviewing the participants follow. The Internet can be useful here – researchers can glean a lot of useful information about individuals from web-based profiles before they begin 'official' data collection. Spending time investigating institutional websites can also offer some useful insights about the culture and ethos of the organisations within which potential participants work, which can be useful knowledge to have before, during and after the interview process. There are a number of sampling techniques that you could use; like most narrative/life history researchers, I tend to favour purposive sampling, as defined by Bryman (2008: 458), to identify appropriate participants:

> Such sampling is essentially strategic and entails an attempt to establish a good correspondence between research questions and sampling. In other words, the researcher samples on the basis of wanting to interview people who are relevant to the research questions.

However, once 'in the field', there are often times when snowball sampling occurs, as participants recommend various individuals to me who they think will be of interest to, and be interested in, my studies.

In order to approach participants, I normally send an introductory email to their work email address inviting them to be involved with the study. I include an information sheet with this initial email which gives more detail on the study and includes information on ethical considerations about data handling, anonymity and the right to withdraw (Chapter 7 examines ethical issues in depth). It also allows me to outline for participants what Goodson and Sikes term the 'research bargain' (2001: 26), in other words, what involvement in the research will mean for the participant.

The number of participants that you will interview depends on your specific research question, but it is important to stress that, as mentioned earlier, by adopting this approach you are not trying to achieve generalisability. Therefore, sample sizes tend to be small, as Lichtman (2010: 142) explains:

> Most qualitative research studies use a small number of individuals and cover material in depth. It is quite common to see studies with fewer than 10 respondents; sometimes only a single person is studied.

Within the field of educational leadership and management, there are several examples of such small sample sizes being used in narrative/life history research projects, including Shapira et al. (2011) who explored the biographical backgrounds of seven female school principals in the Arab education system in Israel, and Dimmock and O'Donoghue (1996) who explored the career histories of six headteachers in Western Australia. There are also occasional examples of much larger sample sizes, such as Smith's (2011) life history study on the career decisions of 40 female secondary school teachers in England. However, this large number of participants is quite unusual in small-scale, unfunded research projects adopting a narrative or life history approach.

Some writers suggest that narrative interviews should begin with a general statement. For example, Flick (2006: 173) suggests that the following might be used: 'I would like to ask you to begin with your life history'. Others suggest conducting interviews by using a semi-structured interview guide to give direction to the interview, but with no fixed order of questions; such flexibility in the interviewing process is seen as an essential element of this type of research (Goodson and Sikes, 2001). The themes that form the basis for this guide should normally be based on the study's specific research questions and link to the underlying theoretical framework developed through your literature review. Nevertheless, some generic questions will probably feature in most life history interview schedules based on key information such as place and date of birth, family background, memories of childhood and perceived educational experiences.

Although there are different approaches to undertaking interviews, I tend to carry them out in stages. First, as highlighted above, the participants receive an information sheet. Second, I set up a face-to-face interview. Some researchers propose undertaking two or three rounds of interviews (see, for example, Seidman, 2006) and there are some life history studies that have involved many more rounds than this (Goodson and Sikes, 2001). However, in the life history studies that I have conducted – my PhD (Floyd, 2009, 2012; Floyd and Dimmock, 2011), a subsequent study into academic department heads in a research-led university (Floyd, 2011), and an ongoing study exploring the career trajectories of Jamaican school leaders – several of my potential participants have not been willing to take part in more than one interview due to time constraints. Therefore, I normally hold one longer single interview and then follow up any outstanding issues and queries through other modes of communication, such as email, telephone or webcam. I have found this approach to be particularly helpful when trying to recruit educational leaders and managers who perceive that they are too busy to commit to more than one meeting. Of course, this practice does not preclude the possibility of undertaking more than one interview if the participant is willing and the researcher feels that it is necessary.

To elicit the whole of an individual's life story, Hollway and Jefferson (2000) argue that several techniques are required. These include using open-ended questions and getting the respondent to tell stories of their experiences. Chase (1995) also highlights this technique as a key method in interview studies, and stresses the need to follow up themes using the respondent's ordering and phrasing. Following suggestions from Kvale (2007) and Seidman (2006) related to interview technique, the researcher should make a conscious effort to ask one question at a time, use open-ended questions and try not to interrupt the respondent. The researcher should also take notes when the respondent uses different styles of language and when key themes are raised that need expansion. These issues can then be followed up at different points of each interview using the respondent's terminology. Additionally, a tick-box schedule should be used to ensure the interview progresses as required. Wherever possible, interviews should be conducted in the participant's office (if they have one) and recorded on a digital voice recorder (with their agreement, of course). For more detail on generic interviewing techniques, please see Chapter 17.

Analysing the data

Before I offer some thoughts on how to analyse narrative and life history data, there are two key points to be made here. First, there is no 'right way' to do this task; based on guidelines from the literature, what I suggest here are examples from my own research that have worked for me. Second, while I agree with writers who argue that narrative and focused description are the cornerstone of good qualitative research (see, for example, Thomas and James, 2006; Wolcott, 1994), I also acknowledge that presenting the narratives on their own is not enough. As Josselson and Lieblich (1993: xii) assert: 'Knowing ... must also include the conceptual. Story cannot stand alone but must be linked to some theoretical concepts or previous knowledge.' Similarly, Bathmaker and Harnett state: 'what is central is the relationship between the individual and wider structures ... narrative inquiry therefore goes beyond the telling of stories ...' (Bathmaker and Harnett, 2010: 4).

Broadly speaking, there are two main approaches to analysing narrative data. The first is to attempt to reduce the data by using coding and thematic analysis techniques, while the second is to attempt to analyse the data as a whole, in narrative form. The two techniques are sometimes seen in opposition in that some researchers view coding and thematic analyses as reductionist and feel that the meaning of the story will be lost if such an approach is taken (Lichtman, 2010). Notwithstanding this tension, one way of making sense of the data that you have collected is to use both of these techniques together (Seidman, 2006). This multi-analysis approach has been used in several narrative studies investigating educational leadership and management issues; examples include Inman's (2007) study on how academic leaders learn to lead in UK universities, Crawford's (2009) study on academics' views on continuing professional development in two English universities, and Dana et al.'s (2010) study exploring experienced teachers' perceptions of assessment and accountability procedures in the US middle-school system.

Analysis begins from the start of the interview process. During the taped conversation, brief notes can be made highlighting any particular interesting details. Notes can also be made about how things are being discussed and recounted. This technique recognises that interview talk is not just about the topic being researched, but is also about the social interaction between the interviewer and the interviewee (Clandinin and Connelly, 2000). Furthermore, this approach can help identify some of the wider cultural influences and narratives of the responses (Silverman, 2006). Wherever possible, the next step in the analytical process is to transcribe and analyse each interview before undertaking the next. This iterative research practice allows interview questions to change as themes and issues emerge from the data and allows the researcher to reflect deeply on each respondent's narrative before undertaking the next interview (Gilbert, 2008). From my own experiences, following each interview, I download each recording onto the computer and then transcribe this into a Microsoft Word document. During transcription, I make notes and cross-references to the notes that have been taken during the interview. Even if someone else is doing the transcription, it is still important to go through the text while listening to your recording to ensure that the conversation has been transcribed correctly. It is worth mentioning at this point that transcription takes time – one hour's worth of talk can take an experienced typist up to six hours to transcribe. However, I contend that it is an essential part of the research process in narrative/life history research; notes, no matter how detailed, are not sufficient. For it is the story, as recounted by the participant, that should form the bedrock of your analysis.

After the transcription is complete, I send it back to the participant for checking and augmentation as discussed earlier. Once the necessary changes and additions have been made to the data, I begin to identify codes in a column to the right of it. This initial coding is undertaken by using gerunds and by keeping the codes active and as close to the original statements as possible (Charmaz, 2006). Each transcript is read through twice during this process and different pens are used each time. At this stage, I normally enter all data into NVivo, a qualitative data analysis software package (also discussed in Chapter 25). While I use the software to help organise the vast amounts of data that have been generated by my interviews (as a very rough guide, one hour's worth of talk will provide you with approximately 8000–9000 words of text), I do not use it to code or sift through the data automatically as I prefer to keep this as a manual process. Next, I revisit the initial codes and begin to identify a list of emerging themes by merging and renaming some codes, keeping others and revisiting the literature (Bryman, 2008). These initial themes are then analysed and contextualised in accordance with the analytical framework of my study and further developed by drawing 'connections with external authority' (Wolcott, 1994: 34). These connections are normally made with key research and writing developed through an initial literature review which I undertake before data collection commences, but which I return to throughout the research process. (Again, this is discussed in full in Chapter 25.)

As mentioned earlier, in order to maintain the holistic narrative of the individual's life story as constructed by themselves (Clandinin and Connelly, 2000; Josselson and Lieblich, 1993, 1995), I also draw on suggestions by Seidman (2006) and construct profiles of each of my participants. First, following the labelling and coding procedures outlined above, I select all the passages for each participant that are seen as important and put these into one document. Then, I create a narrative from this data. This is written in the words of the participant and in the first person:

> One key to the power of the profile is that it is presented in the words of the participant. I cannot stress too much how important it is to use the first person, the voice of the participant, rather than a third-person transformation of that voice. (Seidman, 2006: 121)

Where considered appropriate, I also eliminate any hesitations and repetitions from each participant's oral speech to allow it to read more freely. Once these individual profiles have been constructed, they are analysed to identify interconnections within and between them. By drawing on appropriate theory and previous knowledge, these localised narratives can then be connected to the broader narratives of educational and social change in the country within which they have been constructed (Hargreaves, 1999) and an individual's social constructions of their own experiences can be interpreted and understood in relation to national, social and political contexts.

To conclude this section, I would like to discuss further the notion of attempting to minimise bias in narrative work, picking up on points made earlier in this chapter regarding authors who are critical of the narrative approach. I am always slightly bemused when writers discuss notions of validity and reliability in narrative research, particularly when they suggest that this can be 'improved' by undertaking certain measures, one of which is to 'triangulate' one person's account with other sources of information (Cohen et al., 2011). In my view, this approach of attempting to validate the narrative and achieve some form of objective truth goes against the key ontological and epistemological assumptions of the methodology. I agree with Lichtman (2010: 98) when she says:

> Some writers hold the view that triangulating data, investigators and methodologies can establish validity. I believe, however, that the concept is more appropriate to traditional or positivist paradigms.

This is not to say that other data evidence is not useful in narrative/life history research. Indeed, I would strongly recommend that any researcher planning to use the approach *supplements*, rather than *triangulates*, their data with other sources to provide context and texture to the narrative. For example, analysing key strategic documents produced by institutions could help determine the overall culture and working practices within which participants' narratives are formed. Additionally, before interviews are carried out, it may be useful to analyse web-based information, where possible, for each participant. This task allows the researcher to have a greater knowledge of the interviewee's past and might enable them to tailor questions for each participant; it can also allow researchers to establish a positive and trusting relationship with the participant by founding some common ground and demonstrating knowledge of the topic area, both important aspects of in-depth interviewing technique (Newby, 2010).

When writing up your narrative/life history work, rather than taking steps to minimise the obvious bias present in your research, values and potential biases can be made explicit by providing a short biography that also highlights the epistemological and ontological positions that have underpinned your work early on in your report. This information will then help the reader to appraise the work in a more informed way and help them detect any of the subjective, value-laden assumptions that underpin the study (Goodson and Sikes, 2001; Seidman, 2006). This concept of reflexivity is a key tenet of interpretive research, and is in line with other authors who advocate writing 'yourself into your research' (Lichtman, 2010; Wolcott, 1994).

And finally...

There are several ethical issues involved with undertaking any educational research (Sikes, 2006) and, as noted earlier, these are explored in depth in Chapter 7. Notwithstanding these concerns, one of the most important issues that I have experienced when undertaking narrative research is recognising that each participant's story is still being lived before and after the interview has taken place. Clandinin and Connelly (2000: 63) have termed this as 'being in the midst':

> As researchers, we come to each new inquiry field living our stories. Our participants also enter the enquiry field in the midst of living their stories. Their lives do not begin the day we arrive nor do they end as we leave. Their lives continue ...

These circumstances mean that the researcher may have to negotiate potentially difficult situations that may arise when undertaking each interview. In my research, several situations have arisen during the course of interviewing which have been clearly distressing for those concerned. These situations have included one participant whose husband had died quite recently, one who had just been made redundant, one who felt they were being bullied out of their job, one who admitted to almost having a nervous breakdown and one who was suffering from cancer. Goodson and Sikes discuss these dilemmas in words that provide a useful and thought-provoking conclusion to this chapter:

> Engaging in life history work can sometimes be painful in that informants may find themselves revisiting distressing events. Some informants may be quite prepared to do this because remembering such events has become part of their everyday lives; for others the experience may be shocking, disturbing and unexpected. Life historians need to have thought about the potential implications that being involved in their research has for their informants. Although effects cannot be easily predicted, the fact remains that being in life history work can alter lives. (2001: 109)

Key points

- The use of a narrative and life history approach can be appropriate when investigating research problems in educational leadership and management that are based around exploring perceived, subjective experiences of individuals or groups of individuals and involve understanding complex social situations, such as leaders' career paths and any associated identity formation and changes.

- Careful thought needs to be given to collecting narrative and life history data. Although flexibility is important, the data collection process should be structured and logical in order to address your research question in a meaningful way.

- The use of electronic means can be useful in reducing the time commitment involved for participants, which may encourage potential interviewees to agree to take part in your study.

- When analysing and interpreting your data, a variety of techniques can be used, but whichever is adopted it is crucial to be aware that the story on its own is not enough.

- There are several ethical issues to be aware of when undertaking this type of research, not least of which are the personal relationships established throughout the research process and the potentially sensitive information that participants may share with the researcher during the interview.

Questions and reflections

1 Can you think of a suitable research problem in your own institution that could be addressed by using a life history and narrative approach? What ethical issues do you think may be linked to such a study?

2 What are some of the issues involved with collecting and interpreting somebody else's 'story'? What influence do you think you, as the researcher, will have on the data that emerges? What issues does this raise for your research and how might you address these issues?

3 In relation to analysing narrative and life history data, what are the advantages and disadvantages of using coding and thematic techniques versus more holistic approaches? Can the two approaches be reconciled?

Recommended further reading

Chase, S. E. (2011) Narrative inquiry: still a field in the making, in Denzin, N. K. and Lincoln, Y. S. (eds) *The Sage Handbook of Qualitative Research* (4th edn). Thousand Oaks, CA: Sage. pp. 421–34.

This chapter (recently updated from the original – Chase, S. E. (2005) Narrative inquiry: multiple lenses, approaches, voices – published in the third edition of this landmark handbook) offers a comprehensive starting point to answer the question: what is narrative inquiry? The chapter defines key terms, provides a historical context and discusses the key theoretical issues underlying the approach.

Clandinin, D. J. and Connelly, F. M. (2000) *Narrative Inquiry: Experience and Story in Qualitative Research*. San Francisco, CA: Jossey-Bass.

Seen by many as a definitive text, this book provides a fascinating and thought-provoking overview of the narrative approach, built around the authors' experiences and reflections of undertaking a range of narrative research projects throughout their careers.

Goodson, I. and Sikes P. (2001) *Life History Research in Educational Settings: Learning from Lives*. Buckingham: Open University Press.

This well-written and easy-to-read text by two of the leading scholars in the field is quite simply a 'must read' for those wishing to undertake a life history study for the first time.

References

Ball, S. and Goodson, I. (eds) (1985) *Teachers' Lives and Careers*. London: The Falmer Press.

Bathmaker, A.-M. and Harnett, P. (eds) (2010) *Exploring Learning, Identity and Power through Life History and Narrative Research*. Abingdon: Routledge.

Bozionelos, N. (2004) The relationship between disposition and career success: a British study. *Journal of Occupational and Organizational Psychology* 77(3): 403–20.

Bryman, A. (2008) *Social Research Methods* (3rd edn). Oxford: Oxford University Press.

Charmaz, K. (2006) *Constructing Grounded Theory: A Practical Guide Through Qualitative Analysis*. London: Sage.

Chase, S. E. (1995) Taking Narrative Seriously, in Josselson, R. and Lieblich, A. (eds), *Interpreting Experience: The Narrative Study of Lives* (Vol. 3). Thousand Oaks, CA: Sage.

Chase, S. E. (2005) Narrative Inquiry: Multiple Lenses, Approaches, Voices, in Denzin, N. K. and Lincoln, Y. S. (eds) *The Sage Handbook of Qualitative Research* (3rd edn). Thousand Oaks, CA: Sage. pp. 651–79.

Clandinin, D. J. and Connelly, F. M. (2000) *Narrative Inquiry: Experience and Story in Qualitative Research*. San Francisco, CA: Jossey-Bass.

Clandinin, D. J., Pushor, D. and Orr, A. M. (2007) Navigating sites for narrative inquiry. *Journal of Teacher Education* 58(1), 21–35.

Cohen, L., Manion, L. and Morrison, K. (2011) *Research Methods in Education*. Abingdon: Routledge.

Crawford, K. (2009) Continuing Professional Development in Higher Education: Voices from Below. Unpublished EdD Thesis, University of Lincoln.

Creswell, J. W. (2007) *Qualitative Inquiry and Research Design: Choosing Among Five Approaches* (2nd edn). Thousand Oaks, CA: Sage.

Dana, N. F., Delane, D. C. and George, P. (2010) Reclaiming Camelot: capturing the reflections of exemplary, veteran middle school teachers in an age of high stakes testing and accountability through narrative inquiry, in Malu, K. F. (ed.), *Voices From the Middle: Narrative Inquiry By, For and About the Middle Level Community* (pp. 151–72). Charlotte, NC: Information Age Publishing.

Dhunpath, R. (2000). Life history methodology: 'narradigm' regained. *International Journal of Qualitative Studies in Education*, 13(5), 543–51.

Dimmock, C. and O'Donoghue, T. (1996) *Innovative School Principals and Restructuring*. Abingdon: Routledge.

Flick, U. (2006) *An Introduction to Qualitative Research* (3rd edn). London: Sage.

Floyd, A. (2009) Life Histories of Academics who become Heads of Department: Socialisation, Identity and Career Trajectory. Unpublished PhD Thesis, University of Leicester.

Floyd, A. (2011) Narratives of academics who become department heads in a chartered UK university. Presented as part of a symposium: Barnet, R., Evans, L., Floyd, A., Gornell, L. and Salisbury, J., *Narrating 'Workstyles, Textures and Adaptations' in Academic Work and Workplace.* Paper presented at the Centre for Excellence in Preparing for Academic Practice, 4th International Conference, Academia as workplace: Linking Past, Present and Future, University of Oxford 4–6 April 2011.

Floyd, A. (2012) 'Turning points': the personal and professional circumstances that lead academics to become middle managers. *Educational Management Administration and Leadership* 40(2) in press.

Floyd, A. and Dimmock, C. (2011) 'Jugglers', 'copers' and 'strugglers': academics' perceptions of being a HoD in a post-1992 UK university and how it influences their future careers. *Journal of Higher Education Policy and Management* 33(4): 387–99.

Frazier, C. (1978) The use of life-histories in testing theories of criminal behavior: towards reviving a method. *Qualitative Sociology* 1(1): 122–42.

Gall, M. D., Gall, J. P. and Borg, W. (2007) *Educational Research: An Introduction* (8th edn). Boston, MA: Pearson.

Gilbert, N. (2008) *Researching Social Life* (3rd edn). London: Sage.

Goodson, I. (2001) The story of life history: origins of the life history method in sociology. *Identity* 1(2): 129–42.

Goodson, I. and Sikes, P. (2001) *Life History Research in Educational Settings: Learning from Lives.* Buckingham: Open University Press.

Hargreaves, A. (1999) Schooling in the new millennium: educational research for the post-modern age. *Discourse: Studies in the Cultural Politics of Education* 20(3): 333–55.

Hollway, W. and Jefferson, T. (2000) *Doing Qualitative Research Differently: Free Association, Narrative and the Interview Method.* London: Sage.

Inman, M. (2007) The journey to leadership: a study of how leader-academics in higher education learn to lead. Unpublished EdD Thesis, The University of Birmingham.

Josselson, R. and Lieblich, A. (eds) (1993) *The Narrative Study of Lives* (Vol. 1). Thousand Oaks, CA: Sage.

Josselson, R. and Lieblich, A. (eds) (1995) *Interpreting Experience: The Narrative Study of Lives* (Vol. 3). Thousand Oaks, CA: Sage.

Kelchtermans, G. (1993) Getting the story, understanding the lives: from career stories to teachers' professional development. *Teaching and Teacher Education* 9(5–6): 443–56.

Kvale, S. (2007) *Doing Interviews.* London: Sage.

Lichtman, M. (2010) *Qualitative Research in Education: A User's Guide* (2nd edn). Thousand Oaks, CA: Sage.

Moorosi, P. (2010) South African female principals' career paths: understanding the gender gap in secondary school management. *Educational Management Administration & Leadership* 38(5): 547–62.

Newby, P. (2010) *Research Methods for Education.* Harlow: Pearson Education.

Punch, K. F. (2009) *Introduction to Research Methods in Education.* London: Sage.

Rayner, S. G. and Ribbins, P.M. (1999) *Headteachers and Leadership in Special Education.* London: Cassell.

Seidman, I. (2006) *Interviewing as Qualitative Research: A Guide for Researchers in Education and the Social Sciences* (3rd edn). New York: Teachers College Press.

Shapira, T., Arar, K. and Azaiza, F. (2011) 'They didn't consider me and no-one even took me into account': female school principals in the Arab education system in Israel. *Educational Management Administration & Leadership* 39(1): 25–43.

Sikes, P. (2006) On dodgy ground? Problematics and ethics in educational research. *International Journal of Research and Method in Education* 29(1): 105–17.

Silverman, D. (2006) *Interpreting Qualitative Data* (3rd edn). London: Sage.

Smith, J. (2011) Agency and female teachers' career decisions: a life history study of 40 women. *Educational Management Administration and Leadership* 39(1): 7–24.

Sparkes, A. C. (1994) Self, silence and invisibility as a beginning teacher: a life history of lesbian experience. *British Journal of Sociology of Education* 15(1): 93–118.

Thomas, G. and James, D. (2006) Reinventing grounded theory: some questions about theory, ground and discovery. *British Educational Research Journal* 32(6): 767–95.

Wedgwood, N. (2005) Just one of the boys? A life history case study of a male physical education teacher. *Gender and Education* 17(2): 189–201.

Wolcott, H. F. (1994) *Transforming Qualitative Data: Description, Analysis and Interpretation.* Thousand Oaks, CA: Sage.

Woods, P. (1993) Managing marginality: teacher development through grounded life history. *British Educational Research Journal* 19(5): 447–66.

CHAPTER 16

Learner Voice in Educational Leadership Research

Jacky Lumby

Chapter objectives

This chapter establishes why it may be important to involve learners in research on educational leadership. Learners, of course, are not a homogeneous group and the dimensions of how we might understand their diversity and its implications are explored. The status of learners as children or young adults is argued by some to limit their competence and increase their vulnerability as object and subject in research. The chapter addresses this issue and the methodological issues that arise. It provides examples of research in educational leadership that has involved learners and concludes on the potential purpose and value of learners' contribution to research on educational leadership. The chapter argues that their involvement is often useful and sometimes essential to build knowledge about how leadership is working or could work to the benefit of learners. The first part of the chapter is structured around exploring the answers to a series of questions:

- Why involve learners in research on educational leadership?
- How are issues concerning their competence or vulnerability to be addressed?
- How might we understand learners as a group which is not homogeneous?
- What role might learners play in research?
- What methodological issues arise in involving them?

The chapter then provides examples of learner voice in educational leadership research in practice and reviews the reasons for resistance to the inclusion of learner voice before the chapter conclusions.

Why involve learners in research on educational leadership?

Educational leadership is usually assumed to be primarily the act of adults in nurseries, schools, colleges, universities and other sites of learning. Research about the preparation for and enactment of leadership tends to be primarily concerned with how leaders perceive leadership and its impact, or about other adults' perceptions, or both. While learning is directly experienced by learners, and so something they may be thought to comment on usefully, leadership is seen to have an indirect effect on them. As a result, learners have historically been involved less often in research on leadership than in research on learning; this is despite the fact that they are the intended beneficiaries of leadership. More recently, a rising tide of fashion demands that 'student voice' be heard in national and local policy development, and in running educational organisations (James, 2007). The drivers of this trend are various. Critical theorists have suggested that speaking for the less powerful, such as learners, risks embedding powerlessness further (Alcoff, 1991/92). Consequently, they argue, inclusion of the voice of the less powerful in research should be axiomatic. Slee (1994) depicts schools as habitually creating and sustaining a power differential by means of a culture in which learners are seen as the problem and professionals as the providers of answers. To imbue the voice of learners with importance therefore risks disturbing the power relationship and is consequently perceived as threatening. Others suggest that the greater involvement of learners in the shaping of education is essential preparation for their place in a democratic society (Ruddock and Fielding, 2006). However, the use of learner voice has also been challenged as uncritical (Thomson and Gunter, 2006) or glib and superficial, both in the UK (Fielding, 2006) and in the USA (Lensmire, 1998), or ill thought through (Ruddock and Fielding, 2006).

The belief that learners should have a voice is part of a wider trend in the social sciences where it is increasingly accepted by researchers that groups who have less power should be empowered to speak, no longer to be 'silenced spectators' (James, 2007: 261). As a result of this conviction, children are more likely to be included in studies in particular areas of research such as sociological studies of children in care, or migrants, or educational studies of the learning experience of learners with special learning needs, where powerlessness and vulnerability may be especially evident. The majority of leadership studies do not involve learners and this may be because learners are seen as not competent to judge, or not knowledgeable or not interested, or because there are perceived to be methodological or ethical barriers to involving them.

How are issues concerning their competence or vulnerability to be addressed?

The competence of children to participate in research has been questioned, their age and immaturity rendering them doubtful contributors in the eyes of some (Mahon et al., 1996). Children are viewed as more suggestible than adults and unable to step outside authority relationships with a researcher; they are also seen as potentially misusing power when acting as researchers themselves. A major concern is the potential for children to try to please by affirming what they think is the adult researcher's or teacher's view. It is accepted that adult respondents may also wish to please by their answers or to present themselves in a way that accords with their positive self-image. At issue amongst researchers is the belief that the impetus to please and so distort may be much stronger amongst children. Conolly (2008) suggests also that children and young people are not very competent as researchers themselves, compared to professional researchers or practitioner researchers. Ruddock and Fielding challenge this (2006: 225), suggesting that 'an ideology of immaturity' is reflective of the unequal relation between teachers and learners maintained in schools for control purposes rather than necessarily because of a greater incompetence amongst children.

The vulnerability of children is also a concern (see also Chapter 7 of this volume). It may be difficult in much research to offer absolute anonymity (Walford, 2005). Children and young people may be more vulnerable to negative reactions from adults who learn of views or information provided by the children of which they disapprove or with which they disagree or would prefer not to have had disclosed. There are also concerns about disturbing or upsetting children by questioning that is experienced as invasive due to children's perceived lesser confidence to refuse or divert questions, and adults' greater power to press them. Learners themselves may misuse power, for example in breaching the confidentiality of group interviews. All these are methodological issues that face researchers working with adults in research on leadership. Whether they are perceived as differing in degree to the issues in working with adults or not, as with any methodological issue, the researcher is able to take note and carefully plan to address the challenges.

How might we understand learners as a group which is not homogeneous?

Learners differ across a range of dimensions – by age, developmental stage, gender, ethnicity, socioeconomic class, ability/disability, circumstances (being in care, being migrants, being speakers of English as an Additional Language) and many more characteristics. Despite this, in research 'conceptualizations uncritically clump children together as members of a category. This category is then held to speak with one undifferentiated voice' (James, 2007: 262). Age is assumed sometimes to equate to developmental stage, and that is not always the case. Equally, the life experience of some learners may be more diverse than that of, for example, many teachers. Young people often make clear that they wish to be viewed as individuals and not as an undifferentiated group of learners.

The first issue then is the propensity to distinguish inadequately amongst learners. A second is the propensity to offer unequal access. Rather than the homogenised voice of learners perceived as reflecting the experience and views of all, the voice of particular groups may be privileged. Ruddock and Fielding (2006) argue that some voices are more valued than others – perhaps those who are more articulate or whose behaviour conforms more to the school's or college's formal values. Learners' engagement in research may therefore further embed the differential attention and value accorded to some (Lumby, 2012).

What role might learners play in research?

Levey suggests four roles that children might play in research:

1 as 'wedges', or as instrumentally important in terms of helping adults gain access to fieldsites, relationships, and knowledge

2 as collaborators, when children contribute to the formulation of research questions, collect data, or write reports

3 as objects of study, when the topic of an ethnography is about children's issues but children themselves are not directly observed and/or consulted, and

4 as subjects of study, when children are seen as individuals fully able to answer questions in a worthwhile way. (Levey, 2009: 312)

Educational leadership research, when it engages with learners, typically involves learners as objects of study – for example, the impact of leadership on children's attainment or achievement. Levey argues that not only can children add value to the design of research and the collection of data by working in roles 1, 2 and 4, but their involvement can increase impact. Coad and Evans (2008) offer a similar typology:

Adult research teams plan, collect and undertake data analysis as a group without children's intervention in the process.

Adult research teams plan and analyse the data but involve children in the data collection process through the use of more participatory methods. Children may help to verify adult researchers' understandings of data.

Adult research teams train a group of children to act as a reference or advisory group to consult with and guide the research process and help to interpret the findings.

Adult researchers train a group of children as peer- or co-researchers to work alongside adult researchers at every stage of the research project. They are actively involved in the data analysis stage through strategies such as coding, verification and interpretation.

Child and young person-led research teams plan, collect and undertake data analysis as a group with adults facilitating the process. (Coad and Evans, 2008: 43–5)

An example of the final process is given in the Sharnbrook example in the concluding section of this chapter. It is not suggested normatively that any particular approach is intrinsically of more value than others. Rather, as with all methodology, the appropriate choices are of key importance. The examples that are given in this chapter make it clear that some leadership researchers feel it is of value to involve learners in the range of roles suggested in the above typologies.

What methodological issues arise in involving them?

A number of methodological issues arise in working with children in research. The first of these might be summarised as confining the authority of the researcher, particularly when the latter is a practitioner researcher such as a teacher. This may be particularly testing where the children have special learning needs. Both the child and the parent or teacher may expect the researcher to act in *loco parentis*, adopting a supervisory role, thereby compelling an authority relationship. Some researchers have adopted particular methods to try to avoid this and to relinquish authority. For example, Kelly (2007) recounts the use of 'stop–go' cards to enable young children to stop and restart questions according to their attention span, thereby allowing the child to control the pace of an interview.

Lensmire (1998) explores a more subtle way in which authority may distort, by the researcher's rejection of the authentic views and feelings of the child. In adult mode, an adult may interpret a child expressing, in their view, inappropriate attitudes as deliberately attempting to shock and challenge, or they may feel obligated to challenge and halt such expression, for example of racism (Bragg, 2001). The habitual role of the adult is to shape and guide. The researcher, by contrast, has a different aim: as far as is feasible to step aside from influencing the respondent's thoughts and words. The researcher may need to uncover a range of attitudes in conflict with the researcher's own or that are not generally deemed desirable or acceptable by the community. The roles of both researcher and responsible adult are clear, but in tension. 'Who is speaking to whom turns out to be as important for meaning and truth as what is said; in fact what is said turns out to change according to who is speaking and who is listening' (Alcoff, 1991/92: 12). The issues raised by power distance in relationships, particularly for practitioner researchers, also relate to engaging with adult colleagues, but may be much more acute when engaging with children, as the researcher/teacher may feel professionally obligated to arbitrate and mould views and attitudes. Additionally, the position of the researcher may colour not only the data communicated, but also influence how they are analysed and presented, a process of manipulation of meaning that Fielding (2004: 298) deems 'insidious'. As with research involving adults, there is no simple method or tool to ensure authenticity in engagement with children in research. Rather, what may be required is sustained and deep self-reflection by researchers on the relationship of their position and that of the children involved and acknowledgement of how this has impacted on the research.

The second methodological issue is a frequent failure to adequately situate data from children. The age group to which they belong is often seen as an adequate context, sometimes with added detail on gender or ethnicity. James (2007: 266) suggests:

> The claims that are made about and on behalf of 'children' and the use of 'children's voices' as evidence – and as evidence that might be acted on – need, therefore, to be tempered by careful acknowledgment of the cultural contexts of their production.

The dangers identified by Fielding (2006) of children being used apparently to add authenticity to research, while actually being mere token or decoration, may be reduced if as much care were taken to contextualise a learner sample as would be the case with an adult group. A sample described as comprising Year 9 learners (aged 14 years) does not indicate anything about the diversity of socioeconomic status within the group, the developmental stage in terms of, for example, previous attainment or any other characteristic which might influence their views. The necessity to contextualise is particularly relevant to qualitative studies where, as Alcoff (1991/92: 7) suggests: 'a speaker's location (which I take to refer to their *social* location, or social identity) has an epistemically significant impact on that speaker's claims' (author's emphasis).

Finally, the confining of authority is relevant in both directions; just as learners may feel inhibited in their relations with researchers and particularly practitioner researchers, the researcher may feel overly respectful of learners' views (Thomson and Gunter, 2006).

Researching educational leadership: examples of practice

Early years

Early years education is here defined as for children under the age of 5. This is the age group where concerns about competence and vulnerability might be viewed as most acute. Clark (2005: 491) starts from the question, 'How do you listen to the views and experiences of young children?', and reviews relevant European research and case studies related to early years education to suggest a wide range of methods that have been used with success to involve very young children in expressing their preferences and assessing the provision on offer. These include:

- participant observation, using extended time to interact with and record interaction with and amongst young children, involving them in interpreting the observation
- different forms of interview, including adults interviewing individual children or groups of children, child conferencing, and children interviewing children

- questionnaires on which children can draw
- play activities such as listening on telephones, use of toys or puppets as intermediaries and persona dolls
- ranking games, where photographs of activities are placed in rank order, sometimes using fishing rods to select items
- arts activities using visual and auditory techniques such as cameras and photographs, maps, audio recordings and physical tours.

Practitioners working in early years will recognise such techniques as used within nurseries, playgroups and schools, as Clark (2005) points out, usually for small-scale studies. However, she also cites a study by Dupree, Bertram and Pascal (2001) that involved nearly a thousand young children who were interviewed using child conferencing. 'The children were asked questions relating to five of the dimensions of quality identified in the programme: aims and objectives, learning experiences, learning and teaching styles, staffing and relationships and interactions' (Clark, 2005: 496). Children were contributing to the collection of data along several dimensions of leadership with the aim of improving quality. Even children under the age of 5 were able to provide useful perceptions on instructional leadership, the structure and pacing of learning activities, the balance within the curriculum of different kinds of activity, and on pastoral issues in commenting on relationships with staff. Children here are participating in Levey's (2009) typology, roles 1 and 4; as wedges, allowing researchers to access their play and interactions; and as subjects, contributing worthwhile data in their own right. In common with other commentators on involving children in research, Clark (2005) stresses the obligation to treat the resulting data with respect, to make use of them in adjusting leadership, and to feed back to the participants on how what they have contributed has been used and what the research has achieved.

Secondary school learners

There are many examples of learners' contribution to developing the leadership of secondary schools. In the UK, Thomson and Gunter (2006) engaged learners with school improvement. Working with a small group of learners as consultants, the researchers used a range of methods including questionnaire surveys, mind mapping and interviews to explore in detail multiple aspects of the school as an environment for learning, including not only those factors that directly impact on learning, such as relationships with teachers and pedagogy, but those that indirectly impact, such as the food available. Also in the UK, the Ealing Professional Learning Community Review Team Investigation (Stoll, 2009) set up a formal review led by learners to investigate instructional leadership. Learners researching how learning is led in the school used:

- lesson observations
- staff interviews

- learner interviews
- documentary analysis of curriculum resources – work schemes and plans, and learner work.

The ensuing networking and conversations around what was learned created knowledge about the processes of schooling as well as the outcomes.

The disaffected and disengaged

The voice of those who are disaffected or disengaged may be particularly silent in those forms of research used in schools. Such young people may be absent from School Councils or contribute sparsely or not at all to written evaluation. Despite perceived difficulties, a number of studies have worked with young people to investigate their perspective on the way schools are led. In the USA, Brice Heath and McLaughlin (1994) undertook five years of field-work in 60 youth and community settings where those who had not found schooling a positive experience were enabled to learn. They also interviewed learners of schools in eight metropolitan areas. Amongst much else, they uncovered how schools are led in relation to partnership, the research sug-gesting that schools are perceived as the most difficult category of partner because of their wish to be in control of the partnership and because they see a tight relationship between learners, staff and parents, with other individuals and organisations viewed as outsiders in relation to this closed circle. Young people were also able to provide concrete ideas on how instructional leader-ship might be adapted to enable them to learn in school.

Similarly, in the UK, Lumby (2011) used data from over 60 disaffected young people to uncover how the school environment might be developed to support learning more effectively. Such findings relate to leadership and how leaders might adapt culture, curriculum and pedagogy to make schools more effective. In the USA, Owens and Johnson (2009) focused on the creation of trust, building a conceptual understanding of the stages by which trust was created using multiple sources of data from learners on the Upward Bound Program, a federally sponsored programme that provides academic support to learners preparing for college entrance but at risk of exiting.

Currently, for the methodological and political reasons presented in this chapter, leadership research is often about asking leaders what they think they are doing through interviews or surveys and, more rarely, observation or ask-ing adult colleagues. However, there are compelling reasons for involving learners in research on leadership. Learners are able to structure and contribute to the collection of data about how leadership impacts on the whole learner experience in a way that enhances both research and potentially the learner's development. The latter is an added value in that learners' involvement not only potentially improves research, but offers them opportunities to grow.

In Crane (2001), the author writes as a learner involved in the 'Students as Researchers' project at Sharnbrook Upper School and Community College, Bedfordshire, UK, from when it began in 1996 until she left school in 2000.

She notes the value to students in being involved with research, impacting on how they were viewed and how they saw themselves:

> 'Students as Researchers' had an impact in many ways. It changed how some staff at the school considered their students, encouraging them to think of students more as equals, and a source of help in making the most of their teaching. It also changed how students thought of themselves. They came to feel like a more valued and respected resource. (Crane, 2001: 55)

Another learner from the same group (Harding, 2001: 56) involved in action research on assessment processes at Sharnbrook believes, 'Education is not something that should be done to you, but something that you should be a part of'. He argues passionately for the personal growth and sense of empowerment research gave him, as well as the value of findings which were useful to the senior leadership team.

Resistance

The work cited above exemplifies how learners can contribute to the collection of data and their analysis. They may also work with others to consider the implications of what may need to change in their learning environment. However, the response to evidence-informed suggestions for change is political. There may be acceptance or resistance from staff, from parents and from learners themselves. The grounds for resistance are many. Fielding (2004) notes his experience of staff expressing criticism of the quality of research produced by learners and yet feeling that it was not acceptable to express disquiet. Equally, what is said by learners may be experienced as personally or organisationally threatening by education leaders (Fielding and Ruddock, 2002). As the latter point out, this may relate to a threat to the ubiquitous high power-distance relationship between learner and teacher, but may also be seen as unhelpful in the intense performative environment where leaders feel compelled to run a school or college in a particular way to achieve the results demanded by the market. Schools are predicated on control, of adults controlling the younger, or by cultural guardians deciding what is legitimate knowledge and ways of knowing (Lensmire, 1998). As Slee (1994: 151) suggests, the control is particularly evident in relation to those who do not conform: 'an overriding concern with the mechanics of maintaining authority over the disruptive student'. As the intended beneficiary of leadership, learners are epistemologically well placed to contribute to research, but politically disadvantaged to do so.

Conclusion

Some reading this chapter may believe that the examples given relate primarily to the school environment and the learning that takes place, and that leadership is something other than this. Leadership research may, for example, research the processes of leadership, such as teamwork, staff recruitment and selection, performance management and budgetary control, and the presumption is that learners can contribute little to research of areas such as these. The response to this belief is first to challenge the view that learners can contribute little to research into these areas. They are given little opportunity to do so, but the grounds for this may be disquiet at opening adult behaviour to children's scrutiny rather than any soundly based epistemological reasons. Second, it is arguable that in focusing primarily on management processes, leadership research has somewhat divorced itself from the more important priority of leading learning, or rather created a false division between leadership and learning. Research of assessment processes, for example, as at Sharnbrook, is both research of learning and research of leadership. It involves both technical pedagogical concerns and leadership concerns, such as managing resources and records and public perceptions of results. Increasingly in the UK, leadership is perceived as inextricably embedded in a wide range of children's services. Its impact has been shown to be marginal compared to that of teaching. Leadership is enacted through teaching and to separate the two is untenable, for example researching the recruitment and selection process as if divorced from learning outcomes. Angus presents the argument:

> Leadership is always difficult, and always involves tensions and contradictions. Leadership has to be relational – it is a socially constructed relationship between people. In this sense leadership is more of a dialectical process than a fixed thing, and leads to the production and reproduction (and discarding or assertion) of various organizational practices, norms, and structures. In democratic organizations – indeed in any organizations in which there is genuine leadership rather than merely managerial coercion – such organizational shaping is never just a top-down process but is an engaged process involving all organizational players. (2006: 372)

If leadership is conceived as Angus outlines, enabling learners to contribute to research on leadership becomes one element in the construction of what Fielding (2006: 310) terms 'emancipatory leadership' where researchers do not assume, as Alcoff (1991/92) expresses it, that the right of creating truth relates to our age or letters after our name.

Key points

- There are several arguments for involving learners in research on leadership; critical theorists suggest that speaking *for* the less powerful is not acceptable. Others argue that engagement with research is essential preparation for taking part in a democratic society.
- Learners are often not included in leadership research as they are perceived to be not competent to judge, or not knowledgeable or not interested.

- There are perceived methodological or ethical barriers to involving learners. The barriers are not different in nature to those related to adults, but may differ in degree.

- Learners are not a homogeneous group. Age is not a sufficient proxy for their individual attributes and situation. Careful contextualisation of their role is necessary.

- Learners can play a range of roles in research. Different typologies characterise the varying roles from acting solely as providers of data to leading research in their own right.

- Researchers have employed a range of methods to involve even very young children in research on leadership.

- Resistance to involving learners in research may relate more to reluctance to disturb power relationships rather than any insuperable ethical or methodological barriers.

Leadership research itself may be rather narrowly conceived and based on a view of leadership confined to adults' activities, rather than the impact on learners.

Questions and reflections

1 In what ways might you involve learners in researching the leadership of your own educational organisation?

2 Is the power distance between leaders and learners the most significant barrier to involving learners in research on leaders and leadership?

Recommended further reading

Angus, L. (2006) Educational leadership and the imperative of including student voices, student interests, and students' lives in the mainstream. *International Journal of Leadership in Education* 9(4): 369–79.

Angus provides an argument about how poorly served some young people are by their school and the vital contribution that student voice may make to address their exclusion.

Clark, A. (2005) Listening to and involving young children: a review of research and practice. *Early Child Development and Care* 175(6): 489–505.

Clark focuses on involving early years children in research. As the group might be perceived as particularly problematic to involve, she provides a helpful indication of the methods used and the issues that arise.

Harding, C. (2001) Students as researchers is as important as the National Curriculum. *Forum* 43(2): 56–7.

Harding's paper provides the perspective of a learner on how involvement in research helped him and helped his school.

Thomson, P. and Gunter, H. (2006) From 'consulting pupils' to 'pupils as researchers': a situated case narrative. *British Educational Research Journal* 32(6): 839–56.

This article provides an example of how researchers worked with a group of student researchers and a discussion of how they positioned student voice.

References

Alcoff, L. (1991/92) The problem of speaking for others. *Cultural Critique* 20: 5–32.

Angus, L. (2006) Educational leadership and the imperative of including student voices, student interests, and students' lives in the mainstream. *International Journal of Leadership in Education* 9(4): 369–79.

Bragg, S. (2001) Taking a joke: learning from the voices we don't want to hear. *Forum,* 43(2): 70–3.

Brice Heath, S. and McLaughlin, M. W. (1994) The best of both worlds: connecting schools and community youth organisations for all-day, all-year learning. *Education Administration Quarterly* 30(3): 278–300.

Clark, A. (2005) Listening to and involving young children: a review of research and practice. *Early Child Development and Care* 175(6): 489–505.

Coad, J. and Evans, R. (2008) Reflections on practical approaches to involving children and young people in the data analysis process. *Children and Society* 22: 41–52.

Conolly, A. (2008) Challenges of generating qualitative data with socially excluded young people. *International Journal of Social Research Methodology* 11(3): 201–14.

Crane, B. (2001) Revolutionising school-based research. *Forum* 43(2): 54–5.

Dupree, E., Bertram, T. and Pascal, C. (2001) Listening to children's perspectives of their early childhood settings. Paper presented at the 11th European Early Childhood Education Research Association Conference, Alkmaar, Netherlands, August.

Fielding, M. (2004) Transformative approaches to student voice: Theoretical underpinnings, recalcitrant realities. *British Educational Research Journal* 30(2): 295–311.

Fielding, M. (2006) Leadership, radical student engagement and the necessity of person-centred education. *International Journal of Leadership in Education* 9(4): 299–313.

Fielding, M. and Ruddock, J. (2002) The transformative potential of student voice: confronting power issues. Paper presented at the Annual Conference of the British Educational Research Association, University of Exeter, 12–14 September.

Harding, C. (2001) Students as researchers is as important as the National Curriculum. *Forum* 43(2): 56–7.

James, A. (2007) Giving voice to children's voices: practices. *American Anthropologist* 109(2): 261–72.

Kelly, B. (2007) Methodological issues for qualitative research with learning disabled children. *International Journal of Social Research Methodology* 10(1): 21–35.

Lensmire, T. J. (1998) Rewriting student voice. *Journal of Curriculum Studies* 30(3): 261–91.

Levey, H. (2009) 'Which one is yours?': children and ethnography. *Qualitative Sociology* 32: 311–31.

Lumby, J. (2011) Enjoyment and learning: policy and secondary school learners' experience in England. *British Educational Research Journal* 37(2): 247–64.

Lumby, J. (2012) Disengaged and disaffected young people: surviving the system. *British Educational Research Journal* 38(2): 261–79.

Mahon, A., Glendenning, C., Clarke, K. and Craig, G. (1996) Researching children: methods and ethics. *Children and Society* 10: 145–54.

Owens, M. A. and Johnson, B. L. Jnr (2009) From calculation through courtship to contribution: cultivating trust among urban youth in an academic intervention program. *Educational Administration Quarterly* (45): 312–47.

Ruddock, J. and Fielding, M. (2006) Student voice and the perils of popularity. *Educational Review* 58(2): 219–31.

Slee, R. (1994) Finding a student voice in school reform: student disaffection, pathologies of disruption and educational control. *International Studies in the Sociology of Education* 4(2): 147–72.

Stoll, L. (2009) *Making a difference to learning in city schools: the Ealing professional learning community*. London: The London Centre for Leadership Learning. Available at: www. leru.org.uk/events_and_activities/past_london_seminars/Presentation_2009_ 12_08b_LEARNING_(Ealing_PLC)_-_EALING.ppt#1 (accessed 11 February 2011).

Thomson, P. and Gunter, H. (2006) From 'consulting pupils' to 'pupils as researchers': a situated case narrative. *British Educational Research Journal* 32(6): 839–56.

Walford, G. (2005) Research ethical guidelines and anonymity. *International Journal of Research and Method in Education* 28(1): 83–93.

Part C

Research Tools

CHAPTER 17

Interviews

Marianne Coleman

Chapter objectives

- To identify different approaches to interviewing that may be used in educational leadership research.
- To consider the ways in which interviews can be conducted including:
  - individual interviewer face-to-face with an interviewee
  - individual interviewer carrying out a telephone interview with an interviewee
  - one or more interviewers moderating a group (focus) interview
  - one or more interviewers interviewing individuals or groups online.
- To alert researchers to the need for careful preparation and organisation of the interview.
- To raise awareness of power and ethical issues associated with interviews.

Introduction

The lone researcher working in the field of educational leadership and management is quite likely to conduct interviews as part of their research since interviewing is a flexible research tool. Although we are all familiar with conversing and asking questions and may see interviewing as a more formal version of what comes naturally, interviewing requires the honing of many skills with an emphasis on ensuring that all aspects of interviewing are conducted with integrity. Gillham (2005: 7) points out that 'the interviewer is the research instrument, and this means developing skills in facilitating the disclosures of the interviewee'. However, the interview is 'still one human being interacting with another and using their resources of interpersonal sensitivity to do so'.

Interviewing may be employed in a number of ways, often as the sole research tool, but also as part of a case study. For example, Briggs (2003) conducted case studies focusing on the role of the middle manager in colleges of further education in England. The need for a 360-degree examination of the 'middle' role meant that she undertook individual interviews with senior managers and principals of each case study college and conducted focus group interviews with the middle managers themselves. In this case, the interviews were supplemented by a questionnaire survey of team members of the middle managers and an analysis of college documents. Interviews may also be used as part of an ethnography or to complement the keeping of a diary for research purposes (see Chapters 14 and 22).

The main reason for the choice of research interviews should be the appropriateness of the interview as a tool in meeting the identified research purpose and helping to answer the research questions that arise. However, the practitioner researcher may have pragmatic reasons for the choice of interviewing rather than other research tools. For example, when writing a dissertation or postgraduate assignment, the researcher is faced with time restrictions and is normally reliant on their own efforts. Under these circumstances, the interview is chosen by many sole researchers (Coleman, 1999) to gain relatively speedy insight into a particular problem or issue.

Although such practicalities may play a part, the researchers' epistemological stance (see Chapter 2) is most important in choosing what type of interviews to undertake. Researchers whose purpose involves understanding more about how individuals think and perceive are taking an interpretive approach. Their choice of interview as a research tool is likely to be motivated by: 'an interest in understanding the lived experience of other people and the meaning they make of that experience' (Seidman, 2006: 9). In such an approach, there is no attempt to generalise as there would be, for example, in a large-scale survey. Specialist interviews such as life history interviews obviously fall within the interpretive paradigm and this type of interview is discussed in detail in Chapter 15.

Researchers who take a positivist stance are likely to adopt a quantitative approach and are less likely to use interviews and more likely to use a written questionnaire to reach a large number of research subjects. They may be trying to establish the truth or falseness of a hypothesis and to generalise their findings to a particular population.

Structured, semi-structured and unstructured interviews

Although interviews are usually sited within an interpretive research approach, there is a possible exception, in the form of a structured interview. In effect, a structured interview is similar to a questionnaire and tends to be made up mainly of closed questions. Such structured interviews are then easy to code and if the number of interviews warrants, they can be analysed using SPSS. The difference between a questionnaire and a structured interview is that the latter is administered by a researcher who records the answers, rather than the respondent being asked to do this. Reasons for using a structured interview may be that the researcher wishes to solicit the views of a relatively large number of people which might make other types of interview impractical, or they may be trying to reduce the danger of non-response which might occur with a self-completion questionnaire. However, this type of interview is not conducive to obtaining detailed and in-depth answers. For that, the interviewer will normally use a semi-structured or unstructured interview style and the remainder of this chapter relates to these interview styles.

Working within an interpretive paradigm, or when adopting a mixed methods approach, semi-structured interviews are probably the most common type of interview. The interview schedule often takes the form of a few major questions, with sub-questions and possible follow-up questions. The interviewer may use prompts, offering the respondent a range of choices for their response. Follow-up questions may take the form of probes, trying to extract more information on a topic. Probes may be general, such as 'Could you enlarge on that?' or 'Could you explain that a little more?'. Other probes may be more specific, as in my research on senior women leaders and their support and development (Coleman, 2011): see questions 3 and 4 below; the bullet points of question 6; and the follow-up to question 7:

1 As a woman why do you think you have been successful?
2 What do you think helped facilitate your career progress?
3 Do you think that you encountered barriers in your career progress? If so, please indicate what they were/are.
4 Do you or did you ever feel professionally isolated? If so, could you give me one or two examples?
5 How do you get support and development in your work?
6 Please identify the networks/organisations (if any) that are important to you in providing professional support.

    o Indicate whether they are formal or informal.
    o Are any of them specifically for women?

7 Do you provide or suggest support and/or development for any of the less senior women in your organisation? If so, what do you suggest or offer?

Rather than having a list of questions, the interviewer may make use of an aide-memoire for the interview which might just be a list of the topics that he or she wants to be sure to cover during the course of the interview. In the semi-structured interview, there is general consistency in the questions that are asked of each interviewee, although the probes may differ in response to the detail given by the interviewee. Answers may vary in detail and length, but the interviewer ensures that the same issues are raised in each interview.

Even in the unstructured interview there will be minimal 'structure' as there are likely to be initial questions to start the interview process but then the content of the interview will very much depend on the individual being interviewed, the empathy of the interviewer and the rapport that grows between them. This style of interviewing tends to be used in ethnography, and is also associated with feminist research. Unstructured interviews are also known as non-directive interviews and their origin lies in therapeutic or psychoanalytic interviews. Although particularly suited to ethnography, unstructured interviews may also be useful in initial exploration of a topic, helping the researcher to find their focus and identify their research purpose and questions. Life history interviews may also fall into the category of unstructured interviews. A particular interviewing stance developed by Seidman (2006), known as in-depth and phenomenologically based, involves open-ended questions in a series of three interviews with each participant. The first interview is designed to establish the context of the individual and is normally in the form of a focused life history. The second interview then concentrates on the details of the participant's current experience in the area of interest of the research and the third and final interview allows the individual to reflect on the meaning and make sense of what they are doing in relation to the topic under scrutiny. An example of the use of this type of approach is Crawford's (2009) examination of the role of emotion in school leadership.

In practice, there is no hard and fast division between types of interviews, rather there is a continuum from highly structured to highly unstructured:

Structured interviews   →   semi-structured interviews   →   unstructured interviews

Figure 17.1

At the unstructured end of the spectrum there is what Robson (2002) terms the 'informal interview' and Ribbins (2007) calls 'chats'. These tend to occur casually or by chance and may serve to help the ethnographic researcher understand what they have observed or they might occur when a researcher is conducting a case study. For example, they might arise spontaneously in the staffroom. It is very unlikely that such conversations can ever be recorded, as producing a tape recorder would be likely to end any spontaneity. If the researcher is to make use of such interviews, they must write field notes of what was said as soon as possible after the exchange. If notes are not recorded immediately after the exchange, the data will have very little claim to validity.

Modes of interviewing

Whatever the type of interview adopted for research purposes, there are a number of different approaches that the researcher can take. Variables for an interview include the number of interviewers, the number of interviewees, and whether the interview is face-to-face, by telephone, by video link or online.

Individual interviewer, individual respondent

The most likely mode of interviewing is for an individual interviewer to interview an individual research subject. The interview could take place either face-to-face, by telephone or using a video link. A face-to-face interview enables the interviewer to observe visual clues, for example relating to the layout of an office. It may also allow the interviewer to observe body language which might indicate comfort or discomfort, thus giving the interviewer clues on how to proceed. Observation may also help in the early stages of analysis: 'what a face-to-face encounter does do is to allow the interviewer to make a judgment about how [those] signs are being read and thus to locate their data in the contexts in which they were collected' (Scott and Usher, 1999: 109). However, body language is not always easy to interpret correctly, particularly if people are from differing cultures (Trompenaars and Hampden-Turner, 1997).

In a face-to-face situation, the interviewee also forms an impression of the interviewer. For example, if the pair are both similar in age, apparent status and gender, it may encourage rapport and improve the quality of the interview. In any case, an interviewer needs to be prepared for the fact that they will make an impression on the interviewee which can affect the level of success of the interview.

Interviewing by video link, the interviewer will tend to lose some of the immediacy of the face-to-face encounter, and there may also be technical difficulties to overcome. Telephone interviewing eliminates the possibilities of picking up visual clues in the interview, and may thus limit the development of rapport and the ability of the researcher to fully 'place' the interviewee, although the use of Skype does allow the interviewer to obtain some visual information. Telephone interviewing can be very useful when it proves difficult to arrange a face-to-face meeting because the respondent is geographically distant. It is obviously useful in cutting down on the researcher's own travel time and associated costs. Where access to an interviewee is difficult, a telephone interview may be perceived as less intrusive than a face-to-face meeting. The relative anonymity of the exchange could even encourage a more open dialogue than in a face-to-face meeting. It also offers a busy respondent the opportunity of fitting an interview into their schedule. For example, I have interviewed someone by phone who was a passenger on a car journey, and even someone who took the opportunity to walk their dog whilst talking to me. However, having undertaken both face-to-face interviews and telephone interviews within the same research projects, I have found that the face-to-face interviews usually provide more extensive and memorable responses. The face-to-face meeting tends to be richer than the telephone conversation, although this is not always the case. The relative anonymity of a phone call could encourage more openness in some respondents.

Recording interviews can be by note taking or by recording or both. In the case of telephone interviews, recording requires the use of special equipment that is attached to the phone of the interviewer and this adds a layer of technical difficulty as well as possible expense. In the UK, it is also illegal to use this equipment without the agreement of the respondent.

The group or focus interview

A type of interview that was developed for market research but is growing in popularity in educational research is the group or focus interview. The terms 'group' and 'focus' tend to be used interchangeably. However, a focus group is a group interview on a specific topic where the interviewer guides the group's discussions. The group may be focused in two ways: in terms of a tightly defined topic for discussion and in terms of the individuals who make up the group (Gillham, 2005). These interviews can be more or less structured but are complex to manage, with interviewers acting as moderators. They allow a researcher to access the views of several people at the same time, with the probability that group dynamics and the resulting synergy will produce data which might not have emerged in a one-to-one situation. The fact that the group discussion is focused means that data are in depth. In addition, those who might have been uncomfortable in a one-to-one situation may be empowered in a group to express their opinions.

Although they might be suitable for many research projects, Vaughn et al. (1996) suggest that some occasions might be particularly appropriate for the use of focus groups:

> When a researcher wants to undertake an initial test of an hypothesis before conducting a larger study or to help to produce further hypotheses.
>
> To help in the development of a research instrument such as a questionnaire.
>
> To help researchers make research instruments more user friendly as they enable the researcher to make use of any specific language or terms commonly used by the stakeholders.
>
> To help in fine-tuning research designs.
>
> They may be useful even in the interpretation of findings. This is sometimes known as 'returning to the well' (p. 29).
>
> Groups may also be helpful in generating ideas for follow-up studies.
>
> (adapted from Vaughn et al., 1996, pp. 27–9)

There are decisions to be made about the composition of a focus group, taking into account the impact of members of the group on each other. Does the researcher want groups to be made up of relatively similar people or do they want a heterogeneous mix? Groups tend to work better when individuals identify with each other (Lumby with Coleman, 2007). However, choosing a group that is too homogeneous may not reflect the diversity of the population. In addition, the researcher should be aware of how diversity issues play out in groups. Jehn et al. (2008) point out that both social category diversity (for example gender, age, ethnicity) and functional diversity (job function) affect the ways in which individuals react to each other and how groups and teams work together. Another aspect of diversity lies in the differing personalities of individuals, and the interviewer/moderator may have to ensure that no single individual dominates the group and that without imposing strict 'turn taking' which might bring too much formality to the proceedings, each member gets a chance to speak. Stewart et al. (2007: 99) refer to the 'self-appointed experts' who 'seldom have genuine expertise but offer their opinions as fact and often become dominant talkers in the group'. They may intimidate other group members and it will be up to the moderator to show that she/he is interested in everybody's views and if necessary ignore the individual, cutting off eye contact and showing lack of interest in what they say. It may also be necessary to encourage the group to speak by probing or asking for clarification of the views being expressed. Being skilful in the use of probes also helps with time management issues in the focus groups and in ensuring that all the prioritised questions are discussed. It may be necessary for the interviewer/moderator of groups to give specific guidance to participants – for example, in doctoral research on the role of the pre-school teacher in Iceland, Jonsdottir (2012) prepared a sheet of information for all participants, informing them of the nature and intended outcomes of the research.

The size of focus groups varies. Bryman (2008) reports on research projects where the size varied between three and nine members, but the larger the number of people the more difficult it becomes for one individual to manage the experience. In this type of interviewing, a sole interviewer may need to recruit someone else to help them. Jonsdottir (2012) was able to obtain the help of one of her students as an assistant moderator, to make extensive notes, to operate the tape recorder and to reflect and record her overall impressions after each focus group. In this research, which sought the views of stakeholders, there were separate focus groups, each with five or six members, representing pre-school teachers, pre-school headteachers and assistant headteachers, parents and local politicians. Where the members of the group do not know each other, it is advisable to start with some general and relatively light questioning to get them talking. It is also important to stress that only one person at a time should speak, otherwise transcription becomes very difficult. The visual clues, such as dress, age and gender that the researcher takes into account in face-to-face interviews are multiplied in focus groups with the additional complexities of noting the degree of turn taking, seating arrangements and other factors (Scott and Usher, 1999).

If focus groups include individuals from different cultures, the moderator(s) should be fluent in the common language that is to be used, as shades of meaning may be lost if translation is involved. Also, there are different perceptions of time, punctuality and courtesies between cultures which may need to be taken into account (Trompenaars and Hampden-Turner, 1997). There may be particular issues of sensitivity relating to confidentiality to be considered, including whether the discussion is recorded and what use is made of it (Stewart et al., 2007).

The transcription of focus group interviews presents a considerable challenge, particularly when two or more individuals have been talking at the same time. Transcription of a recording of a focus group will take much longer than that of an individual being interviewed. With the focus group, there are also non-verbal issues to take into account, and thought should be given in advance to exactly what the moderator will record. For example, will they attempt to record the body language of the speakers, and if so what particular aspects?

Focus groups can also operate through video conferencing which again might involve more than one interviewer/moderator.

Online interviews

Interviewing online is an option both for one-to-one interviews and for group/focused interviews. Whether one-to-one or group, online interviews can be either synchronous, that is taking place in real time, or non-synchronous when questions and responses are recorded when it is appropriate and convenient for the interviewer and interviewee.

When the interviewing is one-to-one, the interview can be conducted via email. There are decisions to be made about whether the questions are all posted at the start or whether they are fed to the interviewee singly as they would be in a face-to-face situation. Providing the questions at the start of the process may take away some of the spontaneity of the answers and allow the respondent to pick and choose which questions to answer. Providing them one by one means that there may be delays and communication may break down. One obvious difference from the normal face-to-face interview is that there will be no need for transcription. An implication of this is that the respondent may review and polish their responses in an asynchronous exchange. This provides an authenticated response, but one that may not be as spontaneous and revealing as a response in a face-to-face or synchronous interview. A particular advantage of an online interview is that it may allow the researcher to interview people to whom access might otherwise be difficult. For example, Deem and Ozga (2000) used email as well as telephone and face-to-face interviews in order to access female university vice-chancellors in the UK. Just like telephone interviewing, there are advantages, such as low cost and the elimination of travel, but there are disadvantages in the loss of visual clues and, in the case of online interviewing, the possibility of drop-out and the need for special skills as an online moderator.

Online focus group interviewing can be useful, particularly where members of the group are at a distance, although synchronous group interviews pose difficulties if group members are in different time zones. As long as the group all have access to a shared platform, and a suitable time for the interview can be arranged, there are no limitations on who might be involved. However, there may be technical difficulties in ensuring that individuals have access to equipment and the Internet, and problems of this nature are likely to result in individuals withdrawing from the group. Synchronous discussions demand that the individuals in the group are all available for the same amount of time together. Contributions to the discussion are limited to the speed and dexterity of typing, and this can be frustrating to group members. The role of the moderator/interviewer is vital and demanding in keeping the discussion going and feeding in questions and appropriate probes when necessary.

In many ways, asynchronous groups work better, as individuals have time to decide on and type in their contributions, and differences in time zones do not matter. However, the role of the interviewer/moderator is just as complex as it is with synchronous groups with the added task of keeping the group on track through what is likely to be a number of days or even weeks.

Moderating online focus groups presents different problems. The individuals may know nothing about each other. This could be seen as an advantage since people begin by being free of the stereotyping related to gender, age, ethnicity and so on that is normal in face-to-face encounters. However, people may not be drawn to engage with others if they cannot envisage them as individuals. Having moderated many online discussions, I found that people had to go through a series of stages before they were confident to share information with each other. The stage included familiarisation with the online environment, starting to socialise with others and then moving on to sharing information and even co-constructing knowledge (see Salmon, 2003). The familiarisation and socialisation might include getting to know each other a little, and even posting photographs of each other on the site where the discussion takes place. Although the benefits of anonymity are then lost, individuals are more likely to stay in the group if they are beginning to have some loyalty to individuals in it. As a moderator of online asynchronous groups, you have to be prepared to spend time each day or even several times a day to monitor the discussion, to intervene to summarise, or to get participants to summarise and to ask fresh questions at the right time. The moderator also has to be aware of 'netiquette' and particularly to be sensitive to misinterpretations by participants of what has been posted. This will be particularly necessary where the discussion includes participants from different cultures.

Preparation for and organisation of interviews

There are many practicalities and fine points to bear in mind when preparing for and conducting any interview, whether they are face to face, by telephone or video link or online. For example, for all but asynchronous online interviews, thought should be given to timing, mainly to ensure that interviewees are not stressed by time limits, or exhausted at the end of the day. For face-to-face interviews, attention should be given to the location, particularly to ensure that the interview is not interrupted.

Whatever the type of interview planned, researchers must consider who to interview, how to approach them, how to conduct the interview, how personal dynamics may affect the interview and how they will manage the recording, transcription and analysis of the data.

Sampling and access

The choice of whom to interview will depend on competing tensions between what might ideally and what is actually possible given the resources available. For a single researcher possibly working on a dissertation or thesis, there will be limits on time and money. For a funded project, budgets will have been built into the original design which limit expansion and mean that compromises might have to be made. When sampling for interviews, issues of representation of a particular population are likely to be taken into account, but qualitative interviewing does not aim to generalise other than to the particular group being interviewed. In an evaluation of a professional development course for black and minority ethnic (BME) senior leaders in schools (Coleman and Campbell-Stephens, 2010), we used a sampling frame drawn from two cohorts of the course. Within that population, sampling took account of gender, ethnicity and phase of schooling. It is also common in qualitative research for sampling to be purposive, where the researcher deliberately chooses to interview individuals who have particular expertise or hold a particular office. The research of Jonsdottir (2012) included purposive interviews with individual expert educational consultants. Where accessing individuals is difficult, for example because of the sensitivity of the focus, or the difficulty in accessing elite individuals, snowball sampling might be used. This sampling technique was employed when researching barriers to promotion for Muslim men in schools in England (Shah and Shaikh, 2010) as it was otherwise difficult to identify suitable interview subjects. Finally, there may also be an element of convenience sampling when identifying interviewees. Although this is the least satisfactory sampling technique, limited resources may mean that it is only those individuals who are easily accessed who can be included, and in this case convenience sampling, may occur. (For more information about sampling, see Chapter 10.)

Considering sampling raises the question of how many interviews is the 'right' number. Unfortunately, there is no definitive answer to this question. The number of interviews depends largely on the research purpose, for example if the focus is on the biography of one person, then the interviewing might be several interviews with just that one individual, although a more rounded picture would have to include the testimony of others. To take the example of the study of BME leadership in schools (Coleman and Campbell-Stephens, 2010), 33 individuals (members of two cohorts of a leadership course) were surveyed and 13 of the 33 were then interviewed in-depth. The choice of 13 was partly dictated by sampling, but the interviewing came to a halt after 13 partly because ongoing analysis of the data began to show that major themes were coming through the data and were being reinforced by each successive transcript. Kvale (2007: 44) refers to 'a point of saturation, where further interviews yield little new knowledge'. Qualitative interviewing generates a great deal of data, and a practical concern when deciding on the number of interviews must be planning how the transcription and analysis of data will be managed.

There may be particular difficulties of access where elite interviewing is concerned. When I set out to interview women who were successful leaders at work, sampling was a mixture of purposive, convenience and snowball. Without a defined population to sample, I accessed individual women through a number of relevant networks to which they belonged, seeking the assistance of a 'gatekeeper', a senior person within that network. I also 'cold called', writing letters to women who were named as successful in a variety of published lists, taking care to write a clear letter establishing my purpose and my credentials as an academic researcher. The whole process was complex and long drawn out, but was a fascinating research journey (Coleman, 2011).

Formulating your interview schedule or aide-memoire

Questions to be asked or the list of topics to be covered in the interview will arise from the identified research questions for the project. It is important to limit the number of questions so that the interview should not go on past the specified length which you will have already negotiated with the inter- viewee. It is definitely advisable to pilot an interview schedule with a small number of individuals to check that the questions are relevant and under- standable, and that the interview is manageable within the agreed time. As with a questionnaire, try and word questions clearly and simply, avoiding ambiguity and any leading questions. It is also wise to think ahead to how you might be analysing the data from each question (see Chapter 25) and to avoid collecting information that you will not use.

Dynamics of the interview process

Reference has already been made to the situation where the interviewer is either affected positively or negatively by the interviewee to colour the out- come of the interview. An interview may also be skewed where the interviewer starts with set ideas that they then set out to prove through the interview. Gillham (2005) suggests that interviewers should reflect on how their own views might impact on the interview by asking the following questions:

- What do I expect to find?
- What would I prefer to find?
- What would I hope *not* to find? (Gillham, 2005: 9, original emphasis)

It is always important to be aware of your impact as a researcher on the inter- viewee. It is often the case that practitioner researchers are researching within their own institution. It is then possible that the interview will be influenced by prior knowledge including the status differences between the interviewer and interviewee that arise from their professional roles. In some cultures, it will be difficult for a junior member of staff to interview more senior people. In that case, it may be wise to adjust the research to be less obtrusive, so that such difficulties are avoided. For example, more use might be made of documentary research. Alternatively, a senior person might unwittingly intimidate someone more junior in an interview situation. If the role and status of the interviewer versus the interviewee is not taken into account, questions of validity, reliability, authenticity and research ethics are raised (see Chapters 6 and 7). An interviewer is not a neutral force, and it is wise to recognise that gender, age, ethnicity, institutional status and class of both interviewer and interviewee are relevant to the conduct and outcome of the interview. This may particularly be the case where educational leaders are being interviewed. Gronn (2007: 193) makes the point that it is possible to romanticise leaders and to be too deferential to them so that:

> Interviews can be powerful and compelling in their verisimilitude and may convey the sense that one is, as it were, succeeding in penetrating the consciousness of an informant, the difficulties ... suggest that use of interviews as sole data sources should probably be treated with scepticism.

Conduct of the interview

At the start of an interview, the interviewer normally introduces themselves and indicates the nature of their research before starting on the main part of the interview. However, some of that introduction may have been done when seeking access and in some cases it is appropriate to send the questions to the interviewee in advance, if there is need for them to prepare for the interview or if they request it. On occasions, interviewers may use some sort of stimulus material or ask the interviewee to recall some critical incident in their professional life, if appropriate.

Kvale (2007: 81–2) lists important qualities for a successful interviewer, and amongst them are sensitivity and gentleness, stressing the fact that the interviewer is primarily a listener. Other qualities relate to the strength of the interviewer, being able to steer the interview and exercise critical judgement, for example when dealing with inconsistencies in what the interviewee says. It is also important that the interviewer remembers what has been said and is confident to move from one part of the interview to another, as interviewees may naturally link two areas together, inadvertently answering another question which actually appears further down the schedule. As the interview naturally draws to a close, the interviewer may refer to what will happen next. They may clarify ethical issues, for example the anonymity of the interviewee, confidentiality of the data, their willingness to send the transcript back to the interviewee for verification and their intentions with regard to publication. Above all, they must thank the participants for giving their time and cooperation.

These comments relate to the conduct of all types of interview. Specific practicalities relating to focus groups and online interviews have been touched on in the relevant earlier sections.

Recording

Most interviewers who undertake semi-structured or unstructured interviews will ensure that the interview is recorded so that all nuances of the answers can be retained and the richness of individual statements is not lost. It is important then to ensure that you are familiar with the technology and that the recording is secure. It may be wise to take hand-written notes in addition to the tapes as these might not only act as insurance against technical mishaps, but can also form the basis of the transcription which can then be augmented from the recording. Taking notes also allows the interviewee in the face-to-face interview to see that you are busy writing or that you are no longer writing which signals that what they are saying is no longer relevant to the interview.

Preparing for analysis

Analysis of data is ongoing from the start of the interview process as the interviewer reflects on what they are hearing. However, it is vital to ensure that there are good transcripts of the interviews. Preparing good transcripts is time-consuming and estimates vary from an hour of interview taking 5–10 hours to transcribe with the transcription of group interviews taking longer than the transcription of individual interviews. Reading and re-reading the transcripts allows the researcher to identify possible themes that are emerging. Analysis of qualitative data is the subject of Chapter 25 and reference to the analysis of interview data can also be found in Chapters 15 and 21.

Questions of power and ethics

The principle of informed consent applies to interviewees, which means that individuals should know the likely outcomes and intentions of the researcher. Questions of anonymity and/or confidentiality have to be considered and acted upon. It is good practice to allow the interviewee to approve the transcript of their interviews. Questions of research ethics are the focus of Chapter 7, but the interview does raise particular ethical questions relating to the power balance between interviewer and interviewee. The feminist approach to interviewing sees the traditional one-to-one semi-structured interview as paternalistic and hierarchical, as the interviewer is in charge of the focus and direction of the interview. To this extent, group interviews may be preferred for feminist research as it is harder for a researcher to control the flow of the interview than in a one-to-one situation. In feminist interviews, interviewer and interviewee are regarded as equals in co-constructing the interview.

Feminist-based interview research has already modified social science concepts, and created important new ways of seeing the world. By listening to women speak, understanding women's membership in particular social systems and establishing the distribution of phenomena accessible only through sensitive interviewing, feminist researchers have uncovered previously neglected or misunderstood worlds of experience. (Punch, 2009: 149)

However, the Western feminist researcher will face a dilemma when presenting data from previously silenced women's voices when they represent a culture different to that of an academic Western audience. In this case, there may be a need to 'interpret' (Edwards and Ribbens, 1998).

Finally, research in educational leadership often relies over much on interviews with leaders, without taking into account the voices of other stakeholders or using other research approaches to complement and validate interview data. Although interviewing is a fascinating and useful way to research in educational leadership and management, it is important to take a critical and reflexive approach towards data from a single source.

Key points

Interviewing is repeatedly described by Kvale (2007) as being a 'craft' to be learned, and there is no doubt that the experience of conducting interviews and transcribing them is the best way of honing that craft. However, for the researcher considering the use of interviews in a planned research project, there will be a number of issues to consider. These include:

- their epistemological stance as a researcher
- reflecting on what values and opinions they are bringing to the research
- planning whether interviews will be face-to-face, by telephone or online and whether focus groups would be more appropriate than individual interviews
- the ideal versus the practicalities of sampling
- how best to access their identified interviewees – this could be through an intermediary, through a well-crafted letter or email or a phone call
- designing and piloting the aide-memoire or interview schedule
- the conduct of the interview, ensuring a clear introduction, having clarity about the questions to be asked or topics covered and thanking the interviewee(s) at the end; consideration should also be given to timing and location
- following ethical procedures regarding informed consent, anonymity and/or confidentiality and the consideration of issues of power within the interview
- considering in advance of the interview just how the data will be analysed, and reflecting on analysis of the data throughout the process
- taking a critical and reflexive approach to interviewing, particularly when interviewing leaders.

Questions and reflections

1   What skills do you think that you bring to interviewing? What skills might you need to develop?

2   If you are planning a future research project, what type of interviews might be appropriate? For what purposes might a focus group be more appropriate than single interviews?

Recommended further reading

Gillham, B. (2005) *Research Interviewing: The Range of Techniques*. Maidenhead: Open University Press.

This text provides a useful and practical introduction to the subject.

James, N. and Busher, H. (2009) *Online Interviewing*. London: Sage.

This book provides an in-depth analysis of this relatively new type of interviewing.

Kvale, S. (2007) *Doing Interviews*. London: Sage.

This is a classic text that is both accessible and comprehensive.

References

Briggs, A.R.J. (2003) Modelling aspects of role among middle managers in English Further Education colleges, unpublished PhD thesis, University of Leicester.

Bryman, A. (2008) *Social Research Methods* (3rd edn). Oxford: Oxford University Press.

Coleman, M. (1999) What makes for effective research in a school or college?, in Middlewood, D., Coleman, M. and Lumby, J. (eds) *Practitioner Research*. London: Paul Chapman Publishing. pp. 139–52.

Coleman, M. (2011) *Women at the Top: Challenges, Choices and Change*. Basingstoke: Palgrave MacMillan.

Coleman, M. and Campbell-Stephens, R. (2010) Perceptions of career progress: the experience of Black and Minority Ethnic school leaders. *School Leadership and Management* 30(1): 19–33.

Crawford, M. (2009) *Emotion and Educational Leadership*. London: Sage.

Deem, R. and Ozga, J. (2000) Transforming post compulsory education? Femocrats at work in the academy. *Women's Studies International Forum* 23(2): 153–66.

Edwards, R. and Ribbens, J. (eds) (1998) Living on the edges: public knowledge, private lives, personal experience, in *Feminists Dilemmas in Qualitative Research: Public Knowledge and Private Lives*. London: Sage.

Gillham, B. (2005) *Research Interviewing: The Range of Techniques*. Maidenhead: Open University Press.

Gronn, P. (2007) Interviewing leaders: penetrating the romance, in Briggs, A.R.J. and Coleman, M. (eds) *Research Methods in Educational Leadership and Management* (2nd edn). London: Sage.

Jehn, A.J., Greer, L.L. and Rupert, J. (2008) Diversity, conflict and their consequences, in Brief, A.P. (ed.) *Diversity at Work*. Cambridge: Cambridge University Press.

Jonsdottir, A. (2012) The professional role and identity of pre-school teachers in Iceland, unpublished EdD thesis. London: Institute of Education.

Kvale, S. (2007) *Doing Interviews*. London: Sage.

Lumby, J. with Coleman, M. (2007) *Leadership and Diversity*. London: Sage.

Punch, K.F. (2009) *Introduction to Research Methods in Education*. London: Sage.

Ribbins, P.M. (2007) Interviewing in educational research: conversations with a purpose, in Briggs, A.R.J. and Coleman, M. (eds) *Research Methods in Educational Leadership and Management* (2nd edn). London: Sage.

Robson, C. (2002) *Real World Research* (2nd edn). Oxford: Blackwell Publishing.

Salmon, G. (2003) *E-moderating* (2nd edn). London: Taylor and Francis.

Scott, D. and Usher, R. (1999) *Researching Education: Data, Methods and Theory in Educational Inquiry*. London: Continuum.

Seidman, I. (2006) *Interviewing as Qualitative Research* (3rd edn). Columbia University, OH: Teachers College Press.

Shah, S. and Shaikh, J. (2010) Leadership progression of Muslim male teachers: interplay of ethnicity, faith and visibility. *School Leadership and Management* 30(1): 19–33.

Stewart, D.W., Shamdasani, P.N. and Rook, D.W. (2007) *Focus Groups: Theory and Practice,* (2nd edn). London: Sage.

Trompenaars, F. and Hampden-Turner, C. (1997) *Riding the Waves of Culture*. London: Nicholas Brealey Publishing.

Vaughn, S., Shay Schumm, J. and Sinagub, B. (1996) *Focus Group Interviews in Education and Psychology*. London: Sage.

CHAPTER 18

Developing and Using Questionnaires

Judith Bell and Pam Woolner

Chapter objectives

- To understand the complexity of producing and using questionnaires well.
- To offer guidance for the process of designing a questionnaire.
- To give a sense of how this stage connects back to your research question and forward to analysis.

Introduction

The trouble with questionnaires is that, sometimes, they seem like a very easy way to get hold of a great deal of information quickly and it also seems that anyone can devise one in the time it takes to drink a cup of coffee. With an online version, using one of the increasingly common free packages, new researchers may think there is not even any need to worry about collating or coding responses. These assumptions are wrong on all counts. Questionnaires, on paper or online, are fiendishly difficult to design and then to understand and interpret their results. They should never be considered by anyone who believes that 'anyone who can write plain English and has a modicum of common sense can produce a good questionnaire' (Oppenheim, 1992: 1). Of course, the ability to write plain English is always a help and common sense is a commodity which is good to add to the research armoury, but before any method of data collecting can be considered, decisions have to be made about *precisely what it is you need to find out*. That sounds obvious, but that is the stage which is so often hurried or even overlooked completely and this omission can result in the selection of entirely inappropriate data-collecting instruments which produce responses which you do not understand and have not considered how to analyse.

Begin at the beginning

Throughout this chapter, I will draw on an imaginary example presuming that you have recently taken over responsibility for the Diploma in Foresty Management in your college, and though you are fairly confident that most aspects of the diploma programme are sound, you have reservations about some others. In six months' time, the college is to receive a visit from a team of external assessors who will require evidence of the college claims for quality provision. The only evidence you have is examination results, and they have tended to be ... well ... variable. You discover that records of student feedback and any curriculum discussions between college-based and placement staff are limited. It is clear that the diploma needs a thorough review.

I might also assume that you are halfway through a Masters course and that the dissertation looms. Subject to the approval of the college principal and the dissertation supervisor, here might be an opportunity to achieve two objectives by carrying out an investigation into the quality of the Diploma in Forestry Management.

It is easy to select a topic in general terms but the hard work begins in moving from the general to the specific. You will have your own ideas about the particular aspects which should be considered but you also need to consult colleagues and students about what they consider to be vital elements in the programme. Their views might be different from yours. First thoughts at identifying priorities might include:

- something on the curriculum
- the quality of teaching in the college and on placements
- the quality of student support
- the quality of supervision, particularly on placements
- the relevance of the college course to the work of forestry management
- the balance of theory to practice
- the relationship between college and placement staff
- students' views about all the above – and anything else they consider important
- college social and sports facilities
- the effectiveness of the tutorial system
- library access
- study facilities
- assignment feedback to students
- the overall quality of the programme.

Some or none of these might be selected as being of prime importance but whichever are selected will form the framework for the study. How much time will you have for this investigation? Which items are absolutely essential and which merely desirable? Time has to be spent on this stage of the research, but it's easy to lose sight of the key issues. Punch (1998: 36) reminds us that at this crucial stage in the research planning it's good to remember the 'What are we trying to find out?' question. He warns us that:

> The focus on this question almost always shows that there is 'much more here than meets the eye'. The topic expands, and many questions are generated. What perhaps seemed simple and straightforward becomes complicated, many-sided and full of possibilities.

Not everything can be done, so decisions have to be made about what is essential, what is merely desirable and what can be done in the available time.

It would be impossible to include all the items on the first-thoughts list, so let us assume that you decide to consider students' views on the following priority areas:

- The quality of teaching, support and supervision of students in college and on placements.
- The relevance of the college diploma programme to the work of forestry management.
- The balance of time spent on theory of forestry management and practice.
- Students' overall satisfaction with the diploma programme.

What is the best way of obtaining students' views on these topics? You know what information you require and you now have to decide how best to obtain it. Only when you have considered *precisely* what you want to find out and why, will you be able to decide on which data-collecting instrument will be best for your purposes. If you decide on a questionnaire, work can start on question wording – and that is not as easy as it sounds.

The importance of precise wording

Concepts to variables

All questionnaire items have to be worded in ways which will be absolutely clear to students and which can be *measurable*. Let us start with the most difficult item in the list of priority areas, namely 'students' satisfaction with the diploma programme'. If students are asked 'Are you satisfied with your course?' responses might well be along the lines of 'No', 'Yes', 'Sort of', 'It's all rubbish'. It might be argued that if all that the researcher needed was information about the numbers of students who said they were satisfied, the question would be perfectly all right. But what does 'satisfaction' mean? Might it mean 'It's a darn sight better being warm and dry in college than working in a freezing forest in the pouring rain' or might it mean 'This is the best course I've ever known, the teaching is excellent, the placements and the balance of theory to practice just right', etc., etc.? The Yes/No type of response is of no real value because you need to know more and to discover what 'satisfactory' and 'satisfaction' actually mean to the students. Ways have to be found to overcome this dilemma.

Satisfaction is a concept and we cannot actually observe or measure concepts but we can probably think of ways in which individuals indicate or demonstrate satisfaction. Take time to think about it. Talk about it to colleagues. Brainstorm it. Produce flow charts with ideas because somehow or another ways have to be found to move from the unobservable to the observable.

Muijs provides a useful discussion of ways in which the abstract concepts of 'self-esteem' and 'learning' might be thought about:

> Learning, like self-esteem, cannot be measured directly. Again to be able to do that, we would need to directly plug into people's brains and see what has actually happened there. Tests, essays and whatever other measures we use are always indirect measures of learning. Whether they are good measures is hotly disputed. (Muijs, 2011: 57)

Since it is not possible to 'plug directly into people's heads and know what they are thinking, feeling or experiencing' (p. 57), we need to identify indicators of these concepts or find ways to measure them indirectly. So what indicators might there be of 'satisfaction'? This is quite tricky and you may need several attempts at producing indicators, so once again, ask colleagues and friends for their views, focus the mind and get back to basics and the 'What do I need to know?' question.

Ambiguity, imprecision and assumption

If you were to be asked what you meant by 'curriculum', you would, I'm sure, be able to provide a clear, succinct and comprehensive definition but are you absolutely sure all your colleagues would give the same definition? Ask a room full of people, some concerned with education, some not, and in all probability you would get a variety of responses. Ask students and they might tell you it meant syllabus, subjects or something to do with the course. In other words, you cannot assume they will all have the same understanding of 'curriculum', nor that their understanding is the same as yours. Other wording has to be found which will make it clear what is meant.

Leading and presuming questions

It is surprisingly difficult to avoid leading questions. If the wording is along the lines of 'Do you agree that there is insufficient time spent on forestry practical work?' then that's obviously a leading question, but other questions like 'Does the college make adequate provision for counselling?' may be harder. What is 'adequate'? There's a presumption here that respondents know that a counselling service exists, what it does and whether or not the provision is adequate. In its present form, the question is invalid and if you really want to know something about students' opinions of the service, you will need to work harder to produce wording which will enable respondents to give a clear answer.

Visual methods

Presenting some items more visually might be a way to reduce problems with wording, as well as enlivening the presentation of your questionnaire. This could simply involve presenting a satisfaction scale using icons (see Figure 18.1), making it more appealing and less daunting for younger or less literate respondents. Photographs can also be used to check respondents' knowledge or experience: present pictures and ask, 'Which of these tools have you used during the course?' or 'Indicate your preferred place for independent study'.

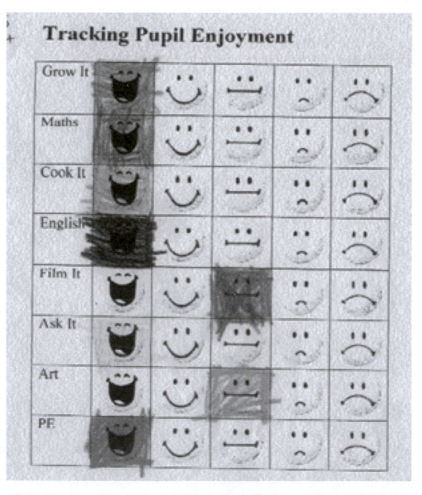

Figure 18.1   The use of icons that children can colour or circle to indicate levels of enjoyment

When you are less certain what to expect and need an open question, an image can be a very successful way to elicit a variety of responses: 'Look at this picture of forest management students on placement. What do you think they are doing? How does this relate to their college work?' (For more ideas of visual items to use in a questionnaire or to mediate an interview, see Woolner, 2010: 60–2, 72–3.)

Double (or even triple) questions

'Has the science component of the programme helped your understanding of pest control and planting techniques?' Well, perhaps it helped my under-standing of pest control but not planting techniques. If information is required about both, then separate questions are needed.

'Is the quality of teaching, support and supervision in college and on place-ments good?' You would not put a question like that, of course; the wording here is just your reminder about what you want to find out. It is a very com-plex question and would need to be broken down into separate components, with explanations about the meaning of 'support' and 'supervision'. However, it is pretty common to come across questionnaires with double questions, particularly in hotel 'feedback' questionnaires such as:

The management is always looking for ways of improving the service to guests. We should be grateful if you would circle the appropriate number below and return the form to reception.

How would you rate the service and cleanliness of the hotel?

Excellent	Very good	Good	Satisfactory	Less than satisfactory
1	2	3	4	5

This was found in the bedroom of a large chain hotel and all the questions followed a similar format. They certainly believed in stacking the odds to emphasise the positive, with only one negative item, but that is not the only criticism. The double question is obvious but there are multiple features of both. You might consider that the service was good in parts: pleasant, helpful personnel at reception, an efficient chamber maid who did a great job, but the porter was surly and the waiters in the dining room were downright disagree-able. As far as cleanliness was concerned, the bedroom was spotless and most public areas were fairly clean except the toilet in the foyer, which was filthy.

It is easy to mock and far more difficult to produce flaw-free questions, but this example is poor in another way. You often see 'excellent' and 'very good' on questionnaires, but it's a fine line between the two and I have never seen an explanation of the difference. Usual practice is for hotels, travel companies and others to group responses. In this case, I don't have much doubt that 'excellent', 'very good' and 'good' would be grouped and the summary of guest comments would be that '80 per cent of guests rated everything under the sun as good or better'.

Memory and knowledge

Your respondents may only have about half an hour or even less to complete the questionnaire and so questions need to be worded in a way respondents can answer without much hesitation. For example, 'What marks did you get for pest control in your first year?' sounds straightforward enough, but if the students are in their third year they may not remember. They would need to check and there is no time to check, so either they will not answer or they will guess. If you decide that you really need this type of information, can you collect it yourself, perhaps through examining college or school databases?

Multiple responses

Indicate which of these items you have been taught to use:

- bow saw
- machete
- chainsaw
- mallet
- first aid kit

For some questions, you might need your respondents to choose their answers from a list, selecting as many as appropriate (see example above). Be warned, though, that multiple response items can be tricky to analyse. If you are purely interested in extent, representing curriculum coverage in this example, then you can just count the ticks. But if you need to consider more complex questions about what has been studied or what combination of skills have been introduced, then you will need to consider responses to each possible choice as a 'yes' or 'no' to an individual item. This results in more data input to do or, if you are using an online survey package, you need to check the format of the output data.

Checking again and considering presentation

Question selection and precision wording are likely to require a good many drafts before final versions come up to standard. Eliminate any item that doesn't comply with the 'what?' rule. There is neither the time nor the space to fill the questionnaire with irrelevancies in case they come in handy. You want every single item to be worded in such a way as to ensure that all items are necessary, that respondents understand what you mean, are able to provide an answer on the spot and are not offended by your wording or assumptions. You may change your mind several times about the order of questions so it's probably a good idea to write questions on cards or separate pieces of paper. As soon as the sorting and eliminating are done, you will be ready to move on to issues of appearance and layout – apart from one last check. Go through each question or item and ask yourself once more:

- Is there any sign of ambiguity, imprecision or assumption?
- Are there any items which require memory or knowledge which respondents may not have?
- Are there any double, leading, presuming, offensive or sensitive questions?

Questions or statements?

Even though you know what you want to find out, the way the questions are worded will influence the usefulness of the responses. Go back to the item relating to the quality of students' supervision while on placements. It wouldn't really be enough to have responses like 'Good', 'Non-existent' or 'Bad', would it? Wouldn't you want more detail? You might decide that ranked items would be likely to produce a greater degree of discrimination and that a Likert scale would be better than straight questions. It would be up to you to decide which approach is best, but consider what a scale might look like.

Likert scales ask respondents to indicate, usually by circling a number, rank order of agreement or disagreement with a statement. There is generally a three-, five- or seven-point range, though researchers frequently prefer an even number of items, as in the following example, mainly to avoid the neutral central point.

In my view, the supervision provided for forestry management practical work is good.					
Very strongly disagree	Strongly disagree	Disagree	Agree	Strongly agree	Very strongly agree
1	2	3	4	5	6

The statement could equally well have begun with 'Very strongly agree', and researchers will sometimes change the order during the course of the questionnaire in order to make sure respondents are awake. Of course, that means that you also have to be awake and to remember what you are doing when you come to score the responses. That also means that you need to decide not only how you are going to score but also what the scores will mean *before* questionnaires are distributed.

We need to be careful about what we can deduce from Likert scales. They certainly arrange individuals or objects from the highest to the lowest but the intervals between each may not be the same (Cohen et al., 2011: 386–7; Muijs, 2011: 41–2). We cannot assume that the highest rating (6 in the above case) is six times higher than the lowest (which is 1). All that can be said is that 'the data in each category can be compared with data in the other categories as being higher or lower than, more or less than, etc., those in the other categories' (Denscombe, 2010). In spite of these limitations, Likert scales can be helpful and as long as the instructions to respondents are clear, useful information can be obtained.

Question order and appearance

If you are satisfied you have done everything possible to ensure that the wording of questions is as clear as you can make it, it will be time to decide on the order in which they are to appear on the questionnaire. There should not be any complex or sensitive questions, but if one or two have slipped in, it is best to place them well down in the order. The last thing you want is for potential respondents to take offence or decide the questionnaire is too hard – and give up immediately.

Appearance is important. If you are producing an online survey, you will be constrained by the package you use. If your questionnaire is on paper, you need to think about layout, both for your respondents' ease and for your own. When it comes to conducting the analysis of responses and producing a report of findings, you need to be able to see and record responses without having to search for them in irregularly positioned boxes or circled numbers which are all over the place.

The online option

Increasingly, researchers are administering questionnaires over the Internet, using widely available and (sometimes) free web-based packages. Generally, the most basic version of the package is completely free to use, with more sophisticated versions available at a monthly or annual rate. Even if you decide that you need to pay to get the features you require, this could still represent a saving if the alternative is a postal survey, requiring postage in addition to printing costs. If you are paying someone to do your data input, a web-based survey becomes even more financially attractive; if you are intending to do your own input, the online option will save you a lot of time. This is because the package will store all responses in a spreadsheet ready for you to download in its entirety or as a summary. More sophisticated versions should allow you to download data straight into SPSS.

You might be concerned that the online presentation will affect who answers your questionnaire, and you should definitely consider this issue. Accumulating research is tending to suggest that response rates should be similar to a postal survey, with a similar profile of respondents, assuming the population you are targeting has ready access to the Internet (see, for example, Kaplowitz et al., 2004). With the continuing spread of available technology, it seems likely that this will increasingly be the case. If you are aiming your questionnaire at staff or students in a school or college, where everyone is provided with Internet access and an email address, making an assumption about access should generally be reasonable.

Considering the advantages of online surveying, you might wonder why everyone is not using the Web for questionnaires. Perhaps you think they are, and it could be that the biggest problem with administering questionnaires in this way is the sheer ubiquity of these surveys. The constraints of the packages mean that it is hard to avoid them all looking the same and perhaps you want to avoid groans of bored recognition from your would-be respondents.

More generally, if you are using the online option, it is still important that you feel in control of your questionnaire. The framework provided by the package may be helpful to you in designing your questionnaire, but ensure that you still consider all the issues addressed in this chapter. The needs of your research should drive your decisions, not the constraints of the package – don't be blinded by the technology!

Respondents' rights

However you carry out your questionnaire, remember that you are asking respondents to do you a favour, even if they are students or staff and you are the boss. They are entitled to know why they are being asked to complete your questionnaire and what you are going to do with their responses. Unless you or a colleague plan to distribute the questionnaires in person, and explain the 'why' and the 'what' on the spot, a letter is required. Be honest and don't promise anything you can't deliver. Many investigations promise anonymity and confidentiality but, occasionally, both have been variously and, to my mind, damagingly interpreted. Sapsford and Abbott (1996: 319) provide what is a helpful definition of anonymity and confidentiality. They write that:

> As we are using the term, *confidentiality* is a promise that you will not be identified or presented in identifiable form, while *anonymity* is a promise that even the researcher will not be able to tell which responses came from which respondent.

So if anonymity is promised, there is no question of numbered questionnaires and a record kept of which number applies to which respondent; and no tricks such as numbers or symbols on the back of the questionnaires. Some online packages make it difficult to provide anonymity so check if you are using one. Be careful not to promise anonymity if you cannot ensure it. Whatever your form of presentation, be clear that anonymity means there is no possibility of reminders. If the forestry management questionnaires were to be answered in class, then any blank returns would mean that the students declined to participate and that would be that. If the questionnaires are distributed via email, internal mail or by post then you have to accept whatever returns you get.

There can be some difficulties over confidentiality. If in your report you say that 'the Director of Resources was of the opinion that ...', you are identifying him/her if there's only one Director of Resources. If your description of a school or department is too explicit, then everyone who works in that area will immediately know which school or department you are talking about. No one minds if the report is complimentary but if your department happens to have poor examination results and high truancy rates, you might be less joyful about the world knowing about it. Sapsford and Abbott (1996: 318) make their views perfectly clear when they write that 'a first principle of research ethics – to be found in all the various codes of conduct imposed by professional and academic organizations – is that the subjects of research should not be *harmed* by it' and, sad to say, there have been cases where individuals and organisations have been harmed. The subject of ethics in research will already have been covered in Chapter 7 of this book but the dangers of loose interpretation of 'anonymity' and 'confidentiality' are worth reinforcing here (see Bell, 2005: 57–8; 167–71).

Piloting the questionnaire

You may feel everything is now done and you are ready to distribute the questionnaires, but there is another important step to take yet. No matter how busy you are, all data-collecting instruments have to be piloted. You may have consulted everybody about everything, but it is only when a group similar to your main population completes your questionnaire and provides feedback that you know for sure that all is well. If you cannot find a similar group, then ask friends, colleagues, anyone you can get hold of. There is another very good reason why you absolutely have to carry out a pilot exercise and that is to practise the collation and analysis of the returns so that when the 'real' questionnaires are returned, you know exactly what to do with them. Even if this is to be a straightforward descriptive study which only requires frequencies (the number of items in each category) and frequency distributions (how often each item occurs), trial analyses need to be made and methods of presentation considered. As Youngman (1994: 248) rightly reminds us:

> The solution lies in accepting that the initial stages of a survey are not independent; the questionnaire structure must include all the facilities deemed necessary for successful analysis.

It might be that for the purpose of the college study, frequencies and frequency distributions will be enough, but your Masters dissertation may well require more sophisticated analysis and that will need to be tried out *before* questionnaires are distributed. You will need to think about statistical techniques and ways to enact them, which will probably involve a statistics package such as SPSS (for ideas, see Chapters 23 and 24, and Mujis, 2011).

Distributing the questionnaire

At last it is time to distribute the questionnaires to your respondent group. It would obviously be best if you or your colleagues were able to distribute paper questionnaires or introduce an online survey and explain the purpose of the study in class time, but that is not always easy to achieve. For a start, you will need access to enough computers for the class if you want them to complete the survey online in class. Furthermore, colleagues may not be willing to lose their class time and even if you have permission from the college management, you will still need to ask your colleagues and obtain their agreement beforehand. Remember that you may need collaboration, assistance or support from your colleagues in future. Involving colleagues in drawing up the questionnaire might mean that they are more likely to lend that support.

If class completion fails, you might be forced to distribute the questionnaires via the internal mail system or send email links to an online questionnaire, but the rate of return will inevitably be lower and you really do need as many completions as possible if the study is to mean anything. Whatever approach is selected, or forced on you, do your utmost to avoid postal distribution. In the first place, you or the college would have to provide a stamped addressed envelope, which is expensive. More seriously, the rate of return for postal questionnaires is generally poor and if questionnaires are genuinely anonymous, it is not possible to arrange a follow-up questionnaire.

Producing the report or dissertation and looking for themes, groupings and patterns

If you were carrying out this study as part of a Masters dissertation, you would already have carried out a review of the literature. As you read, themes would have begun to emerge together with valuable insight as to how others planned their research. In any investigation, we are always looking for patterns and groupings. If all you did was to provide a list of every student's response to each question, you would be left with pages of lists which meant very little and few readers would be willing to spend the time necessary to search for groupings themselves. All data need to be interpreted and if patterns do emerge, they will require particular comment, though *take care not to make claims which cannot be substantiated*. Decide which methods of presentation will best illustrate the data: tables, bar charts, pie charts, box plots, direct quotes – and what else? (see Chapter 12 of Bell, 2005: 203–28 and Chapters 23 to 26 of this volume).

Your aim will be to produce a clear, informative report of the findings which, you hope, will contribute to the college understanding of perceptions of the Diploma in Forestry Management *and/or* be one worthwhile component of the Masters dissertation.

If your preparation has been sufficiently thorough, all will be well. Your questionnaires will be clear and well designed; the comments from your pilot exercise will have been considered and any appropriate changes made; appropriate methods of analysis will have been tried out before distribution of the questionnaire; your report will be well written and will make no unsubstantiated claims – and you will be able to congratulate yourself on a job well done.

Key points

The following points can also be used as a checklist when planning a questionnaire.

- Select a topic which really interests you and is likely to be worth all your time and commitment.
- Spend time refining and focusing your topic and never lose sight of key issues. Set boundaries. Decide which aspects of your investigation are essential and which are merely desirable.
- Make sure you have any permissions necessary to carry out the study.
- Consult relevant colleagues about the topic. They may have good ideas, different points of view and know about useful sources of information, and you may need their collaboration throughout the research.
- Be sure a questionnaire is the best way to obtain the data you need. Refer back to 'What am I trying to find out?'
- Concepts are abstractions and so cannot be observed or measured. Ways have to be found to link concepts to indicators.
- Take time over question wording and order. Think about the responses that will result.
- Consider whether an online option is appropriate and, if so, whether the benefits of the online option will outweigh any costs.
- Make sure the appearance of the questionnaire is attractive and the layout is logical.
- Respondents have rights and they are entitled to know why they are being asked to complete your questionnaire and what you are going to do with the responses.
- If you promise anonymity and/or confidentiality, make sure your respondents *and you* know what you mean. If you promise either or both, you must honour that promise.

- Always pilot questionnaires. Make changes to wording, if necessary, and try out methods of analysis with the pilot returns.
- Decide on methods of questionnaire distribution and possible follow-ups to improve the response rate.
- If your pilot recording and analysis has been well done, you should know beforehand exactly how you intend to record responses or deal with output from an online survey.
- Make sure your report is clear, to the point and highlights key issues. And *never* make claims which cannot be supported by your evidence.
- Thank everyone who has assisted you with the research. You may need their help again some time.

Questions and reflections

1 Think about what your research is trying to find out. Can you write your priorities as a research question (or questions)? Who do you need to ask in order to address these – students, teachers, support staff, others?

2 What are the concepts in which you are interested? Can you identify measurable indicators of them? How might you ask your respondents about these?

3 Can you achieve anonymity for respondents to your questionnaire? Do you need to, or will confidentiality be sufficient? How will you explain your intentions to your respondents?

4 Return to *precisely what do I need to find out?* Which statistical strategies will be necessary in order to provide you with that information? It is best to find out before you are finally committed to the wording of your questionnaire.

Recommended further reading

Bell, J. (2010) *Doing Your Research Project: A Guide for First-time Researchers* (5th edn). Maidenhead: Open University Press/McGraw-Hill.

Part Two of this classic text includes a comprehensive section on questionnaires.

Bell, J. and Opie, C. (2002) *Learning from Research*. Maidenhead: Open University Press.

Parts 1 and 2 consider the approach to research, and in particular the questionnaire design adopted by two postgraduate students. It might be useful to consider the hurdles they faced – and the ways those hurdles were successfully overcome.

Denscombe, M. (2010) *The Good Research Guide for Small-scale Social Research Projects* (4th edn). Maidenhead: Open University Press/McGraw-Hill.

Everything in this book is worth consulting, but in Part II (Methods of Social Research), Chapter 9, 'Questionnaires', is particularly clear and helpful.

Muijs, D. (2011) *Doing Quantitative Research in Education with SPSS* (2nd edn). London: Sage.

So much more than a guide to using SPSS, this book reviews the fundamentals of research design and links them to practices in education. Chapters 2, 3 and 4 are particularly good for thinking about methodology.

Oppenheim, A.N. (1992) *Questionnaire Design, Interviewing and Attitude Measurement* (new edn). London: Cassell.

Chapters 1, 2 and 3 provide guidance about survey design and Chapters 7, 8 and 9 cover questionnaire planning, question wording, basic measurement theory – and much more. This is an excellent book to keep for reference.

Rugg, G. and Petre, M. (2007) *A Gentle Guide to Research Methods*. Maidenhead: Open University Press/McGraw-Hill.

An entertaining read that takes an even stronger line than this chapter on the potential pitfalls of questionnaires. pp 143–51.

References

Bell, J. (2005) *Doing Your Research Project: A Guide for First-time Researchers* (4th edn). Maidenhead: Open University Press/McGraw-Hill.

Cohen, L., Manion, L. and Morrison, K. (2011) *Research Methods in Education* (7th edn). Abingdon and New York: Routledge/Falmer.

Denscombe, M. (2010) *The Good Research Guide for Small-scale Social Research Projects* (4th edn). Maidenhead: Open University Press/McGraw-Hill.

Kaplowitz, M.D., Hadlock, T.D. and Levine, R. (2004) A comparison of web and mail survey response rates. *Public Opinion Quarterly* 68(1): 94–101.

Muijs, D. (2011) *Doing Quantitative Research in Education with SPSS* (2nd edn). London: Sage.

Oppenheim, A.N. (1992) *Questionnaire Design, Interviewing and Attitude Measurement* (new edn). London: Cassell.

Punch, K.F. (1998) *Introduction to Social Research: Quantitative and Qualitative Approaches*. London: Sage.

Sapsford, R. and Abbott, P. (1996) Ethics, politics and research, in Sapsford, R. and Jupp, V. (eds) *Data Collection and Analysis*. London: Sage.

Woolner, P. (2010) *The Design of Learning Spaces*. London: Continuum (Chapter 5 has some pointers for those interested in using visual methods in research).

Youngman, M. (1994) Designing and using questionnaires, in Bennett, N., Glatter, R. and Levačić, R. (eds) *Improving Educational Management through Research and Consultancy*. London: Paul Chapman with The Open University.

CHAPTER 19

Making Use of Existing Data

Anna Vignoles and Shirley Dex

Chapter objectives

- To introduce readers to the possibility of doing research using existing data – most often large-scale survey data.
- To consider different types of data that could be used and their implications.
- To describe the general ways of constructing, assembling and accessing statistics and data for research in educational leadership and management.
- To provide pointers to the locations of accessible educational data and statistics.

Introduction

Sole practitioners and researchers involved in educational leadership and management are likely to neglect the possibility of making use of existing data sets, and yet for educational leaders concerned with levels of academic achievement or social and economic changes which might impact on their institution the analysis of such data can provide valuable insights. The investigation of existing data may also be particularly appropriate for those who wish their research to be unobtrusive (see also Chapter 4).

In this chapter, we examine the use of data that has already been collected by someone else or by another organisation. In some cases, it is possible to get hold of a data set that is just ready and waiting to be analysed. In other cases, work has to be done to assemble and prepare the data before it can be analysed and, in a sense, therefore, you as researcher will need to create or assemble the data set. We consider both these alternatives and give a few examples of data sources that are available. In practice, there are huge numbers of sources of data that are waiting to be assembled by the researcher. The advent of the Web has led to a proliferation of these sources of data and statistics and made them more accessible.

One important distinction to bear in mind is that data can be at the micro or macro level. Micro data usually have individuals as the unit of analysis, although other common examples of micro data include data on firms or schools. When the units of analysis are macro data, there has been some aggregation process over a set of individuals or a set of schools. Examples of macro data might relate to the country as a whole, or a local authority – for example, the percentage of private schools or faith schools in an area. Data are available nationally and internationally and a list of accessible data sets can be found in this book's website materials, at http://www.sagepub.co.uk/briggs. In this chapter, the examples of national data mainly relate to England, but similar national data sets are likely to be accessible through other government websites. References to international data sets are towards the end of the chapter.

In this chapter, we first consider the type of analysis that makes use of existing data, along with some definitions about the types of data possible. We then consider the general ways of constructing, assembling or accessing statistics and data.

Secondary data analysis

Carrying out analysis on existing data is called *secondary data analysis*. Since someone has already collected the data, or at least decided on the categories under which the data are stored, the researcher has to work within these categories. These categories may not always be exactly what the researcher would have chosen but, at the most basic level, this is not alterable. Sometimes it is possible to modify data definitions by constructing new variables out of the existing ones. This might be done by aggregating more than one variable, for example. This is only possible where you can obtain an electronic copy of the data set stored inside a statistical package like SPSS (you will need to have access to the same software on your own PC in order to read the data and manipulate and analyse it). Secondary data analysis is also described below under the sub-heading 'Ready-made data'. Some examples are provided in Figure 19.1.

However, there is an important caveat to bear in mind before you start creating new variables. You need to check the frequencies of the existing variables before you start to combine them. In Example 2 (Figure 19.2), you may have found that 70 per cent of people gave code (1) as their response and a further 20 per cent gave code (2). If this were the case, you would not be advised to combine them because, by then, nearly all of your sample would be covered, and this would leave you with no variation to examine or analyse. For the same reason, you would not want to analyse a single code (for example, code (1) from Example 2), if 95 per cent or more of the people surveyed gave the same, one response. This would indicate that the question was not useful for distinguishing between people and offered little prospect for analysis.

Millennium Cohort Study Sweep 1 Question: Does anyone look after *Jack <child's name> while you are at work? Tick all that apply. (18 specific codes)			
1	Respondent	11	Friends and neighbours
2	Husband/partner	12	Live-in nanny/au pair
3	Child's non-resident father	13	Other nanny/au pair
4	Your mother	14	Registered childminder
5	Your father	15	Unregistered childminder
6	Your partner's mother	16	Workplace/college nursery – crèche
7	Your partner's father	17	Local Authority day nursery – crèche
8	Child's non-resident father's or mother's mother	18	Private day nursery – crèche
9	Child's non-resident father's or mother's father	95	Other (Specify)
10	Other relatives		

You might be interested in defining 'Formal childcare use'. This could be done by combining codes to make a new variable 'Formal care' coded '1' when any of the following codes were used: (12), (13), (14), (15), (16), (17), (18), and otherwise zero. However, if you wanted to investigate 'Out of the home formal care', you would not include codes (12) or (13).

Figure 19.1 Example 1: Childcare while mother is at work

How important do you think it is for your child to have a good education?	
1	Very important
2	Quite important
3	Do not have a strong view
4	Not very important
5	Very unimportant

Here you might create a new variable 'Important' out of people who gave either code (1) or code (2).

Figure 19.2 Example 2: Importance assigned by parents to education

So, the first stage of any secondary data analysis is to give a thorough examination of the data that have already been collected, before you start to alter anything or analyse it. This means that you should first print out, for all the variables you are interested in, the frequencies for each of their codes. By so doing, you may discover that some variables of interest are unable to be analysed.

For further information about carrying out secondary data analysis, a good reference book is Hakim (1982a, 1982b). You may also like to refer to Chapters 23 and 24 in this book.

Cross-sectional, longitudinal or time series data

An important distinction to bear in mind about data is whether they were collected at one point in time or over a period of time.

A *cross-sectional* data set or survey refers to one point in time. This is like a snapshot photograph. It captures the subject once. Cross-sectional data can allow the researcher who, for example, wanted to monitor the progress of a particular group of students, to compare subjects within the time period it refers to. So, for example, a survey which contained UK pupils' Key Stage 1 or 2 scores in 2000 alongside some of their characteristics, for example, their age group, ethnic group, parents' education levels, would allow an investigation and identification of whether there were statistical correlations between Key Stage scores and ethnic origin, or Key Stage scores and parents' education level. It does not allow you to infer that parents' education level causes the child's Key Stage score. In order to get closer to identifying causal relationships, as close as it is possible to get in social science, you generally need to have longitudinal data to analyse.

Longitudinal data are like the cine or video camera moving picture, as opposed to the cross-sectional snapshot. Longitudinal data follow the same subjects as they age and develop over time. For example, linking up the yearly test scores of a pupil as they progress, year by year, through a school creates a longitudinal data set about them. The analysis can be richer if you have some more personal information about the pupils, as well as their outcome data. For example, parental characteristics can be useful, as can the pupil's sex, whether they have any health problems or disability and other characteristics that might affect their learning. Having this record over time about an individual, when you have sufficient sample sizes of such data, allows you to start to unpick causality – for example, to answer the question about what factors affect a child's outcomes in life. One interesting British study found that the extent to which parents express interest in their child's education when the child was in early primary school (age 5 and 7) was an important determinant of their educational achievement at age 16. In fact, parental interest in their child's education was more important in determining the child's educational achievement than other parental variables, such as the socio-economic status of the parent (Feinstein and Symons, 1999).

A hybrid between these two types of data is the *repeat cross-section* data set. This is where you have a regular sample survey which collects data from individuals at a cross-sectional point in time, and then goes back to collect data at a later cross-section in time using the same questions. However, the repeat data collection is based on a new sample and it is not the same individuals telling you about themselves each time. The regularity of such surveys does start to offer greater possibilities for examining change than the one-off cross-sectional survey. For example, a random probability cross-sectional sample of headteachers in 2005 could give you a picture of headteachers' pay and conditions in 2005. And if done again on an annual basis, even though asking a different random probability sample of headteachers, it would provide information about the changes over time in headteachers' pay and conditions.

As well as offering insights into change, repeat cross-section surveys, where they use the same questionnaire, can be pooled to create more cases for analysis. In this way, a smaller sample size for any one cross-section can become bigger by pooling, and allow analysis of groups that would be too small in size for robust analysis of any one survey. An example of this could be pupil cross-section surveys that wished to focus on separate minority ethnic groups, or disabled pupils, although the latter group are so small in number that pooling would still not produce sufficient sample sizes, without employing some over-sampling procedure for disabled people.

Time series data are similar to repeat cross-sectional data. They consist of statistics or data over time, one per time period, which most often is per year. However, it is aggregate, or macro data, rather than micro data. For example, researchers interested in looking at the wider context of educational change might consider the proportion of children who receive primary education in every year from 1982 to 2008 in a developing country, which would create a time series of data. These could be put together for a number of countries, alongside the fertility rate and the Gross National Product (GNP) for that country and that year. It would then be possible to look for statistical relationships between the extent of education and GNP, or education and fertility. Because there is a time reference to the data, it is possible to analyse the association of education in year t with the outcome of GNP in year $t + 1$, or $t + 2$, etc. It is also possible to subtract one year's data from another year (1999 GNP – 1998 GNP) to produce a difference (or percentage growth) that can be analysed. In this way, again, it is possible to get closer to testing out hypotheses that are causal – for example, the hypothesis that an increase in the percentage of the country's population that have primary education will cause growth in its GNP, or changes in the fertility rate.

Having set out above the main types of data and the analyses they offer, the rest of this chapter charts some of the resources that are available with some examples of how they have been or could be used to research particular topics.

Ready-made micro data sets

These data are already collected in large-scale surveys and are available in electronic form in a statistical package (most often in social science this is SPSS) from a data archive which in Britain is housed at Essex University, The Economic and Social Data Service (ESDS) (found at www.esds.ac.uk/). ESDS offers a search facility as well as the ability to investigate some data sets for descriptive statistics online. This archive also contains some pre-collected anonymised qualitative interview data sets. Data sets can be downloaded after registration and permission are granted, and are free to access for academic use.

Once one gets a copy of the survey data and the appropriate software, it is a fairly quick route to carrying out an analysis. However, learning about the statistical package will slow down the process, though many standard statistical packages can offer a transfer write-out of the data into an Excel (or other regular) spreadsheet. The data can then be manipulated and many standard analyses carried out in Excel.

A set of existing, ready-made data sets and their contact details are listed in Table 19 which can be found at http://www.sagepub.co.uk/briggs. Some examples of potential analyses of ready-made British and international data are:

- The relationships between pupils' educational attainment and their earlier educational and family background experiences: National Child Development Study (NCDS), British Cohort Study (BCS), National Pupil Database/Pupil Level School Census (NPDB/PLASC), Longitudinal Survey of Young People in England (LYSPE).

- The educational attainment of pupils from different minority groups by gender: Universities Statistical Record, Higher Education Statistics Agency data; LSYPE, NPD, NPDB/PLASC.

- The economic value of gaining a degree or other educational qualification: Labour Force Survey, NCDS, BCS, Destination of Leavers from Higher Education Longitudinal Survey from the Higher Education Statistics Agency, various Graduate Surveys commissioned by the Department for Education and Skills, General Household Survey (GHS) – a number of these surveys were commissioned by what was the Department for Education and Employment.

- Who gets involved in lifelong learning: National Adult Learning Survey, International Adult Literacy Survey (IALS).

- Whether educational attainment varies by region: GHS.

- The relationship between quality assessment grades awarded by the Office for Standards in Education (Ofsted) and the area of the school (Ofsted data).

- How pupils' test scores vary across countries with different educational systems, and ages at which children start school: Programme for International Student Assessment (PISA), IALS.

- The effects of types of childcare used in infancy on the child's later development: the Effective Provision of Pre-School Education (EPPE) Project, Millennium Cohort Study (MCS), the Avon Longitudinal Study of Parents and Children (ALSPAC).

- How children's scores in maths vary by country and whether these relate to economic indicators; or whether they relate to spending on education or to pupil–teacher ratios. PISA data, which are downloadable from OECD, contain the pupil scores on maths across countries, and other international organisations provide data on the other macro educational measures (see online resources at http://www.sagepub.co.uk/briggs).

Assemble your own micro data set

In some cases, researchers are stimulated to research a particular topic about which there is no existing data set. For example, it might be interesting to know, as a school leader, whether children's assessments have changed over successive generations, or whether the intake into your school or other education institution has the same sort of socio-economic profile as other institutions and how this relates to students' examination or assessment scores. This may suggest the only way to proceed is to try to collect new data, for example as a one-off or repeat survey. But it is always worth considering first what data are already available in administrative records. Administrative records will usually provide robust information and are generally reasonably complete in the sense that they do not suffer from the problem that often people will not participate in surveys. However, even if administrative data are not complete, they are likely to be far more complete than any data you could collect yourself. Also, if you wanted more than one year of data, there would be a long wait to assemble sufficient data in order to be able to analyse change. So even though the administrative records may not contain all the data you would like, it is often worth compromising to get (often) better quality and more systematic data than a lone researcher could start to collect for themselves.

PLASC is a pupil-level census of English schools. These data provide quite detailed information on the teaching resource input into individual schools and on some pupil characteristics – for example, age, gender, ethnicity, eligibility for free school meals, whether the pupil has English as an Additional Language or has Special Educational Needs (SEN). The teaching resource variables include the ratio of qualified teachers to pupils, as well as the ratio of support staff to pupils. Prior to PLASC, this kind of data was available at school level from what was known as 'Form 7'. There is, therefore, a long time series of school-level data (one can aggregate PLASC to school level) which researchers can analyse in a number of different ways. An English school will have an electronic version of its recent PLASC submissions and may hold data from its earlier Form 7 submissions. Assembled into a spreadsheet, they would offer the opportunity to do some simple descriptive analyses of change in your school over time. PLASC data for all schools can be obtained from the Department for Education (DfE) and, when combined with National Pupil Database (NPD) information on pupils' Key Stage scores, enable various kinds of analyses, particularly value-added analyses. For example, one could undertake an investigation of how the value added across different schools varies with the level of resource inputs.

PLASC and the National Pupil Database now provide extremely comprehensive individual-level data on pupil attainment, pupil characteristics and indeed school characteristics. However, well before the advent of PLASC/NPD, some schools had been collaborating and pooling data to provide schools and indeed researchers with data on all schools in a particular area. At least one such scheme was initiated by the headteacher of Harrogate Grammar School in the north of England in 1995 as a data set exchange and, at the time of writing, it is still going on. It now includes comparative expenditure data, income information and staffing cost data on more than 60 secondary schools (Mayston and Jesson, 1999). It is also possible to do this, one school at a time, from the DfE website, entering schools and their postcode and the data you require (www.education.gov.uk/inyourarea/). The data can be obtained for KS2, KS3, GCSE and several other statistics or scores (on, for example, pupils with special needs; school initiatives; class sizes; school work-force; early years; post-16; children's social services) currently for some years between 2005 and 2009. The DfE website also offers downloadable perform-ance tables (www.education.gov.uk/performancetables) from 2004 onwards. Another alternative is that you obtain national educational statistics from the DfE website, and you collect the data for your own school and present it in the context of the national profile. Where your school differs, you could investigate why this might be the case. One possible analysis (available from the Office of National Statistics website at www.statistics.gov.uk) is to examine the sick leave rate at your school and see whether staff in your organisation have sick leave absence rates that are the same as, lower than or above the national or regional average.

Macro data: existing data enhanced by collating

In the same way that a researcher can assemble a micro data set, it is also pos-sible to assemble a macro data set. This has got easier since the advent of websites with downloadable material. But there have, for many years, been books of statistical data which can be drawn on and entered into a spread-sheet for analysis. Collecting the data points (statistics) from books can be more laborious than analysing an existing electronic data set already entered into a statistical analysis package, but it is still not usually as time-consuming as collecting new data by carrying out your own survey using a questionnaire.

The DfE website in England offers time series data on a large number of statistics (www.education.gov.uk/rsgateway/DB/TIM/). These are downloadable in the form of one Excel file per statistic. Currently, some are not very long time series, but they will gradually increase over time. They include the following, among a larger number of topics:

- Average salaries of full-time teachers.
- Total teachers in maintained schools.
- Initial teacher training available places.
- Number of schools in England in January of each year.
- Pupil–teacher ratios.
- Primary KS1 class size data.
- Secondary class size data.
- Spending per pupil in real terms.

- Spending per pupil in cash terms.
- UK educational expenditure per pupil as a percentage of Gross Domestic Product.

Just using these data, it would be possible to examine whether there are correlations over time with spending per pupil in real (or cash) terms and pupil–teacher ratios, for example. Also available at the rsgateway are:

- Outcomes for children looked after by Local Authorities in England.
- Qualifications and participation in learning at a local level.
- Provision for children under 5 years of age in England.
- Surveys of information and communication technology in schools.
- Higher education statistics.

It would also be possible to construct a model of whether an increase in average teacher salaries year on year is associated with a change in the achievement rate of pupils in the following years. This involves creating explanatory variables that are lagged in time behind the dependent variable. In this case, you would also need to be calculating the change in any variable from year to year (see Figure 19.3, Example 3).

	% pupils achieving Level 2 in KS1 Maths	% pupils achieving Level 2 in KS1 Reading	Average class size (primary and secondary school)	Average salaries (£) FT primary teachers	Expenditure (£) per pupil in real terms (primary and secondary schools)
1995	79	78		20,860	2920
1996	82	78		21,370	2880
1997	84	80		22,080	2840
1998	84	80	27.1	22,700	2770
1999	87	82	26.5	23,570	2800
2000	90	83	25.8	24,550	2930
2001	91	84	25.2	26,210	3130
2002	90	84	25.2	27,590	3410
2003	90	84	25.2	29,290	3380
2004	90	85	25.7	30,510	2620
2005	91	85			
....					

Figure 19.3 Example 3: The beginnings of a time series spreadsheet containing some example data

Source: Collated from separate series in www.education.gov.uk/rsgateway/DB/TIM/

	Below Level 1b (less than 262.04 score points)		Level 1b (from 262.04 to less than 334.75 score points)		Level 1a (from 334.75 to less than 407.47 score points)		Level 2 (from 407.47 to less than 480.18 score points)		Level 3 (from 480.18 to less than 552.89 score points)		Level 4 (from 552.89 to less than 625.61 score points)		Level 5 (from 625.61 to 698.32 score points)		Level 6 (above 698.32 score points)	
	%	S.E.	%	S.E.	%	S.E.	%	S.E.	%	S.E.	%	S.E.	%	S.E.	%	S.E.
OECD																
Australia	1.0	(0.1)	3.3	(0.3)	10.0	(0.4)	20.4	(0.6)	28.5	(0.7)	24.1	(0.7)	10.7	(0.5)	2.1	(0.3)
Austria	1.9	(0.4)	8.1	(0.8)	17.5	(1.0)	24.1	(1.0)	26.0	(0.9)	17.4	(0.9)	4.5	(0.4)	0.4	(0.1)
Belgium	1.1	(0.3)	4.7	(0.5)	11.9	(0.6)	20.3	(0.7)	25.8	(0.9)	24.9	(0.7)	10.1	(0.5)	1.1	(0.2)
Canada	0.4	(0.1)	2.0	(0.2)	7.9	(0.3)	20.2	(0.6)	30.0	(0.7)	26.8	(0.6)	11.0	(0.4)	1.8	(0.2)
Chile	1.3	(0.2)	7.4	(0.8)	21.9	(1.0)	33.2	(1.1)	25.6	(1.1)	9.3	(0.7)	1.3	(0.2)	0.0	(0.0)
Czech Republic	0.8	(0.3)	5.5	(0.6)	16.8	(1.1)	27.4	(1.0)	27.0	(1.0)	17.4	(1.0)	4.7	(0.4)	0.4	(0.1)
Slovak Republic	0.8	(0.3)	5.6	(0.6)	15.9	(0.8)	28.1	(1.0)	28.5	(1.1)	16.7	(0.8)	4.2	(0.5)	0.3	(0.1)
Slovenia	0.8	(0.1)	5.2	(0.3)	15.2	(0.5)	25.6	(0.7)	29.2	(0.9)	19.3	(0.8)	4.3	(0.5)	0.3	(0.1)
Spain	1.2	(0.2)	4.7	(0.4)	13.6	(0.6)	26.8	(0.8)	32.6	(1.0)	17.7	(0.7)	3.2	(0.3)	0.2	(0.1)
Sweden	1.5	(0.3)	4.3	(0.4)	11.7	(0.7)	23.5	(1.0)	29.8	(1.0)	20.3	(0.9)	7.7	(0.6)	1.3	(0.3)
Switzerland	0.7	(0.2)	4.1	(0.4)	12.1	(0.6)	22.7	(0.7)	29.7	(0.8)	22.6	(0.8)	7.4	(0.7)	0.7	(0.2)
Turkey	0.8	(0.2)	5.6	(0.6)	18.1	(1.0)	32.2	(1.2)	29.1	(1.1)	12.4	(1.1)	1.8	(0.4)	0.0	(0.0)
United Kingdom	1.0	(0.2)	4.1	(0.4)	13.4	(0.6)	24.9	(0.7)	28.8	(0.8)	19.8	(0.8)	7.0	(0.5)	1.0	(0.2)
United States	0.6	(0.1)	4.0	(0.4)	13.1	(0.8)	24.4	(0.9)	27.6	(0.8)	20.6	(0.9)	8.4	(0.8)	1.5	(0.4)
OECD total	1.1	(0.1)	4.8	(0.1)	13.8	(0.3)	24.4	(0.3)	27.9	(0.3)	19.9	(0.3)	7.0	(0.2)	1.0	(0.1)
OECD average	1.1	(0.0)	4.6	(0.1)	13.1	(0.1)	24.0	(0.2)	28.9	(0.2)	20.7	(0.2)	6.8	(0.1)	0.8	(0.0)

Proficiency levels

Figure 19.4 Example 4: OECD Programme International Student Assessment: Percentage of students at each proficiency level on the reading scale

Source: www.oecd.org/document/53/0,3746,en_32252351_46584327_46584821_1_1_1_1,00.html#tables_figures_dbase

S.E = Standard Error

However, a researcher could go to other sources to supplement the data. Annual aggregate statistics on many areas of the UK are available from the General Lifestyle Survey (formerly the *General Household Survey*) and *Social Trends*, dating back to the 1970s. These are available in large libraries, especially university libraries, as annual volumes. It would be possible to trawl through these volumes year by year to construct a time series of variables which could then be examined to see how they were correlated. But such time series are also available, in some cases, on websites – for example, from the Office of National Statistics (ONS) website (www.statistics.gov.uk/StatBase). The areas covered by these volumes include economy, crime, education and training, employment, sick leave, social welfare and information on families, among other subjects. Some sample time series statistics from the education and training section which are also available on the ONS website include:

- participation rates of children aged 3 and 4 in maintained nursery and primary schools, by region
- teacher training/newly trained teachers
- pupil exclusions from school.

In addition, there are other international organisations (such as the United Nations, UNICEF, UNESCO, World Bank, International Labour Office/ILO, OECD, Eurostat) with similar annual volumes that cover international statistics, one per country per year, which could be assembled in the same way (see Figure 19.4: Example 4, and Figure 19.5, which lists useful publications in book volumes). These volumes are increasingly being made available on websites.

More and more statistics are becoming available on websites. For example, UNESCO's website (www.unesco.org) offers a range of annual statistics for a minimum of 50 countries (see www.uis.unesco.org/) on measures such as:

- school life expectancy
- indicators on teaching staff
- demographic indicators
- economic indicators
- literacy rates among 15–24-year-olds

and many other educational measures.

In some cases of educational statistics, there are also historical series dating back to 1970 – for example:

- pre-primary education
- new entrants to primary education
- enrolment and teaching staff in primary education
- secondary education.

Eurostat

Europe in Figures is the EUROSTAT Yearbook. Issues from 2010 dating back to 1996 are available at:
http://epp.eurostat.ec.europa.eu/portal/page/portal/publications/recently_published

General LiFestyle Survey (GLF), formerly General Household Survey (GHS)

The GLF is a continuous multipurpose national survey of people and has been carried out continuously since 1971, published by HMSO and the Office of National Statistics. Statistics from these volumes are also available at: www.statistics.gov.uk/StatBase/Product.asp?v1nk=57 56&Pos=3&ColRank=2&Rank=416

International Labour Office

Yearbook of Labour Statistics. Available annually since 1935–36 in two volumes. Volume 1 contains time series statistics going back the previous 10 years; Volume 2 contains country profiles: www.ilo.org/public/english/bureau/stat/child/actrep/yearbook.htm
   There is also an ILO Statistics and database portal at: www.ilo.org/global/statistics-and-databases/lang--en/index.htm

OECD

Education at a Glance is an annual report providing a full range of education statistics for most OECD countries. 2010 is available at: www.oecd.org/edu/eag2010 (for earlier versions, change the year.)

Social Trends

An annual volume of official statistics published by HMSO/The Stationery Office. Statistics from these volumes are also available by theme online in 2010 and back to 1999 at: www.statistics. gov.uk/StatBase/Product.asp?vlnk=5748&Pos=2&ColRank=1&Rank=272

United Nations

One annual publication is the *Human Development Report*. The annual report in 2010 (and back issues to 1990) are available at: http://hdr.undp.org/en/reports/global/hdr2010.
   See also United Nations, *Demographic Yearbook*, annually from 1948 to 2008 at: http://unstats.un.org/unsd/demographics/products/dyb/dyb2.htm
   Yearbook of the United Nations is an annual collection from 1946 to 2005, available at: http://unyearbook.un.org/unyearbook.html?name=2005index.html
   Economic Survey of Europe has annual surveys available at: www.unece.org/ead/survey.htm

World Bank

One annual publication is its *World Development Report* which has a statistical appendix. Available online, from the 1978 issue to the 2010 report, at:
http://econ.worldbank.org/WBSITE/EXTERNAL/EXTDEC/EXTRESEARCH/EXTWDRS/

Figure 19.5 Tertiary education: useful publications in book volumes

The Office of Economic Cooperation and Development (OECD) offers a range of downloadable macro-level educational and other statistics from its website (www.oecd.org). These statistics are presented by country and include comparisons over a range of more developed countries, which are internationally comparable. For example, under the *Statistics* section, 'Composite leading indicators' on 'Education and Training', we can find:

- educational personnel per country
- educational expenditure by funding source
- foreign student enrolments
- graduates by age
- total population by age and sex
- students enrolled by age and by type of institution
- teachers' salaries.

Your research may still involve collating these separate statistics and series into a data set that can be analysed. Often, this involves a bit of data manipulation and interrogation of the website or published data to get a series that overlaps in time, for the same years, with all the data points from all the various variables you are interested in. There are sometimes inconsistencies or gaps in the series; also, definitions of variables and measures, frustratingly, can change over time. It is possible to handle some of these problems in the analysis – for example, one can handle changes in variable definition in regression analysis by entering a dummy variable to show where the definition of your dependent variable has changed (this is done by creating a zero 1 dummy which takes the value '1' in years from the change in definition onwards, but zero in the years before the change). In other cases, you may have to miss out the year that does not have full information on all of your variables, or enter the mean for cases that are missing.

In the case of higher education, the Observatory on Borderless Higher Education website under its *Resources and Services* section, *Key Resources* sub-section, has a review of free higher education statistics sources, providing links by country to more information and how to access it (www.obhe.ac.uk).

Conclusion

There is no shortage of data, and accessible data sources are multiplying through the ease of website access. It is important to remember that data assembled by the researcher, while needing time to be assembled, is usually a much quicker route to analysis than collecting primary data via a survey. For those involved with issues of educational leadership and management, accessing and interrogating existing data sets can be an important and instructive research method.

Key points

- There are already many sources of existing data sets, many downloadable from websites, that can be used to address a wide range of educational research questions and data sources are increasing all the time.

- To make use of these data sets in research, once obtained, requires familiarity with quantitative multivariate data analysis (covered in Chapters 23 and 24 of this volume).

- Data can be about aggregate macro-level trends or time series (such as the percentage of young people leaving school at 16 year by year) or about micro or individual units of analyses (such as individual pupils' achievements in the light of their school, parental background, etc.)

- It is far easier to use an existing data set than to start to collate data across years or areas for yourself.

- A range of accessible data sets and their Web and access addresses are provided in this chapter and further suggestions are given in the online resources (see http: www.sagepub.co.uk/briggs).

Questions and reflections

1 Could you employ existing data about your school or college to analyse a problematic issue in your role as an educational leader?

2 What international comparisons could you make that might be helpful in examining a leadership/management issue in your educational institution?

Recommended further reading

Earl, L. and Fullan, M. (2003) Using data in leadership for learning. *Cambridge Journal of Education* 33(3): 383–94.

This article gives suggestions and examples of analyses you can carry out using readily available data about leadership and learning.

Goldstein, H. (2001) Using pupil performance data for judging schools and teachers: scope and limitations. *British Educational Research Journal* 27(4): 433–42.

This article assumes that you want to evaluate schools and teachers and demonstrates ways of carrying out quantitative analyses to do this, given you have data about schools (or teachers) already. It also warns you about what you cannot do with specific data.

Leithwood, K., Aitken, R. and Jantzi, D. (2006) *Making Schools Smarter: Leading with Evidence*. London: Sage.

This book shows you how to use and analyse available data to provide schools with information and tools which will help their decision making and their ability to achieve specified goals.

Marsh, C. and Elliott, J. (2008) *Exploring Data* (2nd edn) Cambridge: Polity/John Wiley and Sons.

This provides a textbook treatment of carrying out analyses on existing data about a set of cases (e.g. individuals or institutions) from surveys or administrative sources. It takes a step by step approach to questions you might want to ask of the data and how to answer these questions using data analyses and statistics.

References

Carey, S., Low, S. and Hansbro, J. (1997) *Adult Literacy in Britain*. London: The Stationery Office.

Dex, S. and Joshi, H. (eds) (2004) *Millennium Cohort Study First Survey: A User's Guide to Initial Findings*. London: Institute of Education, University of London.

Dex, S. and Joshi, H. (2005) *Children of the 21st Century: From Birth to Nine Months*. Bristol: The Policy Press.

Dolton, P.J. and Makepeace, G.H. (1992) *The Early Careers of 1980 Graduates, Work Histories, Job Tenure, Career Mobility and Occupational Choice*. Department of Employment, Research Paper 79.

Dolton, P.J. and Vignoles, A. (2000) The incidence and effects of over-education in the graduate labour market. *Economics of Education Review* 19: 179–198.

Feinstein, L. and Symons, J. (1999) Attainment in secondary schools, *Oxford Economic Papers* 51: 300–21.

Ferri, E., Bynner, J. and Wadsworth, M. (eds) (2003) *Changing Britain, Changing Lives*. London: Institute of Education, University of London.

Hakim, C. (1982a) *Secondary Analysis in Social Research: A Guide to Data Sources and Methods with Examples*. London: Allen and Unwin.

Hakim, C. (1982b) Secondary analysis and the relationship between official and academic social research. *Sociology* 16(1): 12–28.

Mayston, D. and Jesson, D. (1999) *Linking Educational Resourcing with Enhanced Educational Outcomes*. Department for Education and Employment, Research Report 179.

OECD (1997) *Literacy Skills for the Knowledge Society*. Paris: Organization for Economic Cooperation and Development.

United Nations (1996) *Human Development Report, 1996*. New York and Oxford: Oxford University Press for the United Nations. Published annually.

World Bank (1996) *From Plan to Market*. World Development Report. New York and Oxford: Oxford University Press for the World Bank. Published annually.

CHAPTER 20

Documents and Documentary Analysis

Tanya Fitzgerald

Chapter objectives

This chapter will address the following:

- What is documentary research and why are documents useful?
- What types of documents can researchers in educational leadership and management use and why?
- What tools might be used for documentary analysis?

Introduction

Documents litter the worlds in which we live and provide evidence that narrates the details of our personal and professional lives. Birth certificates, school attendance records, examination results, passports, drivers' licences, bank statements, insurance policies, correspondence, blogs, emails, Web pages, photographs, video clips and wills contain numerous personal details that assist in building a portrait of an individual. Similarly, employment and tax records, curriculum vitae, committee minutes and institutional records contain the minutiae of the professional work and contribution of individuals. As leaders and managers in education, documents such as employment applications, teacher registration, performance management records, curriculum books and statements, school inspections, institutional website data, marketing and publicity materials, policies, meeting agendas and minutes, correspondence, memoranda, speeches and media interviews all form part of the public professional record. Documents from schools, colleges and universities therefore can provide valuable information about the context and culture of these institutions and frequently provide another window for the researcher in educational leadership and management to read between the lines of official discourse and then triangulate information through interviews, observations and questionnaires, possibly within a case study.

At the macro level, documents such as education policy, speeches of politicians, official websites (such as the Department for Education in England, Ministry of Education in New Zealand, Department of Education, Employment and Workplace Relations in Australia), league tables, official statistics, regulations and legislation can provide another level of public narration and insight into how organisations and institutions work, and what values and practices guide decision making.

What is documentary research?

One of the advantages of documentary research is that documents have been produced and preserved as a record of the past; but this is not to suggest that documents are any less time-consuming or easier to deal with than data from interviews, questionnaires or a focus group. It takes considerable skill to locate elusive documents and considerable interpretative skills are required to uncover the meaning of the contents. Accordingly, researchers need to ask critical questions to evaluate the document, its author and its place in the public record and be mindful of the fact that documents are written so that an author can record his/her view of what occurred. In terms of research in the field of educational leadership and management, at times it may be less difficult to establish the accuracy and credibility of documents if researchers are able to contact and/or interview authors.

For researchers in the field of educational leadership, documentary research might be primarily used as a data collection strategy for case studies. It is unlikely that a researcher in this field would undertake documentary research in the same way as an historian. Historical research is primarily based on archival and documentary research and so the methodological demands of this field of research are different. Researchers in educational leadership might adopt a number of the tools of documentary research to supplement other data collection methods. For example, policy documents might be used as a way of triangulating interview data.

Scott (1990) cautions researchers to adopt the position that documents cannot be regarded as objective accounts. Documents are required to be examined and interrogated in the context of other sources of data. Data from documents can be used to highlight a range of perspectives on a particular event, activity, group or individual and can be further utilised to determine the representativeness of such a document. For social science researchers, documents offer a form of voice – a voice on past events and activities that provides a level of insight for the reader into these events, activities and participants. Their interpretations may vary as researchers engage in their work with different and differing epistemological and ontological frameworks. This is true of all social science data whereby conclusions are derived from particular interpretations of data.

Documentary analysis is a form of qualitative analysis that requires researchers to locate, interpret, analyse and draw conclusions about the evidence presented. Documentary research is a form of interpretative research that requires researchers to collect, collate and analyse empirical data in order to produce a theoretical account that either describes, interprets or explains what has occurred. If documentary research is the main research approach, researchers must engage in systematic activities to ensure the reliability of their evidence and conclusions. This will involve the following 10 stages:

1 Identify the research problem or issue.

2 Devise a list of possible aims and research questions.

3 Identify the relevant theoretical and methodological frameworks.

4 Develop a list of key words or themes from the literature.

5 Locate physical (library, archives) and electronic documents.

6 Classify documents.

7 Collect and collate data.

8 Identify emerging themes from the data.

9 Interpret evidence and link with research questions and literature themes.

10 Structure and write a report.

Bear in mind too that this process can be applied to other forms of enquiry. There are endless variations as to how these 10 steps might be applied; what is important to note is that researchers should be systematic about their data collection activities. As indicated in Table 20.1, there are several advantages and limitations to documentary research that I have outlined. This is not to dissuade researchers from these data collection activities but to highlight the potential of documents to offer another means to address and answer research questions.

As a general rule, the majority of documents are written and available in the public domain (libraries, archives, museums, institutional holdings, websites). These sources might be further classified as primary or secondary, and that can predetermine ways in which analysis might occur. There is considerable debate, however, as to whether these two binaries are appropriate or adequate (McCulloch and Richardson, 2000), as not all documents 'fit' these classifications. Accordingly, there is no rigid distinction between primary and secondary sources and the kinds of questions asked to 'read between the lines' are of critical importance. There is not the space here to provide an overview of the methodological debates surrounding 'primary' and 'secondary' sources and researchers are urged to consult the literature that traverses these debates, some of which are listed in the section entitled 'Additional Sources' at the end

Table 20.1 Advantages and limitations of documentary research

Advantages	Limitations
Allows researcher to gather data from the words of the participant	Documents can be subjective
Can be accessed at a time convenient to the researcher	Documents can be protected, unavailable for use or not catalogued correctly, or at all
Contain facts that may not be readily available – for example, names, dates, specific event details	Can be difficult to locate, may be stored in several places geographically distant, may be difficult to access
Can provide access to information that may be difficult to gain via interview	May not be accurate and have been created to present a particular view of events, activities or individuals
Use of electronic tools to store and analyse data can provide ease of use for researcher	Can be time-consuming and require methodical analysis
Can be unobtrusive	

of this chapter. While I am not suggesting a rigid classification here, primary sources can be regarded as data in much the same way as interview or focus group transcripts because these sources contain raw (that is, not yet inter-preted) data. Secondary sources, on the other hand, can be generally regarded as literature as they have been subjected to a level of interpretation and analysis.

The major difference between 'primary' and 'secondary' sources lies in the question of authorship. Primary sources are usually first-hand accounts pro-duced by a witness to a particular event. For example, this might include notes taken from a committee meeting or attendance statistics; records that are produced close to an event, depending on the type of record, may be easy or difficult for researchers to locate. A primary source would not contain any analysis of an event whereas secondary sources provide an interpretation of that event. In both cases, there is potential for bias not only in terms of what was recorded for example in minutes, but what was omitted and the particu-lar epistemological view of the author. In recent years, methodological debates across the humanities and social sciences have raged concerning what 'counts' as a primary source (see, for example, Burton, 2001; Fitzgerald, 2005). The range of primary sources most likely to be used by researchers in the field of educational leadership include:

- official letters and correspondence
- parliamentary debates (for example on education budgets)
- public submissions on a particular policy
- government reports

- policy documents (such as performance management policies)
- institutional documents such as school rolls, strategic plans, staff lists
- minutes of meetings
- newspaper articles, letters to/from the editor, editorials
- pamphlets (such as advertising material from schools and institutions)
- virtual documents (such as institutional websites).

Locating documents

Whatever documents are used, it is important to conduct as exhaustive a search as possible for these sources. While this might involve a physical presence in archives, libraries and institutions, the Internet has also opened up possibilities for documentary research from desktops. However, caution must be exercised as records and resources that appear on the Internet are usually subject to decisions about what information might be made public, how this information might be presented, and what, if any, information ought not to be in the public domain. In other words, Internet sources should be read with a critical eye as they have usually been subject to a level of interpretation and analysis. A further disadvantage of Internet sources is that funding decisions about what documents and resources can be digitised are frequently made. The consequence of finite resources is that librarians, archivists and officials have to determine which documents to release, and which documents might be of interest. As lamented by feminist historians, too frequently papers for/ about women and their lives are not deemed to be important enough to store electronically, catalogue or digitise (Fitzgerald, 2005). One of the immediate advantages of the Internet is that it can provide a level of access to repositories, libraries and archives that might prove otherwise impossible due to time constraints or geographical location. Additionally, researchers can locate catalogues online in preparation for a visit to an archive or library. Not only does this save time, but requests for access can be made prior to any on-site data collection and any necessary approvals for access to material can be obtained.

Documents are reasonably convenient records to locate and access, particularly in the digital age. Library catalogues are available online to all users, irrespective of geographical location, and contain bibliographic and archival sources. For researchers in the field of educational leadership, the main sources for documents will be local institutions (such as a school or college), local government offices and organisations such as:

- the DfE in England (www.education.gov.uk)
- the Department of Education, Employment and Workplace Relations in Australia (www.deewr.gov.au)
- the Office of Standards in Education (Ofsted) (www.ofsted.gov.uk)
- the Education Review Office in New Zealand (www.ero.govt.nz).

All of these organisations have policy documents, media releases, speeches, statistics and research reports that are publicly available through their websites. However, care should be exercised as documents that have been released are frequently those that the author/institution/organisation wishes to be in the public domain. Most archives and libraries have policies with regard to access to their collections that prevent unauthorised disclosure of private information (such as raw census data) so researchers are urged to discuss their project with a librarian or archivist. Librarians and archivists are exceptionally helpful and can frequently assist with locating relevant catalogues and finding aids.

Analysing documents

It might seem as if documents are reasonably uncomplicated sources of data to locate and analyse. Scott (1990) has suggested that all documents should be assessed according to four criteria:

1 Authenticity.
2 Credibility.
3 Representativeness.
4 Meaning.

The issue of *authenticity* concerns the soundness and authorship of documents. One of the first steps is to determine whether the document is an original or a copy. If a copy, it is important to verify that no material has been added, replaced or deleted. The process of reproducing the original by hand, photocopy, scanning or microfilming may have resulted in missing text or unreadable text. It might well be the case too that institutional documents, invariably filed in a variety of places, might not be a complete record, and details such as page numbers, section numbers and reading previous and subsequent meeting minutes can point to the existence of other documents a researcher might wish to access.

Credibility refers to assessing a document for its accuracy. This refers to the factual accuracy of reports and whether they do, in fact, report the true feelings of the author. All documents are, in the main, selective or distorted as it is difficult to construct accounts that are independent of any particular viewpoint. This is not to suggest that documents are not credible accounts and it is therefore important that information about the author(s) is known. Documents can be exercises in reputation building or reputation restoration and, consequently, researchers are advised to read secondary source material about the specific event or activity as well as about the individual(s) or groups involved. This will assist in establishing a level of credibility.

The *representativeness* of a document is determined by its survival and availability. It might not be the case that a representative sample of documents about a particular policy, for example, is required but it is important to determine whether the selected documents are representative of the contemporary environment. This is not to suggest that all documents on a particular issue or problem have either been stored correctly (Fitzgerald, 2005) or not consigned to a shredder. Computerised records are not immune from deletion as current files can be over-written or stored in an unreadable format. Document writing is an activity for the literate and, consequently, there is likely to be bias in terms of authorship. Selective retention is therefore another issue that researchers need to take into account when making claims about the representativeness of a document.

The *meaning* of a document is its interpretation. This involves, on the surface, the literal or surface reading of the text. It is important to know the accepted definitions of the key words, phrases and concepts and to decipher any handwriting accurately. Once this literal reading has been produced, the next level of interpretation involves both *content* and *textual* analysis. Content analysis (Robson, 1993), a form of quantitative analysis, requires a count of the number of times a particular word/term or image is used. On the other hand, textual analysis (Jaworski and Coupland, 1999) concentrates on deriving an understanding from the qualitative significance of the words/terms and images. Both content and textual analyses require classification of data and reading for embedded meanings. Electronic programmes such as NVivo can assist with the extraction and retrieval of key words, particularly if there are an extensive number of documents under examination (see also Chapter 25 in this book). The template in Figure 20.1 can be used in the initial phase of documentary research.

Analysing documents involves the systematic identification of underlying themes in materials, analysing these themes and providing an interpretation that augments a theoretical argument (see also Chapter 24 on discourse analysis). What is less explicit, however, is *how* themes are extracted, coded and thus made retrievable. One strategy for searching for themes in data is to develop a coding system that will readily permit the development of categories that can then be used to formulate conclusions. Altheide (2004) has developed an approach that he has labelled ethnographic content analysis (ECA) that represents a codification of certain procedures that might be viewed as typical of any kind of qualitative content analysis, although he argues for the constant revision of themes based on data collection activities and emerging interpretations. This is, accordingly, a form of grounded theory in which data are constantly revised to assist with conceptualisation, interpretation and the development of a narrative (see also Chapter 13 in this book). This is a useful framework, particularly for case study research that depends on what I term the situatedness of the case and data. Altheide (2004) describes the six steps researchers should undertake:

1 Generate a research question.
2 Understand the context in which the documents were generated.

1. **TYPE OF DOCUMENT** (Check one)

___ Newspaper	___ Map	___ Advertisement
___ Letter	___ Telegram	___ Meeting minutes
___ Legislation	___ Press release	___ Census report
___ Memorandum	___ Report	___ Other (specify)

2. **UNIQUE PHYSICAL QUALITIES OF THE DOCUMENT** (Check one or more)

___ Logo, letterhead	___ Notations
___ Handwritten	___ Stamps (date received)
___ Typed	___ Signature(s)
___ Seals	___ Other (specify)

3. **DATE(S) OF DOCUMENT**

   REFERENCE (for retrieval purposes)

4. **AUTHOR (OR CREATOR) OF THE DOCUMENT**

   POSITION (TITLE)

5. **FOR WHAT AUDIENCE WAS THE DOCUMENT WRITTEN?**

6. **ANALYSIS**

   A. *List three key ideas/themes/issues identified in the document*

   1.
   2.
   3.

   B. *Why was this document written and what evidence is there for this conclusion?*

   C. *What questions are left unanswered by the document?*

Figure 20.1 Template for documentary analysis

3 Read a range of relevant documents.
4 Generate categories that will guide the collection of data.
5 Test categories by using them to collect and collate data.
6 Revise categories.

These steps will assist in the development of a grounded theory; the theoretical argument is grounded in the data. What is also important is for researchers to adopt a critical stance in their reading of documents, in much the same way as this critical lens is applied to any form of data. Useful questions that can be asked from the outset are:

1 What type of document is it?
2 Does it have any particularly unique characteristics?
3 When was it written?
4 Who was the author and what was his/her position?
5 For whom (what audience) was the document written?
6 What is the purpose of the document?
7 Why was the document written?
8 What evidence is there within the document that indicates why it was written?

As I have mentioned, documentary research is one of the tools that can be employed in case study research. The examples I have used above can be used to collate and analyse case data. In 2005, I was involved in a collaborative research project with a New Zealand school practitioner and an academic colleague in England. Our project examined links between middle leadership and learning and was a case study of two schools in New Zealand and two in England (Fitzgerald et al., 2006). This involved 96 interviews that included the heads/principals, senior managers, middle leaders, teachers, teaching assistants and pupils. In order to provide the contextual background, we examined the school prospectus, ERO and Ofsted reports, and websites and had access to the SEF (self-evaluation form). To assist with our analysis, we constructed tables that collated this wealth of data and provided a mechanism to create a plausible and trustworthy account of our findings. One of our research questions was: What is the link between leadership and learning? As mentioned, we interviewed the heads/principals of the four schools and were particularly interested in how schools organised teaching and learning.

One of the first interview questions was: How are teachers organised in this school? Figure 20.2 shows the transcribed responses from the two secondary school heads (ES refers to the English secondary school and NS, the New Zealand school). The third column is an example of our analysis that builds on the literature review and the documentary analysis that occurred in the first stage of the project. The comments noted below the black line triangulate the interview data and assist with the emerging narrative and theorisation of links between leadership and learning. What we were looking for was the 'persistence' of such examples from multiple sources (Lincoln and Guba, 1985), and in this case, the documentary research complemented other forms of qualitative enquiry.

Collecting, collating and analysing data in documentary research is an iterative process that requires checking, re-checking and refining key themes, concepts or ideas. This can be illustrated by the diagram in Figure 20.3.

Case study question: How are teachers organised in this school?

Identifier	Text	Coding
NSH	Basically, they're organised around departments. We've never gone to the faculties in fact which is a disappointment to me. Because to go to faculties you really got to throw all the units away in a basket and re-build. I've watched a lot of schools struggle with the whole Head of Faculty thing so I've stuck with traditional departments and tried to transform them into a co-operative model so that when you make key appointments you make sure they understand the integration that you're looking for in the department and so if we've stuck with traditional departments and we've tried to restructure them so that the whole structure is of a small and interactive with a dynamic team and you say 'Right! You're in this level, use the experiences and responsibilities … anything that you want to have a go at to grow at' … and so they shift the well structured department and shift the responsibilities around in order to grow the whole business of that professional growth, the whole dynamics of professional growth. What would you like to grow at? …. responsibilities ... resources … shape it the way we want to so that it's an effective delivery and it's got good outcomes for students. And then pastorally it's quite different because it was the first school in NZ to have Deans and we cherish that. We cherish that for a number of reasons. First of all it does mean we got many (mini) schools, we've only got 300 students and when somebody who knows the kids – we've got one person who says, 'These are my kids'. And their knowledge of them is incredible. Their knowledge of the kid, the understanding of them becomes formidable … you are there to care and encourage and grow ... again they're growing.	Structural Cooperative model Shift responsibilities Innovation Risk taking Aligns with website and prospectus content analysis Organisation of teachers commented on in ERO report
ESH	Around learning and teaching. Learning Centres with a Director and Assistant Director and report to leadership group in school of 15. HT, Deputy, Bursar and everyone responsible for an area of learning and whole school responsibility. Teachers attached to Learning Centre. All behaviour, management, guidance and welfare part of Student Services. Leading tutor monitors learning and achievement of pupils. Tutor teams – focus on learning.	L and T the focus Learning focus Responsibility and accountability Aligns with SEF

Identifier: of the school (NSH = New Zealand, secondary head; ESH = England, secondary head)

Text: Column 2 contains a transcript of the interview response; no words are omitted, and the language is unaltered. Any direct quotes used in our analysis and discussion were extracted directly from Column 2.

Coding: Column 3 contains the key words or themes that have been extracted from the interview transcript. In addition, this column has also been used to record any questions that arise for a researcher to further check or verify; to make a note of links with possible relevant literature or to assess the document according to Scott's (1990) criteria; and to record the 'count' of key words (content analysis).

Figure 20.2 Example of case study analysis

> Research questions lead to raw data →
> raw data are stored with relevant location reference and prompt →
> reflective thinking that leads to content analysis and →
> generation of key themes →
> that are tested, refined and amended and lead to →
> textual analysis that leads to →
> empirical findings and the →
> generation of the final report.

Figure 20.3   From research questions to report

Conclusion

This chapter has provided an overview for researchers in educational leadership and management of the possible ways in which documentary research might be conducted. As I have stressed, it is important to approach research in a systematic, critical and informed way and this may further involve learning new sets of skills to assist with asking questions of the evidence (data), analysing that evidence and formulating conclusions. For those new to documentary research, it is important to read the methodological debates in the field to gain an understanding of the complexities of research, in any form, and at any level. I have provided a number of key questions in this chapter to assist with critical thinking about the research and the evidence and suggested a format for electronically collating and analysing data. In conclusion, I would suggest that, whatever documentary research is undertaken, it is manageable within the time available, that the research design 'matches' the questions posed and that an iterative process is employed that subjects the data and conclusions to critical scrutiny. Whatever the strengths and limitations of documentary research, it can be innovative and illuminating and prompt an enthusiasm for research that is infectious.

Key points

In summary, this chapter has:

- given an overview of the potential uses of documents and documentary analysis for educational leadership researchers
- suggested possible types of documents to consult
- indicated physical and virtual sources that house a range of documents
- examined advantages and limitations of documents
- suggested methods for data collection and analysis
- provided a template for researchers to adopt or adapt

- scoped a list of reflective questions to assist with documentary analysis
- alerted researchers to bias within documents
- offered examples for researchers
- critically examined the use of documents and documentary research.

Questions and reflections

This chapter has outlined possible ways in which researchers in the field of educational leadership might incorporate documentary analysis within their own work. While many of the data collection strategies draw from the toolkit of educational historians, the use of documents can add a refreshing level of analysis to research projects. Readers and researchers are therefore encouraged to consider the following questions when scoping a project:

1 What is the background to this topic/issue/question and where might I locate that information?
2 Why might it be important to seek this background information? How will this information assist with my analysis?
3 What tools might I use to source and analyse the document?
4 What can I learn from this document?
5 How can documents provide a level of triangulation for the project data?

Recommended further reading

This is not a definitive list of texts but offers researchers an abridged list for their guidance.

For more information on the Internet:

Gorst, A. and Brivati, B. (1997) The Internet for historians, in Butler, L. and Gorst, A. (eds) *Modern British History: A Guide to Study and Research*. London: IB Tauris Publishers.
Hooley, T., Wellens, J. and Marriott, J. (2011) *What is Online Research? Using the Internet for Social Science Research*. London: Bloomsbury.

For further discussion on methodological debates:

Bohnsack, R., Pfaff, N. and Wellwe, W. (2010) *Qualitative Analysis and Documentary Method in International Educational Research*. Harlow: Longman.
Goodson, I. and Sikes, P. (2001) *Life History Research in Educational Settings: Learning from Lives*. Buckingham: Open University Press.
McCulloch, G. (2004) *Documentary Research in Education, History and the Social Sciences*. London: RoutledgeFalmer.
Prior, L. (2003) *Using Documents in Social Research*. London: Sage.
Steedman, C. (1999) *Dust*. Manchester: Manchester University Press.

For more coverage of photographs and visual sources:

Lawn, M. and Grosvenor, I. (eds) (2005) *Materialities of Schooling: Design, Technology, Objects, Routines*. Oxford: Symposium Books.

References

Altheide, D. (2004) Ethnographic content analysis, in Lewis-Beck, M., Bryman, A. and Liao, T. (eds) *The Sage Encyclopedia of Social Science Research Methods*. Thousand Oaks, CA: Sage.

Burton, A. (2001) Thinking beyond the boundaries: empire, feminism and the domains of history. *Social History* 26(1): 60–71.

Fitzgerald, T. (2005) Archives of memory and memories of archive: CMS women's letters and diaries, 1823–1835. *History of Education* 34(6): 657–74.

Fitzgerald, T., Gunter, H. and Eaton, J. (2006) Leadership of learning: middle leadership in schools in England and New Zealand. *A Report to the National College for School Leadership as part of the International Research Associate Programme*. Manchester: Manchester University Press.

Jaworski, A. and Coupland, N. (eds) (1999) *The Discourse Reader*. London: Routledge.

Lincoln, Y.S. and Guba, E.G. (1985) *Naturalistic Inquiry*. Newbury Park, CA: Sage.

McCulloch, G. and Richardson, W. (2000) *Historical Research in Educational Settings*. Buckingham: Open University Press.

Robson, C. (1993) *Real World Research: A Resource for Social Scientists and Practitioner-Researchers*. Oxford: Blackwell.

Scott, J. (1990) *A Matter of Record: Documentary Sources in Social Research*. Cambridge: Polity Press.

CHAPTER 21

Discourse Analysis

Jane Perryman

Chapter objectives

In this chapter, I will focus on three key questions:

- What is discourse analysis?
- Why do discourse analysis?
- How do we do discourse analysis within education leadership and management research?

Introduction

The purpose of this chapter is to discuss the importance of discourse analysis for researchers in educational leadership and management, drawing on my own experiences researching into school inspection and government education policies in England. This chapter will argue the case for the importance, relevance and usefulness of discourse analysis and answer the question: What is the link between discourses and everyday practices in schools and other educational establishments? I will examine in detail the meaning of discourse analysis later, but broadly speaking it is a method of examining and interpreting written or spoken words to uncover otherwise concealed feelings, messages and motivations. Thus, for the educational researcher, discourse analysis, in any educational context, can be a vital tool to enable the researcher to understand an issue at a deeper level.

What is discourse analysis?

Discourse itself is a difficult topic to define. Hyland and Paltridge (2011: 1) write that:

> [Discourse] concerns the ways that language works in our engagements with the world and our interactions with the world and each other, so creating and shaping the social political and cultural formations of our societies.

I first became interested in discourse when I was undertaking a post-structuralist analysis of a school undergoing inspection, as discourse is central to Foucault's work. A discourse and its counter-discourses shape what it is possible to say about a subject. If the subject were 'good schools', the discourse would encompass information from researchers, teachers, parents, pupils, government ministers, inspectors, journalists, etc. From this body of created knowledge come beliefs about what a school should be like, and this defines what we know and think about schools. Discourse shapes power-knowledge. Phrases such as 'experts say ...', 'studies show ...' and 'research has concluded ...' give power to those who hold the knowledge and decide how it should be acted upon. Thus, Foucault claims that:

> The judges of normality are everywhere. We are in the society of the teacher-judge, the doctor-judge, the educator-judge, the social worker-judge; it is on them that the universal reign of the normative is based; and each individual, wherever he may find himself, subjects to it his body, his gestures, his behaviour, his aptitudes, his achievements. (Foucault, 1977b: 304)

Discourse in social structures creates the new truths, the specialist knowledge which gives power to those who hold it:

> Discourses are practices that systematically form the objects of which they speak ... discourses are not about objects, they do not identify objects, they constitute them and in the practice of doing so conceal their own intervention. (Foucault, 1977a: 49)

Ball (1990: 2) explains that this is because 'discourses constrain the possibilities of thought. They order and combine words in particular ways and exclude or displace other conditions'. Gold and Evans (1998: 9) agree, writing of discourse construction in education that 'dominant discourses are often so powerful that the dissenter finds it hard to voice dissent articulately or objectively'.

Jeffrey and Woods (1998), writing specifically about discourses in leadership and management, describe a power struggle between a complex mixture of two discourses which can be defined as professional and managerial. They argue that a professional discourse views schools as different from each other, sees accountability as mutual and auditing as an active ongoing process. It sees evaluation as subjective, and observation as validation. It instructs that targets should be set internally, and external expertise used as an aid to professionalism. In contrast, the managerialist discourse treats schools as mechanisms which can be treated as the same, with hierarchical accountability, passive auditing, objective evaluation, systematic grading, observation as control and the setting of external targets by external expertise. There seems little doubt that if these are competing discourses, then the managerialist approach has triumphed. Schools and other educational institutions in England and elsewhere are subject to an approach that discounts socio-economic factors and judges their effectiveness as if they are all the same (and thus 'failing' if not reaching set measurements of effectiveness). This management-oriented running of education establishments has been made possible by what Lowe (1998: 97) refers to as 'the colonisation of school discourses' through school development plans and performance tables. The increased accountability within education means that systems have to be developed to monitor the success of the new discourse. An example of this from higher education is cited by Morley (2003), who wrote about the accountability discourse in British universities. She found that university leaders saw the new audit culture as a way of strengthening their position. She quotes one university pro-vice chancellor as saying:

> in terms of the leadership of this university, it, of course, gives greater power to my arm. There is no question whatsoever about that. I can get people to listen more carefully to the need, for example, to have some kind of accountability framework ... it's strengthened my arm. (Morley, 2003: 7)

Discourse is relevant to all research in educational leadership and management. In asserting its importance in higher education research, Morley (2003: 72) writes that 'as with any powerful meta-narratives assuming "truths", other "truths" are silenced and excluded from the quality discourse'. Perhaps an example from my own research will help to clarify the importance of discourse and discourse analysis in educational leadership and management research. In a previous paper (Perryman, 2002), I researched a school under the intensive inspection regime of Special Measures. The 1992 Education Act established a framework for school inspections in England and created Ofsted (Office for Standards in Education) to oversee a system of inspections of schools. Inspection was based on an explicit framework and required extensive classroom observation. It was to be undertaken by a team of independent inspectors trained for the task. Following the inspection, the school would be required to produce an action plan. If a school was not seen to be providing an acceptable standard of education, it would become subject to Special Measures and subsequently receive termly visits from Her Majesty's Inspectorate to monitor progress. If the school was judged to have made sufficient improvements, it would be removed from Special Measures following a full inspection. In extreme cases, if Ofsted did not observe improvement, the school would be closed down.

I concluded from my research that teachers and governors live in fear of going into Special Measures and it is seen as something that needs to be survived. This may have the consequence of schools struggling to come out of Special Measures and making changes that can be short-term and cosmetic. I called the experience of being under Special Measures one of 'panoptic performativity' using Foucault (1977b) to argue that, like prisoners in Bentham's (1787) Panopticon, schools and teachers alter their systems and behaviour so that when they are inspected, they can perform in a way likely to 'pass' inspection. Documentation is manipulated, perfect lessons devised, displays created, meeting records augmented and briefings rehearsed. Teachers conspire to unite against an external enemy. The school is presented in its best light, as the inspection system invites a fabricated performance (Ball, 2003) rather than an honest appraisal. Because of the fact that the inspection is of performance and not of reality, schools do not get the intervention and support they really need.

Given the focus on normalisation, I realised the importance of discourse when I started my case study, as it seemed it was the standards and quality discourse of Ofsted, the discourse of derision and the discourse of accountability that were shaping teachers' responses to inspection. The 'discourse of derision' (Ball, 2001: 15) in education justifies criticism of teachers and schools to the extent that it is hard to argue against the prevailing opinion without seeming to be anti-education. The discourse of Ofsted involves standards, quality, efficiency, value for money and performance and 'it can become the means by which power relations within a school and between the school and external agencies can be established and maintained' (Lowe, 1998: 97). A change in discourse to the Ofsted discourse must occur in a 'failing' school for normalisation to take place.

During the early stages of my research, I decided that as well as producing a descriptive case study of a school and its response to inspection, I also wanted to attempt to examine the relationship between the school and the discourse of inspection. I thus needed to analyse the texts produced by the school preparing for and responding to OfSTED, as well as examine my interview findings through the lens of discourse, to see how discourses of inspection were accommodated and resisted/challenged.

Why do discourse analysis?

If we accept that discourse is a framework in which society works, then discourse analysis can be defined as an examination of data in order to gain familiarity with the social processes behind the words. As Phillips and Hardy (2002: 2) argue: 'without discourse there is no social reality, and without understanding discourse we cannot understand our reality, our experiences or ourselves'.

Simply put, discourse analysis is about uncovering the socially constructed context in which words are spoken and written. Since research in the field of education leadership and management is so often about power relations, it is an area that is particularly relevant. Discourse analysis can help us to understand the political dynamics of organisations and the real dynamics of leadership structures. As MacLure (2003: 9) puts it: 'a discourse based educational research would set itself the work of taking that which offers itself as common-sensical, obvious, natural, given or unquestionable and trying to unravel it a bit – to open it up to further questioning'.

There are many different sorts of discourse analysis. Hyland and Paltridge (2011: 1) state that:

> People who study discourse might therefore focus on the analysis of speech and writing to bring out the dynamics and conventions of social situations or take a more theoretical and critical point of view to consider the institutionalised ways of thinking that define social lives.

Sometimes the term critical discourse analysis (CDA) is used interchangeably with discourse analysis. I would argue that discourse analysis is the umbrella term for all aspects of the methodology, of which CDA is one. Critical discourse analysis started in the early 1990s and as Wodak (2011: 40) notes:

> unlike some forms of discourse-based research, CDA does not have a fixed theoretical and methodological position. Instead the CDA research process begins with a research topic that is a social problem; for example, racism, democratic participation, globalisation, workplace literacy and so forth ... this entails a diversity of approaches to CDA research drawing on various linguistic analytic techniques and different social theories.

Locke (2004: 9) describes CDA thus: 'in respect of educational research, it has the potential to reveal the way power is diffused through the prevalence of various discourses throughout an education system, at both the micro-level of the individual classroom and the macro level of large-scale reform'. Hence, in studying the discourses implicit in policy and classrooms, critical discourse analysis, especially when focusing on issues of power, is another avenue worth exploring.

There is also conversation analysis (CA), in which power relations between participants are analysed through studying such issues as interruptions and pauses. There are six key structural features of talk, which Wilkinson and Kitzinger (2011: 25) list as 'turn-taking, action-formation, sequence organisation, repair, word selection and structural organisation'. In conversational analysis, conversations are transcribed and annotated, often several times and by different researchers looking for new meanings and new interpretations. MacLure (2003: 190) notes:

> Like critical discourse analysis, conversation analysis has come in for criticism from commentators on both sides of the discourse debate ... it has long been the target of acerbic critique from sociologists and cultural theorists on

the grounds that its intransigent focus on interaction as the sole locus of social order renders it impotent to address issues of power and dominance.

It is the notion of linguistics that many researchers find off-putting about discourse analysis. There are different approaches to discourse analysis, but because of the centrality of the researcher as interpreter of text there are likely to be different kinds of interpretations and methods of interpreting the same text. In the examples I give below, I hope that my methods are apparent – but I would argue that there is no one correct way to do discourse analysis. Once you have decided in your research that it would be useful to know more about the context within which you are researching, then examine the texts produced as you wish. Hopefully, the following examples will help and there are suggestions for further reading at the end of the chapter.

Documentary discourse analysis: an example of a school case study

As discussed earlier, for a school like Northgate, adopting the discourse of Ofsted was a key strategy in terms of getting out of Special Measures and continuing to 'pass' in inspection terms. The discourse analysis I undertook initially was that of documentation. Under an inspection regime, a school's documentation becomes part of the surveillance. In schools and other educational establishments, this can be seen in constant clarifications of policies and procedures, in departmental handbooks, school and departmental action plans. Ball (1997: 319) notes: 'documents produced in these technologies become increasingly reified, self referential and dislocated from the practices they are "meant" to stand for or account for'. To take an example from higher education, a principal lecturer in a new university told Morley (2003: 57) that they had not been totally truthful in their preparation for Quality Assurance, saying 'I mean I'm not saying that we told lies, but we cemented over certain issues, and those weren't picked up'. Poulson (1998: 429) argues that teachers are free to represent themselves as they wish: 'they chose what and how they would represent themselves, their work, values and practices in written documentation and, to a large extent, also defined the audience for these texts'. However, under the Ofsted regime, and particularly under Special Measures, there is no such freedom – unless a school 'behaves' and 'jumps through the hoops', it will not be released from the regime.

In order to perform a discourse analysis of the school's documentation, I physically collected everything produced by the school over the inspection period (before, during and after). Before getting round to reading, I looked at the documentation, noting the self-presentation, the images used, the size of the documents and such details as the weight/glossiness of the paper. I then examined in detail the language used, looking for repeated phrases and developments. I was particularly interested in how the school documentation mirrored the language of Ofsted. In order to identify the actual words and phrases I regarded as the language of Ofsted, I examined in detail the framework for inspection, compared this with the school's inspection reports and literally highlighted and counted recurring words. I then created a list that I could look out for in the school's documentation, such as 'standards', 'policy', 'quality', 'teaching and learning'. Beyond this mechanistic process, I was also interested in looking for tone and mood.

The following is an example of the conclusions reached following the physical examination of the documentation:

> The self-evaluation documentation produced by Northgate over the inspection period increasingly mirrored the language of Ofsted. Even the appearance of the documentation differed. The first Headteacher's Report, produced in November 2000 is five sides of closely typed paper, stapled together. The ninth report, by now grandly entitled 'Headteacher's Self Evaluation of Progress Under Special Measures' is spiral bound with laminated covers, has a three-colour title page, and is 47 pages long. (Field notes)

The next extract draws conclusions based on what is actually written in the documentation:

> The short comment on key issue 2 (Raise Standards across the Curriculum) in the first report is a practical guide to developments such as the introduction of lesson observations and the standardisation of schemes of work. The ten pages allocated to this issue in the ninth report detail self-review, performance review, teaching and learning policy, monitoring of teaching, training and improved planning and is clearly a direct response to the Ofsted report following the previous inspection. Successive Headteacher's Reports demonstrate the increased adoption of the discourses of the inspection, in part through a direct emulation of the language of the Ofsted reports. For example, the first Headteacher's Report (November 2000) comments briefly on 'the introduction of a school based schedule of lesson observations'. In March 2001, Ofsted remark that 'there is no clear consensus as to the aims of teaching and learning – there is a need for a teaching and learning policy which should guide each department's teaching'. Similarly in one inspection HMI note 'a system is needed which can judge conclusively the proportion of good and satisfactory teaching'. The Headteacher's Evaluation then notes 'the quality of teaching will be monitored by a structured programme of lesson observations', and the following inspection report responds 'the school has responded positively to criticism in the previous monitoring visit report by implementing an appropriate system for monitoring the quality of teaching'.

Thus, a discourse analysis of the documentation was useful for analysing how the school responded to Ofsted, and at a deeper level had absorbed the discourse of Ofsted itself.

Discourse analysis and questionnaire/interview responses

In order to further discover how much of the Ofsted discourse of standards, targets and failure had been absorbed and imbibed by staff and pupils, I analysed the responses of students to a questionnaire for the appearance of such language. On being put into Special Measures, one student responded, 'We were given Special Measures because our school was the worst school in [the LEA]'. Commenting on the reasons for the constant inspections, some students responded, 'it had failed to meet targets' and 'its standards were too low'. Asked whether they thought the school should be taken out of Special Measures, one response was, 'yes because at first it was failing to reach standards, but now it has settled' and another agreed 'the school has progressed'. The use of language about progression, targets, standards, failing, etc. are perhaps a result of being in such a high-profile 'failing school' where the language had become normalised even for pupils.

It must be noted here that discourse analysis can only be undertaken in what Phillips and Hardy (2002: 70) call 'naturally occurring texts'. The students in the above example were being asked what they thought of their school, if it had deserved to fail, etc. Their use of the Ofsted discourse occurred naturally – i.e. the questionnaire did not in any way use such language. Initially at Northgate, the teachers also echoed the sense that what was happening in the school was not 'normal' and that the school also lacked the expected systems of a 'good' school. Asked in interviews to explain why the school had been put into Special Measures, some teachers responded: 'the school had become out of control and in order to gain a sense of normality, severe action was required'; 'someone finally realised how much of a mess we were in'; 'at the time there were inadequate systems in place and ineffective management; the school lacked leadership, a common ethos, structures, procedures etc. The expectations did not match reality. Basically it was unsafe'.

It is when analysing such responses that discourse analysis becomes particularly appropriate. In the comments above, these respondents are echoing the discourse of failure that they have inculcated through the process of Special Measures. Similarly, even given that the general consensus at Northgate was that inspections were 'demoralising and exhausting', as the school 'improved', teachers were able to welcome some of the effects of being in Special Measures, often in the framework of an 'improvement' discourse. Several welcomed the extra support given to the school; 'outside support and the focus provided by inspections', 'extra funding is provided to the school to bring in projects that are exciting through the use of outside providers'. Others commented on the 'frequent push for improvement and monitoring this improvement. Evidence that we are improving'. A further group mentioned the 'enforced systems set up and monitored' echoed in the statement 'they have forced us to build the framework for a successful school' and 'the absolute necessity to address weaknesses that could otherwise be subtly ignored'. Many acknowledged the development of good practice under the regime, praising the 'Whole school approach to important key skills i.e. literacy and numeracy. Development of good practice and support within faculties'.

There is a sense that, towards the end of the process, the inspection regime was cautiously welcomed, again using the improvement discourse of 'push for improvement', 'systems', 'monitoring' and 'good practice'. At the same time, as teachers became practised in the use of the improvement discourse, so they were able to demonstrate improvement to the inspectors. Thus, the discourse change could be said to have 'worked' for them. There seems little doubt that, according to the criteria laid down and then judged by Ofsted, in the short term, Northgate had sustained its improvement following its release from Special Measures. The middle and senior managers at the school generally concurred that the school was a better place to work, behaviour had improved, teaching was easier and leadership was dynamic. There is evidence to suggest that the inculcation of the Ofsted discourse during Special Measures had led to a management and staff skilled in making successful improvements which would meet with inspectors' approval, particularly in terms of teaching lessons in the accepted Ofsted style. If school improvement is to be judged by the criteria laid down by Ofsted, then the process of inspection and Special Measures had secured Northgate's improvement. By all the relevant bench-marking criteria, examination results, pupil recruitment and community esteem, the school had improved.

However, I questioned Northgate's ability to improve according to its own specific development needs. In the medium term, the sheer effort made to 'pass' Ofsted and the resultant sense of exhaustion and complacency leads to the conclusion that improvement was hard to sustain. More crucially, as so much of Northgate's efforts were put into 'performing the good school', and producing the correct discourse, suppressing many of its genuine problems and development needs, 'sustained improvement' was difficult. Discourse analysis was crucial to this finding, as it enabled me as a researcher to look beyond what was being said and written.

An example of analysing policy discourses

Within a different research project, looking at how schools in England respond to policy (Ball et al., 2012), I conducted a discourse analysis of policy, an area highly relevant to leadership and management research. The study had two main objectives, one theoretical, that is to develop a theory of policy enactment, and one empirical, that is a critical exploration of the differences in the enactment of policy in 'similar' contexts. The research focused on four main issues: (1) the localised nature of policy actions, that is the 'secondary adjustments' and accommodations and conflicts which inflect and mediate policy; (2) the ways in which many different (and sometimes contradictory) policies are simultaneously in circulation and interact with, influence and inhibit one another; (3) the interpretational work of policy actors; and (4) the role of resource differences in limiting, distorting or facilitating responses to policy. We collected four kinds of data: (a) contextual information from each school; (b) policy texts – national, local and school-centred; (c) observations of meetings, training, etc.; and (d) semi-structured interviews. The research generated a data set of 93 digitally recorded and transcribed interviews, together with a wide range of documentary and observational data.

One of my tasks was to perform a discourse analysis of government publications on a policy called 'Personalised Learning' or tailoring teaching and learning to individual needs. I searched the DCSF (Department for Children, Schools and Families, since renamed Department for Education) website for personalised learning and there were over 100 results. The most significant were links to speeches made by then education secretaries David Miliband and Ruth Kelly, an analysis of which helped me to outline the discourse and rhetoric behind personalised learning. I looked for repeated phrases and asked questions of the language, which was not neutral but used to persuade, particularly at the outset of the policy. It may be helpful to give an example of the sort of extracts I was looking for, and the questions and comments they led to.

A speech by David Miliband in 2004 is worth looking at in detail. (The emphases in bold are mine.)

> Personalised learning enables us to pursue the **standards agenda** from the **perspective of the child**. The child with an aptitude for maths who has the potential to get an A, but whose talent is **squandered** through **lack of attention** and ends up with a pass that is only just good enough ... The child who lacks confidence and self-belief but who is quiet and well-behaved so is just left alone. **Personalised learning is about making education more than a numbers game**. More than the annual scramble over the pass or fail line. Through personalised learning, we can **reach out to the children** behind the statistics. We have lived for many months with this personalisation as a distant dream – offering the promise of a **warm, fuzzy, comfortable** future. This is the point in time when our ideas about personalised learning are put to the test.

This is stirring rhetoric, and designed to persuade. Miliband wants to distance this policy from the standards agenda. There is a sense that children (note the use of 'children' and 'child', rather than the more depersonalised 'pupils' and 'students') are being left behind. There is an implied sense of blame on the teachers who ignore their well-behaved but underachieving students. There is a call to 'reach out' to those left behind and make the 'warm, fuzzy, comfortable future' dream a reality. Analysing speeches is always rewarding, as, unlike the interviews I discussed above, they are not comments made spontaneously. Speeches have been drafted, designed, honed to convince and persuade. Doing a discourse analysis on speeches over time can be very interesting, as it can reveal the meanings behind the messages.

For example, in a speech from October 2005, Ruth Kelly pledged to fund personalised learning:

> Personalised learning is a key part of the government's central aim to promote excellence and equality in education, giving pupils strength in the basics in literacy and numeracy, stretching their aspirations, and focusing on their individual strengths, weaknesses and interests.

It was interesting to note that personalised learning is now very much centralised as a key policy with links to literacy and numeracy, and key government education policies, and firmly back in the standards agenda. Nothing fuzzy here!

A later speech from the Innovation Unit's Next Practice Project stated:

> Although the Gilbert Review has offered schools greater clarity about the ambitions of personalised learning, and the practical steps needed to deliver it, there is still some confusion among the workforce about what this actually looks like. Some think they have heard it all before and are doing it already. Others are worried that it means individualised teaching for everyone, all the time. The 2020 review ... reminds us that 'Personalisation is a matter of moral purpose and social justice'. So personalised learning isn't a something that will be nice to have. Rather it is an essential component of modern education – what every parent wants and what every child deserves.

This speech seems very defensive, alluding to resistance from teachers who were presumably wondering what was new in the policy. I was also particularly interested in the use of the term 'moral purpose and social justice'. This is presumably attempting to create a discourse whereby one cannot be against the policy, as that would be to be against morality and justice. As part of my research into this policy area, I also analysed documentation given to schools to explain and support the policy, and guidance on the Internet. There really isn't the space to go into great detail here, but as one further example, I examined the personalisation FAQ (frequently asked questions) section on the DCSF website (http://nationalstrategies.standards.dcsf.gov.uk/node/48435). FAQs are a rich source of analysis as they are pre-posed questions, presumably anticipating criticism and responding in advance. One question, pertinent to my comments above about links with the standards agenda, is 'Does the move to personalisation imply a shift away from the focus on standards?' The response is as follows:

> Quite the reverse. The central purpose of personalised learning is to reconcile excellence and equity, with high expectations for all achieved by tailoring provision to pupils' needs and aspirations ... There will be renewed impetus to meet the national targets, with increasingly focused attention to different pupil groups who are underachieving at every level of attainment.

The emphasis on excellence, attainment and targets rather indicates, that the policy is not so warm and fuzzy any more.

As I hope the above illustrates, discourse analysis was used to look at inconsistencies, contradictions and infirmities in a current government policy and proved useful to examine the context within which policy was enacted. To those interested in researching educational leadership and management, discourse analysis of policy can be a highly rewarding source of information.

Conclusion

At the start of this chapter, I asked the question 'What is the link between discourses and everyday practices in schools and other educational establishments?'. The key importance is that discourses endow those who have specialist knowledge with power. In terms of inspection, the example I gave first in this chapter, this knowledge is provided by the school effectiveness discourse, and inspectors have the power to enforce adherence to its principles. Unsurprisingly, when applied to inspection, discourses are essential components of power.

More generally, discourses and their influences are crucial throughout all aspects of education. An example from education is the now almost universal acceptance in English schools of the 'three-part lesson'. A relatively new label, this describes the good practice of a lesson with a beginning, middle and end. This is common sense in many ways and, I am sure, was widely practised before it was enshrined as 'good practice', but with alarming rapidity it has become the hallmark of a good lesson, and seemingly the only way to teach. For teachers under 40, there is almost no collective memory that there used to be acceptable alternatives for lesson planning. Similarly, teachers trained in England since the 1990s simply cannot imagine teaching without the existence of a National Curriculum, nor how contentious this was when it was introduced.

I would argue then that it is appropriate that research into educational leadership and management takes discourse into account, and that researchers consider incorporating discourse analysis as part of their methodology.

Key points

- Discourse analysis is useful in putting education leadership and management research findings into a wider context.
- Discourse analysis is important in any research which would benefit from an analysis of power relations.
- Discourse analysis can help us to understand the political dynamics of organisations and the real dynamics of leadership structures.
- Discourse analysis can be done across a plethora of sources, written and verbal, in as much detail as is required. You do not need to be a linguistic analyst to identify overarching and underlying societal themes.

Questions and reflections

1 How might you make use of discourse analysis in a planned research project?
2 Could discourse analysis be the main component of your methodology or a contextual support?
3 Are there other ways to get 'under the skin' of power relations without using discourse analysis?

Recommended further reading

Hyland, K. and Paltridge, B. (2011) *The Continuum Companion to Discourse Analysis.* London: Continuum.

This book guides the researcher through key terms, methods and current research topics and directions in the field of discourse analysis.

Phillips, N. and Hardy, C. (2002) *Discourse Analysis: Investigating Processes of Social Construction.* London: Sage.

This book reflects on the practice of analysing discourse and its potential for revealing processes of social construction.

References

Ball, S.J. (1990) Introducing Monsieur Foucault, in Ball, S.J. (ed.) *Foucault and Education: Disciplines and Knowledge.* London: Routledge.
Ball, S.J. (1997) Good school/bad school: paradox and fabrication. *British Journal of the Sociology of Education* 18(3): 317–36.
Ball, S.J. (2001) Better read: theorising the teacher! in Dillon, J. and Maguire, M. (eds) *Becoming a Teacher: Issues in Secondary Teaching.* Buckingham: Open University Press. pp. 10–22.
Ball, S.J. (2003) The teacher's soul and the terrors of performativity. *Journal of Education Policy* 18(2): 215–88.
Ball, S., Maguire, M. and Braun, A. with Hoskins, K. and Perryman, J. (2012) *How Schools Do Policy: Policy Enactments in Secondary Schools.* London: Routledge.
Bentham, J. (1787) *Panopticon: Or the Inspection-house.* Dublin: Thomas Byrne.
Foucault, M. (1977a) *The Archaeology of Knowledge.* London: Tavistock.
Foucault, M. (1977b) *Discipline and Punish: The Birth of the Prison.* Harmondsworth: Penguin.
Gold, A. and Evans, J. (1998) *Reflecting on School Management.* London: Falmer.
Hyland, K. and Paltridge, B. (2011) *The Continuum Companion to Discourse Analysis,* London: Continuum.
Jeffrey, B. and Woods, P. (1998) *Testing Teachers: The Effect of School Inspection on Primary Teachers.* London: Falmer Press.
Locke, T. (2004) *Critical Discourse Analysis.* London: Continuum.

Lowe, G. (1998) Inspection and change in the classroom: rhetoric or reality, in Earley, P. (ed.) *School Improvement after Inspection? School and LEA Responses*. London: Paul Chapman. pp. 97–109.

MacLure, M. (2003) *Discourse in Educational and Social Research*. Buckingham: Open University Press.

Morley, L. (2003) *Quality and Power in Higher Education*. Maidenhead: Open University Press.

Perryman, J. (2002) Surviving special measures: a case study of a 'Fresh Start' school. *Improving Schools* 5(3): 46–59.

Phillips, N. and Hardy, C. (2002) *Discourse Analysis: Investigating Processes of Social Construction*. London: Sage.

Poulson, L. (1998) Accountability, teacher professionalism and education reform in England. *Teacher Development* 2(3): 419–32.

Wilkinson, S. and Kitzinger, C. (2011) Conversation analysis, in Hyland, K. and Paltridge, B. (eds) *The Continuum Companion to Discourse Analysis*. London: Continuum. pp. 22–37.

Wodak, R. (2011) Critical discourse analysis, in Hyland, K. and Paltridge, B. (eds) *The Continuum Companion to Discourse Analysis*. London: Continuum. pp. 38–53.

CHAPTER 22

Reflection as Research: Using Diaries and Blogs

Marlene Morrison

Chapter objectives

The purposes of this chapter are:

- To introduce the research diary/log/journal as a distinctive research genre and 'thinking tool'.
- To focus upon diarists as researchers and research participants.
- To consider the emergence of new forms of 'diary' data, and their implications.
- To assess strengths and weaknesses of diary use, drawing upon examples.

Introduction

Diaries are among a wide range of data sources of potential interest to researchers of education leadership and management. A distinctive genre, its purposes straddle quantitative and qualitative approaches that, historically, prioritise patterns of time use (Gershuny et al., 1986; Szalai, 1972); health and sexual behaviours (Coxon et al., 1992); workplace and learning activities (Marsh and Gershuny, 1991; Zimmerman and Wieder, 1977); and life history (see also Chapter 15). Personal chronicling is strongly implicated in its autobiographical aspects. More recently, the burgeoning of electronically generated social networks in which blogging and tweeting are new forms of communication, has enhanced the phenomenon of journal/log keeping (Suzuki, 2004) as a record of activities and events and as a:

- personal diary
- daily 'pulpit'
- political soapbox
- breaking news outlet
- build-up of 'private' thoughts, and/or
- memo to the wider 'world'.

(see www.blogger.com/tour_start.g – what's a blog?)

This chapter considers diaries in more traditional formats as well as newer forms of electronic communication. Consideration is of their use as reflective tools for researchers and for research participants although, in increasingly virtual environments, the distinctions between the two forms of reflection may be less clear-cut than previously. Advantages and challenges are discussed, not least their practical implications. Of particular interest is the extent to which 'new' diary forms allow researchers and research participants not only to 'walk through' self-narrated, retrospective 'life' accounts by leaders and managers, for example, but also 'to walk into' those lives, using weblogs or smaller online posts like tweets, as interactive synchronous and asynchronous communications, described elsewhere in terms of 'constructive participation' (Berkowitz, 1997: 1).

Diary/journal keepers might be researchers or research participants or both. Most recently, the potential for a wider range of visitors/readers/'outsiders' to 'lurk' within interactive cyberspace has increased. In other than the most closed environments, this diminishes even further the sense in which it might be possible, or indeed desirable, to view diaries as intimate or personal (Morrison and Galloway, 1996). In whichever form, diaries have always been 'motivated by a variety of reasons' that have involved 'various attempts at self-presentation' for unspecified or specified 'others' (Scott, 1990:177). For the purposes of this chapter, diary keeping is seen as *essentially* social and reflective, most attention given to diary use as research data that are solicited rather than unsolicited accounts.

Initial consideration is given to the importance of researchers' diaries, especially those of qualitative researchers.

Researchers' diaries

In early methods textbooks, references to diaries related mainly to their importance for researchers (Burgess, 1984; Griffiths, 1985) where distinctions were made between *logs, diaries* and *journals* (for example, Holly, 1984, 1989). Holly differentiated between a log, which is a (truncated) record of information that relates to specific situations, rather like an aide-memoire, and a diary, which is seen to contain more 'personal' information, and includes interpretation as well as description (Holly, 1984: 5). According to Holly, journals are a third form of research record, carefully structured to combine both objective notes and free-flowing accounts. As Burgess (1984) has suggested, such distinctions have been more useful analytically than in practice, since the umbrella term – diaries – can frequently comprise substantive, methodological and analytic research elements.

A diary serves a range of elementary yet critical purposes for the researcher. Integral to research audit and reflection, it is a tool for charting progress and critical research moments; these can be plotted against the planning checklist agreed among the research team, or with the research supervisor. It might include contact dates with the supervisor or research team, and record research agreements and progress. Not all researchers have the time, resources or epistemological 'will' to record in the detail favoured by anthropologists like Judith Okely in her 1994 seminal study of gypsies in England (discussed in Bryman and Burgess, 1994), for example. However, such accounts remind readers of decisions that need to be made in relation to the structuring of a researcher's diary and the contribution of 'jottings' to data collection, analysis and/or the final report/dissertation/thesis.

From my earliest experiences as a researcher, I have kept a diary for every project in which I have been involved. While format and style vary, the basic structure has remained. Column 1 is a daily record of all events, frequently substantive, sometimes methodological, and usually completed at the end of the day; column 2 is used for analytic memos, records, emerging themes and ideas, and poses questions; column 3 is what I call the R&I column (for retrospection and introspection). This provides the opportunity to note and refine ideas and thoughts after time has elapsed from the original diary entry. The columns that used to be found in paper notebooks would subsequently become document files on computers. More recently, software packages for qualitative data analysis provide further opportunities for the researcher/diarist. For example, Bazeley and Richards (2000: 96–111) describe the various approaches used in qualitative computing, in their case referring to NVivo (see also Chapter 25). Here, the processes of creating and recording 'jottings' as 'node memos' are described; advocacy is for 'memos' to log the development of 'thoughts' at 'nodes' or categories for analysis. Such entries are never 'mere doodling' (p. 96); neither are they complete or neutral records that are unaffected by other writing and reading (Atkinson, 1992). Pragmatically, Miles and Huberman (1994) have argued strongly against allowing such data to accumulate without engaging in early analysis. Their advice remains pertinent today, since iterative analysis continues to allow 'the possibility of collecting new data to fill in the gaps, or to test new hypotheses' (p. 50) that emerge in fieldwork.

Diaries are important tools for action researchers (see also Chapter 12), and a basis for self-reflection to provoke changes in the practices of self and others. For example, Brown and Dowling (1998: 65–6) discuss how a single practitioner researcher might use either structured or unstructured diaries to reflect and then act. Structured diaries, for example, can be used to investigate how headteachers allocate time to different aspects of their work, drawing on the number and types of activities in order to record the times such activities took place (event sampling) or at specified moments (interval sampling). A less structured, more exploratory approach would be for the practitioner researcher to keep 'unstructured, free flowing notes on their activities' (p. 66). For Brown and Dowling, this requires appreciation of the extent to which research subjects 'might present idealized versions of what they do' (p. 66), or about who they purport to be.

For ethnographers (see also Chapter 14), diaries are central to the research account itself. For example, a project during 1993–1994 investigated the ways in which adults, children and young people in English primary and secondary schools experienced food and eating. Conducted by Burgess and Morrison, the study formed part of a larger ESRC programme entitled *The Nation's Diet: The Social Science of Food Choice* (Burgess and Morrison, 1998). Morrison spent a term in each of four schools, observing the dynamics of food and eating in a range of formal and informal settings for teaching and learning: classrooms, dining halls, playgrounds and school corridors, journeys to and from school, neighbouring ice-cream vans and chip shops. Events were recorded daily in diary form; extracts were published in the final report, and subsequently. In the following example, diary data were used as illustrative vignettes of lunchtime eating experiences in a secondary school:

Thursday

Those in receipt of FSM [free school meals] are not checked to see what they purchase, so chips in combination with three or four cakes is not uncommon. There is a shortage of knives and forks, and no water. Cheap coloured drinks are very popular. Latest habit appears to be to ignore the straw supplied with drinks, turn the carton upside down, suck plastic carton, tear into with teeth, and suck contents from the resultant tear. Interesting noises! Some pupils leave the dining hall with half eaten purchases. Two observed with bags of chips in coat pockets. (Morrison, 1995: 246)

In such ways, ethnographic accounts using the researcher's diary illustrated ways in which schools remain important arenas for assessing the ambiguities and contradictions of food consumption which are still replicated more widely in adult populations.

In a recent research example, focused upon senior leadership team meetings as communication vehicles for productive (or unproductive) decision making in an English secondary school, Coleman and Glover (2010: 113–16) draw readers' attention to reflective notes taken by a headteacher alongside more formal meeting records. In the former, the head records his reflections about unresolved tensions and role ambiguities evidenced in the conduct of meetings, when he notes:

We really are faced with a problem. Edward [joint deputy head] is becoming more difficult and obstinate … and is constantly undermining any attempt to get vitality into the place … and his antagonism to Peter [assistant head] is obvious ... Peter is obviously feeling he hasn't got a chance in school ... Anne [joint deputy head] has a loyalty to Edward and yet ...

I really believe we need a new vision for the school, and that is greater than one training day, and so my inclination is to go with Peter ... and have a day looking at our contributions and ways of working as a team. (p. 115)

More recently, researcher blogs have emerged as important aspects of online research. Discussed by Wakeford and Cohen (2008), newer forms of reflexive writing are akin to 'field-notes-in-public'. For example, some doctoral students of education leadership have used blogs not only to post the development of their research thinking and empirical research over time but also to invite comments from others. Davis (http://leadershipliteracies.wordpress.com/blogs/) records the development of her PhD research, sharing with other Internet users her research objectives to identify 'leadership literacies' for the knowledge sector and 'test them out against the Higher Education sector in Australia'. As Lee et al. (2008: 14) suggest, it may be the case that blogs are more appropriate for 'relatively unsensitive research topics', where they 'serve as a focus for engagement between researcher and research participants [see below] as well as the means ... by which widely dispersed research teams can collaborate', and/or single researchers seek engagement (frequently international) with others showing similar interests.

Having introduced aspects of the usefulness of diaries for researchers, the chapter now turns to diary keeping by research informants/participants.

Research informants' diaries

Like all personal accounts, diaries share the strengths and weaknesses of information that is solicited from research informants. In education leadership research, where there has been a tendency to privilege the 'oral' – what people say they think and do – over the literary, diaries provide an interesting counterpoint, since diarists are invited to write what they do and/or think. Whether the relative neglect of diary use is because we tend to assume that 'the spoken account is more "authentic" or "spontaneous" than the written account' (Hammersley and Atkinson, 1995: 165), diaries have specific uses in exposing the minutiae of vicarious experience, in ways which other major forms of solicited written information, such as questionnaires, do not. Figure 22.1 provides an example.

A number of fundamental issues about diary keeping warrant careful consideration. Diaries:

- rest on the view that participants are in especially advantageous positions to record aspects of their lives and work
- allow researchers to access evidence that may not be otherwise available, whether on *logistical* (researchers cannot be everywhere) or *ethical*

(researchers should not be everywhere) or *pragmatic* (researchers need to be elsewhere) grounds. The extent to which diary data constitutes 'substitute observation' (Morrison and Galloway, 1996) is considered below

- provide, in combination with other tools, a wider and/or deeper picture of what educational experience means to groups, as well as individuals
- produce large amounts of data. Researchers need, therefore, to convince themselves *and* potential diarists that diaries are worthwhile
- require agreement with diarists about which aspects will be open to public scrutiny
- tend towards a 'degradation in accuracy over time' (Suzuki, 2004), not least because of diarist fatigue, and drop-out
- elicit 'hidden' costs in obtaining agreements, in briefing diarists and in making progress calls/visits (repeatedly).

Q. How might primary school managers improve the effectiveness of temporary (supply) teacher use in school?

Time	Main activities	Other activities
13.00	Children in. Did register. Didn't tally. Incorrect from morning! Took ages to sort out; some children's names difficult to pronounce. Register not very clear. Need to be accurate for swimming.	A mum came with me – an older lady – very nice but not very effective. Very noisy in changing areas. I was dotting from one to the other.
13.20	Eventually set off. Took a while to get there as kept starting and stopping. Worn out when I arrived!	
14.00	Eventually we got there down to the pool instructor. He took the more able group – leaving me alone with 20 children in a small pool. We worked hard but they didn't tire. Changing took ages. Walked back after a great lecture from me.	I have never felt so worn out after swimming. Only I had to get out of the water for a short while.
	Got back 14.40. Too late for play.	Miracles never cease.
15.00	I kept them out for 10 min. play while I had a drink. An ESN teacher took a group for reading. I let rest finish off any work then get an activity while I heard readers. Behaviour improving.	Didn't think they'd settle to a story and they hadn't read all week.
15.30	Dismiss children. Write note for teacher.	Dep. wished I was going back as I'd controlled class.

What was the most demanding task or situation you had to deal with today?

Any additional comment on today's activities?

Swimming – very dangerous situation – particularly at the baths. 13:20. Ridiculous.

Figure 22.1 A diary extract: a supply teacher's afternoon

(Morrison and Galloway, 1996: 50; reproduced with permission of Palgrave Macmillan)

In summary, there are at least six practical pointers for maximising successful outcomes. For potential diarists, these include:

1 clarity in instructions for use
2 relative ease in completion
3 assurances about potential benefit

For the researcher, they include all of the above, as well as:

4 early decisions about diary communications as online, off-line or both
5 clarity in the analytical approach to be taken which will, in turn, be reflected in diary formats
6 clarity about how and why points 1–5 link to the methodological orientation of the research.

Diary designs

Diaries can be analysed qualitatively and quantitatively to illuminate a range of educational issues. In interpretive and action research, where the focus is often upon daily accounts, reflections or 'confessionals', the notion of 'designing' diaries might seem contradictory. Yet, design frameworks are essential, not least to inform child and adult participants who may have different perceptions about their purpose(s). So, some guidance narrows the focus to specific, limited uses. For example, Bell (1999) asserts that diaries:

> are not records of engagements or personal journals of thoughts and activities [why not?], but rather logs of professional activities ... Do you really want to know that someone had a cup of tea, paid the milkman, or had a bath [depends on the research problem, and, in any case, such data is part of an inevitable research compromise, or alternatively useful contextual information] or are you only interested in professionally related activities [perhaps]? (pp. 148–9, insertions are mine)

If the core intention is to examine the ways in which school departmental and faculty heads manage time for professional activities (Earley and Fletcher-Campbell, 1989), then the use of a timed weekly log of professional activities seems apt. But if research purposes are to investigate the ways in which managers, teachers and/or students make connections between the public and private spheres of their lives, then 'personal' activities take on a specific significance, and warrant inclusion. For example, part of the rationale for using diaries in a project entitled *Supply Teaching: An Investigation of Policy, Processes and People,* was 'to make connections between private and public aspects of supply teachers' lives which showed infinite variation' (Morrison and Galloway, 1996: 35).

Temporality

Diaries have the potential for non-completion which is partially overcome by meticulous attention to cosmetic appearance and clear instructions. In many large-scale time budget surveys, the period covered is usually either one or seven consecutive days; but there can be two to four non-consecutive day and part-day diaries. 'Time slots' can be open or fixed and activity categories pre-coded or open. Earlier, Gershuny et al (1986) described the 'Szalai' system (with 190 activity codes) as a de facto standard for time budget surveys (Szalai, 1972). A large-scale one-day survey of the distribution of activities in a popula-tion might be very useful descriptively, but less useful interpretively than diary surveys over a longer period. Large-scale designs are clearly not an option for the single-handed researcher. But some challenges are similar. Objections to lengthy diary periods are that agreements to participate become more difficult to secure, and the quality and rate of response declines. The propensity to respond may vary at different times of the day/night, and the gap between the event and its record and interpretation by the diarist may widen.

'Substitute' observation

Researching supply teaching, diary accounts were used by Galloway and Morrison to investigate supply work in schools, a phenomenon that is both ordinary (occurring frequently, if irregularly) and extraordinary, in that it sometimes brings into schools teachers who are strangers to the pupils for whom they are fleetingly responsible (Galloway, 1993). Explaining the mechanics of diary use, they comment:

> Seventeen supply teachers completed diaries, enabling experience to be tracked in detail. The selection did not purport to be a representative sam-ple; rather they exemplified a range of different situations pertaining to individuals doing supply work *that went beyond what researchers could observe given the practical constraints affecting the field work* … However, unlike interviewing (where self-report sometimes occurs over a lengthy time span), daily accounts would add an immediate and alternative dimension to verbal accounts of experience. (Morrison and Galloway, 1996: 37, my emphasis)

Not only did Morrison and Galloway (1996) give detailed attention to the extent to which 'writing about experience adds an element of artificiality and superficiality to already complex features of data recording in "natural set-tings"' (p. 41), they also caution against simplistic assumptions about diary data as *necessarily* straightforward substitutes for observation. On occasion, diary accounts were at variance with observations recorded by researchers. In other circumstances, Oppenheim (1966) noted the tendency either for diarists to record what they think researchers would wish to read, or amend 'usual' behaviour during the recording period. In this sense, diaries share the strengths and weaknesses of all forms of self-report.

Children's diaries

In Chapter 16, Lumby provides a very important rationale for including the voices of children and young people in research about education leadership and management. Using diaries to undertake research with children presents opportunities and challenges. Studying food and eating in schools, for example, Burgess and Morrison (1995) designed diaries to be used by primary school children. It was important to talk with children about the research topic and to design a booklet that was both appropriate and attractive. Diary keeping was restricted to one week, including a weekend, and a cover letter inside the diary, signed by the researcher, was addressed personally to each child. As Bell (1999: 150) notes: 'diarists must be at a certain educational level to understand the instructions, let alone complete the diary'. In the example referred to above, the method posed questions about the capacity of a mixed-ability group to articulate a written record at similar levels of detail. Qualitatively, 60 diaries produced rich data about children's lives, but they also presented challenges. Some accounts from children were free-flowing accounts; others treated each of the questions raised in the introductory letter from the researcher as topics to be answered, often in brief responsive sentences. This also posed issues about comparing data across diaries, an important issue if the research intentions are to track the use of time, in this case for eating, or the extent to which children exercised 'choice' in the selection of foods they record as having eaten.

Such diaries might also be considered to pose ethical concerns in terms of the level of intrusion into the lives of diarists and their families. Albeit as an early example, the approach taken does suggest the ongoing potential for diaries to allow children and young people to give voice to their various understandings of lives within and beyond formal education 'boundaries', not least in terms of how they experience the exercise of leadership and/or control. More recently, Hessler et al (2003) discuss a research project in which children and young people were invited to submit diaries online, allowing, it is argued, better rapport with and disclosure from young people, in this case a study of adolescent risk-taking behaviour.

Leading and managing

For researchers of education leadership and management, diaries have often been used to explore time use for professional activities on a daily or weekly basis; in more personal, exploratory accounts, interest extends to how leaders decide upon what is more (or less) important to attend to. Bell (1999: 151–3) recorded a range of approaches that have been applied in the area of management, for example the critical incident approach (Oxtoby, 1979) or 'problem portfolios' (Marples, 1967) that recorded 'information about how each [management] problem arose [and] methods used to solve it'.

More recently, 'shared' or group diaries have been suggested for research into leadership as senior management team activity. Earlier, Burgess (1994) suggested that 'diary groups' offered the potential to share day-to-day practice. Similarly, Galloway et al (1995) used a diary/log to investigate the use of interactive video in educational and training institutions. Diary booklets attached to workstations invited users to record date, time and place used, start and finish times, software used and whether the equipment was used by a group, on a course or individually. Given space for qualitative comment, contributors made entries, some minimal, others more extended reflections. The potential for 'group' diaries has risen dramatically with 'new' forms of diaries, logs and journal writing in online research, not least in relation to leadership communities of practice.

Online research

Computer mediated communication gives rise to new forms of diary/log/ journal keeping and for a range of research purposes. Most commonly known as weblogs or blogs, two main kinds of blog/Internet diary use predominate: the diary blog; and the 'group' blog, access to which is commonly filtered to specific participants in order to track and discuss various forms of activity, frequently related to learning, whether of developing leaders or other education actors. In relation to the first, similarities are to the autobiographical account, often written by a single author in the first person, and are accessible as diaries-in-process. Scheidt (2007) describes such accounts as a kind of blog 'sub-genre', in which a specific (broadly or narrowly framed) audience gains access to the daily, reflective thoughts and activities of the individual blogger/ diarist. Researchers' access to and interest in such accounts shows partial resemblance to documentary research; here, the researcher's interest is in diary blogs as archival sources. In the second, the focus, if researcher/tutor or leader-initiated, is upon specific 'topics', whether these are to investigate learner motivation, the quality and/or pace of leadership development and experience, and so on. For virtual ethnographers, the interest may lie primarily in the kinds of participation and cultural communications that develop, often centred upon online communities of practice, and their forms of interaction (Hine, 2008). For action researchers, online diaries may provide learning tools or leadership prompts to generate participants' learning or leadership development outcomes, for example.

Suzuki (2004) used online diaries as a way of exploring students' learning motivation in English as a Foreign Language (EFL) teaching and learning; McAlpine et al. (2004) developed a WebCT site in order to document the first-year experiences of undergraduate physics students. Applying action research frameworks, participants' discussions were used to frame subsequent intervention programmes that would allow leaders to improve course design and enhance student motivation. In a succession of US studies, Werner et al. (2007) have used daily blogs with education principals/administrators to track their coping strategies, not least during periods of accelerating State regulations relating to competences and standards for education leaders. In a joint leadership development programme between the Universities of Calgary, Canada and Waikato, New Zealand, Robertson and Webber (1999) described how electronically mediated discussion groups between potential and actual education leaders and leadership development providers in both countries called *Change Agency* (www.acs.ucalgary.ca/~~cl/CAN/frameset.htm) provided a cross-cultural dialogic basis for a 'boundary-breaking leadership development model' that would subsequently combine online leadership learning with study exchanges.

Such developments are, in one sense, unsurprising. As Lee et al. (2008: 2–5) comment, researchers have usually responded 'readily to shifts in ... the scope of technologies available to them' (p. 3). Yet, enlarged scope brings new challenges as well as opportunities, not least when the distinctions between being a professional/'real' researcher and a 'lay' or 'citizen' researcher, who can access a myriad of Internet sources at the click of a button, become less tenable. Moreover, while judgements about the 'quality and accuracy [of data/information] become much more difficult' (p. 5) when there is a plethora from which to select, online research methods themselves have become more 'variegated' and complex (p. 5).

Applied to diaries, Suzuki (2004) points to differences and similarities between diaries used as online research tools and those formerly constituted in paper, print and/or audio-recorded forms. The most obvious distinction is in the mode of data entry where diarists or bloggers now enter data via the computer keyboard, typing online onto Web pages and/or by emailing entries. Yet, similarities pertain. For example, in each form there remains the potential for writing style to be informal and reflective and for writing accounts to develop by date, with the newest first. However, it is in relation to issues of accessibility, interactivity and publication that the main distinctions lie. Where there is unlimited online access, the time delay between the writing and reading of diaries is greatly reduced. Especially in group diaries, synchronous and asynchronous discussion proliferates, not least because reading and writing become much more than research collaborations between readers and writers; rather, they become interactive communications, similar to online focus groups in which the geographical locations of participants and the flow and spread of interactions increase significantly. Simultaneously, communications often mean 'an absence of visible presence [by the researcher] ... which the moderator must confront in a conscious and reflexive way' (Lee et al., 2008: 13). Depending upon access and filtering mechanisms, readership is wider, and, as significantly, publication that might previously have been disseminated as end-points to research, becomes, instead, an accessible publication of process and 'progress', regardless of whether formative interaction is viewed as a key rationale underpinning the research.

Analysis and report

Whether diary accounts are off- or online, epistemological and methodological emphases affect diary analyses and forms of report; each are also imbued with ethical concerns. Formerly:

> The ethicality of research practice is seen to depend largely on professional self-regulation … In pro-active systems … researchers are required to comply with certain standards of research before they begin their research.

Now:

> Online methods [increasingly] challenge [such] assumptions, given the usually remote presence of the research participant, and the ease with which the Internet facilitates both the disclosure and accessibility of information. (Lee et al., 2008: 7)

Elsewhere, Eynon et al. (2008) and Charlesworth (2008) provide important analyses of the ethical and legal implications of Internet research in general.

By whichever means diary data are captured, diarists create texts that are open to descriptive or perspectival analysis by researchers (Purvis, 1984). In descriptive analysis, diary participants are 'witnesses' to education phenomena. But diary data can also be used as representative indicators of the perspectives of the group to which the diarist belongs; accuracy in description is key. Like any document, then, diaries can be considered in terms of their 'authenticity, representativeness, credibility, and meaning' (May, 1993: 144), and analysis is increasingly supported by computer software packages. Yet, whilst the balance of concerns and the means of articulation may differ, the essential components remain the text (in increasingly varied forms), the audience and the diarist(s).

Quantitative analysts derive categories from the data in order to compare and count them, whereas qualitative analysts tend to view diary writing as a process in which diarywriters address potential and actual readers. Some diary analysts have focused upon the complementarities of both approaches (Dex, 1991; Marsh and Gershuny, 1991). As introduced above, Internet research adds further dimensions, not least in relation to the relative costs, reach, levels of control and 'particularities of data collection' as blogs or tweets (Lee et al., 2008: 18).

From the outset, researchers need to consider how diaries will feature in the final report. Platt's (1981) early advice remains instructive, especially her suggestion for a clear enunciation of the role of diaries, and the use of diary extracts as illustrative data for general themes emerging from the research overall. Sampling and coding procedures require careful explanation that applies equally to research in and about virtual environments (Hine, 2008).

Neither stand-alone nor for everyone?

Readers will be aware that diaries are rarely used alone, and are frequently accompanied by pre- and post-diary interviews and other tools such as questionnaires and observation. Post-diary interviews help to verify diary data, contributing to 'triangulation' procedures and/or as channels for interim feedback. Some limitations inherent in the diary method extend to diary interviews, since the quality of diary data partly shapes the success or otherwise of subsequent interviews.

Researchers have tended to request diary information from certain groups, and culture, power and status can play a part. Diarywriters have been predominantly people with adequate writing/communication skills, often communicators who are at ease with reflecting on paper or online, and/or those whose cultures value documented rather than spoken accounts. Increasingly, online communications draw upon new linguistic codes and means of expression, about which both readers and writers require familiarity. At first sight, education leaders seem particularly well-suited as diary writers. However, the method has been seen as less appropriate for very 'busy' people with 'limited time'. Of course, this depends on whose interpretation of busyness is accepted; refusal to participate may relate more to the power and status of potential diarists to decline engagement with research diaries than to work/life schedules.

Key points

Diaries and blogs have a growing potential to illuminate a range of leadership issues. This is an essentially interactive genre, and increasingly experimental. Diary writing, reading and interpreting are complex processes involving larger numbers of participants, who are increasingly familiar with the activities of blogging and tweeting in both their professional and personal lives. Because there are methodological challenges about the genre's various procedures, technologies and applications, researchers will need to ensure that their use is securely grounded and understood.

Questions and reflections

1 International conferences are frequently locations where leadership researchers meet to consider leadership activities across cultures and nations. Think about the possibilities of diary use as the means to investigate leadership and/or enhance communities of practice post-conference.

2 Your school is embarking upon a leadership development programme. Think about how and why weblogs might be a useful means to research and evaluate progress and outcomes.

3 Your organisation is committed to student voice as integral to decision-making activities. Can you think of ways in which diaries with children and young people might enhance such activities?

Recommended further reading

Holly, M.L. (1984) *Keeping a Personal Professional Journal*. Deakin, Melbourne: Deakin University Press.

This is a seminal piece on the early use of diaries, and distinctions between diaries, logs and journals.

Lee, R.M., Fielding, N. and Blank, G. (2008) The Internet as a research medium: an Editorial Introduction to *The Sage Handbook of Online Research Methods*, in Fielding, N., Lee, R.M. and Blank, G. (eds) *The Sage Handbook of Online Research Methods*. London: Sage. pp. 3–20.

This chapter by Lee et al. draws to readers' attention important issues relating to online research, not least to new forms of research communication.

Morrison, M. and Galloway, S. (1996) Using diaries to explore supply teachers' lives, in Busfield, J. and Lyons, E. S. (eds) *Methodological Imaginations*. London: Macmillan in association with the British Sociological Association. pp. 34–57.

This chapter provides educational examples of the use of dairies as research tools, including challenges in use and their role as 'substitute observation'.

Suzuki, R. (2004) Diaries as introspective research tools: from Ashton-Warner to Bloggs, TESL-EJ 8(1). Available at: www.kyoto-su.ac.jp/information/tesl-ej/ej29/int.html (accessed 27 May 2011).

This piece offers important insights into the growing online and off-line diary genre.

References

Atkinson, P. (1992) *Understanding Ethnographic Texts*. Qualitative Research Methods Series 25. London: Sage.

Bazeley, P. and Richards, L. (2000) *The NVivo Qualitative Project Book*. London: Sage.

Bell, J. (1999) *Doing your Research Project: A Guide for First Time Researchers in Education and Social Science* (3rd edn). Buckingham: Open University Press.

Berkowitz, R. (1997) Analysing qualitative data, in Frechtling, J. and Sharpe, L. (eds) *User-friendly Handbook for Mixed Method Evaluations, Directorate for Human Resources, nsf*. Available at: www.ehr.nsf.gov/EHR/REC/pubs/NSF97-153/CHAP_4.htm (accessed 24 May 2011).

Brown, A. and Dowling, P. (1998) *Doing Research/Reading Research: A Mode of Interrogation for Education*. London: Falmer Press.

Bryman, A. and Burgess, R.G. (eds) (1994) *Analysing Qualitative Data*. London: Routledge.

Burgess, R.G. (1984) Methods of field research 3: using personal documents, in *In The Field: An Introduction to Field Research*. London: George Allen and Unwin. pp. 123–42.

Burgess, R.G. (1994) On diaries and diary keeping, in Bennett, N. Glatter, R. and Levačić, R. (eds) *Improving Educational Management through Research and Consultancy*. London: Paul Chapman and the Open University.

Burgess, R.G. and Morrison, M. (1995) 'Teaching and learning about food and nutrition in school', Report to the ESRC as part of *The Nation's Diet Programme: The Social Science of Food Choice*. Harlow: Addison Wesley Longman.

Burgess, R.G. and Morrison, M. (1998) Ethnographies of eating in an urban primary school, in Murcott, A. (ed) *The Nation's Diet: The Social Science of Food Choice*. Harlow: Addison Wesley Longman. pp. 209–27.

Charlesworth, A. (2008) Understanding and managing legal issues in Internet research, in Fielding, N., Lee, R.M. and Blank, G. (eds) *The Sage Handbook of Online Research Methods*. London: Sage. pp. 42–57.

Coleman, M. and Glover, D. (2010) *Educational Leadership and Management: Developing Insights and Skills*. Buckingham: McGraw Hill/Open University Press.

Coxon, A., Davies, P., Hunt, A., Weatherburn, P., McManus T. and Rees, C. (1992) The structure of sexual behaviour. *Journal of Sex Research* 29(1): 61–83.

Dex, S. (ed.) (1991) *Life and Work History Analysis: Qualitative and Quantitative Developments*. London: Routledge.

Earley, P. and Fletcher-Campbell, F. (1989) *The Time To Manage? Department and Faculty Heads at Work*. Windsor: NFER-Nelson.

Eynon, R., Fry, J. and Schroeder, R. (2008) The ethics of Internet research, in Fielding, N., Lee, R.M. and Blank, G. (eds) *The Sage Handbook of Online Research Methods*. London: Sage. pp. 23–41.

Galloway, S. (1993) 'Out of sight, out of mind': a response to the literature on supply teaching. *Educational Research* 35(2): 159–69.

Galloway, S., Budge, A., Burgess, R.G., Haworth, R., Pole, C. and Sealey, A. (1995) *School Management Training with Interactive Technology*. Coventry: National Council for Educational Technology.

Gershuny, J., Miles, I., Jones, S., Mullings, C., Thomas, G. and Wyatt, S. (1986) Time budgets: preliminary analyses of a national survey. *Journal of Social Affairs* 2(1): 13–39.

Griffiths, G. (1985) Doubts, dilemmas, and diary keeping, in Burgess, R.G. (ed.) *Issues in Educational Research: Qualitative Methods*. Lewes: Falmer Press. pp. 197–215.

Hammersley, M. and Atkinson, P. (1995) *Ethnography: Principles in Practice* (2nd edn). London: Routledge.

Hine, C. (2008) Virtual ethnography: modes, varieties, affordances, in N. Fielding, Lee, R.M. and Blank, G. (eds) *The Sage Handbook of Online Research Methods*. London: Sage. pp. 257–70.

Hessler, R.M., Downing, J., Beltz, C., Pellicio, A., Powell, M. and Vale, W. (2003) Qualitative research on adolescent risk using email: a methodological assessment. *Qualitative Sociology* 26(1): 111–24.

Holly, M.L. (1984) *Keeping a Personal Professional Journal*. Deakin, Melbourne Deakin University Press.

Holly, M.L. (1989) *Writing to Grow*. Portsmouth, NH: Heinemann.

Lee, R.M., Fielding, N. and Blank, G. (2008) The Internet as a research medium: an Editorial Introduction to *The Sage Handbook of Online Research Methods*, in Fielding, N., Lee, R.M. and Blank, G. (eds) *The Sage Handbook of Online Research Methods*. London: Sage. pp. 3–20.

McAlpine, I., Wilson, K., Russell, C. and Cunningham, M. (2004) An online diary as a research and evaluation tool for 1st year physics undergraduate students. Proceedings of the 21st ASCILATE Conference, Perth, December, pp. 616–22. Available at: www.ascilate.org.au/conferences/perth04/pwcs/pdf/mcalpine.pdf (accessed 25 May 2011).

Marples, D.L. (1967) Studies of managers: a fresh start. *Journal of Management Studies* 4: 282–99.

Marsh, C. and Gershuny, J. (1991) Handling work history data in standard statistical packages, in Dex, S. (ed.) *Life and Work History Analysis: Qualitative and Quantitative Developments*. London: Routledge.

May, T. (1993) *Social Research: Issues, Methods, and Process*. Buckingham: Open University Press.

Miles, M.B. and Huberman, A.M. (1994) *Qualitative Data Analysis. A Source Book* (2nd edn). London: Sage.

Morrison, M.B. (1995) Researching food consumers in school: recipes for concern. *Educational Studies* 21(2): 239–63.

Morrison, M. and Galloway, S. (1996) Using diaries to explore supply teachers' lives in Busfield, J. and Lyons, E. S. (eds) *Methodological Imaginations*. London: Macmillan in association with the British Sociological Association. pp. 34–57.

Okely, J. (1994) Thinking through fieldwork, in Bryman, A. and Burgess, R.G. (eds) *Analysing Qualitative Data*. London: Routledge. pp. 18–34.

Oppenheim, A.N. (1966) *Introduction to Qualitative Research Methods*. London: Wiley.

Oxtoby, R. (1979) Problems facing heads of departments. *Journal of Further and Higher Education* 3(1): 46–59.

Platt, J. (1981) Evidence and proof in documentary research 2: some shared problems of documentary research. *Sociological Review* 29(1): 53–66.

Purvis, J. (1984) *Understanding Texts*. Open University Course E205, Unit 15. Milton Keynes: Open University Press.

Robertson, J.M. and Webber, C. (1999) Graduate learning: a leadership development model. Available at: www.aera.du.ac/99paper/rob99500.htm (accessed on 25 May 2011).

Scheidt, L.A. (2007) The personal journal or diary weblog. Available at: http://indiana.academia.edn/loisscheidt/Papers/169344/Diary-weblogs-as-genre (accessed 26 May 2011).

Scott, J. (1990) *A Matter of Record: Documentary Sources in Social Research*. Cambridge: Polity Press.

Suzuki, R. (2004) Diaries as introspective research tools: from Ashton-Warner to Bloggs, TESL-EJ 8(1). Available at: www.kyoto-su.ac.jp/information/tesl-ej/ej29/int.html (accessed 27 May 2011).

Szalai, A. (ed.) (1972) *The Use of Time*. The Hague: Mouton.

Wakeford, N. and Cohen, K. (2008) Fieldnotes in public: using blogs for research in Fielding, N., Lee, R.M. and Blank, G. (eds) *The Sage Handbook of Online Research Methods*. London: Sage, pp. 307–26.

Werner, A.Z., Wahlström, K.L. and Dikkers, A.G. (2007) An investigation into the daily lives of education principals. Available at: www.cehd.edu/edpa/licesnsure/Research/blogs.pdf (accessed 27 May 2011).

Zimmerman, D.H. and Wieder, D.L. (1977) The diary: diary-interview method. *Urban Life* 5(4): 479–98.

Part D

Analysing and Presenting Data

CHAPTER 23

Quantitative Data Analysis: Using SPSS

Pauline Dixon and Pam Woolner

Chapter objectives

- To enable you to understand when using quantitative methods might be useful.
- To enable you to use descriptive statistics to add to a study, research paper or report.
- To provide ideas of some statistical techniques that can be employed for different types of variables and when utilising uni- or bi-variate analysis.
- To provide you with more confidence in managing quantitative data, at whatever level of sophistication is appropriate to your research needs.

Introduction

Why use quantitative methods?

The short answer to this question is: 'Why not...?' The longer answer should become evident from this chapter.

Essentially, educational establishments of all kinds collect information of all sorts. It makes sense when carrying out research to make use of these data, and much of it is quantitative in nature; that is, things are counted or measured. Teachers, managers and other staff spend a considerable amount of time recording numerical information. This can be institutional-level data, such as the number of students enrolled on a particular course, the percentage of learners who achieve at a certain level or attendance across year groups. Much of the information comes from the records of individual students, which provide student-level data, such as the number of assignments completed, scores in end-of-unit assessments or annual attendance. Chapter 19 of this volume offers information about national and international data sets which are also available for your use.

While conducting your research, you will of course find there are additional data you need, which may be collected in the course of your work through methods such as direct observation, questionnaires and interviews. Yet, aspects of these data could also be quantitative in nature. For example, you might observe the number of learners on task at intervals through a session or count how many of various sorts of questions are asked by learners. Questionnaires can be designed to produce more quantitative data through the use of closed questions and rating scales (see Chapters 10 and 18) and, even if you choose to conduct interviews, your analysis of transcripts may involve counts of key issues or themes.

So the collection and analysis of quantitative data could be central to your research or it may be intended to complement other, qualitative, methods. Such triangulation is useful to you as the researcher, trying to make sense of your data, but may also come in handy when you present your findings to others. Some audiences particularly value the apparent objectivity of numerical information, while with others you may be more successful in conveying ideas through qualitative data, such as choice quotations from your participants.

Given that there are potentially useful quantitative data available, the problem for the researcher is what to collect, from whom and how to make use of it. In considering this challenge, it is important to keep in mind the central aim of your research – what question are you trying to answer? This is generally about trying to find evidence that something is *making a difference*. Many statistical techniques centre on testing whether there are patterns in the data which suggest differences between groups of people, or between occasions. The issue then for the researcher is whether the difference can be explained by the object of the research or whether it is just as likely to have occurred by some other means. For example, we might ask whether test results are increasing year on year because of better teaching, or because of a change in the characteristics of the student intake.

Types of variable – nominal, ordinal and continuous or scale

These aspects of the educational world that we are measuring or counting are referred to as *variables* and it is possible to distinguish three broad types:

Nominal variables are based on classification or groupings, such as gender or course of study. To simplify recording and to carry out quantitative analysis, it is often helpful to refer to the possible values that nominal variables can take using numbers. So 'male' is recorded as '1' and 'female' as '2'; 'science subjects' are '1'; 'arts and humanities' are '2'; 'vocational' is '3', etc. These numbers, however, are not to be understood as quantities – being female is not somehow 'twice as much' as being male. This is important when it comes to generating statistics and conducting analyses. An 'average gender' is clearly nonsense, but we need to be careful that we don't accidentally treat the values of a nominal variable as if they are quantities.

Where quantity is involved, it is likely that we are dealing with an ***ordinal variable***. Here, the values are again whole numbers, but in this case '3' really is more than '2', which is more than '1'. You might have assigned numbers to lengths of teaching experience, so '1 year or less' is coded as '1'; '2–5 years' is coded as '2'; '6–10 years' as '3' and 'over 10 years' as '4'. Or, if you are asking for opinions on a questionnaire, you may use a five-point rating scale for positions from 'strongly disagree' to 'strongly agree'. Ordinal variables have values that can be thought of as a ladder or staircase, where '4' is consistently above '3', but there is *no certainty that the steps are equal distances apart*. A rating scale from 'strongly disagree' to 'strongly agree' might be measuring opinion in some sense but it is not like a ruler or tape measure. Again, it is important, when we come to generating and understanding statistics, to keep this distinction in mind.

If our measurements are like those produced by a ruler, where the values are evenly spaced and there is a meaningful zero, then we are dealing with a ***scale variable***. Unfortunately, these are fairly rare in education. There is some debate about just how rare, and the consequences of this for research. Since there is more flexibility in dealing statistically with scale variables, there is a temptation to consider some ordinal variables as scale. This seems reasonable in the case of some standardised tests which produce results along a fairly long range (say 0 to 100) and where attempts have been made to ensure that intervals along the scale are approximately equal. It seems much more dubious if an opinion-rating scale, even if long, is considered to be a scale variable.

Misconceptions, misunderstandings and inflated claims

If a change in practice is having an effect, *something* must be changing. It should be possible to identify this something, devise a way of measuring it (or other factor closely related to it) and make meaningful comparisons.

Numbers, however, do not guarantee meaningfulness. Remember the old adages: 'Garbage in, garbage out' and 'Correlation does not prove causality'. You need to think about possible relationships between variables and possible mechanisms for a potential cause to produce the effect you are claiming for it. For example, a correlation could occur because of direct cause and effect (in either direction), it could be due to some underlying (and probably unmeasured) causal relationship(s) or it might be spurious. More concretely, does completing homework cause higher achievement or does achieving highly make you more likely to complete homework? Or are both effects caused by some aspect of students' home situations?

As this example demonstrates, identifying causation is rarely straightforward in education research. It might be possible to measure changes but more difficult to be certain that they are due to particular input and not other variations. Appropriate comparisons between the group in question and some other group can help, but this needs to be built into the design of your research. Often, it is only really possible to say that one variable is associated with another in a particular way. You should beware of this when reading reports and articles, which sometimes claim they have evidence of causation when they do not.

In your own research, you may find that quantitative results sometimes do not show a change that you are convinced is genuine. If there is no sign of an effect, review again what you expected, and why, and what you measured. If the effect is only slight, or not statistically significant, but it is backed up by other results, it may be appropriate to acknowledge it. Further research might produce results in the same direction and so add weight to tentative conclusions. It is particularly important in such cases to describe your analyses thoroughly, being clear about what you are doing and why. If you're not sure, try to find out rather than fudging the explanation.

In any case, you need to make sure your tables and graphs convey the information effectively. This can be affected by such factors as different arrangements of bars in bar charts, different ways of combining data from several categories, different ways of labelling tables. Also ensure that descriptions and titles are adequate for someone who doesn't know the area as well as you do. It can be helpful to ask someone who is not involved in the research to comment on your tables and figures, or try to draw conclusions from them.

Handling your data: collection and entry

The beginning ...

From your understanding of your area, you will have generated some research questions or hypotheses to investigate or test. These need to be your starting point when you begin to consider how you will collect data. They will suggest who you need to collect data from (your sample) and the sort of data you need. They will also imply the types of analysis you will need to do and this needs to be kept in mind when you plan data collection. Considering the homework example above, if you want to explore the possibility of home situations influencing the success of a classroom intervention, then you will need to try to measure some aspects of participants' home situations.

Data entry – creating a framework for data

First, you need to be clear about your **variables** and your **cases**. Identify your variables – what aspects of the situation are you collecting information about? Consider which are nominal, ordinal and scale variables. Identify your cases – who or what does the information refer to? They are likely to be individual people, perhaps represented by questionnaires, but could be homework samples or groups of people such as classes or tutorial groups.

You will need to code some data to turn it from words or ideas into a numerical form. Designing and coding a questionnaire need to inform each other, so that you are not faced with information that you cannot think how to code and enter into a database (for more detail on questionnaires, see Chapter 18).

Next, decide what you are going to do about 'missing data'. This is where you don't have a value for a particular variable, perhaps because a respondent has missed out an item on a questionnaire. You can invent a code for missing data – '99' used to be suggested – so that you can distinguish it from accidents at the data entry stage. However, this can cause problems if you forget that you've done this and fail to register '99' as 'missing data' with your database. In that case, the 99s will be treated as real data. If, for instance, the variable is 'age', you might find that your sample appears to be much more elderly than you expected ...! It might be safer to just leave missing data spaces as blanks. SPSS copes very happily with gaps like this and if you are using an online survey tool, the output from that will tend to come with spaces.

You'll need to think carefully about how to code your particular data but there are some common mistakes to avoid:

- Time and participant ages – remember that units of time do not come in tens, so you can't convert simply into decimals: '2 years and 3 months' is not equal to 2.3.

- Data inputted as strings (words) – be consistent with spellings, including capital letters: 'teacher' and 'Teacher' will be treated as different job categories.

- Likert scales – be consistent. Most people code low as '1' and high as '5'. If it makes sense to you the other way round, with '1' as 'top', that's not a problem as long as you keep to this coding.

Cleaning data: spotting errors

Once your data are all entered into your database, you need to check for accuracy before you begin your analysis. To spot errors, it is helpful to produce some outputs, such as descriptive statistics and charts (see below), for individual variables. Check these are sensible, given what you know about the variables (highest and lowest points on the scales) and what you might have noticed about your data set (lots of people circled 'option 2' on that item). If you produce a mean of 110 for a set of examination scores entered as percentages, then it's clear you've made some mistakes!

Getting to know your data set

Univariate analysis

Introduction

Before tackling the relationship between variables, it is always a good idea to start by looking at individual variables and generating some descriptive statistics. We may be interested in how students or staff have performed on certain tests or how they have responded to certain questions. Descriptive information, such as the gender of our respondents or their age, is useful in providing us with important statistics that may help us answer our research questions or provide vignettes about our participants. When looking at one variable at a time, the term we use is *univariate analysis*. As set out in the section below, not only do we learn about our data set by carrying out univariate analysis, but we can also look for errors that could have occurred during data input where codes outside of the code values are easily visible.

Frequency distributions

Once you have collected and inputted your data into a statistical package such as SPSS, one possible next step is to take a look at how the data look using frequency tables and graphs, such as histograms (if the variable is scale) or bar charts (where the variable is ordinal or nominal). A histogram is a graph made up of vertical bars, with frequency on the vertical axis and the horizontal axis representing the variable value. A bar chart is similar but is

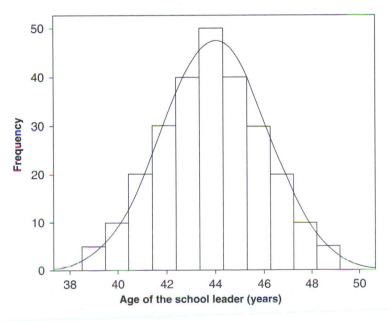

Figure 23.1   A normal distribution curve (bell-shaped curve)

used for variables that can be grouped into categories and would include Likert scale type variables where the category is on the horizontal axis and the vertical axis is the frequency or percentage of each category. This is known as looking at the frequency distribution of your data. A frequency distribution will show the number of times the variable values occur in your data set. First, this will allow you to see if there have been any problems at

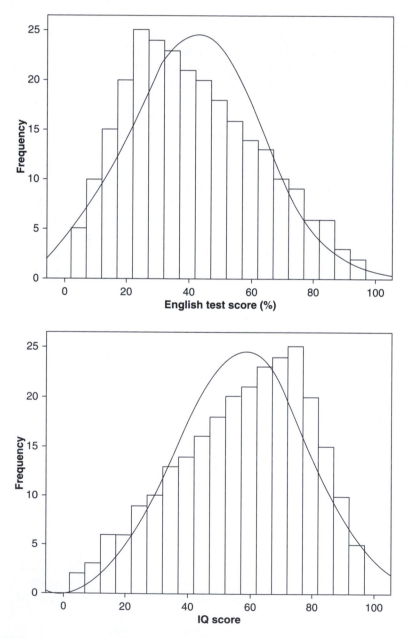

Figure 23.2 A positively and negatively skewed distribution

the inputting stage and enable you to go back to your original data to check why certain values or codes seem to be missing or not consistent with your coding. This would include outliers in the data set or codes that are not consistent with your coding values. An outlier is an extreme value, either high or low, which is isolated from the main group of values and needs to be checked against the original data. Second, by looking at the diagrams your data produces, you will be able to assess if the data produce a normal or skewed distribution. Figure 23.1 shows a normally distributed distribution curve where the mean, mode and median are the same. In general, a normal distribution illustrates a situation where 50 per cent of cases lie on one side of the arithmetic mean and the other 50 per cent on the other side. The curve will peak at the mean.

It is also interesting to note that for a perfectly normal distribution, 68.26 per cent of cases will be within one standard deviation of the mean, 95.44 per cent of cases within two standard deviations of the mean and, finally, 99.7 per cent of cases will be within three standard deviations of the mean.

Some data will not follow the pattern of a normal distribution, thus these are termed *skewed*. A skewness of the distribution implies that the values cluster at one end of the scale with the frequency of values tailing off towards either the right or left end. A positive skew indicates that there is a long tail to the right and the values cluster to the left and a curve that is negatively skewed is where the values cluster to the right and the long tail is to the left (Figure 23.2).

Histograms can be generated in SPSS using a variety of methods. One such method is as follows. Find 'Data Set I' in this book's website materials (http://www.sagepub.co.uk/briggs) and follow these steps:

Graphs ➡ **Legacy Dialogs** ➡ **Histogram**

which opens the dialog box in Figure 23.3. Select the variable from the list by either highlighting and using the arrow to insert into the variable box or dragging the variable from the list into the variable box. Click OK and the output file should now contain a histogram as shown in either Figures 1 (age) or 2 (englishs or iqscore) depending upon the variable chosen.

Bar charts are more appropriate to use where the variable is ordinal. Take the example from Data Set II, where we are looking at the satisfaction levels of school leaders with their role and their salary levels generating bar charts in an alternative way to the procedure set out above in SPSS:

Analyse ➡ **Descriptive statistics** ➡ **Frequency**

which opens the dialogue box shown in Figure 23.4. Select the variables from the data set for which you wish to produce bar charts and frequency tables (in this case *satleader* and *satsalary*). Highlight these and use the arrow in the centre to shift them into the *variable(s)* box on the right (as illustrated). Now click the button marked '*Charts*'. Choose the bar chart option (as in Figure 23.5), then continue and finally click OK and in your output folder both simple frequency tables and bar charts will be produced for these two Likert scale variables.

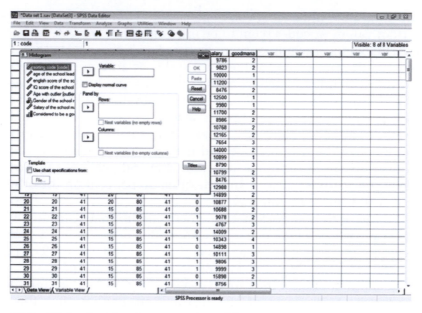

Figure 23.3 Dialog box for the generation of histograms

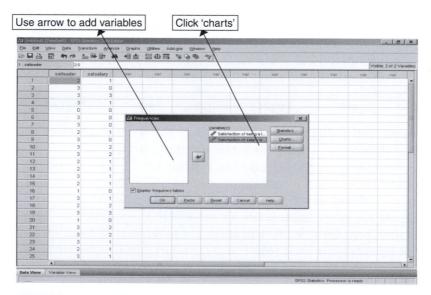

Figure 23.4 Producing bar charts and frequency tables – dialog box

Measures of central tendency and dispersion

Now that you have started to look at the distribution of some of your data, the next step is to explore the variables further by summarising their *central tendency*. Three measures of central tendency are the arithmetic mean, the median and the mode. The arithmetic mean is what is typically described as the 'average'. All values are added together and divided by the number of values. The median

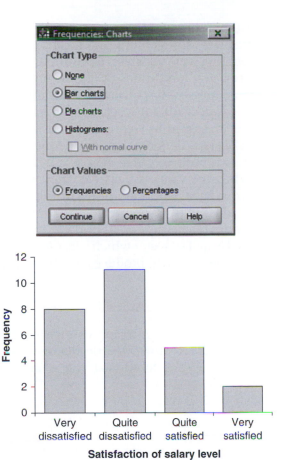

Figure 23.5   Frequency chart options in SPSS

is the mid-point in the distribution when the values are set out in order, splitting the distribution of values in half. The third measure of central tendency is the mode that is the value which occurs most often in the distribution. Arithmetic means and medians may be very similar or indeed equal in two sets of values, however the *dispersion* of the distribution should also be of interest to us and considered together with the measures of central tendency.

Measures of dispersion or spread include the *range, the inter-quartile range* and *the standard deviation.* When providing information regarding measures of central tendency, you should also provide the measures of dispersion in order to provide an indication of the shape of the distribution. The *range* of the data is the highest minus the lowest value within our data set. The *inter-quartile range,* is the difference between the third and first quartile after the data have been arranged from the lowest to the highest values. Finally, the *standard deviation* will illustrate the amount of deviation from the mean and allows you to interpret whether the values cluster around the mean or are more spread out along the scale of values. The larger a standard deviation or inter-quartile range, the more spread out the values. Hence, the smaller the standard deviation the more clustered the values around the mean. A standard deviation is only used when considering scale variables. For ordinal variables, the range or inter-quartile range are better indications of dispersion and for nominal variables there is no need to measure dispersion at all as this makes little sense.

For scale data, the skewness and kurtosis are both valuable measures. For a normal distribution, as illustrated in Figure 23.1, both the skewness and kurtosis would be zero. Skewness denotes the 'lopsidedness' of the distribution. If the value of skewness is positive, then there is a heap of values to the left of the distribution; when the value is negative, there is an accumulation to the right. The kurtosis provides information regarding the peakedness of the distribution. Positive values imply a pointed distribution and negative values a flat one. SPSS allows the calculation of all of these measures of central tendency and dispersions. Using Data Set I which sets out the age, English ability and IQ of 260 school leaders, we will produce a table with all of this information for each of these variables:

Analyse   ➡   Descriptive Statistics   ➡   Frequencies

Now transfer each of the variables for which you wish to generate the statistics. Then click on statistics as shown in the dialogue box in Figure 23.6. Finally, once all the measures are ticked that you wish to appear in a table, click continue and finally click on OK.

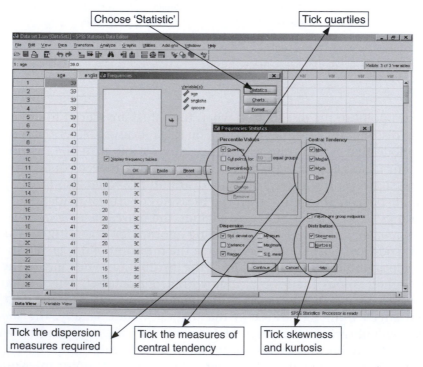

Figure 23.6   Measures of central tendency and dispersion in SPSS

Table 23.1 Output measures of central tendency and spread

Statistics

		age	englishs	iqscore
N	Valid	260	260	260
	Missing	0	0	0
Mean		44.00	42.04	57.96
Median		44.00	40.00	60.00
Mode		44	25	75
Std Deviation		2.197	21.069	21.069
Skewness		.000	.411	−.411
Std Error of Skewness		.151	.151	.151
Range		10	90	90
Percentiles	25	42.25	25.00	45.00
	50	44.00	40.00	60.00
	75	45.75	55.00	75.00

Table 23.1 will be produced in the output folder. In one table then, we have generated the figures for each of the variables concerning the school leader's age, English score and IQ measure. The histograms for these data were produced at the beginning of this section. From this table, you can now put these values into your report or paper, providing informative statistics and presenting the reader with a good level of description concerning single variables – that is their measures of central tendency and spread.

Boxplots and the outlier
Other charts that could be produced at this stage include boxplots and pie charts. Pie charts should be used for ordinal and nominal data and boxplots for continuous or scale data. Boxplots again help the cleaning of data in these initial stages of analysis, especially when looking for outliers in continuous or scale data. These may constitute an input error that you will need to correct. Taking Data Set I, use the variable that has been inputted where there are examples of outliers. A boxplot is made up, as the name suggests, of a box where the bottom line of the box represents the top of the 1st quartile and the top line of the box the top of the 3rd quartile. The whole box then represents the middle 50 per cent of the observations (inter-quartile range), and the thick black line is the median value. 'Whiskers' are lines that denote the lowest and highest values excluding outliers. Outliers are extreme values within the data set. Like the histogram, the boxplot provides a pictorial representation of the dispersion and shape of the distribution. The boxplot provides you with a feel for the data in the initial stages. To generate a boxplot for your data select Graphs then Legacy Dialogs and Boxplot.

This provides you with access to the dialog box as above. Select *Summaries of separate variables*, then click on Define, bringing up the second dialog box which shows all of the variables in your data set. Highlight the variable *'age with outlier [outlierage]'* and use the middle arrow to transfer it to the *Boxes represent* box (Figure 23.7). Now click OK to produce a boxplot as shown in

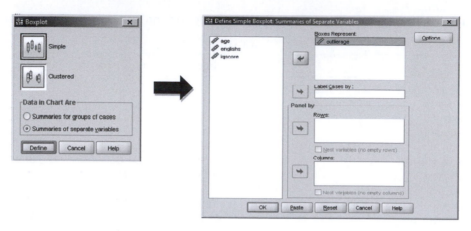

Figure 23.7   Dialog boxes to generate boxplots

Figure 23.8. Outliers are shown either by a circle or a star. Next to these are numbers which inform you which case in your data set (i.e. on which row of your SPSS spreadsheet) has these outlier values. So, for example, if you go to row 260, you will see that the age has been inputted as 54 years old. You should still have your original questionnaires (the raw data) and having labelled each of the questions with the number stating the order in which the data were inputted, then a quick check will allow you to ascertain whether 54 is the correct age or an error. If need be, a correction can be made.

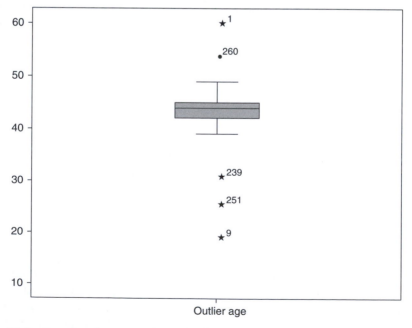

Figure 23.8   Boxplot showing school leader age with outliers

One final word of advice would be always to use a caption for your table or figure. These can be generated automatically using the 'insert caption' feature in Word. Never assume that your reader can understand your diagrams or interpret your tables. You will need to explain what your data are showing in the text but focusing on main issues rather than everything the table or figure is showing.

Bivariate analysis

Introduction
Having looked at individual variables and cleaned the data, the next step is to look for relationships or differences between two variables that are *statistically* significant. Yes, using percentages and tables, we can often see by eye what look like differences, but we need also to show if relationships, positive or negative, are statistically significant. Examples of questions that could be answered using bivariate analysis include:

- Do female school staff earn less than their male counterparts?
- Do females have the same opinions regarding their ability to manage as males?
- Do scores in one student test correlate with scores in another?
- Is there a statistically significant difference between baseline and endline scores in an intervention?

There are a number of tests that can be used to determine whether the relationship between two groups is significant.

Crosstabs and chi squared tests
Where the dependent and independent variables are either nominal or ordinal, cross-tabulation and the chi squared test can be used to determine whether membership in one category has a bearing on membership in another. A cross-tabulation is a table that sets out how cases are distributed between each combination of category. The chi squared test is based on comparing the expected with the observed frequency in each cell. Table 23.2 is an example of cross-tabulation from Data Set I.

Table 23.2   Cross-tabulation of gender and self-perception of managerial ability

| | | Gender of the school manager | | |
		Male	Female	Total
Considered to be a good manager	Agree strongly	47	22	69
	Agree	59	51	110
	Disagree	20	45	65
	Disagree strongly	9	7	16
Total		135	125	260

This table can be generated by following this procedure:

Analyse ➡ **Descriptive Statistics** ➡ **Crosstabs**

Place the 'considered to be a good manager' variable in the row box and the gender variable in the column box by highlighting the variable and using the arrows (Figure 23.9). Clicking OK will produce the table as in Table 23.2.

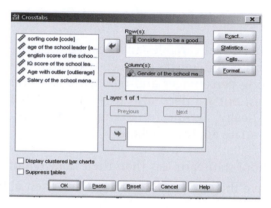

Figure 23.9 Dialog box to create a cross-tabulation table

By looking at the table that has been produced, it would seem that there are some differences between male and female leaders and the way they answer this question regarding their ability as a manager. However, we wish to calculate the significance level of any difference that may exist. The chi squared test tells us if there is a statistically significant difference between how the different genders answer this question. It tests the hypothesis that the row and column variables are not related to one another and are independent. In order to carry out the chi squared test and obtain the significance level in SPSS the following steps need to be undertaken:

Analyse ➡ **Descriptive Statistics** ➡ **Crosstabs**

This should bring us back to the dialog box as above. Now click on Statistics and the crosstabs statistics box will become visible. Check the chi squared box in the left-hand corner (Figure 23.10). Click on Continue and then OK. This will now produce an output as shown in Figure 23.11.

The tables produced by this procedure are the cross-tabulation table and another table which has the chi squared test results. There are two pieces of information we require here. First of all, we need to look at the 'Pearson Chi-Square' row and the final number in the third column labelled 'Asymp. Sig. (two-sided)' (where asymp.sig is asymptotic significance). This shows the test statistic or p-value. In statistics, it is typically accepted that a p-value of less than 0.05 reveals a statistically significant difference and this difference has a 95 per cent confidence level. Where the p-value is less than 0.01, this indicates a 99 per cent confidence level and less than 0.01 99.9 per cent confidence level.

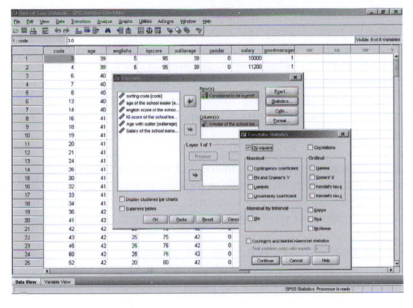

Figure 23.10   Crosstabs statistics dialog box

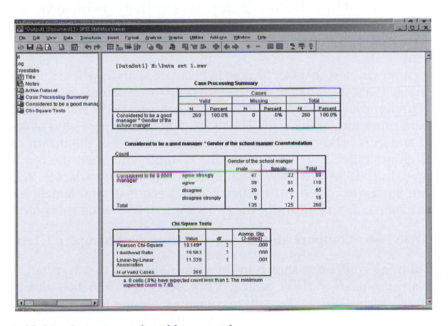

Figure 23.11   Outputs produced by crosstabs

In this case, as shown in our 'Chi Squared Tests' table, in the output the
p-value is 0.000. We can therefore state that there is a statistically significant
difference between the way men and women answered this question.
However, the second important piece of information is that given below the
table in this case: 'a. 0 cells (.0 per cent) have expected count less than 5.' The

cut-off point for this statement is 20 per cent in the brackets. If such a case occurs, you will need to carry out an exact test in order to ascertain whether the statistical significant difference is held, or combine columns in order to eradicate smaller values. This may sometimes occur if your data set is small. In order to report the above finding, one could use the following sentence:

'carrying out a chi squared test shows that there is a statistically significant difference between the way men and women respond to the item "considered to be a good manager"' (chi square = 19.149, df = 3, p = 0.000).

Parametric methods: T-test – comparing the means of two groups

There are some unresolved issues when looking at data analysis. These include when to use what are termed 'parametric' and 'non parametric' tests. There are those who argue that parametric tests can only be used when:

- variables are normally distributed.
- variables are continuous; and
- the variance of both variables is equal.

It is beyond the scope of this chapter to set out the arguments and evidence. However, it should be noted here that parametric tests are often carried out on variables that do not conform to the above three conditions. If one wished to be cautious, one could compare the results of non-parametric tests with parametric tests.

One parametric test that can be used in bivariate analysis where the dependent variable is a scale variable and the independent variable is nominal is the t-test. This test could be used, for example, to compare the test scores, salaries, marathon times, etc., of male and female participants or those who have been trained and those who have not. The test looks at whether the means of two sample groups differ. It is the p-value that is important when the results are generated. In Data Set I, we have a number of continuous variables. We shall carry out a t-test to consider the difference between male and female leaders' salaries (comparing the means of the two samples). Following this procedure:

Analyse ➡ **Compare Means** ➡ **Independent Samples T-Test ...**

This will bring up the box shown in the Figure 23.12. In the 'Test Variable(s)' box, place the salary variable which is our dependent variable, and in the 'Grouping Variable' box, as we want to compare male and female leaders, enter 'gender'. Click on the 'Define Groups ...' sub-dialog box shown in Figure 23.12 and in the box beside Group 1 type 0 and in the box beside Group 2 type 1 (male and female codes), now click Continue and this closes the 'Define Groups' sub-dialog box. Finally, click OK. The output that is generated by this is now shown in Table 23.3. on p 358. The first table under the heading of 'Group Statistics' shows us how many male and female participants answered the question, the mean for those respondents, the standard deviation and the standard error for males and females. The next table sets out the results of the t-test.

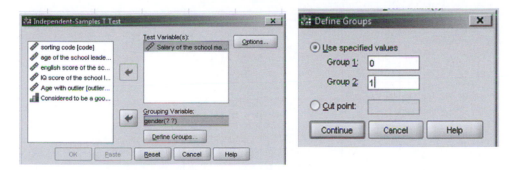

Figure 23.12   Independent Samples T-Test dialog box

The first thing that needs considering in Table 23.3 are the two columns that state 'Levene's Test for Equality of Variance'. If the variance is not significant, then we can assume that the variances are equal in the data. Where the variance is significant (as in this case, i.e. the Sig. value < 0.05) then we need to look at the figures in the lower row of the table, that is the 'Equal variances not assumed'. The findings from the t-test are then reported in the following columns. The most important information reporting-wise are those figures set out in the t, df and Sig. (two-tailed) columns. We need to report the t and df, but the most important statistic is the Sig. value showing the significance. The cut-off point is 0.05. Therefore, regarding male and female salary levels, we have found a statistically significant difference between salaries and gender of school leaders/managers. When reporting these findings, we would set out the following: 'when considering our data and using an independent t-test we found that there was a statistically significant difference between male and female salary levels (t = 16.548, df = 246.387, p<0.05)'.

As stated above, there are those who believe that where the distribution of the continuous data are not normal and there are violations to the assumptions of the t-test, then a non-parametric test such as the 'Wilcoxon' (for paired sample t-tests) and the Mann-Whitney test (for the independent sample t-test) should be used. Parametric tests should be utilised first, and only where the violations are serious should the alternative non-parametric test be used (see, for example, Muijs, 2004 for more details). Both tests can be performed in SPSS.

Correlation: continuous variables
When initially looking for an association between two continuous variables (two test scores or height and weight, or salary level and test scores, for example), it is often helpful to construct scatterplot diagrams. These will show visually if there is a linear association between two variables and if this association is positive or negative. In a scatter diagram, each of the plots for an individual are shown where the two variables intersect and hence all of the respondents' individual plots make up a pattern. Where there is a positive correlation, the pattern of the points will move upwards from left to right and

Table 23.3 Unrelated T-test comparing salaries for male and female leaders in education

Group Statistics

Gender of the school manger		N	Mean	Std Deviation	Std Error Mean
Salary	Male	135	13174.71	2058.277	177.148
	Female	125	9433.22	1524.835	136.385

Independent Samples Test

		Levene's Test for Equality of Variances		T-test for Equality of Means						
									95% Confidence Interval of the Difference	
		F	Sig	t	dif	Sig (2-tailed)	Mean Difference	Std Error Difference	Lower	Upper
Salary of the school manager	Equal variances assumed	16.835	.000	16.548	258	.000	3741.487	226.096	3296.258	4186.716
	Equal variances not assumed	.000		16.735	246.387	.000	3741.487	223.568	3301.140	4181.835

accumulate around the regression line. This would imply that as one variable increases so does the other and there is a positive association between the two variables. Where there is a negative correlation, the pattern will move downward from left to right implying that as one variable increases the other decreases and a negative association exists. Figure 23.13 shows scatterplot diagrams with different degrees of linear association. Scatterplot diagrams can be generated in SPSS using:

Graphs → Legacy Dialogs → Scatter/Dot → Define

and then, inserting the variables for which you wish to generate a scatterplot in the Y Axis and X Axis boxes, click OK. Relationships are not always positive or negative, but at times take on what is termed a curvilinear association. That is where the relationship curves as one or more point.

The correlation coefficient measures the strength of this association. The most commonly used correlation coefficient when considering continuous variables is the Pearson's r correlation. A Pearson correlation can take a range within −1 and +1. A perfect correlation would be indicated by + or − 1. Where r = 0 there would be no association. It is generally accepted that the strength of the relationship can be determined utilising the following interpretation:

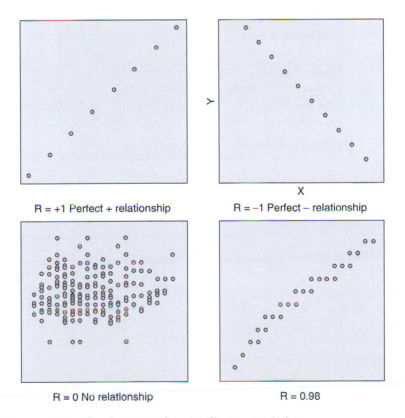

Figure 23.13   Scatterplot diagrams showing linear associations

0.00-0.19 (±) weak; 0.20-0.39 (±) low; 0.40-0.69 (±) modest; 0.70-0.89 (±) high; 0.90-1 (±) very high (see Cohen and Holliday, 1982).

Computing Pearson's r in SPSS is carried out as follows:

Analyse ➡ **Correlate** ➡ **Bivariate**

This will open a box titled 'Bivariate Correlations' as in Figure 23.14. Select the variables that you want to correlate from the list on the left. In this case, using Data Set I the two variables are English scores and the age of the school leader. Ensure that the Pearson box is ticked and click OK (Figure 23.14).

The correlations table will be generated as in Table 23.4. What is of importance for reporting the findings are the figures set out in one of the numerical cells which is the top right-hand cell. This tells us that the Pearson's r is 0.98 which implies a very high relationship between English scores and age. After the Pearson's r are two asterisks showing that the correlation is significant at the cut-off level of 0.01 (set as default in SPSS) and, in this case, the statistical

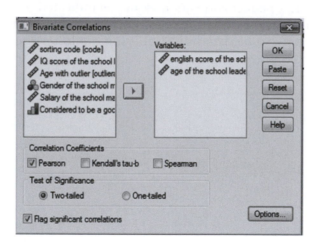

Figure 23.14 Pearson's r correlation dialog box

Table 23.4 Pearson's r output

Correlations		English score of the school leader	Age of the school leader
English score of the school leader	Pearson correlation	1	.980**
	Sig. (2-tailed)	260	.000
	N		260
Age of the school leader	Pearson correlation	.980**	1
	Sig. (2-tailed)	.000	
	N	260	260

** Correlation is significant at the 0.01 level (2-tailed).

significance is p<0.000. The number of leaders with test scores is shown by N = 260. This could be written up as r = 0.980; n = 260; p<0.000.

Correlation: rank variables

When investigating correlations between ordinal variables, typically Spearman's rho and/or Kendall's tau are utilised. Once the above procedure for calculating Pearson's r is known, then it is straightforward to calculate either Spearman or Kendall in SPSS. Follow the same procedure as set out above (Analyse, Correlate, Bivariate), and in the dialog box you will need to uncheck the 'Pearson' box and check either the Kendall and/or Spearman box. A matrix of correlation coefficients will be generated. You need to look again for correlations that achieve statistical significance at the p<0.05 level and report accordingly.

And finally...

We have covered a lot of detail above but it's important not to lose sight of the bigger picture. Keep returning to your research question, which should also help you to think about analysis. Why are you collecting the data? What are you trying to find out? Which quantitative methods will enable you to answer your research questions? Ensure you understand why you are conducting a statistical procedure so you can explain your reasoning in your write-up.

Key points

- From the beginning of your research, think about how you are going to manage your data.
- Get to know your data. What descriptive statistics or charts can you produce that best illustrate your findings and how do you write about this in your text?
- Make sure your analysis is appropriate for the types of variables and that it helps you answer your research questions.

Questions and reflections

1 Can you remember what the different types of variables are? What sort are your data going to be?

2 What descriptive statistics can you generate with SPSS? Do you know how to get the ones you need?

3 Will you be comparing your respondents with themselves or with a comparison group? Therefore, what sort of analysis will you be undertaking?

Recommended further reading

Connolly, P. (2007) *Quantitative Data Analysis in Education: A Critical Introduction Using SPSS*. Abingdon: Routledge.

This text is useful in developing an understanding of quantitative methods of analysis. Someone with existing statistical expertise would definitely find the detail useful in broadening their knowledge of what the SPSS package can do, and how to get it to do it.

Kosslyn, S.M. (2006) *Graph Design for the Eye and Mind*. Oxford: Oxford University Press.

If you can get hold of this little book, it will help you make sensible decisions about visual representation of your data.

Morrison, K. (2009) *Causation in Educational Research*. London: Routledge.

This provides some thought-provoking background reading for anyone considering research in an educational context.

Muijs, D. (2004) *Doing Quantitative Research in Education with SPSS*. London: Sage.
Muijs, D. (2011) *Doing Quantitative Research in Education with SPSS* (2nd edn). London: Sage.

This book (either edition) is much more than a guide to using SPSS, though it is good on that front (for which the latest edition is recommended). Muijs reviews the fundamentals of research design and statistics, linking them to examples from education, in a very readable way.

References

Cohen, L. and Holliday, M. (1982) *Statistics for Social Scientists*. London: Harper and Row.
Mujis, D. (2004) *Doing Quantitative Research in Education with SPSS*. London: Sage.

CHAPTER 24

Advanced Quantitative Data Analysis

Daniel Muijs

Chapter objectives

In the previous chapter, we saw how we could analyse quantitative data. In this chapter, we will build upon that knowledge to further develop quantitative methods. In particular, the aims of this chapter are:

- To enable you to understand when using advanced quantitative methods might be useful.
- To enable you to choose the appropriate statistical methodology for your research question and variable.
- To develop an understanding of the concept of statistical modelling.
- To develop an understanding of some of the advanced statistical methods used in leadership research.

What is statistical modelling?

In the previous chapter, we learnt how we can statistically test whether there is a relationship between two variables. This is obviously extremely useful, but limited. In many cases in educational leadership research, we will be interested in research questions that entail rather complex situations. Think, for example, of the relationship between educational leadership and student attainment. Theoretically, it is clear that a lot of variables may intervene in this relationship, for example school climate, teaching quality and student intake. We will therefore have to develop a strategy to deal with this level of complexity.

That strategy is called *statistical modelling*. A statistical model is essentially a way of representing processes that occur in the real world, and can be defined as a simplified representation of reality showing the interrelationships between selected variables. Essentially, we are trying to accurately represent the actual relationships between variables in our data, while attempting to be *parsimonious*, that is to use as few variables as possible to explain the dependent variable of interest (student attainment in our example) (Tolmie et al., 2011).

Modelling is an important part of quantitative research. We know it is impossible to fully account for everything that may influence our dependent variable in reality. Thinking of student attainment, for example, many contingencies may intervene. Students may be influenced by the temperature in the exam room, poor sleep and numerous other circumstances. Of course, we cannot collect and analyse data on all possible contingencies, so what we try to do instead is work with an initial hypothesised model, collect data on the variables we think are relevant, and then test our model with the data collected. For our study on the relationship between school leadership and student outcomes mentioned above, we might, for example, hypothesise the model shown in Figure 24.1.

This admittedly somewhat simple model proposes that school leadership has an indirect effect on student attainment through its influence on school climate and teaching quality. The other main factors influencing attainment are student intake characteristics like gender and ability. School climate is hypothesised to influence teaching quality. If we collect data on these variables, we can then start to test this relationship, using some of the methods outlined below.

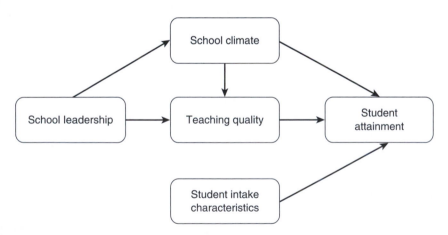

Figure 24.1   School leadership and student outcomes (1)

Multiple linear regression

What is multiple linear regression?

The first method we will look at is called multiple linear regression. In multiple linear regression, we look at the relationship between one 'effect' variable, called the *dependent* or *outcome* variable, and one or more *predictors,* also called *independent* variables. In our example, we will look at the relationship between student attainment, our dependent variable, and the independent variables school climate, teaching quality, school leadership, student gender and student ability (Muijs, 2010).

How regression works can best be demonstrated by looking at just two variables, for example English grades and Maths grades. If we look at these variables, we can make a scatter plot that shows each child's Maths grades on the X-axis, and each child's English grades on the Y-axis (see Figure 24.2).

Regression works by trying to fit a straight line between these data points, so that the overall distance between the points and the line is minimised (it does this using a statistical method called least squares), in this example the diagonal line in Figure 24.2.

The basic regression equation is the following:

$$Y = a + bX$$

Where:

Y = the dependent variable
X = the predictor variable

a = the intercept, or the value of Y when X is zero (what English grades would a student be predicted to get if they scored a 0 in maths?). When you use more

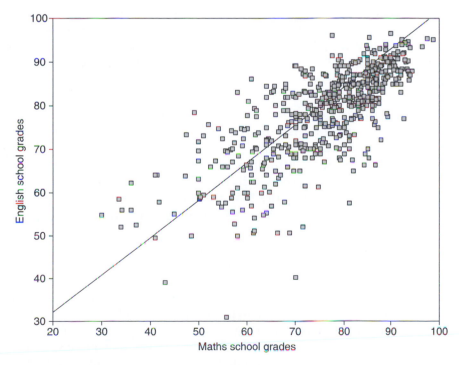

Figure 24.2 Scatter plot of English and Maths scores

than two predictor variables, this value doesn't have a substantive interpretation, and we can ignore it. b = the slope, or the value that Y will change by if X changes by 1 unit. For example, if X was Maths grades, Y was English grades and b was 0.5, this would mean that when a student's maths grades go up by one, we would predict that their English grades go up by 0.5 points. This value is known as the regression *coefficient.*

We can also calculate a *standardised regression coefficient.* This basically rescales all variables to the same scale to make the effect sizes more easily comparable. Standardised regression coefficients, known as Beta values, vary between –1 and +1, and are interpreted in the same way as a correlation coefficient.

When we use more than one predictor, our regression equation becomes:

$$Y = a + b1X1 + b2X2 + b3X3 + \ldots + BnXn$$

where b1 is the coefficient for variable X1, b2 for variable X2, etc. The interpretation is the same as when we had only one predictor, although obviously we cannot graph the relationship, as we are now working in multi-dimensional space.

As well as giving us a coefficient, we can calculate a *p-value*, which, as in correlation analysis, tells us whether or not the relationship is statistically significant (in other words, how likely it is that this relationship would exist in our sample if there was no relationship in the population).

As well as finding out whether the specific variables we have put in our analysis individually are related to the dependent variable, we might also want to know how well all our variables *taken together* (our model) predict the outcome. This is also calculated in regression analysis, as the amount of variance in the dependent variable explained by all the predictors together. This measure is called R squared.

Remembering how important levels of measurement are (is our variable nominal, ordinal or continuous?) and that different levels of measurement call for different types of analysis, you will be asking what type of variables we can use in regression analysis. Multiple linear regression requires the dependent variable to be continuous. The predictor variables can be either continuous, ordinal or nominal, although if they are nominal we have to transform them if they have more than two categories (see below). If our predictors are ordinal, we have to be careful with our interpretation (again, we will discuss this further below).

What multiple linear regression allows us to do is therefore to model the relationship of all our predictors with the dependent variable simultaneously. Essentially, the model we have is as shown in Figure 24.3.

This model, which doesn't allow for indirect effects, is obviously quite a lot simpler than the one we originally hypothesised, and this is one of the main limitations of multiple linear regression. Also, you will see that student gender has not been included in the model. In this book's website materials, (at http://www.sagepub.co.uk/briggs) you can follow how to do this analysis in SPSS.

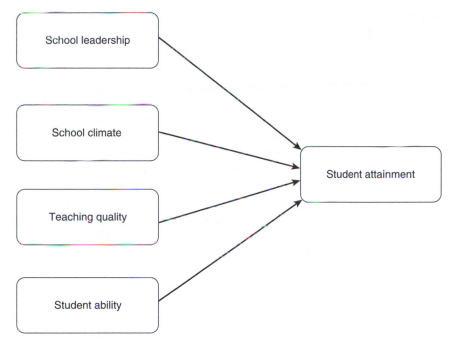

Figure 24.3   School leadership and student outcomes (2)

Using ordinal and nominal variables as predictors

In theory, regression analysis is designed to be used with continuous variables. Both the dependent and independent variables are supposed to be continuous. This obviously limits the extent to which this method can be used to construct models that properly explain the variance in the dependent variable. In our example, this means that there are a number of variables we can't use, like the variables on student attitude (which are ordinal) and the variables that are nominal, like gender.

Ordinal independent variables
Luckily, regression as a method is what we call 'robust'. This means that it works quite well when certain assumptions have not been met. In practice, we can even use ordinal variables in our regression analyses quite successfully. This is good news, as at least one variable in our model is likely to be ordinal. School climate will typically be measured using Likert scales in a questionnaire, and will therefore be ordinal.

Nominal independent variables
The situation with regards to nominal variables like gender is a bit more complicated. Because they are not ordered, we have to create something called *dummy variables* before we can use them in regression. What does this mean? Basically, what we are going to have to do is compare the categories to one

another. For example, if we look at a variable like school type, we may need to compare Catholic, Church of England and State schools. To do this, what we need to do is make one category into our reference category, to which the others are going to be compared. Let's take State schools as our reference category in this example. We are first going to compare children in Catholic schools with children in State schools, and then children in Church of England schools with children in State schools. How do we do this? We will have to make two new variables, one for Catholic and one for Church of England schools. We will have to recode our variable school type so that all Catholic schools are coded as 1, and all other schools as 0 for the first variable, and then we will have to recode our variable school type so that all Church of England schools are coded as 1, and all other schools as 0 for the second variable. As gender, the nominal variable in our model, only has two categories, all we will need to do is make sure one category (for example, boys) is coded 0, and the other (girls) is coded 1.

Assumptions in multiple linear regression

As with most other methods, a number of conditions need to be met before we can use regression analysis with confidence. The two most important conditions are that the relationship between independent and dependent variables must be linear, and that the independent variables shouldn't be too strongly correlated to one another.

1. *Linearity.* This method is not called multiple linear regression for nothing. Multiple linear regression imposes a linear relationship on the data points that describe the relationship between the two variables (see Figure 24.2). If the relationship is non-linear, the model will not fit the data properly. There are many relationships that are not linear, for example where we need to pass a threshold to find any effect, or where the strength of the relationship tails off.

One way of finding out whether the relationship is linear or not is by looking at how many large *residuals* there are. What is a residual? Basically, a residual is the observed value of the dependent variable minus the value predicted by the regression equation, for each case. Or, in other words, how well does our model predict the value of the dependent variable for an individual case? If we look at Figure 24.2, we can see that regression draws a straight line through the data points. This is our predicted regression line. Each individual point (which represents the scores of an individual on the two variables) can be close or further away from that line. The closer to the line, the better the score of that person is predicted by the model. The further away, the worse our prediction. The higher our residual, the further away from the regression line the data point is. Obviously, we want to have as few high residuals as possible, as having many high residuals would suggest that our model does not fit the data, possibly because our relationship is not linear. What we are looking for is how many residuals there are that are more than three standard deviations away from the predicted score. These are cases for which the predictors predict the value of the dependent variable (scores in English) very badly. We need to worry if the number of outliers rises to 10 per cent of the sample or more.

2. *Multicollinearity.* A second major precondition for doing and interpreting regression modelling is that our predictor (or independent) variables mustn't be too strongly correlated with one another. If they are, this will cause serious problems in estimating the relationship between the dependent and predictor variables, as it becomes hard to calculate the individual contribution of each variable. When predictor variables are very highly correlated, we have to wonder whether they are not in fact measuring the same thing, and would be better combined into one new variable. This problem is called *multicollinearity.* We will therefore need to check the correlations between our independent variables. If any two variables have a correlation of .7 or above, we are likely to have multicollinearity problems.

Logistic and ordinal regression

As we saw above, multiple linear regression is only a suitable method if our dependent variable is continuous. However, we might in many cases want to explain ordinal or nominal dependent variables. For example, we might want to look at student attainment in terms of whether or not students get a pass or fail grade. This would make it an ordinal rather than continuous variable. Likewise, we might want to predict what subject choices students will make when they choose to go into higher education. This would be a nominal variable.

Logistic regression

If we have a dependent variable with two categories (for example, pass/fail), we use a method called *logistic regression.* The underlying premise is that we are looking at the probability of getting a certain outcome given certain values of the independent variable. That is, what is the probability of getting a pass or fail given different levels of the independent variables? So, for example, are we more likely to gain a pass if we are female than if we are male, or if we agree strongly rather than agree somewhat that we like school? In logistic regression, there is therefore no assumption that the relationship between the independent and dependent variables is linear, as was the case in multiple linear regression.

The formula for logistic regression is:

$$Y = \log \frac{p}{(1-p)} = b_0 + b_1 x_1 + b_2 x_2 + \cdots + b_n x_n$$

where p is the probability that $Y = 1$ and X_1, X_2, ... ,X_k are the independent variables (predictors). The letters b_0, b_1, b_2, ... b_k are known as the regression coefficients (see above).

Log $(p/(1–p)$ is a predictor of whether the event (for example, pass/fail) is likely to occur, based on the combined values of the independent variables. The values of this predictor variable are then transformed into probabilities by a logistic function, which has the shape of an S. (See Figure 24.4.) On the horizontal axis are the values of the predictor variable, and on the vertical axis the probabilities of the event occurring (Kleinbaum, 1994).

Logistic regression also produces odds ratios (O.R.s) associated with each predictor value. The 'odds' of an event is defined as the probability of the outcome event occurring divided by the probability of the event not occurring. The odds ratio for a predictor is defined as the amount by which the odds of the outcome increase (O.R. greater than 1.0) or decrease (O.R. less than 1.0) when the value of the predictor variable is increased by one unit. So, if the value of the predictor goes up by one unit, do the odds of the event occurring increase or decrease, and by how much?

This is obviously a different method of looking at the relationship between one dependent and several independent variables. However, many aspects will be familiar, for example the regression coefficients, b. Similarly to multiple linear regression, we can calculate p-values for significance. We will, however, also want to have a measure of how well our overall model fits, or, in other words, how well our independent or predictor variables taken together accurately predict the probability of the event happening (or not happening).

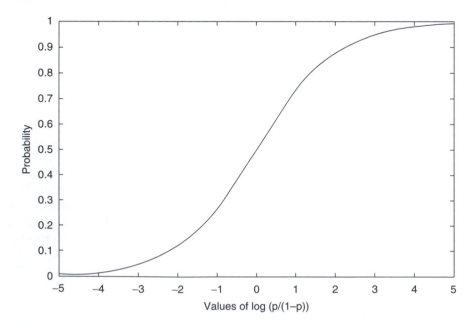

Figure 24.4 The logistic function

Obviously, we can't use the R^2 measure we used in multiple linear regression, as the concept of explained variance doesn't map neatly onto this probability approach. There are two alternative *goodness of fit* measures that have been developed to do this.

The first and most intuitive way of doing this is to compare the predicted result (such as pass or fail) for each individual in our sample with their actual result. This works as follows: on the basis of each individual's ratings on the independent variables, we can predict whether they are likely to get a pass or fail. We have, of course, got their actual score as well, so we can see whether they have in fact passed or failed. We can then easily calculate how many of our predictions were right, and use this as a way of judging how well our model fits. We do need to remember though that, as we have only two possible outcomes (pass or fail), we would expect to randomly be able to accurately predict group membership of 50 per cent of our sample. A well-fitting model should therefore substantially improve on that.

The second type of goodness of fit measures are so-called *Pseudo R^2* measures. As the name implies, these have been designed to 'mimic' the properties of R^2. They will therefore also vary between 0 and 1, with a value of 1 indicating perfect fit and a value of 0 indicating no fit (see above for effect size interpretations). What they essentially do is compare the improvement of the fit of the model that includes our independent variables with a model that does not include any independent variables – the so-called baseline model. What it does *not* do is indicate a percentage variance explained, and it cannot be interpreted in this way!

Ordinal regression

So we now know how to use regression analysis if we have a binomial outcome variable. But what about ordinal variables? For these variables, we will need to use a different method called the *Polytomous Universal Model* (PLUM). What is specific about this model is that instead of considering the probability of an individual event (such as the likelihood of getting a response of 'agree somewhat'), it considers *the probability of that event and all events that are ordered before it.* So, if we had a four-point scale (such as do you agree or disagree that school leadership is the most important factor in improving schools?), our probabilities would be as follows:

- prob. of getting a score of 1 (disagree strongly)
- prob. of getting a score of 1 or 2 (disagree strongly or disagree somewhat)
- prob. of getting a score of 1, 2 or 3 (disagree strongly or disagree somewhat or agree somewhat)
- prob. of getting a score of 1, 2, 3 or 4 (disagree strongly or disagree somewhat or agree somewhat or agree strongly).

The ordinal logistic model is then: $\ln(\theta_j) = \alpha_j - \beta X$

Where (θ_j) is the odds of obtaining a score of category X or lower (see above), j goes from 1 to the number of categories minus 1, and β is the regression coefficient. The method is therefore based on probabilities of reaching thresholds of the dependent variable, depending on the response to the independent variable. This does mean that independent variables can't have too many categories, which means that we usually have to recode continuous variables into variables with four or five categories.

In terms of output, there are many similarities to logistic regression. We will get regression coefficients and significance levels, though these will be calculated for each category of the independent variable. We will also have global measures of fit and *Pseudo R²* measures which are interpreted in the same way as in logistic regression.

Multilevel modelling

What is multilevel modelling?

Another extension of regression modelling, and one that is particularly important in education, is multilevel modelling. Multilevel modelling, also known as hierarchical linear modelling (HLM), is in many ways very similar to multiple regression, in that it is also used to look at the relationship between a dependent variable and one or (usually) more predictor variables. If multilevel analysis essentially does the same thing as regression, why are we bothering with it?

There are two main reasons: one is statistical, the other more substantive and related to fundamental research questions we might want to ask.

The statistical reason is related to sampling. Multiple linear regression (along with most related methods) assumes that we have a random sample from the population of interest. This means that if we want to look at the relationship between school leadership and student achievement with the intention of generalising our findings to the population of students of that age group nationally, we would have to randomly sample students from the whole of the country. This hardly ever happens in educational research, as it would mean that we would end up with 1000 students in something like 900 different schools! This would have obvious cost implications and mean that we would not be able to say anything about the effect of school leadership as we would have too few students in each individual school. After all, if we have only one child in a particular school, that hardly allows us to say anything about children in that school more generally!

Therefore, we usually sample schools, and look at all or a sample of students in those schools. This means we no longer have a random sample. What we now have is a *hierarchical* or *cluster* sample. In that kind of sample, students are *nested* in schools.

This of course may, and usually in educational research will, mean that we are faced with a situation in which students within a school or classroom are more similar to one another on a variety of characteristics than they are to the sample as a whole. One reason for this is that school catchment areas tend to be more homogeneous in terms of the society as a whole.

This has an important statistical consequence. Whenever we have clustered samples, it means that if we just use multiple linear regression and pretend we have a random sample, we will probably be underestimating the extent of standard error of the variance (the standard deviation of the predicted true value for a given observed value). Does this really matter? Yes, as this will lead to the effect of certain predictor variables wrongly being classified as statistically significant when they are not (Snijders and Bosker, 2011).

The second reason to use MLM is substantive. Often in educational research, we are interested in finding out about certain characteristics of schools and classrooms, and how they relate to student characteristics. In our example, we might want to know whether school leadership affects student attainment. What multilevel modelling allows us to do is to look at how much of the variance in students' achievement is explained at the individual level, how much at the classroom level and how much at the school level, for example, and then accurately model variables at the right level. Leadership is, for example, a school-level variable (it affects the whole school), while student ability is a student-level variable (it is a characteristic of an individual student) (Muijs, 2010).

An example of multilevel modelling

In our example, we have a number of student-level variables, in particular student gender, student ability and the outcome variable student attainment and a number of school-level variables, school leadership and school climate (for simplicity, we will leave out teaching quality, which is a classroom-level variable and would introduce an extra level into the analyses). Results of our model are given in Tables 24.1 to 24.3. It is important to point out here that multilevel options in SPSS are very limited, and it is usually better to use bespoke programmes like MLwin or HLM to conduct multilevel analysis. It falls outside the scope of this chapter to discuss this software, but the further reading provides some useful sources.

Table 24.1 Base model

Variable	Coefficients	
Constant	16.97 (1.87)	
Level		**% variance to be explained**
School	18.90 (3.34)	12.3%
Student	134.11 (3.65)	87.7%

In Table 24.1, we can see the predictor variables listed under 'variables'. Here, there is only one 'constant'. The constant is the intercept, just like in multiple regression, and does not have a strong substantive meaning.

The next part of the output is called 'level'. This will tell us how much of the unexplained variance in student achievement (once the effect of beginning-of-year test scores is taken into account) is due to differences between the individual students, and how much is due to the fact that students attend different schools. The first number is again the coefficient, the amount of variance to be explained at that level. The number between brackets is the standard error. As the coefficients in themselves don't mean that much, we usually convert them into percentages. These are given in the final column. As you can see, most of the variance (87.7 per cent) is due to individual differences between students, with a smaller (but significant) percentage being due to the fact that students go to different schools.

In the next step, in Table 24.2, we are going to add some of our independent variables.

Table 24.2 Multilevel model: student attainment predicted by gender and student ability

	Coefficients		
Variable			
Constant	26.18 (6.88)		
Ability	−2.93 (0.59)		
Gender	−0.15 (0.02)		
Level		**% variance to be explained**	**% variance explained**
School	16.31 (3.59)	13.9%	13.7%
Student	101.29 (3.51)	86.1%	32.4%

In the column under 'variable', we can now see the names of the three variables we have added. In the next column, we can once again see the coefficients and the standard errors. The coefficients are similar to our 'b's in multiple regression, and are interpreted in the same way. They are significant if the coefficient (for example, −0.15 for gender) is at least twice as large as the standard error (the number in brackets, for gender that is 0.02).

Gender and ability both have coefficients more than twice as large as the standard error (in brackets), and are therefore statistically significant predictors of the outcome. If we look at the dummy variable gender as an example, we can see that the coefficient for this variable is −.15. This means that boys are predicted to have a score that is 0.15 lower on the end-of-year test.

Under levels we can again see the variance to be explained at the two levels. We can see that in all cases this variance has decreased compared to Table 24.1. For example, variance to be explained at the student level has gone down from 134.11 to 101.29. In the last column, this has been converted to a percentage (32.4). This means that the two variables we have introduced have explained 32.4 per cent of the variance between individual students. Or, put another way, part of the reason for the fact that individual students perform differently on the end-of-year test can be explained by their ability and gender. We can also see that notwithstanding the fact that these variables are measured at the individual student level, they also explain variance at the school level (13.7 per cent). This suggests that schools are somewhat homogeneous with respect to these student variables.

Finally, in Table 24.3, we will introduce the two school-level variables to see whether those can explain some more variance.

Table 24.3 Multilevel model: end-of-year test scores predicted by beginning-of-year test scores, pupil, school and classroom variables

Coefficients			
Variable			
Constant	22.83 (6.88)		
Ability	−2.85 (0.59)		
Gender	−0.14 (0.02)		
School climate	0.32 (0.14)		
School leadership	0.52 (0.15)		
Level		**% variance to be explained**	**% variance explained**
School	5.45 (1.94)	5.1%	66.5%
Student	100.43 (3.48)	94.9%	0.8%

We can now look at the coefficients for the three new variables in the same way. We can see that both school climate and school leadership have a coefficient that is more than twice as large as the standard error (between brackets), and so are statistically significant. The coefficient of .52 suggests that an increase of 1 on the leadership scale is predicted to lead to an increase of 0.52 in student attainment. If we look at the variance for the two levels, we can see that these variables have explained most of the remaining variance at the school level and hardly any of the differences at the individual student level. So leadership and school climate explain differences in attainment caused by students going to different schools, rather than differences due to their individuality, as we would predict.

This example shows that multilevel modelling is useful in telling us more about how our variables are related to one another. We can see that, for example, most of the differences between how students perform are explained by individual differences between students, rather than school or classroom factors. School and classroom factors are significant, however, and can largely be explained by differences in teaching quality.

Structural equation modelling

Why use structural equation modelling (SEM)?

Another method that is being used increasingly in quantitative educational research is structural equation modelling. Like multilevel modelling, it brings the discipline further by solving both substantive and statistical problems that the traditional methods we discussed earlier cannot handle. Like multilevel modelling, it is based on principles used in regression analysis.

A major substantive issue relates to the model we are using to relate our dependent variable to our predictors. In both multiple regression and multilevel modelling, we are basically saying that all our predictors have a direct effect on the dependent variable (see Figure 24.2). This means that we are not directly testing our theoretical model as depicted in Figure 24.1.

Obviously, it would be interesting to test a model like that, as most of our theoretical models in education are likely to look more like the one shown in Figure 24.1 than the one shown in Figure 24.2, because of the complexity of the field. That is exactly what we can do in structural equation modelling.

Another reason why we use structural equation modelling has to do with the issue of measurement error. As you know, whenever we measure anything in education and the social sciences more generally, we do this with a certain amount of error. Our measurement instruments are imperfect, and human beings somewhat unpredictable. Therefore, whenever we measure something like school climate (using a questionnaire item, for example), the scores we get for each respondent will contain two elements: the 'true' score and the measurement error. Obviously, we want our measurement error to be as small as possible. Nevertheless, some measurement error always remains. In our standard regression procedures, we basically ignore this element, and pretend that our scores are accurate. In structural equation modelling, we can go one better and actually take the measurement error into account in our analyses.

This is where the concept of *latent variables* comes in. The underlying idea behind the concept of latent variables is that most of the time we cannot, in the social sciences, directly measure what we want to measure. Think, for example, of school climate. This is not a concept we can directly measure, as it is not a physical object. Instead, we use questions or rating scales to try and measure this, such as 'In this school teachers can ask the head for advice at all times' and 'In this school everyone's opinion is valued'. Each such question or rating scale we call a *manifest variable*. This is what we are actually measuring. We are, as researchers, not necessarily directly interested in these specific items though. What we actually want to know about is the latent variable, school climate. What we can do in structural equation modelling, that we can't do in multiple regression, is look at the relationship between the latent rather than the manifest variables. How do we do this? Well, we tell the software program we are using to do the structural equation modelling that we are going to make a new variable, for example school climate. Then we tell it that this item is made up of a number of manifest variables, such as the ones we gave as examples above (Tolmie et al., 2011).

The SEM program will then tell us whether these manifest variables do indeed form a latent variable, by giving us the fit of this model to the data. It will also be able to partial out the measurement error to a reasonable extent by

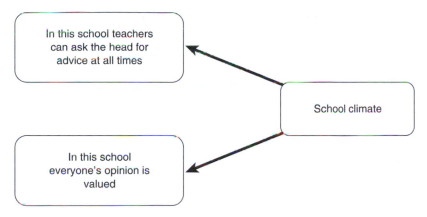

Figure 24.5 Latent and manifest variables

looking at the relationship between the manifest variables and the latent variable. This method is called *confirmatory factor analysis* and is one part of SEM.

As mentioned above, SEM is an extension of multiple regression. Like multiple regression, it will provide us with both coefficients telling us how much Y would change if X increased by 1 (e.g. in our model above, how much would achievement at time 1 go up by if the measure of parental background went up by 1), and a measure of how well the model fits the data. The former are given by the regression coefficients or 'b's. The second, the measure of overall fit to the data, is given by the chi square test (remember that we encountered the chi square test in Chapter 23). There is one important difference between the chi square test as we used it earlier and as we use it here: in order for us to say that the model we have designed fits our data, chi square has to be *non-significant, or >.05*. There is a problem with this chi square measure though, in that with these complex models it is very sensitive to sample size. If our sample is large enough, it will detect even very small divergences of our model from the data, and models tested with large sample sizes almost never fit the data. Therefore, a variety of fit indices have been developed that are less sensitive to sample size, and are now more commonly used to look at whether our model fits the data. We will discuss a few of these below.

An example of the use of structural equation modelling

Like multilevel modelling, SEM is best done using bespoke programs such as LISREL, AMOS or EQS. Our theoretical model, given in Figure 24.1, is a perfect example of the type of relationships we can model. What we would do first is create a measurement model, where the scores on the manifest variables are hypothesised to be determined by the latent variables. Then we would model the way the latent variables affect one another. This is what we have done in the example in Figure 24.6. The numbers next to the arrows are the standardised coefficients, or betas, like the ones we discussed in the section on multiple linear regression analysis (we can get the software to provide us with both the unstandardised 'b's, and standardised betas). If they are in italics, the betas are statistically significant. So, we can see that most of our standardised regression coefficients are statistically significant, with the exception of the relationship between school climate and teaching quality. The strongest relationship, with a standardised coefficient of .44, is that between ability and attainment.

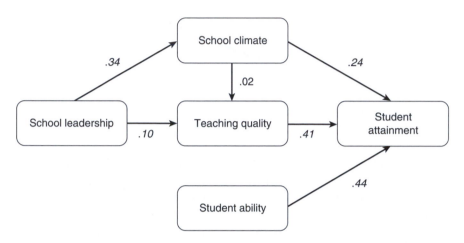

Figure 24.6 Structural equation model

Does our overall model fit the data? As I mentioned earlier, we will have to look at some fit indices to find out. Our chi square test is significant. This means that our model does not fit the data. However, we do have a large sample (over 2000 students), so that might be causing the lack of fit. Because we have a large sample, we will look at some of the alternative fit indices I mentioned earlier that have been designed to be less sensitive to sample size. Three indices that we can look at are the Goodness of Fit Index, the Comparative Fit Index, and the Root Mean Square Error of Approximation. All are calculated in a different way (it goes beyond this book to discuss those different methods here), and it is good practice to look at a number of different indexes to see whether they contradict or confirm one another. As a rule of thumb, we say our model fits the data well if GFI and CFI, which both vary between 0 and 1, are above .95, and if RMSEA is below .05. In this case, GFI was .99, CFI .98 and RMSEA .04. This suggests that our model fits the data quite well.

The conclusion that we can draw is that our hypothesised model is not rejected. However, some important caveats need to be taken into account: first, our model can only test those variables we have collected. There may be variables that we have not included that are more influential than those that we have included. Also, one important thing we need to take into account is that while this model is not rejected by the data, there may be equivalent models which fit the data equally well. For example, it may be that, rather than teaching quality leading to higher attainment, it is the case that teachers are able to perform better when they are teaching a high attaining class. Only if we replicate our model, and do not find any other models that fit the data as well or better, can we be totally confident of our findings. Also, remember that in this example we have got a hierarchical sample (students in classrooms in schools), so because we have not used multilevel modelling we might be overestimating the significance of our relationships. While attempts are ongoing to merge these two useful methods, at present this is still quite difficult to do with real data.

As you can see, structural equation modelling is an extremely useful tool, which allows us to model the complex realities of educational research better than traditional techniques.

Key points

In this chapter, we looked at ways we can model more complex statistical relationships:

- Multiple linear regression can be used to look at the relationship between one continuous dependent variable and several independent variables, allowing us to more accurately look at what can affect outcomes.
- If we have categorical or ordinal outcome variables, we need to adapt our models using, respectively, logistic regression and its extension to ordinal variables, PLUM.
- One issue we often have in educational research is the nested structure of our data, with students grouped in schools, for example. Multilevel modelling allows us to accurately model this structure.
- Many relationships we want to model are complex, with variables having indirect effects on outcomes through mediating variables. Structural equation modelling allows us to model this type of situation.

Questions and reflections

1 Distributed leadership is often said to improve organisational performance. Can you develop a model of the relationship between distributed leadership and an outcome variable related to organisational performance, using whatever mediating variables are appropriate?
2 What statistical method is best suited to testing your model? Why?

Recommended further reading

Draper, N. and Smith, R. (1998) *Applied Regression Analysis*. New York: Wiley.

A classic textbook on regression analysis, this will allow you to develop an in-depth understanding of the method.

Kleinbaum, D. G. (1994) *Logistic Regression*. New York: Springer.

This is a comprehensive statistical description of logistic regression, which does contain significant amounts of maths.

Snijders, T. A. B. and Bosker, R. (2011) *Multilevel Analysis: An Introduction to Basic and Advanced Multilevel Modelling*. Newbury Park, CA: Sage.

This is the best introductory text on multilevel modelling.

Schumacker, R. and Lomax, R. (2010) *A Beginner's Guide to Structural Equation Modeling*. London: Routledge.

There are many textbooks on SEM, but this one manages to be both accessible and comprehensive.

References

Kleinbaum, D. G. (1994) *Logistic Regression*. New York: Springer.
Muijs, D. (2010) *Doing Quantitative Research in Education* (2nd edn). London: Sage.
Snijders, T. A. B. and Bosker, R. (2011) *Multilevel Analysis: An Introduction to Basic and Advanced Multilevel Modelling*. Newbury Park, CA: Sage.
Tolmie, A., Muijs, D. and McAteer, E. (2011) *Quantitative Methods in Educational and Social Research using SPSS*. Ballmoor, Bucks: Open University Press.

CHAPTER 25

Qualitative Data Analysis: Using NVivo

Rob Watling and Veronica James with Ann R.J. Briggs

Chapter objectives

This chapter offers guidelines for the principles and practice of analysing qualitative data, including the use of data analysis software. In particular, the authors seek to clarify and explore:

- The function of data analysis throughout the research process.
- The nature and key elements of qualitative data analysis:
    - defining and identifying data
    - collecting and storing data
    - data reduction and sampling
    - structuring and coding data
    - theory building and theory testing
    - reporting and writing up research.
- Using data analysis software.

Introduction

Analysis is the researcher's equivalent of alchemy – the elusive process by which you hope to turn raw data into nuggets of pure gold. And, like alchemy, such magic calls for science and art in equal measure, whether you are analysing manually or using data analysis software. It might seem that this transformation of data into wisdom is something that can only be done in the later stages of a research project, once the raw material has been safely gathered in: the sorts of analysis you do in your project inevitably depend on the types of research you have undertaken, and the types of data you have collected.

But analysis is not, in practice, something that *can* only be considered towards the end of the project. This is for two main reasons. First, the types of analysis that you are in a position to carry out may determine the types of research you are able to do. If, for example, you do not have the time or resources to analyse 100 in-depth, face-to-face interviews, or to process 1000 text-based questionnaires, or to use diaries with 25 managers, you had better choose another approach. If you feel that qualitative analysis will be too imprecise for your purposes or too vague to act as the basis for generalisation, or too conceptual to have credibility, you may already have chosen to adopt a more quantitative approach which will require different analytic techniques. So the first point to recognise is that some decisions about analysis may actually *precede* important decisions about methods. But the second point is just as important. The analysis of data, particularly of qualitative data, takes place throughout the project. It is an iterative and persistent part of the research process. This is true whether you are using an electronic package or not.

Imagine that you are going to conduct a series of interviews with managers at a further education college. In selecting the college that you want to visit, you will already be considering some of its key features (its size, its general type, its suitability for your project, and so on). You will certainly do some basic background research about its policies and practice. When you arrive at the college to conduct your interviews, you will form some important first impressions of the place, such as the neighbourhood in which it is located, the state of the college buildings, the demeanour of the students, whether it is welcoming to visitors, and so on. Before you start the interviews, you may have general discussions with the people you have come to meet, and these are likely to give you more information about the place. By now, you will understand quite a lot about the college you have chosen for your research. Indeed, you will have started to analyse some important qualitative data. Throughout the interviews, you will be 'reading' the situation – making sense of the interviewees' words and interpreting their body language. You are bound to form judgements, hunches, prejudices, theories, hypotheses and further questions as you go along.

By the end of the day, you will have conducted the interviews, responded to the managers' answers in order to get more detail, probably added a new question to your schedule, formed some key judgements, come to some tentative conclusions about their management style, left the building, reflected on the visit, challenged some of your own assumptions and written up your field notes. You will, in the process, have analysed a huge amount of qualitative data. And that is just one field visit.

This key recognition that analysis pervades every aspect of qualitative enquiry is an important one. Whether they realise it or not, all qualitative researchers have to analyse parts of the data while they are designing the project; when they are conducting their desk-based research; when they are doing their fieldwork; while they are storing, retrieving and handling their records; when they are building and testing theories; and when they are writing up their report. This chapter considers some of the ways in which analysis can take place at any or all of these stages and encourages you to realise that data analysis is rarely a separate or distinct activity in its own right.

Systems and software

Some people are free-thinking, free-floating individuals who can live with the organic mess produced by most qualitative research, and come out at the end with a seamless and well-rounded research report. But most people fall back on systems of one sort or another, be it field notes, diagrams, computer templates and files or data analysis software. Throughout this chapter, we emphasize the use of systematic and secure methods of data collection, storage and retrieval. It is important also to use analytical processes and systems which you understand, which are reliable and which you can justify.

When you choose to use data analysis software, remember that software cannot 'do analysis for you'. The analytical thinking is yours, assisted by the software. What data analysis packages can do is enable you to handle and analyse qualitative data more systematically, comprehensively and effectively than you may be able to achieve by other methods. You may read accounts of researchers' frustration and disappointment with earlier versions of analytical packages; however, software currently available is user-friendly and can greatly enhance your analytical capability. Many qualitative researchers find that the practical benefits of data analysis software, particularly for the management of large quantities of data, far outweigh the disadvantages of learning a new system.

The introduction of software for qualitative data analysis has, however, been controversial. It has been challenged for distorting the epistemological basis of qualitative research, and for fragmenting and potentially quantifying what should be regarded as free-flowing text. On the other hand, it offers transparency to the analytical process, enabling the researcher to clarify and track their theoretical thinking, and militates against a tendency towards anecdotalism which had been a feature of some qualitative research (see Bryman, 2008: 566–7 for a summary of these debates).

At each stage of the chapter, we consider the links between the principles of qualitative analysis and the process of analysis, including analysis using computer-assisted (or computer-aided) qualitative data analysis software (CAQDAS). The commercial package chosen, for example, is NVivo, as it is widely used at the time of writing. Theory-building software of this kind includes code-and-retrieve facilities, which emphasise relationships between categories and (where appropriate) enable numerical counting of data. They help users to develop higher-order themes, and formulate propositions which can then be tested. During the lifetime of this book, this type of software will no doubt be further expanded and developed: our purpose therefore is to offer generic advice as to how using such software can enable the analytical process.

Methods and methodology

As most chapters in this book affirm, researchers are constantly faced with a series of choices and options about research methods. What they are doing in response to these options is less about making the 'right' choice than about making the 'best' choice in their particular circumstances – they are seeking the optimum choice. It is not necessarily 'right' to take a positivist or interpretivist position, to use a standardised measure of literacy or to organise a focus group. The decision needs to be made and justified in the particular context of the research you are undertaking.

The same is true of the approach that you take to analysing your data, whether these data are qualitative, quantitative or – as is likely – a mixture of both. The important thing is that you, the researcher, make the decisions thoughtfully, systematically, critically and in ways which can be accounted for. In this way, when you come to defend your work, you will be able to justify your choice of methods (the tools, techniques, instruments and approaches you have adopted) through a clear methodology (a study and an account of the arguments and the philosophical underpinnings of your work). In the analysis of qualitative research, that means making a series of deliberate, critical choices about the meanings and values of the data you have gathered, and making sure that your decisions can be justified in terms of the research, the context in which it was carried out and the people who were involved in it. Nothing less will do.

Denzin and Lincoln (2003) describe this collection of processes as bricolage – 'a pieced-together, close-knit set of representations that are fitted to the specifics of a complex situation' (2003: 5) and go on to look at some of the key skills of the bricoleur – the flexible, creative, intuitive qualitative researcher who seeks to produce an in-depth understanding of complex social phenomena:

> The ... bricoleur is adept at performing a large number of diverse tasks, ranging from interviewing to observing, to interpreting personal and historical documents, to intensive self-reflection and introspection. The ... bricoleur reads widely and is knowledgeable about the many paradigms that can be brought into any particular problem.

> The ... bricoleur understands that research is an interactive process shaped by his or her personal history, biography, gender, social class, race, and ethnicity, and those of the people in the setting. The ... bricoleur knows that science is power, for all research findings have political implications. There is no value-free science. ... The bricoleur also knows that researchers all tell stories about the worlds they have studied ...

> The product of the bricoleur's labour is a complex, quiltlike bricolage, a reflexive collage or montage – a set of fluid, interconnected images and representations ... connecting the parts to the whole. (2003: 9)

In carrying out our research, we should aim to contribute new knowledge: something that was not already known. New information, by itself, has limited value: it is about 'what' rather than 'why'. The process of analysis seeks to 'explain the nature of the thing being studied' in order to arrive at general principles which can be applied elsewhere to other situations (Denscombe, 2007: 256). In other words, analysis 'involves the study of complex things in order to identify their basic elements. It calls on the researcher to discover the key components or general principles underlying a particular phenomenon so that these can be used to provide a clearer understanding of that thing' (Denscombe, 2007: 106).

The six elements of qualitative data analysis

In order to understand and analyse your own data in the context of what is already known and understood, you need to read widely, not just in the educational leadership literature, but more broadly within the field of education and outwards into the whole range of the social sciences. This will enable you to make reflective, systematic and critical judgements which will give insight into your data and enable your process of analysis.

When we look at other people's research, and at our own, we can identify a series of different stages where analytic processes can be found. For the purpose of this chapter, we have chosen six (see Figure 25.1) though some research projects will have more or fewer than this. We will discuss them in turn, giving examples from published research, suggesting the types of analysis that might occur under any of them and linking this thinking to the use of analytical software. We do not want to imply that Figure 25.1 represents a blueprint for action. Rather, it is a guide to some of the ways in which analysis might be located throughout a qualitative research project.

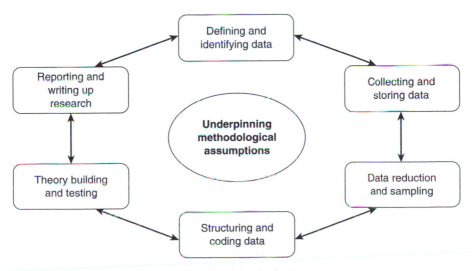

Figure 25.1 Six elements of qualitative data analysis

Defining and identifying data

What do we mean by 'data' – especially in a qualitative study? It is a term with distinctly positivist origins, coming from the Latin and meaning 'things that are given'. It implies a scientific, objective approach to reality in which there is a fixed (a given) world of known and knowable facts for us to discover. It has been argued that with new technologies for qualitative analysis, the practical differences between qualitative and quantitative analysis will diminish (Ryan and Russell Bernard, 2003). However, as we have seen elsewhere in this book, such a view is not always accepted, especially by those who argue that reality is socially constructed and that truths are negotiated by actors in specific contexts:

> Fundamentally, we think that social phenomena exist not only in the mind, but in the objective world as well, and that there are some lawful, reasonably stable relationships to be found among them. The lawfulness comes from the sequences and the regularities that link phenomena together; it is from these that we derive the constructs that account for individual and social life. (Huberman and Miles, 1998: 182)

The qualitative researcher, especially one working within such an epistemological framework, is likely to be searching for understanding, rather than facts; for interpretations rather than measurements; for values rather than information. And the scientific notion of 'data' sometimes sits uncomfortably in such discussions. Some researchers are not happy with the word at all, preferring to write about evidence, information or material rather than data. For the purposes of clarity within this chapter, however, we have retained the term.

Whatever term you decide to use for 'data', it is important to acknowledge what, for you, the term includes. Once you move away from the analysis of given, measurable and objectively verifiable facts, to the analysis of thoughts, feelings, expressions and opinions which are open to debate, there is a clear requirement to make justifiable choices about what to include and what to leave out of your account. In doing so, you are already involved in a process of analysis – weighing up the value and worth of specific things and deciding whether or not they are likely to 'count' in the research. How much of an interview, for example, will you count as evidence? Is it only the spoken words? Is it also the gestures and body language of the interviewee (Keats, 2000)? Is it also the things people omit to say which you will regard as important? And how will you record and analyse the non-spoken evidence?

Even at the design stage, we can see that researchers are weighing up alternatives and making choices. For example, Eslea and Mukhtar (2000) identify what needs to be researched, partly by analysing what others have left out of their work:

> The study reported here is an attempt to address some of the problems identified in the bullying and racism research to date. Clumsy definitions, inappropriate questionnaires, white researchers and the unnecessary

lumping together of non-white ethnic groups mean that little can be concluded about the real experiences of ethnic minority children in British
schools. Any hypothesis must therefore be tentative: experiences of racism
and bullying may vary according to country of origin, language, religion,
clothing, food, rituals, and so on. On the one hand, one might expect the
political tensions between India and Pakistan to be reflected in hostility
between children of these nationalities, and on the other hand, that tension between Hindu and Muslim children might be found regardless of
nation. Another possibility is that bullying may reflect the relative propor-
tions of different ethnic groups in the local population. This study
attempts to begin the process of untangling these possibilities, in order to
provide a richer understanding of bullying among Asian schoolchildren in
Britain. (2000: 210)

In a further example, when describing the methods used in their study of
English Local Education Authorities (LEAs) and their role in carrying out
teacher capability procedures, Marchington et al. (2004) make a series of
points about their sample, all of which we may presume are relevant to their
ultimate analysis. We have inserted italics in Marchington's account to indicate where key stages of analysis may have taken place:

First a postal survey of all English LEAs was used to ascertain the numbers
of heads and teachers on capability procedures during 1999–2000. *Using
data provided by the postal survey* over 20 LEAs were asked to participate in
a second stage of the project, *selected on the basis of usage of procedures, a
geographical spread, type of LEA and mix of urban and rural areas* ...

The next stage involved brief structured telephone interviews with
headteachers ... Five hundred and twenty telephone interviews were then
carried out with a random sample of headteachers in the chosen LEAs ...
Using the data from the telephone interviews, the research team selected case-
study schools so as to provide a spread of *size and type of school, the type of
'capability' issues, and the outcome for the individual teacher*. Fifty three case
studies in 45 schools were carried out, all of which involved face-to-face
interviews with the headteacher. Additionally, over 100 further interviews
were held with LEA officers, personnel managers and advisors, officials
and representatives of six teacher associations, and with teacher colleges.
Finally, *seven different LEA capability procedures were itemized alongside several from voluntary-aided schools.* (2004: 28–9)

This process shows how analysis and sampling are inextricably linked, and are
not only carried out at the beginning of the project.

Defining and identifying data using NVivo

Your sampling – of locations, respondents and data types – is reflected and
recorded in the framework which you set up in NVivo. The software invites you
to import data – for example, interviews, field notes, documentary data – from

standard software such as Word for textual analysis. The different types of data – interviews, field notes, etc. – may be kept in different sets of folders. By allocating attributes to each document, you can retrieve and analyse items of data easily, and you will also be able to sort and link your data sets as your analysis progresses. Other sources, such as video files, audio files and Web pages, may be linked externally to your project folder and still be readily available for analysis.

From your initial thinking about the project – What do I want to find out? Within what critical frameworks? – you start to construct a sequence of nodes, which are the routes by which coding of your data will be undertaken. This process of setting up the project within the data analysis package offers useful frameworks for thinking and for project organisation. The choices you make about the organization and labelling of your data sets, and your initial thinking about node labels, reflect and inform your analytical process.

Collecting and storing data

During the collection of qualitative data, most researchers start to form opinions and judgements. Let us look briefly at some of Watling's own field notes written after a semi-structured interview with a group of teachers piloting a new curriculum project. He was exploring the extent to which the curriculum project was trying to be informative (introducing new areas of knowledge into the curriculum) or transformative (supporting social change):

> The discussion then moved on to consider some aspects of the distinction between two aspects of the project identified in the interim report as its informative and transformative goals ... During the first few minutes of this part of the discussion, I detected a reluctance on the part of the team to acknowledge a transformative ambition. I was not sure whether to put this down to humility, reservation or disagreement with my basic question.

> The team began by suggesting that the pilot was interested first in transforming the teachers and the assumptions of teaching and learning that are inherent in some other subjects. There has also been a transformative element of the work as it is carried out in schools, and this needs to be linked (hopefully) to a wider view of what schools are, how they operate, and what they are 'for'. This, in turn, is linked to the wider aspirations of the current review of the curriculum. (Watling, personal field notes)

We can see that it is *during* the interview itself that theories start to form in the researcher's mind. These theories may be tentative, provisional or unfinished. They may be dispensed with later on or may prove to be key elements of the final analysis. But, once again, it is important to recognise that they are not left till the end of the research, and that their 'value' needs to be judged by the researcher within the context of the data collection. It is also advisable, at times like this, to check your analysis by sharing these observations with the people you are working with – whether that is your research and work colleagues, or the participants in your research.

Finally in this section, consider the ways in which you store your data and make them accessible for analysis. Whether your data are on paper, in note-books, on proformas, on digital, audio or video recordings, on computer files or anywhere else, it is important to organise them early on in the research process in ways that will be helpful to you later.

Denscombe (2007: 298–9) offers sound advice on the organisation and storage of data, which we have edited and annotated below. In each of the points, Denscombe's text is the first statement, with italics as in the original:

First and foremost, *back-up copies should be made of all original materials.* Label the raw data-recordings, field notes, original documents – to identify their source (see below), copy them and store the originals carefully in a separate location from the working copies, using the back-up copies for analysis. This advice applies just as strongly for electronically recorded and stored data as for other media.

Second, as far as possible, *all materials should be collated and organised in a compatible format.* For example, use the same software templates for all text files. This is important whether using paper-based methods of analysis or electronic packages. Standardised formats allow for easier analysis across data sets.

Third, where possible, *the data should be collated in a way that allows researchers' notes and comments to be added alongside at a later stage.* Set up your field notebook – paper or electronic – with a wide right-hand margin. Where line-by-line analysis of text is to be carried out, number each line and leave a wide right-hand margin for notes. Alternatively, insert text data into a table with extra columns added for labelling and annotation. NVivo has space for coding stripes at the side of the screen linked to sec-tions of text, and for further notes at the bottom, also linked to the section of text under analysis.

Fourth, it is very important that *each piece of 'raw data' material should be identified with a unique serial number or code for reference purposes.* This will enable you to locate material easily and to move back and forth through the data without confusion. The serial code or 'Document Attributes' in NVivo should indicate the research site, date and time, respondent(s) and other key descriptors.

You will find further advice on the storage and preparation of data in Chapter 11.

Collecting and storing data using NVivo

As you can see, much of the generic advice about safe storage and retrieval applies equally when you are using a software package. When preparing data for importing into NVivo, consider to what extent the text needs to be 'tidied up', with hesitations and colloquialisms removed, or whether these 'messier' elements are essential to the analytical process. It is good practice at this stage to also carry out whatever anonymisation of data is needed. Your original files, with the authentic names (and authentic language) are safely stored elsewhere. Where you have undertaken to present your research data in anonymised form, it is best to have the anonymised version as your working document.

The initial theory building referred to above in relation to Watling's research is reflected in the further development of the nodes created for data analysis. We will discuss nodes (and codes) further in the section on coding.

Data reduction and sampling

It is unlikely that any researcher will present all the data gathered during their project, especially if they are using approaches discussed elsewhere in this book which are likely to produce large amounts of rich, deep data. In your data collection process, you may have reached 'saturation point', where new data added do not enable you to learn anything new. All data are reduced, filtered and sampled through the process of analysis. It is sometimes necessary to reduce the data by purposive methods, working on the basis of what you already know to be important or relevant, and the intended purpose of the investigation. There may be sections of data which are not relevant to the line of analysis which you are following. On the other hand, there may be data sets which seem to encapsulate what is evident in the other data, and upon which you wish to focus for more detailed analysis. You need to weigh up carefully the value of evidence to your project as you go along, taking informed judgements on its relevance to your work, to interpret it and to use it as the basis for your understandings and your explanations. Never exclude data simply because they seem to offer 'inconvenient truths'.

One aspect of data reduction concerns the use of respondent quotations. Judicious use of quotations brings your research account alive, providing vivid and rich word pictures which can be very exciting and offer direct contact between the reader and respondent. It is important not just to 'cherry-pick' quotations, but to use those which best sum up an important point which is emerging through your analysis, or which are unique but illuminating. At this stage of the research process, it is a good idea to mark a number of quotations which may be of particular illustrative use.

Data reduction and sampling using NVivo

One advantage of using an electronic package is that it can enable you to handle larger and more numerous data sets in your analysis, so you may not need to reduce your data at all. You could choose to import all of your data files into NVivo, and evaluate their relevance to the project during the process of coding (discussed in the next section). It might still be a good idea to exclude material which falls clearly outside the purpose of your research, or which you feel is not authentic or trustworthy. NVivo also offers an easy way to mark the quotations you have chosen, and to link them through your coding or notes.

Structuring and coding data

Almost everything that we have considered so far is what we might call *formative analysis*. It reflects the epistemological and ontological aspects of qualitative research projects which seek to provide understandings and explanations, and actively shape the types of data collection carried out. These perspectives *allow* and *require* the researcher to analyse aspects of their subject iteratively and reflexively. The more easily recognisable processes of analysis begin once we have safely collected and stored our data. As we listen to our recordings, as we prepare and read our transcripts and other documents, as we revisit our research journals, we have to start to make some sense of it all. At this listening and reading stage, you have a real opportunity to build in the originality of research that Denscombe (2007) refers to. The structuring and coding of data underpin the key research outcomes, and can be used to shape the data to test, refine or confirm established theory, apply theory to new circumstances or use it to generate a new theory or model.

The ways of proceeding with this stage of analysis are varied, and some are highly specialised. They include indexing, coding, content analysis discourse analysis, and others. In Chapter 13, you will find advice about the various types of coding used in grounded research. Fielding (2002) uses the term 'coding' generically when he notes:

> 'Coding' is fundamental to qualitative data analysis. The corpus has to be divided into segments and these segments assigned codes ... which relate to the analytic themes being developed. Researchers aim for codes which capture some essential quality of the segment, and which apply to other segments too. (2002: 163)

Coding involves putting tags or labels against large or small pieces of data, in order to attach meaning to them and to index them for further use. Codes may be pre-specified, based upon the aims of the project and the concepts upon which it is based, or they may emerge as the analysis proceeds, or a combination of both these approaches may be used. As an example, the following list of NVivo codes was used for the analysis of the Baseline Report for 14–19 reforms (Gorard et al., 2009):

> Partnership; Employers; Resources: staffing; Resources: physical; Values; Learning support; Curriculum range; Curriculum pathway; Curriculum uptake; Learning process; Learning; Student voice; Staff workload; Staff stress; Learner outcome: enjoyment; Learner outcome: achievement; Learner outcome: participation; Learner outcome: citizenship; Effectiveness; Efficiency.

Basic coding, carried out as a first step in the analysis of data, is both useful in itself and acts as a preparation of the data for more advanced analysis at higher levels of abstraction (Punch, 2011). At each stage, a clear definition for each code is needed, so that codes may be applied consistently over the period of analysis and over a range of data. This is as important for the single-handed researcher as it is for researchers acting as part of a team. Inevitably, codes are re-assessed as the process of analysis proceeds and understanding of the topic deepens. Where this happens, code definitions have to be reworked and initial drafts of analysis re-coded.

Accounts of coding techniques are easy to find in any of the quality research methods handbooks and in data analysis software manuals. But we stress that the techniques you choose to manage your own data are intricately related to the methodological choices you make elsewhere in your work. It is important to use them critically and not just instrumentally.

Structuring and coding data using NVivo

Coding lies at the heart of data analysis software such as NVivo, and it is an increasingly powerful tool as new versions of software are developed. Coding in NVivo is carried out by creating a set of nodes. These tags and labels can be free-standing code descriptors or can be arranged in families and hierarchies to indicate levels of association between the coding concepts identified. Text is imported into NVivo from standard software packages, and the researcher adds document attributes for easy collation, comparison and retrieval of data. Users are also encouraged to use a range of fonts, formats, colours and highlights to identify and mark passages for review.

The researcher analyses the text of the imported interview, field description, case document or other source by applying coding stripes, based upon the node descriptions, to large or small sections of text. Multiple stripes can be applied to any section of text. *In vivo codes* can be derived from the language of research participants, and applied in response to specific words in the text under analysis. To aid the process of analysis, memo links can be entered against your document, linked to the text you are considering.

As you build up your set of analysed documents in NVivo, you can search across the documents for occurrences of specific codes, and you can also search for instances where two or more codes occur together. Specific items of text can also be searched – and counted, if you wish. These processes of collation and analysis across documents (even across the work of separate research teams) are much more easily and accurately carried out through software such as NVivo than through manual techniques. One important factor to bear in mind, however, is that your analysis is only as good as your choice and application of codes. It can be a useful (and sobering) practice to have more than one researcher analyse a section of text, to ensure parity of analysis and to clarify understanding of the concepts behind the codes.

Theory building and theory testing

We commented earlier that an important purpose of research is to generate new knowledge. So how do we do this? Huberman and Miles (1998) describe a set of 'tactics' for generating meaning from qualitative data which they summarise as follows:

Numbered 1 to 13, they are roughly arranged from the descriptive to the explanatory, and from the concrete to the more abstract: *Noting patterns and themes* (1), *seeing plausibility* – making initial, intuitive sense (2) – and *clustering* by conceptual grouping (3) help one to see connections (between the various pieces of data). *Making metaphors,* a kind of figurative grouping of data (4), is also a tactic for achieving more integration among diverse pieces of data. *Counting* (5) is a familiar way to see 'what's there' – and to keep oneself honest.

Making contrasts and comparisons (6) is a classic tactic meant to sharpen understanding by clustering and distinguishing observations. Differentiation is also needed, as in *partitioning variables,* unbundling variables that have been prematurely grouped, or simply taking a less monolithic look (7).

More abstract tactics include *subsuming particulars into the general, shuttling back and forth between first-level data and more general categories* (8); *factoring* (9) and analogue of a familiar quantitative technique, allowing the analyst to move from a large number of measured variables to a smaller set of unobserved, usually hypothetical, variables; *noting relations between variables* (10); and *finding intervening variables* (11). Finally, assembling a coherent understanding of a data set is helped through *building a logical chain of evidence* (12) and *making conceptual/theoretical coherence,* typically through comparison with the referent constructs in the literature (13). (Huberman and Miles, 1998: 187)

You will notice that Huberman and Miles's 13 tactics take us from simple labelling of patterns and themes in the data (basic coding) through to theory building, which is the subject of this section. In their description, we can identify an iterative process whereby theories about the data are generated, tested and applied at various stages. Some may need to be rejected, or adapted if they are going to be retained. If there is space in your research report, you can describe these changes in your theory base – discussing the alternative viewpoints you have considered and explaining why some of them were not thought suitable. To build and test your theories in this way, as you progress through the research, is one way of showing your critically analytical approach to your work. You will find further accounts and examples of theory building through modelling in Chapter 26 of this text and in the online annex to Chapter 26.

Theory building and theory testing using NVivo

NVivo enables theoretical thinking in a variety of ways. We have already noted the capacity of the software for collation and comparison of data. The nodes that you use for coding can be arranged in hierarchies or trees (see tactics 10, 11 and 12 above) and relationship nodes can be inserted where the researcher notes a significant link between the concepts being analysed. Once portions of data have been coded, queries can be used to test out hunches about your data, to investigate patterns and connections. Models can be created to display and explore what you have been investigating in your project, giving a visual display of the links between the concepts you have used. All of these tools enable you to 'stand above' your data to see the bigger patterns of knowledge you have been exploring, and to formulate theory.

Reporting and writing up research

Some of the 'findings' of qualitative research (again, this term has a positivist heritage that not everyone is comfortable with) only really start to emerge when you begin drafting the final report. As you construct an argument based on what you have done, the things you have seen and heard, the people you have worked with, and the data you have handled, some more analysis is not just permissible, it is almost inevitable. The final threading together of the piece, the weight you give to each part of the argument, the elaboration of a line of thought – all these constitute a final round of analysis. Richardson (2003) considers our approach to writing as the final frontier in our efforts to make research come alive to a wider audience:

> I write because I want to find something out. I write in order to learn something that I didn't know before I wrote it. I was taught, however, as perhaps you were, too, not to write until I knew what I wanted to say, until my points were organized and outlined. No surprise, this static writing model coheres with mechanistic scientism and quantitative research. But, I will argue, the model is itself a sociohistorical invention that reifies the static social world imagined by our 19th-century foreparents. The model has serious problems: it ignores the role of writing as a dynamic, creative process; it undermines the confidence of beginning qualitative researchers because their experience of research is inconsistent with the writing model; and it contributes to the flotilla of qualitative writing that is simply not interesting to read because adherence to the model requires writers to silence their own voices and to view themselves as contaminants.
>
> Qualitative researchers commonly speak of the importance of the individual researcher's skills and aptitudes. The researcher – rather than the survey, the questionnaire, or the census tape – is the 'instrument' … Yet they are taught to conceptualize writing as 'writing up' the research, rather than as an open place, a method of discovery. (2003: 501–2)

Richardson goes on to propose a whole range of creative writing practices that can support analysis in these stages of research. She also suggests a series of writing exercises which might encourage you to be more versatile and to adopt new processes for analysis. Our only caveat would be to remind students that their work is likely to be assessed by people who are firmly rooted in the writing traditions she is trying to challenge. It may be a strategy which delivers risk as much as it offers liberation.

Reporting and writing up research using NVivo
The main advantage of NVivo when you come to write your final report is the relative accessibility both of your analysed documents and your emergent thinking. You may choose to import into your text 'screen dumps' of analysed data, or the models you have created, in order to illustrate your methods of working and its theoretical outcomes. You have ready access to illustrative quotations, linked to the concepts you are exploring. In visual presentations, the 'live items' behind elements of NVivo models can be accessed to demonstrate the data behind the theory. The structure which you have created for your project in NVivo can also suggest a structure for your writing, working your way through the interconnected themes and concepts recorded in the linked nodes, in order to present the theory you have built.

Conclusion

We have argued that analysis is an integral part of the whole research process – especially when you are dealing with qualitative data. It informs and responds to the types of research you are able to conduct, it shapes and is shaped by the subject of your work, and it pervades each and every aspect of the research process from project design to the writing of the report. Most important, the processes of analysis, whether they are manual or electronic, are inextricably linked to the other methodological choices you make throughout your work. As such, they need to be accounted for, justified, critically evaluated and (we hope) celebrated.

Key points

- Analysis is integral to every stage of the research process.
- Analysis is inextricably linked to choices about methodology.
- Qualitative analysis should be as rigorous, transparent and systematic as quantitative analysis.
- Data analysis software can increase the researcher's capacity to analyse and theorise, but it cannot 'analyse data for you'.

Questions and reflections

1 Why do I undertake qualitative research?
2 How can my analysis of qualitative data reflect and support my purposes in undertaking qualitative research?
3 How can I best use my chosen methods of analysis to create new knowledge?

Recommended further reading

Bell, J. (2010) *Doing Your Research Project* (5th edn). Milton Keynes: Open University Press.

This classic text is helpful in all aspects of your research, including data analysis.

Bryman, A. (2008) *Social Research Methods* (3rd edn). Oxford: Oxford University Press.

This comprehensive text has a useful chapter on computer-assisted qualitative data analysis.

Denscombe, M. (2010) *The Good Research Guide: For Small-scale Social Research* (4th edn). Buckingham: Open University Press.

This is another essential for understanding how to undertake small-scale research, with a helpful chapter on qualitative data analysis.

References

Bryman, A. (2008) *Social Research Methods* (3rd edn). Oxford: Oxford University Press.

Denscombe, M. (2007) *The Good Research Guide: For Small-scale Social Research,* (3rd edn). Maidenhead: Open University Press/McGraw-Hill Education.

Denzin, N. K. and Lincoln, Y. S. (2003) *Collecting and Interpreting Qualitative Materials.* London: Sage.

Eslea, M. and Mukhtar, K. (2000) Bullying and racism among Asian schoolchildren in Britain. *Educational Research* 42(2): 207–17.

Fielding, N. (2002) Automating the ineffable: qualitative software and the meaning of qualitative research, in May, T. (ed.) *Qualitative Research in Action.* London: Sage.

Gorard, S., Lumby, J., Briggs, A. R. J., Morrison, M., Hall, I., Maringe, F., See, B. H., Shaheen, R. and Wright, S. (2009) *14–19 Reforms: QCA Centre Research Study – Commentary on the Baseline of Evidence 2007–2008.* London: Qualifications and Curriculum Authority.

Huberman, A. M. and Miles, M. B. (1998) Data management and analysis methods, in Denzin, N. K. and Lincoln, Y. S. (eds) *Collecting and Interpreting Qualitative Materials.* London: Sage.

Keats, D. M. (2000) *Interviewing: A Practical Guide for Students and Professionals.* Buckingham: Open University Press.

Marchington, L., Earnshaw, J., Torrington, D. and Ritchie, E. (2004) The Local Education Authority's role in operating teacher capability procedure. *Journal of Educational Management Administration and Leadership* 32(1): 25–44.

Punch, K. F. (2011) *Introduction to Research Methods in Education.* London: Sage.

Richardson, L. (2003) Writing: a method of enquiry, in Denzin, N. K. and Lincoln, Y. S. (eds) *Collecting and Interpreting Qualitative Material.* London: Sage.

Ryan, G. and Russell Bernard, H. (2003) Data management and analysis methods, in Denzin, N. K. and Lincoln, Y. S. (eds) *Collecting and Interpreting Qualitative Materials.* London: Sage.

CHAPTER 26

Academic Writing

Ann R. J. Briggs

Chapter objectives

This chapter offers guidance for those who are relatively new to academic writing, and for more experienced writers who wish to consider their practice. Its objectives are as follows:

- To encourage writers to consider the purpose of their writing, and especially to prioritise the needs of the reader.
- To examine the critical and analytical nature of academic writing, considering ways in which new insights and understandings are grounded in the material presented and set in the context of previous knowledge.
- To discuss the writing process itself: the ways in which text is created from a range of working documents to present an appropriate flow of argument.
- To look at the process of drafting and editing, and finally of dissemination.

The purpose of academic writing

Why am I writing? What am I writing about? Who am I writing for? These questions, and their answers, are an important basis for how and what we choose to write. In the context of this book, the purpose of academic writing is to communicate the outcomes of research into some aspect of educational leadership or management. This communication might be in any of the following forms:

- a Masters or Doctoral dissertation or thesis
- an article for an academic journal
- a book

- a conference paper
- a research report to a funding body
- an evaluative report for an employer
- teaching materials
- web-based dissemination of any of the above.

This list is not exhaustive, and it is easy to see that the purpose, and therefore the form, of the writing differs from one to another. An evaluative report for your own organisation is written differently from an academic journal article. The overall structure, the contents and language change according to context and purpose. Even within communication types, there may be a range of potential purposes, which affect the way we choose to write. A conference paper might focus on one discrete element of a research project, or it could aim to give a 'helicopter perspective' of what has been learned from the project as a whole. It might therefore focus upon the fine detail of the data, their analysis and implications, or have a stronger focus on concepts and theory.

So what is your purpose in writing? Are you aiming to do one or more of the following?

Describe: present qualitative or quantitative data with an explanatory commentary

Narrate: 'tell the story' of a sequence of events, usually to probe for deeper meaning

Compare: explore the likenesses and differences between two or more sets of data

Synthesise: draw together sets of data or published material to explore their collective meaning

Evaluate: assess the quality or degree of success of a particular leadership activity

Theorise: place findings within a current theoretical framework, or present the knowledge gained from research as a new aspect of theory.

Whether the writing is extensive (as in a Doctoral thesis or a book) or concise (as in an academic paper), achievement of its over-arching purpose is likely to entail elements of other purposes. A paper which seeks to present new theory may necessarily involve description or comparison. Moreover, the over-arching purpose may change as we write. For example, we might seek to compare the effectiveness of one educational leader's response to a particular government policy initiative with that of another leader. Once we have decided how we might evaluate effectiveness (a thorny problem in itself), and collected our data on leadership approaches and indicators of effectiveness, our over-arching purpose is comparison: considering the likenesses and differences between the data sets, and what we may learn from comparing them. However, during the process of analysis and writing, theorisation might become more important than the initial purpose of comparison: we realise that the construction of theory has become the main purpose of the paper. We now have to reconsider the structure and wording of the paper, in order to suit the new purpose of theorisation – and re-think the title and the abstract. It is important to understand the element of discovery which the writing process engenders, and be prepared to treat early drafts as an initial exploration of the subject, rather than the finished article.

Remembering the reader

A repeated theme in this chapter is: 'Remember the reader'. There is little point in writing if the reader cannot follow our arguments or understand the nature of the data we present. All of our readers have their own expectations, some easy to assess, others less so. All expect to be presented with something new and engaging: new insight into known situations, new concepts or areas of knowledge.

More experienced writers may understand the main characteristics of their readership – headteachers or principals, academic journal readers, conference delegates, funding bodies, degree programme examiners – although each of these categories of reader could encompass a wide range of prior experience of the subject and capacity to deal with the issues and ideas presented. Newer writers may find it helpful to focus on a particular person as they write, who characterises the type of intended reader. How much prior knowledge can be assumed of this reader? What writing conventions do they expect us to follow? How can we best engage them with the new ideas we are presenting? Why are they reading what we write?

As we will see in later sections of this chapter, the reader's needs are paramount as we organise and structure our material, shape our paragraphs and sentences, and include appropriate illustrative material to communicate our chosen theme.

Types of communication

> Research in isolation serves no purpose. Effective communication, both to other research workers and to teachers and other educationists, is the essence of good educational research. (Nisbet and Entwistle, 1984: 256)

The findings of a research project may be presented many times in different formats according to the intended readership. The heart of the research – its aims, the investigation itself, the analysis of findings and conclusions – is likely to be there in each case, but the balance of what we present to each readership differs, as does the level of detail, depending on the expectations of the reader.

In many cases, the entire project is published in pdf form on a website, including research tools, anonymised data, analysis, findings and (where appropriate) recommendations. It is important to design the website for easy access, with clear navigation routes between the various pages. It is also helpful to the reader to be informed about other projects which are relevant to one they are reading.

For theses and dissertations, there are normally conventions and regulations to be followed, which influence the expectations of the examiners. It is therefore advisable to study the appropriate guidelines concerning the format and approach of your thesis, and to browse through examples of completed Masters and Doctoral work at your university. If, after discussion with your supervisor, you feel that your work needs to be presented differently, make it clear in your thesis text why you are deviating from conventional practice.

The expectations of academic journal editors, their reviewers and readers can largely be gauged by reading academic papers which have received their approval, and by consulting the journal website. The content and presentation of published articles consulted during your research will guide you in developing a style, structure and approach to your own article writing that is appropriate for the journal in which you wish to publish.

In planning to write a book, it is important to carry out some market research to see which publishers are likely to be interested in your material. Each publisher has their own specialisms, and their own requirements for book proposals. Be prepared to include information about the potential market for the book as well as its contents, and to offer a sample chapter. It is unwise to write the whole book before getting agreement from the publisher.

When writing shorter pieces for publication, a selective approach is needed, rather than one which seeks to tell the whole story of the research. This is especially true of conference papers or chapters in edited books. Conference delegates expect to be stimulated to think and debate, but within relatively tight time constraints. It may therefore be wise to focus on one particularly intriguing aspect of a research project: preferably one that ties in with the theme of the conference. A book chapter likewise needs to tie in with the theme of the book, and might deal primarily with the outcomes of the research, or its contribution to theory in relation to the book theme, using referencing to indicate where fuller accounts of the project may be found.

Your research findings may need to be pared down still further. In a formal research report, the main details – including the conclusions – are generally presented first as an executive summary: the reader then chooses whether to read the full text, or sections of it, to access further information. Similarly, senior staff at your workplace may need a concise and accessible report which summarises all your findings, together with clear recommendations for action. This may mean that months of investigation, analysis and writing must be distilled into 1000–2000 words for easy access by a range of staff. If the intended outcome of your research – school or college improvement, for example – is to be guided by what you have learned, then a format is needed which motivates the maximum number of people to read and respond.

Analytical writing

Whatever the format, academic writing is characterised by its focus upon analysis. We may not know what we have found until we have written about it: we rarely 'write up' a cohesive body of knowledge that we have accumulated during the process of data analysis. As Punch (2009: 341) observes, writing can be seen as: 'a way of learning, a way of knowing, a form of analysis and enquiry' where the writer is 'constructing a map or theoretical picture of the data which emerges as the analysis proceeds'. This approach is often linked to qualitative analysis; however, in both qualitative and quantitative research, the writer draws back from the ana-lysed data in order to interpret, understand and communicate what has been found. This mental process is enabled by exploratory drafts of ana-lytical writing.

Analysis, particularly in qualitative research, often draws sequentially upon other forms of writing. In the presentation of research findings, descrip-tion often precedes analysis: the reader needs to understand *what* has been found before becoming involved in our analysis of concepts and meanings. Narrative writing – story-telling – may also perform a descriptive, clarifying function, but it can further be used as a methodological technique which encompasses the process of analysis: narrative enquiry. Here, information is gathered for the purpose of research through story-telling. The researcher then writes a narrative of the experience, which encapsulates the meanings revealed through the collected stories. In this context, the construction of narrative is a form of analysis. (For further discussion of narrative enquiry, see Chapter 15.)

Critical writing or 'writing a critique' is a further type of analytical writing. It involves giving a reasoned assessment: perhaps evaluating the thinking set out in a published article or judging the appositeness of a particular meth-odology to a piece of research. Here we offer our critical appraisal – of a published text, or of our own research and writing – in order to discuss its merits and weaknesses within defined criteria. The ensuing judgement is not whether this is a 'good' or a 'poor' piece of writing or methodology per se, but the extent to which it is useful or insightful within the context we are considering.

Conceptualisation

The process of analysis – of the content of published texts, of our own and others' data, of the ideas which emerge when our own research is considered in the context of previous enquiry – involves the consideration and formation of concepts. Conceptualisation essentially involves a process of the distilla-tion of ideas. For example, preliminary work for a research paper on student transition to Higher Education (HE) (Briggs et al., 2012) first involved the identification of topics covered in published articles. A sub-section of the topic list is shown below:

Student expectations of HE/reality of first year

Student aspiration/reality of HE

Student identity/perception of a successful student

Decision making among entrants

Issues faced before and during HE experience

Knowledge about/of HE

Preparation for transition/choice of institution and programme

Lack of planned transition – liaison between schools and universities

Preparedness and student retention

Making connections with pre-university experience

Collating these factors and considering them in relation to other topics discussed in the literature resulted in them collectively being categorised as: *student expectations, aspirations, decision making.* This category was then used as a set of concepts within which to analyse the new data collected in the research project. (For further information about this process, see Chapter 26 on this book's website materials, http://www.sagepub.co.uk/briggs)

The formation of a conceptual framework may be carried out before data analysis, or even before data collection, if the purpose of the research is to examine concepts which have been identified from earlier investigation. The conceptual framework may equally be drawn up through analysis of the project data, using a grounded theory approach, as discussed in Chapter 13, or by a process of modelling, described below. Where a preliminary conceptual framework is drawn up, it functions as a structure through which to consider the data. The concepts and the ways in which they interact within the framework may then be challenged, modified, re-assembled or extended as a result of the data analysis. If a key purpose of educational leadership research is to arrive at new insights and construct new knowledge, the function of a conceptual framework is to enable, not to constrain.

Modelling

Modelling as a process of reduction and 'mapping' can be used to identify underlying principles and concepts and the ways in which they relate to each other. In the research context, modelling can be integral to the process of analysis, both the analysis of quantitative data as described in Chapter 24 and qualitative data as discussed in Chapter 25. Huberman and Miles (1998) describe modelling as a developmental interaction between display and analytical text, where display enables the researcher to summarise data, identify themes, patterns and clusters, discover relationships and develop explanations. There is no single 'right way' to undertake modelling of qualitative data: Figure 26.1 presents a simple example for researchers who may not have considered this technique before.

Step 1: Search

Run through the analysed data looking for underpinning ideas and processes. Look methodically at the data, asking yourself, 'What's going on here?' and record it as succinctly as possible. This first list of ideas is likely to be relatively unsophisticated; you may hit a few concepts on the first run-through, but it won't all be as neat as that.

Step 2: Shuffle

Put your unsophisticated list of words and phrases into a list that you can easily manipulate. Shuffle and sort them into groups of ideas which are closely related within the context of your research. Then sort the groups into a meaningful order, and allocate a label to each group. During this process, split groups or re-allocate items if necessary.

Step 3: Check

Consider the labels carefully. At this stage, there is probably a mixture of concepts and more descriptive statements. Is anything missing? If necessary, go back to Steps 1 and 2 and try to see what underpinning idea has got lost.

Step 4: Organise

Put the Step 3 list of labels into a meaningful pattern, showing relationships, influences, developments, whatever it is you are trying to record. Talk with your fellow researchers. Is it starting to make sense? Is anything missing? A good test at this stage is to try to 'talk someone through' the emerging diagram. Which parts don't quite fit? Which are in the wrong place?

Step 5: Conceptualise

Look at your research aims: what are you trying to identify and explain? Which of the elements of your diagram can be reduced further to identify simpler underlying concepts? Aim for single words as far as possible. Now re-assess the links between them: this is a process of analysis, and you may see something new.

Step 6: Model

Tidy up your Step 5 diagram and discuss it with colleagues. They may recognise in your model aspects of scenarios which they have experienced or investigated. You may have a model which crystallises and clarifies some underlying social system. Even if this is not the case, you have reduced your analysed data to its clearest possible factors and the systems in which they operate.

Step 7: Use

Use the model to re-assess the raw or partly analysed data, now that you have identified the underpinning processes. You can use it to explain what you have found, to assess, evaluate or even predict, within other related contexts.

Figure 26.1   Example of the modelling process

What this example demonstrates is that, as David (2001: 462) points out, a model has 'two complementary indissociable functions': a function of 'abstraction, based on reality', moving from reality to the model, and a development function, a 'means of action', which moves from the model to reality. The knowledge constructed in this way can be used as a tool for understanding and as an agent for change. (See this book's companion website for an extended example of this process.)

Presenting new insights

In presenting research, our aim is to achieve new insight and understanding of aspects of educational leadership and management, to explore existing concepts and offer new ones and to reveal new areas of knowledge. 'The essential feature of any research report is to make a claim to knowledge' (Bassey, 1999: 89).

How can we be sure that our insights are new? From where do we draw the authority to write on our chosen subject? We need to demonstrate that the research has been properly carried out; that it recognises and builds upon what has been previously researched and understood; that the data have been methodically collected and thoughtfully analysed; and that conclusions bear in mind the research findings, the extent of previous knowledge and the constraints imposed by the scale of the research.

Given the extent of the literature which is potentially relevant to any educational leadership research, and the constraints upon both large and small research projects, any claim to knowledge has to be appropriately worded. We cannot speak with authority on the development needs of school principals worldwide on the basis of a small-scale study in one country. But we can show how the results of our small-scale study fit in with, challenge or extend what is known internationally. Murray (2002: 52) has some useful guidance about originality:

- You say something that has not been said before.
- You synthesise things that have not been put together before.
- You look at topics that people in your discipline have not looked at.
- You test existing knowledge in an original way.

In order to give credence to the insights presented, research writing needs both internal and external coherence. The train of thought – the argument or story – has to be carefully and purposefully constructed, enabling new insights to be constructed and presented, which are both grounded in the discussion of the new findings and set in the context of previous knowledge. In this way, we provide a basis for our claims to originality.

The process of writing

The issues we have considered so far – the purpose of writing, the ways in which research writing might be presented, and the particular demands of analytical writing – all point towards the need to consider the process of writing itself. One piece of academic writing may differ substantially from another, but both should display the same degree of mental rigour. In undertaking research, try to allocate as much time as possible to the writing process, so that you have time to think and to construct successive drafts; your ideas will develop as you write.

Building an argument

When you start to write, you will probably draw upon a number of source documents which you have created. These may include your research proposal, notes on related literature, field notes, research diaries, sets of analysed data and early drafts of sections of your work. A useful activity is to familiarise yourself with these source documents, stand back from them, and ask yourself: What does it all mean? What does it add up to? If these are my base documents, what is my argument? What is the story that I want to tell? It might be helpful to draw a mind-map of the different themes indicated by your source documents, explore linkages between them and take some time to consider what collectively they suggest. This activity should help you to construct an argument: a logical line of thought which runs through your writing, giving it coherence and purpose. The process of writing enables us to develop our ideas, as well as simply to express them, and it is likely that the argument will change as you write. It might therefore be helpful if initially you write your argument down, and revise it as you work. This should enable you to match the final draft of your work with the final line of argument.

Creating a structure

A clear overall structure – the macro structure – for a piece of writing enables writer and reader to follow a train of thought which runs through the document and gives credence to the conclusions. It also enables the micro-structure – the paragraphs and sentences – to be constructed in such a way that it supports and carries through the argument. A generic macro structure for presenting research in the educational field is set out by Punch (2009: 338):

- clear identification of the research area and its topic
- a statement of the research purpose(s) and research questions
- a setting of the study in context, including its relationship to relevant literature
- a description of methods, including strategy and design, sample and the collection and analysis of data
- a presentation of data and of its analysis
- a clear statement of the findings and a consideration of what can be concluded from these findings.

Developing a good macro structure depends not only on following conventional patterns such as these, but also on considering the major themes of your research report. These are the main ideas that have shaped your thinking: the research questions, key issues derived from the literature and the conceptual framework which you have devised to analyse and present your data. Consider this advice from Blaxter et al. (1996: 215) about the themes of your research:

> The themes of your report or thesis are the key issues, concepts or questions you identify as being of relevance and interest. These will both inform the research you undertake, so will be evident in your contextual discussion, and help to structure your analysis and findings. They are the aspects of your field or discipline to which your research is contributing.

Within the larger sections of the writing, a consistent internal structure can be achieved by using these themes to frame the sub-sections. The structure can be both externally visible – as sub-headings replicated in different sections – and embedded, where the concepts are dealt with in the same order in each section. If the structure of your argument is clear, the reader is 'freed up' to become interested in your findings; if there is no clear 'map' of the pattern of ideas you present, the reader may struggle to follow your train of thought and may not engage with the key points you are trying to make.

Within each sub-section, a finer degree of structuring is also essential. In order to organise your writing, ask questions such as 'What do the readers need to know next?' and 'What do they need to know already in order to understand what I am writing here?' Use 'signposting' to help the reader to make connections between different parts of the text. Put link paragraphs to act as bridges between sub-sections, and summaries to enable the reader – and the writer – to take stock of what has just been presented. Using words and phrases such as 'but', 'however', 'therefore', 'on the other hand' or 'in addition' helps to build a cumulative argument, rather than simply presenting a succession of statements, and helps to move the document towards the intended destination.

Presenting analysed data

However fascinating you may find your individual data sets, the reader does not need to be presented with them all. A selection of analysed data, often in the form of tables, figures, illustrative vignettes or sets of representative respondent quotations, is used to support the argument for a specific piece of writing. In Masters or Doctoral work, all analysed data might be presented, with figures and tables that form an essential part of the discussion in the main body of the text, and those that provide further evidence or illustration placed in the appendices. In other writing, data sets are treated as source documents and drawn upon as needed. There can be a temptation to 'cherry-pick' illustrative quotations, or to 'smooth over' inconvenient irregularities in data sets: it is therefore important to select items of data honestly and representatively, and to admit to ambiguities. In many cases, ambiguity provides a valuable basis for discussion.

Presenting data in the form of tables and figures (each one labelled with number and caption) is often essential to your argument, making points which it would be difficult to convey in continuous prose. However, the flow of your text is enabled or impeded by the way in which the tables and figures are placed, and each one is likely to need some form of commentary. It is not helpful for the reader to encounter a 'brick wall' of tables or figures when trying to follow an argument. The reader is dependent upon you to draw material from the figures and tables into the discussion and to cross-reference appropriately. In this way, the data tables become an integral part of the argument.

Writing about your data

In reporting research, it is important that the choice of language matches the scope of the investigation. For example, a survey which elicited replies from all the teachers at one primary school could be reported as: 'Three-quarters of the teachers at the school agreed that ...' or 'Few of the teachers at the school considered X to be important.' Where the sample comprises the whole population, given reliable research tools, the results can be reported as representing the views of the whole population. It may still be wise to acknowledge that there might be personal variations in perception which the sampling design did not detect.

However, a survey which sampled lecturers from two faculties of a university would be reported differently, for example: 'Half of the respondents agreed with the statement ...', 'All of the staff sampled for the survey reported ...' or 'The overall impression given by respondents from Faculty Y was ...'. If robustly designed probability sampling has been used, then inferences could be drawn for the whole of each faculty, or for the pair of faculties, but not for the university as a whole, unless the two faculties represented a reliable sample of the whole staff.

Where the probability samples are small, or where non-probability sampling is chosen, assertions cannot be made about the whole population. Instead, the perceptions would be presented as a 'snapshot' of opinion, or as elements of a 'rich picture' of part of the organisation. Sampling design is fully discussed in Chapter 10 of this book, and the issues of reliability and validity of data in Chapter 6; both chapters will help you to understand the methodological issues underlying this advice. What is emphasised here is that the choice of words used to describe and present the data must match the parameters set by the research design. Your argument will be more convincing if you stay within the limits of the authority provided by your data.

Writing conventions

The success of your writing depends upon the ability to work within academic conventions without losing a sense of your own personal voice. This can involve choosing – in grammatical terms – which 'person' to write in. In areas of ethnographic research, in research which engages in a large degree of self-reflection, and in research where a narrative approach is adopted, the use of the first person 'I' and 'we' is appropriate. In research where an objective viewpoint is paramount, a neutral third-person stance, combined with use of the passive voice, helps to maintain objectivity. This neutral language need not be stilted: the statements 'Five teachers were selected for interview' or 'The college has three main sites' are no more difficult to follow than 'I selected five teachers for interview' or 'Our college has three main sites.' If you are not sure which 'person' to use, pay attention to the style of other writing in your discipline, and take advice from academic colleagues. In the end, as Blaxter et al. (1996: 221) comment: 'Whether you use the first or third person will depend upon your discipline, your politics, your purpose and your audience.'

Having carried out a research project, it is sometimes tempting to adopt a rather 'imperative' style in presenting the findings and conclusions, saying that something 'must' be so or 'should' happen. This is probably unwise, given the scope of the research, the limitations of the methodology and the wide range of un-investigated phenomena which may have impacted upon the researched situation. A stance which balances confidence in making recommendations based upon the data whilst acknowledging the limitations and boundaries of the research is probably a good option. Think through the issues presented by Tony Bush in Chapter 6 before asserting claims too strongly.

New researchers sometimes ask, 'When can I express my own opinion?' The simple answer is that your own opinion, unsupported by data, is not valid. The deeper answer is that your own opinion – in the form of your own interests, ethics, values and priorities – shapes the whole of your research: it guides you in choosing what questions to ask, what literature to read, what methodology to adopt, what factors to analyse in your data and what importance to place upon your findings. The complexity for you as researcher lies in your ability to balance your opinion – what you feel is right or fitting – with a 'research attitude' that is prepared to accept a broad range of possible outcomes for the research.

Finally in this section, there are some specific features of style to note. A consistent model of referencing is needed, both within the text and in the reference list: advice on achieving this is offered in Chapter 5. Gender-neutral language should be used, unless the discussion is necessarily gender-specific. Abbreviations such as 'it's' and 'don't' should usually be avoided. Professional abbreviations such as 'SLT' for 'Senior Leadership Team' are acceptable, provided that they are written out in full and followed by their abbreviation where they first appear in the text. Specialised terminology, even simple phrases like 'subject leader' or 'homework club', needs at least a brief explanation. Try to avoid using jargon that is very specific to your own institution: these words may mean little to an outsider. Similarly, when writing for an international audience, remember that educational terminology varies from country to country, so it is good practice to offer a brief explanation of specific terms and abbreviations.

Drafting and editing

Achieving the necessary complexity in your writing may seem daunting. If you find it difficult to get started, the best advice is: 'Just write something!' Whatever you write will have to be re-drafted, probably three or more times, so the quality of the first draft is not really important. Remind yourself that a house is built one brick at a time, and it may be necessary for you simply to prepare your bricks (sentences, paragraphs, drafted sub-sections) and lay them out in front of you before you can see how they all fit together. Writing in manageable chunks is particularly useful if you only have limited periods of time in which to write. Once you have written something and looked at it critically, you will begin to see what is missing, what is in the wrong place, what needs to be better expressed. Even a clumsy attempt at writing can produce an engagement with the topic which is the key to successful communication. Above all, allocate time in the writing process for producing several drafts, and accept that the final version may look nothing like the first one.

Critical friends

It is good practice to ask other people to read your draft material and offer critical comment. If you are part of a research team, or have a reference group for your research project, these people need to be consulted about the content of what you write. Ask a critical friend to comment on the clarity of your argument, and to point out sections which are difficult to understand. However much you would like the current version of your writing to be 'just fine', asking others to read it is a valuable test for the probity of what you say, as well as its clarity.

Writing to a word limit

When writing to a word limit, there seem to be two main stances. The first is to write what you want to say, then edit it down to the necessary word limit. The second is to set notional limits for each sub-section, and try to keep the material under control from the beginning. You may feel that the latter stance may limit the scope of your thinking: conversely it may offer a secure framework within which to work. Whatever stance you choose, remember that most early drafts are not succinct; most writing benefits from being pared down to make the essential parts of the argument more visible. Make sure also that the length of each section of your paper is appropriate to its importance. A beginner-writer may write expansively describing the context of the research, and may subsequently not 'have enough space left' for analysing and discussing the findings.

Introductions and abstracts

All sections of your writing are important, but particular care should be taken with introductions and abstracts. The introduction prepares the reader for what is to come: it introduces the whole work. It answers the question: what does the reader need to know, in order to follow this article, thesis or book? The final version of the introduction therefore is written late in the process, when you know what has to be introduced. At this point, it is also a good idea to check that your title reflects what you have actually presented.

The abstract is written last of all. It is a document which can be separated from the article or thesis and is often stored separately in electronic form, as an indication of the nature and scope of the whole work. It is *not* an introduction. It summarises the salient features of the whole research: its context and purpose, methodology, main findings and conclusions. Through the choice of words in the abstract, the writer also indicates the originality, rigour and potential impact of the research.

Dissemination

As we have noted, your research may be presented in a number of different ways. The important point is that it *is* disseminated, to local and wider colleagues, and to others who may benefit from the work you have done. When disseminating research findings within and beyond your organisation, the following media may be appropriate:

- A developmental workshop based on the research, presented to colleagues and staff from neighbouring educational institutions.
- A summary of the research published on your organisation's website, or submitted to an appropriate Internet discussion group.
- An electronically published research paper.
- An article submitted to an educational newspaper or magazine.
- A paper submitted to an educational or academic conference.
- A paper submitted to a refereed academic journal.

One important principle is to match the message you are offering to the audience and medium that you choose, and another is not to under-rate yourself. However you disseminate, you will probably be surprised at the amount of interest your research generates, and the stimulus you receive to undertake more research. Pushing forward the frontiers of understanding, even in a small way, can be addictive!

Key points

- Make the purpose of your writing clear to yourself and your reader.
- Write analytically, constructing an argument by considering deeply the material and data you have collected.
- Match the style and content of your writing to the medium in which you intend to disseminate.
- Allow time to draft, reflect, consult and draft again.

Questions and reflections

1 Why are you writing?
2 What is your argument?
3 Who is your reader?
4 How can you best convey your argument to your reader?

Recommended further reading

Bryman, A. (2004) *Social Research Methods* (2nd edn). Oxford: Oxford University Press.

This excellent methodology text has a helpful chapter devoted to 'Writing up social research'.

McNiff, J. and Whitehead, J. (2009) *Doing and Writing Action Research*. London: Sage.

Although this text focuses on action research, the academic writing advice can be applied more generally.

Thomas, G. (2009) *How to do Your Research Project*. London: Sage.

Most of the chapters in this text include advice on writing about a particular aspect of the research project.

Finally, most universities have student support websites which offer advice on academic writing skills. Use the one for your own university, or shop around!

References

Bassey, M. (1999) *Case Study Research in Educational Settings*. Buckingham: Open University Press.

Blaxter, L., Hughes, C. and Tight, M. (1996) *How to Research*. Buckingham: Open University Press.

Briggs, A.R.J., Clark, J. and Hall, I.R. (2012) Building bridges: understanding student transition to university. *Quality in Higher Education*. Available at http://dx.doi.org/10.1080/13538322.2011.614468 (accessed 18 January 2012).

David, A. (2001) Models implementation: a state of the art. *European Journal of Operational Research* 134: 459–80.

Huberman, A.M. and Miles, M. B. (1998) *Collecting and Interpreting Qualitative Materials*. London: Sage.

Murray, R. (2002) *How to Write a Thesis*. Buckingham: Open University Press.

Nisbet, J.D. and Entwistle, N.J. (1984) Writing the report, in Bell, J., Bush, T., Fox, A., Goodey, J. and Goulding, S. (eds) *Conducting Small-scale Investigations in Educational Management*. London: Paul Chapman/Open University.

Punch, K.F. (2009) *Introduction to Research Methods in Education*. London: Sage.

Author Index

Subject Index

Added to a page number 'f' denotes a figure and 't' denotes a table.